International Series in Operations Research & Management Science

Volume 173

For further volumes
www.springer.com/series/6161

Elena Tànfani
Angela Testi (Eds.)

Advanced Decision Making Methods Applied to Health Care

Springer

Elena Tànfani
Department of Economics and Quantitative Methods (DIEM)
University of Genova, Italy

Angela Testi
Department of Economics and Quantitative Methods (DIEM)
University of Genova, Italy

ISSN 0884-8289
ISBN 978-88-470-2320-8 ISBN 978-88-470-2321-5 (eBook)
DOI 10.1007/978-88-470-2321-5

Library of Congress Control Number: 2011941624

Springer Milan Heidelberg New York Dordrecht London

Typesetting with LaTeX: PTP-Berlin, Protago TeX-Production GmbH, Germany (www.ptp-berlin.eu)

Springer-Verlag Italia S.r.l., Via Decembrio 28, I-20137 Milano
Springer is a part of Springer Science+Business Media (www.springer.com)

Preface

This book collates some applications of quantitative methods, in particular operational research, statistical and economic decision-making tools, to different concrete situations and problems arising in the broad field of health care delivery. Though presenting "advanced" methods, requiring specialised skills, this book is addressed to an interdisciplinary and wide audience, not just quantitative researchers and economists. It is an excellent reference for practitioners because it presents possible approaches for more informed, and therefore more responsible, decision-making.

Decisions in health care delivery are becoming more and more difficult in the presence of budget cuts and shortages of resources, but overall because of increasing demand and progress in health care delivery models, requiring integrated answers to meet the complex needs of citizens.

The two main features of this book are to collate contributions dealing with new problems and to focus on practical applications.

From the first point of view, the contributions in this book represent the more recent ways of tackling the new challenges in current practice. They do not necessarily require new methods. Traditional methods, such as simulation, optimisation or data envelopment analysis, which are already widely used in the literature, are presented, applied in new ways.

Simulation is largely present because of the intrinsically uncertain context of healthcare and is used for both single facilities and clinical pathways (Chapters 12 and 13), a system where birth centres are seen as a network at a regional level (Chapter 7) and multiobjective comparison in decision making, as in Chapter 5, in an emergency department where the consideration of average and extreme operating conditions are both important.

Optimisation methods are applied to some relatively new topics, such as to team composition and rostering driven by demand in an emergency department (Chapter 1) and to the nurse-to-patient assignment problem (Chapter 8), that is a crucial aspect in meeting the high variability of demand in Home Care. They are also applied in tools for testing the impact of modification of different strategies for the scheduling of interventions in operating rooms to account for uncertainty a posteriori (Chapter 2).

Data envelopment analysis proves, as always, to be a very effective tool in assessing technical and scale efficiency and identifying the determinants of efficiency when used with other statistical instruments, as in Chapter 6. This model can be used, as shown in Chapter 11, also to measure fairness of access and clinical effectiveness together with technical efficiency, allowing a complete assessment of the performance of health care delivery.

Chapter 9 presents methods that are less commonly used in health care. In this chapter multicriteria analysis is used for prioritising community care programmes, taking into consideration both health gains and equity. Chapter 10 presents quite a new method, graph mining, which proves to be a very effective tool to address the actions of policy makers. In Chapter 4 the authors propose an original model to coordinate pharmaceutical industry research on new drugs for rare diseases.

From a methodological point of view, the contributions presented in this book suggest that today an integrated holistic approach is preferable for problem solving. This is the specific aim of Chapter 12, where the clinical pathways of surgical elective patients are considered together within a hospital across the three main subprocesses they follow, that is, waiting list management, operating room planning and stay organisation. This is also the approach followed in Chapter 13, where multiple resources (beds, operating rooms, personnel and intensive care capacity) are taken into consideration to plan admissions of surgical patients by means of many consecutive models.

A holistic approach is even more necessary when all the levels of assistance are involved, as in Chapter 3, where the authors emphasise that alternatives to hospital care require new services, but also corresponding changes to clinical practice and care pathways. This means a participative approach to the whole system and not only a focus on planning and control of the single facility or organisation.

The second key feature of this book is combining, for each topic, a clear explanation of methodological and theoretical concepts together with some reminders of practical applications, and a description of the impact on and benefits to health-care policy. This book proves that whilst the application of quantitative methods in a health care context has its difficulties, due to uncertain conditions and lack of proper data, it also has great potential to provide valuable information to help decision-makers improve services. Rigorous methods are needed and problems should be tackled to make quantitative methods useful and not limited to theoretical exercises.

Genova, November 2011

Elena Tànfani
Angela Testi

Contents

Chapter 1

Workforce management based on forecasted demand

Bernardetta Addis, Roberto Aringhieri, Giuliana Carello, Andrea Grosso, and Francesco Maffioli

Abstract. Health care delivery has a dramatic impact on the quality of life of every community. Hence, in the past years in many countries, a great effort has been spent in order to rationalize the management of limited resources, such as operating rooms, ambulances or workforce. Nevertheless, to the best of our knowledge, the idea of using demand for driving the workforce optimization process has received little attention in the literature. In this work we address the problem of managing workforce taking into account forecasted demand. We focus on the management of the operators working at the Operations Center of the Emergency Medical Service of Milano, Italy, for which a huge amount of accurate data is available.

Keywords: workforce management, forecasted demand, optimization, emergency medical service

---

B. Addis
Department of Computer Science, Università degli Studi di Torino, Corso Svizzera 185, 10149 Torino, Italy
e-mail: addis@di.unito.it

R. Aringhieri (✉)
Department of Computer Science, Università degli Studi di Torino, Corso Svizzera 185, 10149 Torino, Italy
e-mail: roberto.aringhieri@unito.it

G. Carello
Department of Electronics and Information, Politecnico di Milano, P.zza L. Da Vinci 32, 20133 Milano, Italy
e-mail: carello@elet.polimi.it

A. Grosso
Department of Computer Science, Università degli Studi di Torino, Corso Svizzera 185, 10149 Torino, Italy
e-mail: grosso@di.unito.it

F. Maffioli
Department of Electronics and Information, Politecnico di Milano, P.zza L. Da Vinci 32, 20133 Milano, Italy
e-mail: maffioli@elet.polimi.it

Tànfani E., Testi A. (Eds.): Advanced Decision Making Methods Applied to Health Care.
International Series in Operations Research & Management Science 173
DOI 10.1007/978-88-470-2321-5_1, © Springer-Verlag Italia 2012

1.1 Introduction and problem addressed

Health care delivery has a dramatic impact on the quality of life of every community. Hence, in the past years in many countries, a great effort has been spent in order to rationalize the management of limited resources, such as operating rooms, ambulances or workforce. Health care delivery covers many aspects, and among them, emergency medical services play a fundamental role in the quality of the health services provided to citizens. Emergency Medical Services (EMS) usually deal with limited resources and variable demands. EMS must guarantee a 24 hours answer to citizens, and, moreover, the provided service must be fair and efficient at the same time. Of course, ambulance availability plays a fundamental role in the service provided by an EMS, but the first answer to patients is given by the operators of the Operations Center (OC). The OC is in charge of receiving the phone calls from citizens who need immediate medical assistance. The OC operators answer the calls, evaluate the seriousness of the disease or injury, and assign emergency vehicles to the patients. The probability of survival is strictly related, for very serious cases, to the quickness of the assistance. Thus, the OC must provide a quick and high performance service.

In this work we address the problem of managing OC workforce taking into account forecasted demand. We focus on the management of the OC of the EMS of Milano. Milano EMS collected reports on everyday activity over the past years; thus a huge amount of data is available. Although we take into account some specific problem features, the solution provided can be easily extended to more general cases of medical workforce management.

The Milano EMS operators work in teams according to predefined shift patterns. The OC workforce management problem consists in assigning operators to teams and teams to shifts with the aim of guaranteeing the needed number of operators with respect to the forecasted demand, while providing the best service to citizens. In [19], the authors provide a perspective of the current health-care literature, focusing on recent papers in planning and scheduling, and describe the following stages in the temporal scale affected by the managerial decisions: Planning, many years to a decade; Staffing, 6 months to a year; Scheduling, 4 to 6 weeks; Allocation, a single shift; Assignment, patient level. In this work, we focus on staffing and scheduling stages in an integrated approach [17]. The aim is to provide Integer Linear Programming (ILP) models which can be used as a planning tool by the management of the EMS. We propose ILP models to divide OC staff in teams and to assign teams to shifts, taking into account the overall quality and fairness of the provided service, even in case of reduced workforce.

The medical workforce management belongs to the class of the personnel and staff rostering problem. Indeed, the Milano OC staff works according to ward shifts, as it is part of a hospital, and it is subject to the same contractual agreements as the hospital staff. Thus, the considered problem can be seen as a nurse rostering problem. On the other hand, it has features which are not usually considered in nurse rostering problems. In fact, beside coverage, fairness and efficiency must be guaranteed and variable demand must be taken into account. From this point of view, the problem is related to call center staff managing problems, and, in general, to personnel management problems with uncertain demand.

Staff rostering problems have been widely investigated in the literature and we refer to [9, 10], and to the two volumes [15] for detailed surveys on such topic. The nurse rostering problem has also been widely addressed in the literature, starting from the first works of the seventies [18, 20], as reported in surveys such as [7] and [8]. Many applications in real life cases have been investigated in [16] and, among them, an italian case [4].

As pointed out in [1], the management based on forecasted demand gains more relevance when the medical workforce have to guarantee the efficiency and fairness of the delivered service. To the best of our knowledge, the idea of using demand for driving the optimization process has received little attention in the literature. Demand based planning has been considered with respect to call center staffing problems, rather than to nurse rostering.

In [6] the problem of scheduling a hierarchical workforce with variable demands is discussed considering a problem in which a higher qualified worker can substitute a lower qualified one, but not vice versa. An ILP model has been proposed which is solved using a general purpose solver.

In [2, 3], the authors consider the problem of minimizing staffing costs in an inbound call center, while maintaining an acceptable level of service in multiple time periods. The staffing level in one time period can affect the service levels in subsequent periods. The authors present an iterative cutting plane method for minimizing staffing costs in a service system which must meet service level requirements over multiple time periods. Furthermore, it is assumed that the service level cannot be a-priori computed, but it is evaluated using simulation.

More recently, in [14] the problem of staffing call centers with multiple customer classes and agent types operating under quality-of-service (QoS) constraints and demand rate uncertainty has been addressed. A formulation of the staffing problem is introduced according to which the QoS constraints must be met with high probability with respect to the uncertainty in the demand rate. Furthermore, the solution approach transforms the problem with uncertain demand rates into one with known arrival rates which is easier to solve.

Forecasted demand is crucial in [11, 12] where the author focus on the long-term supply of employees in the company, which is adapted to the forecasted needs by recruitments, layoffs or retraining the current workforce.

Other papers take into account concepts close to that of the forecasted demand. In [13] the authors deal with the problem of assigning individual employees "who differ in cost and productivity to labor tour schedules, that is, schedules that specify each employee daily starting time and days-off during the week". Finally, a similar modelling approach to the one in [1] is reported in [5], where a network flow approach is discussed for maximizing workforce diversity in project teams.

The chapter is organized as follows. In Section 1.2 a complete description of the problem is reported, and the two models are introduced and commented. In-depth discussion on the results of the computational tests on real life data is provided in Section 1.3. Conclusions end the chapter in Section 1.4.

1.2 Materials and methods

As mentioned, OC staff is considered, in Milano EMS, as hospital staff, and therefore it is subject to the same contractual agreements and shift patterns as hospital staff. However, the OC staff is in charge of particular kind of tasks, and therefore the management of OC staff must take into account different constraints and requirements, such as efficiency and fairness of the provided service.

Operators of the EMS work accordingly to standard ward shifts; specifically, such shifts are **M**orning (7 am–2 pm), **A**fternoon (2 pm–9 pm), **N**ight (9 pm–7 am) plus one **R**est day. Each operator is assigned to one of the five teams which work according to the five-days basic pattern reported in Table 1.1. The pattern is cyclically repeated. Each team must have at least one member with particular skills (a foreman). In Table 1.1, a special shift, denoted A/M, is reported, in which each team "splits" in order to partially support both the morning staff and the afternoon staff. As the pattern is cyclically repeated, each team splits once in the sequence.

Beside receiving the emergency calls, the OC is in charge of other tasks, such as managing the transport of organs from organ donations, or keeping contact with the volunteering associations operating on the ambulances. Thus, the set of operators on work in each time period is divided in two sub-teams: one is in charge of the phone calls, the other is in charge of the other tasks. Since the two groups alternate in managing the emergency calls, both must provide a suitable quality of service. Although the composition of the two groups may vary, we assume it fixed over all the planning horizon, so as to provide well balanced assignment.
The considered problem calls for composing the teams in order to satisfy a forecasted demand of service. To provide a fair service, the problem aims at maximizing the minimum amount of additional demand that can be served. This objective matches a robustness requirement.

The Milano EMS keeps daily logs of the emergency calls, with time and duration of each call; the 24 hours time horizon is divided in a set of time intervals – or time spans – for each of which the maximum number of simultaneous calls is computed. This allows to compute a forecasted demand, as the maximum number of calls within a given time span. Figure 1.1 depicts the cumulative emergency demand in terms of number of calls received during each time span over a period of three months: it proves the need of taking into account the demand when planning the workforce management.

Table 1.1. Five-days patters for EMS teams

Day	*1*	*2*	*3*	*4*	*5*
Team 1	A	A/M	M	N	R
Team 2	A/M	M	N	R	A
Team 3	M	N	R	A	A/M
Team 4	N	R	A	A/M	M
Team 5	R	A	A/M	M	N

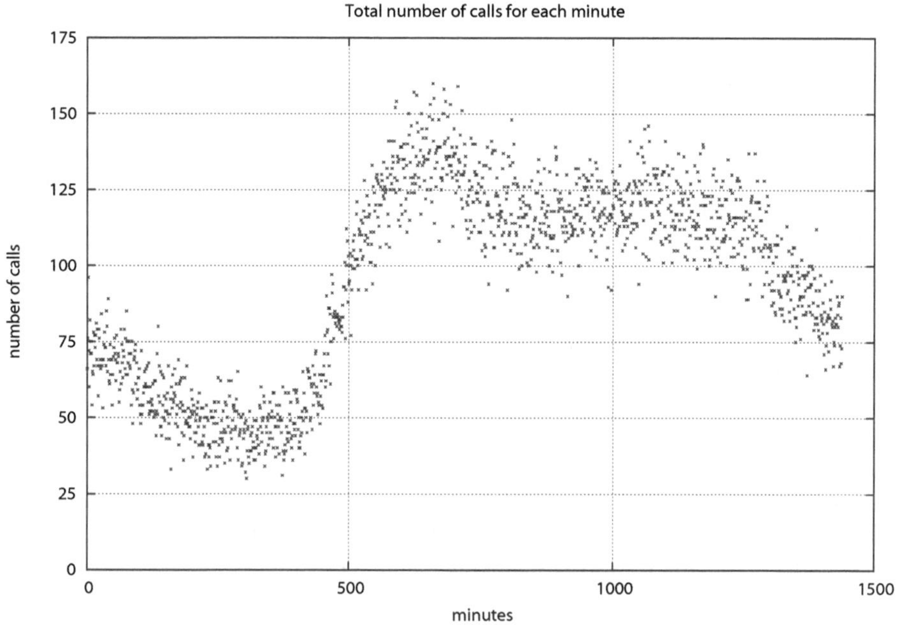

Fig. 1.1. Cumulative emergency demand in terms of number of calls received during a day

We use the following notation to model the problem. O is the set of operators, $O_c \subset O$ the set of foremen, S the set of possible shifts. For each operator $i \in O$ an *efficiency* e_i is given, estimated as the average number of calls he/she answers per hour. F is the set of time intervals in which the 24 hours time horizon is divided: for each time interval (or time span) the demand is known, as well as the set of shifts covering it. The set of shifts covering each time span is represented with binary parameters with the following meaning: $\mu_f = 1$ if time span $f \in F$ is covered by the morning shift, 0 otherwise, and $\phi_f = 1$ if $f \in F$ is covered by the afternoon shift. K is the number of operators required in each team, while k_f is the number of used phone operator positions in each time span, and thus it represents the cardinality of each sub-team. Due to the number of operators, some operators may belong to both sub-teams, namely they may be in charge of the phone calls with both sub-teams. We allow at most τ_f operators to belong to both sub-teams in each time span. The demand level forecasted for the time span $f \in F$ is denoted by r_f.

Note that all teams follow the same pattern and the pattern is cyclically repeated, thus the meaningful decision is assigning each team to the shift to be performed in the first day of the considered time interval. Hence we can identify teams with the first day shifts. Besides deciding the assignment of operators to shifts, the subteams in which each team is split must be decided as well. To represent the composition of each team and sub-team we use six sets of binary variables: $\{x_{is} : i \in O, s \in S\}$, with $x_{is} = 1$ if operator i is assigned to team s as the foreman of the shift; $\{w_{is} : i \in O, s \in S\}$, with $w_{is} = 1$ if operator i is assigned to team s but he/she is not the foreman;

$\{\delta_{isf}: i \in O, s \in S\}$, with $\delta_{isf} = 1$ if operator i is assigned to shift s and to the first sub-team in the time span f; $\{\gamma_{isf}: i \in O, s \in S\}$, with $\gamma_{isf} = 1$ if operator i is assigned to shift s and to the second sub-team in the time span f. Besides, we use a binary variable for each operator, time shift and time span, η_{isf}, which is equal to one if the operator belongs to shift s and to both sub-teams with respect to time span f. We define another set of binary variables $\{y_{is}: i \in O, s \in S\}$, where $y_{is} = 1$ if operator i is assigned to the morning shift when his/her team splits.

Finally, a continuous non negative variable z represents the relative increase, of the number of manageable calls. As such increase must be managed in each time interval, z represents the minimum increase over all the considered time intervals. The choice of this objective function is twofold. First, the resulting team composition allows to satisfy the largest demand increase in the worst time interval; this modeling choice gives a better balance in team composition with respect to the use of average values, since it tends to guarantee equity in the service access. Second, since even if the data on forecasted demand changes, as soon as their proportion is constant, the optimal solution found by the model is still meaningful. We can then consider this feature as a robustness one with respect of the data collected.

We then obtain the following mathematical model:

$$\max z \qquad (1.1)$$

$$\sum_{i \in O}(x_{is} + w_{is}) = K \qquad \forall s \in S \qquad (1.2)$$

$$\sum_{s \in S}(x_{is} + w_{is}) \leq 1 \qquad \forall i \in O \qquad (1.3)$$

$$\sum_{i \in O_c} x_{is} \geq 1 \qquad \forall s \in S \qquad (1.4)$$

$$y_{is} \leq x_{is} + w_{is} \qquad \forall i \in O, s \in S \qquad (1.5)$$

$$w_{is} + \mu_f y_{is-1} + \phi_f(x_{is+1} + w_{is+1} - y_{is+1}) \geq \delta_{isf}, \qquad \forall i \in O, f \in F, s \in S \qquad (1.6)$$

$$w_{is} + \mu_f y_{is-1} + \phi_f(x_{is+1} + w_{is+1} - y_{is+1}) \geq \gamma_{isf}, \qquad \forall i \in O, f \in F, s \in S \qquad (1.7)$$

$$\sum_{i \in O} \delta_{isf} = k_f, \qquad \forall f \in F, s \in S \qquad (1.8)$$

$$\sum_{i \in O} \gamma_{isf} = k_f, \qquad \forall f \in F, s \in S \qquad (1.9)$$

$$\delta_{isf} + \gamma_{isf} \leq 1 + \eta_{isf}, \qquad \forall i \in O, f \in F, s \in S \qquad (1.10)$$

$$\sum_{i \in O} \eta_{isf} \leq \tau_f, \qquad \forall f \in F, s \in S \qquad (1.11)$$

$$\sum_{i \in O} e_i \delta_{isf} \geq r_f(1+z), \qquad \forall f \in F, s \in S \qquad (1.12)$$

$$\sum_{i \in O} e_i \gamma_{isf} \geq r_f(1+z), \qquad \forall f \in F, s \in S \qquad (1.13)$$

$$x_{is}, w_{is}, v_{is}, y_{is} \in \{0,1\}, \forall\, i \in O, \forall\, s \in S, \qquad z \geq 0. \qquad (1.14)$$

Constraints (1.2) state each team is composed of K operators, including the selected foreman, inequalities (1.3) ensure each operator belongs to at most one team, and constraints (1.4) guarantee that each team has at least one foreman assigned to it. Constraints (1.5) state that each team is split in two in the A/M shift. Constraints (1.6) and (1.7) describe the division in sub-teams of the operators on work in each time span, namely those assigned to the shift, plus those assigned to the previous shift and belonging to the part assigned to morning shift, if the considered time span belongs to the morning, plus those assigned to the following shift and assigned to the part covering the afternoon, otherwise. Equations (1.8) and (1.9) state that k_f phone operator positions are used. Constraints (1.10) force the suitable value of variables η_{isf}, while constraints (1.11) guarantee that at most τ_f operators belong to both sub-teams in each time span. Constraints (1.12) and (1.13) are the demand coverage constraints. The left hand side of each inequality represents the efficiency of those operators covering the considered time span f. Note that each team faces each time span and therefore such constraint is to be written for each team and time span. Further, as each subgroup may be in charge of the emergency calls, the constraint is to be written for both subgroups. The right hand side represents the forecasted demand increased by fraction z. Thus, the value of z is forced to the minimum fraction of increase which can be faced in each time span. The value of z is maximized, according to objective function (1.1).

During the working time, operators can take short breaks, thus becoming temporarily unavailable. We modified our model to take into account the possible unavailability of one operator, thus introducing a further robustness feature. In particular, we select the operator with highest value of e_i in each time span. We introduce variables q^{δ}_{sf} (q^{γ}_{sf} respectively) representing the efficiency of the best operator in team δ (γ respectively) in shift s and time span f. Then we modify constraints (1.12) and (1.13) to guarantee that each team can deal with the amount of traffic even if the best operator is not available, obtaining:

$$q^{\delta}_{sf} \geq e_i \delta_{isf}, \qquad \forall i \in O, s \in S, f \in F \qquad (1.12')$$

$$q^{\gamma}_{sf} \geq e_i \gamma_{isf}, \qquad \forall i \in O, s \in S, f \in F \qquad (1.13')$$

$$\sum_{i \in O} e_i \delta_{isf} - q^{\delta}_{sf} \geq r_f(1+z) \qquad \forall s \in S, f \in F \qquad (1.12'')$$

$$\sum_{i \in O} e_i \gamma_{is} - q^{\gamma}_{sf} \geq r_f(1+z) \qquad \forall s \in S, f \in F. \qquad (1.13'')$$

1.3 Results and discussion

The Milano EMS keeps daily logs of the emergency calls, with time and duration of each call. We divided the considered 24 hours horizon into to a set of time intervals or time spans. Initially, the time spans are three, corresponding to the shifts. For each time span f the forecasted demand level r_f is computed as the 99% percentile of the number of calls over one minute intervals. This allows to compute a maximum forecasted demand, as number of calls within a given time span.

Table 1.2. Results on the first model, with three time spans

Instance n.	*LB*	*UB*	*gap %*
0	0.6994	0.7034	0.57%
1	0.7730	0.7773	0.55%
2	0.7669	0.7782	1.45%
3	0.7301	0.7368	0.91%
4	0.7055	0.7080	0.35%
5	0.7423	0.7564	1.86%
6	0.7301	0.7374	0.99%
7	0.7730	0.7810	1.02%
8	0.7301	0.7380	1.07%
9	0.7362	0.7454	1.23%
average	0.74		1.00%

The team cardinality K was fixed to 7 operators, while the number of available phone positions k_f is set to 5 during morning and afternoon shifts and 3 during the night shift. We recall that due to the split, during morning and afternoon there are more operators availables than during the night. Ten instances were randomly generated selecting 35 operators on a pool of 54, so as to model a certain amount of unavailability, due, for instance, to illness or vacation.

Our models were implemented in OPL and solved by CPLEX 12.10, setting one hour time limit and mipgap 0.005, and the tests have been run on a dual Six-Core AMD Opteron Processor, with 16GB RAM. First, we ran tests involving model (1.2)–(1.14). The results are shown in Table 1.2, where for each instance the best bound on the optimal solution (UB) and the best integer solution found by CPLEX (LB) are reported, together with the gap, in percentage, computed as $\frac{(UB-LB)}{UB}$. Table 1.2 shows that the gap provided in the considered CPU time is reasonable, being always below 2%, even though CPLEX cannot prove optimality in any instance. The needed CPU time may appear significant, also because of the features of the used processor. However, the teams planning is to be run once a month in the worst case, and thus some hours of computational effort can be spent. Although the optimality of the integer solutions is not proven, the results show that the optimized teams can manage a significant increase in the demand amount (70% on the average).

An analysis of the obtained solutions shows that the bottleneck time span is the night one, as the number of operators is reduced. However, according to the data on demand and on the real life based experience, the night is usually a quiet period. The worst part of it is between 9pm and 11pm. During these hours, all the available operators may be required to answer the emergency calls. Thus, a second set of tests have been run, in which one time span is added, between 9pm and 11pm. For this time span the value of k_f is set to 5, while for the rest of the night is kept as in the former tests. The results obtained applying this strategy are reported in Table 1.3. Also in this case, the gap il limited, even if CPLEX cannot prove optimality in any of

Table 1.3. Results on the first model, with four time spans

Instance n.	*LB*	*UB*	*gap %*
0	1.2893	1.2950	0.44%
1	1.3884	1.4041	1.12%
2	1.3802	1.3959	1.12%
3	1.3306	1.3397	0.68%
4	1.2975	1.3008	0.25%
5	1.3471	1.3661	1.39%
6	1.3306	1.3405	0.74%
7	1.3884	1.3992	0.77%
8	1.3306	1.3413	0.80%
9	1.3388	1.3512	0.92%
average	1.34		0.82%

the instances. Allowing to use more operators in the evening significantly increases the objective function. In fact, the optimized teams may face a more than double demand.

Further, by adding constraints (1.12′)–(1.13″), the model can be modified to guarantee that the increase represented by z can be faced even without the best operator. We tested the second model, with three and four time spans, as well: results are reported in Table 1.4 and 1.5, respectively. Results on the modified model show that the gap significantly increases, rising up to about 85% in the worst case. On the other hand, the value of z decreases. Especially for the three time span case, it drops below 0.1. We must note that they are heuristic solutions; still, even the upper bound dramatically decreases. The gap is improved for the four spans case. The bearable increase in the demand peak is improved with respect to the three spans case. The model seems however difficult to solve. Nevertheless, it seems to represent well the real life case, and it is therefore worthy of further studies.

Table 1.4. Results on the model with best operator unavailable, with three time spans

Instance n.	*LB*	*UB*	*gap*
0	0.0491	0.2270	78.37%
1	0.0920	0.2883	60.09%
2	0.0798	0.3090	74.17%
3	0.0491	0.3336	85.28%
4	0.0368	0.2883	87.24%
5	0.0552	0.3497	84.22%
6	0.0675	0.2883	76.59%
7	0.0920	0.3065	69.98%
8	0.0552	0.3250	83.02%
9	0.0675	0.3103	78.25%

Table 1.5. Results on the model with best operator unavailable, with four time spans

Instance n.	*LB*	*UB*	*gap*
0	0.4132	0.8429	50.98%
1	0.4711	0.7702	38.83%
2	0.4380	0.8182	46.47%
3	0.4132	0.7865	47.46%
4	0.3967	0.7839	49.39%
5	0.4215	0.8945	52.88%
6	0.4380	0.7427	41.03%
7	0.4876	0.8182	40.41%
8	0.4050	0.9135	55.57%
9	0.4380	0.8017	45.37%

Finally, we apply our models to partially given solutions. We started using an example of team composition given by Milano EMS (November 2010). We fixed the foreman and shift assignment variables (x_{is} and w_{is}), and optimize the model to find the best splitting and sub-teams composition. As a term of comparison we optimize the full model. The given team composition, even if optimized with respect to splitting and sub-teams composition may bear an increase in the demand up to 1.124 (0.306, without the best operator). On the other hand if also team composition and shift assignment are optimized, then a larger increase 1.364 (0.463) can be reached.

1.4 Conclusions

We proposed mathematical programming models to deal with the problem of workforce management based on forecasted demand arising in an Operation Center of an Italian Emergency Medical Service. In particular, we take into account the team composition and the rostering problems of OC operators. We show that such approach can be used to solve the problem in real life cases in reasonable computational time.

The models allow to take into account quality and fairness of the provided service, as the overall efficiency of the OC is considered in the constraints formulation. Besides, the proposed models aim at maximizing the increase which can be faced: in fact OC would, in the future, deal with an increase in the demands amount due, for instance to the population aging. Furthermore, the models compose teams in order to satisfy the largest demand gain in the worst time interval: this approach gives a better balance in team composition guaranteeing the equity in the service access.

Finally, the models are flexible as they can be modified to take into account different shifts, or more robust requirements.

Acknowledgements. Bernardetta Addis, Roberto Aringhieri and Andrea Grosso acknowledge support from the Italian Ministry of Education, University and Research (MIUR), under the grant n. RBFR08IKSB, "Firb – Futuro in Ricerca 2008". The authors wish to thank Andrea Pagliosa and Rodolfo Bonora of Milano EMS.

References

1. Aringhieri, R.: Composing medical crews with Equity and Efficiency. Central European Journal of Operations Research **17**(3), 343–357 (2009)
2. Atlason, J., Epelman, M.A., Henderson, S.G.: Call center staffing with simulation and cutting plane methods. Annals of Operations Research **127**, 333–358 (2004)
3. Atlason, J., Epelman, M.A., Henderson, S.G.: Optimizing call center staffing using simulation and analytic center cutting-plane methods. Management Science **54**(2), 295–309 (2008)
4. Bellanti, F., Carello, G., Croce, F.D., Tadei, R.: A greedy-based neighborhood search approach to a nurse rostering problem. European Journal of Operational Research **153**, 28–40 (2004)
5. Bhadury, J., Mighty, E.J., Damar, H.: Maximizing workforce diversity in project teams: a network flow approach. Omega **28**(2), 143–153 (2000)
6. Billionnet, A.: Integer programming to schedule a hierarchical workforce with variable demands. European Journal of Operational Research **114**(1), 105–114 (1999)
7. Burke, E.K., Causmaecker, P.D., Berghe, G.V., Landeghem, H.V.: The state of the art of nurse rostering. Journal of Scheduling **7**, 441–499 (2004)
8. Cheang, B., Li, H., Lim, A., Rodrigues, B.: Nurse rostering problems – a bibliographic survey. European Journal of Operational Research **151**, 447–460 (2003)
9. Ernst, A., Jiang, H., Krishnamoorthy, M., Owens, B., Sier, D.: An annotated bibliography of personnel scheduling and rostering. Annals of Operations Research **127**, 21–144 (2004)
10. Ernst, A., Jiang, H., Krishnamoorthy, M., Sier, D.: Staff scheduling and rostering: A review of applications, methods and models. European Journal of Operational Research **153**, 3–27 (2004)
11. Feyter, T.D.: Modeling heterogeneity in manpower planning: dividing the personnel system into more homogeneous subgroups. Applied stochastic models in business and industry **22**, 321–334 (2006)
12. Feyter, T.D.: Modeling mixed push and pull promotion flows in Manpower Planning. Annals of Operations Research **155**, 25–39 (2007)
13. Goodale, J.C., Thompson, G.M.: A comparison of heuristics for assigning individual employees to labor tour schedules. Annals of Operations Research **128**, 47–63 (2004)
14. Gurvich, I., Luedtke, J., Tezcan, T.: Staffing call centers with uncertain demand forecasts: A chance-constrained optimization approach. Management Science **56**(7), 1093–1115 (2010)
15. Jiang, H., Krishnamoorthy, M., Sier, D.: Staff scheduling and rostering: Theory and applications, part I and II. Annals of Operations Research **127–128**(1–4) (2004)
16. Kellogg, D.L., Walczak, S.: Nurse scheduling: From academia to implementation or not? Interfaces **37**(4), 355–369 (2007)
17. Li, Y., Chen, J., Cai, X.: An integrated staff-sizing approach considering feasibility of scheduling decision. Annals of Operations Research **155**, 261–390 (2007)
18. Miller, H.: Nurse scheduling using mathematical programming. Operations Research **24**, 857–870 (1976)
19. Turner, J., Mehrotra, S., Daskin, M.S.: Perspectives on health-care resource management problems. In: Sodhi, M.S., Tang, C.S. (eds.) A Long View of Research and Practice in Operations Research and Management Science, pp. 231–247. International Series in Operations Research & Management Science, vol. 148. Springer, New York (2010)
20. Warner, D.: Scheduling nursing personnel according to nursing preference: A mathematical programming approach. Operations Research **24**, 842–856 (1976)

Chapter 2

Operating rooms scheduling under uncertainty

Isabelle Beaulieu, Michel Gendreau, and Patrick Soriano

Abstract. Operating rooms (OR) are considered as one of the most resource consuming services of hospitals. OR managers must face conflicting constraints in order to build schedules which maximize resources utilization while minimizing cancellations and overtime. In this work, a four steps approach is proposed. First, surgery cases are assigned to a given day. Second, they are scheduled according to different strategies, which are evaluated through a simulation tool in the third step. If needed, feedback and rescheduling occur in the fourth step. Uncertainty is taken into consideration implicitly twice. First through the load level of the schedule built during the assignment problem and second, in the simulation step. Each scheduling strategy is evaluated according to different performance criteria. Computational experiments performed on sixteen sets of randomly generated data (based on real data provided by a large hospital center located in Montreal) are used to compare the different strategies.

I. Beaulieu (✉)
Department of management sciences (MQG), HEC Montréal, 3000 chemin de la Côte-Sainte-Catherine, Montréal (Québec), H3T 2A7 Canada
Interuniversity Research Center on Enterprise Networks, Logistics and Transportation (CIRRELT), Université de Montréal, C.P. 6128, succ. Centre-ville, Montréal (Québec), H3C 3J7 Canada
e-mail: isabelle.2.beaulieu@hec.ca

M. Gendreau
Department of mathematics and industrial engineering, Ecole Polytechnique, C.P. 6079, succ. Centre-ville, Montréal (Québec), H3C 3A7 Canada
Interuniversity Research Center on Enterprise Networks, Logistics and Transportation (CIRRELT), Université de Montréal, C.P. 6128, succ. Centre-ville, Montréal (Québec), H3C 3J7 Canada
e-mail: michel.gendreau@cirrelt.ca

P. Soriano
Department of management sciences (MQG), HEC Montréal, 3000 chemin de la Côte-Sainte-Catherine, Montréal (Québec), H3T 2A7 Canada
Interuniversity Research Center on Enterprise Networks, Logistics and Transportation (CIRRELT), Université de Montréal, C.P. 6128, succ. Centre-ville, Montréal (Québec), H3C 3J7 Canada
e-mail: patrick.soriano@cirrelt.net

Tànfani E., Testi A. (Eds.): Advanced Decision Making Methods Applied to Health Care.
International Series in Operations Research & Management Science 173
DOI 10.1007/978-88-470-2321-5_2, © Springer-Verlag Italia 2012

Keywords: surgery planning, case assignment problem, scheduling criteria, detailed surgery schedules, operating rooms, stochastic surgery times, integer programming, simulation

2.1 Introduction and problem addressed

2.1.1 Introduction

Aging population puts an extra burden on health care systems as evidenced by recurring reports since several years. Expenses are increasing faster than governments' budgets for medical services. In 2006, health expenditures accounted for 10.4% of GDP in Canada [19]. Out of this, 43% was invested in medical and health care [13]. Knowing that the surgery department usually accounts for around 10% [4, 15] of a hospital budget, one can understand the importance of an optimal usage of operating rooms (OR). However, this is a challenging task because it is almost impossible to predict the exact duration of a surgery. In order to help OR managers build robust schedules, we develop in this study a tool which takes into account uncertainty and needs for specialized equipments. This tool compares eight different scheduling strategies and evaluates them based on various performance criteria. Thus, each surgery department can select a scheduling strategy that performs well with regards to its objectives. The tool also allows for the adjustment of various parameters to achieve established goals. Our contribution is mainly focused on the assignment of cases. Indeed, surgeons' choices are respected regarding priority (or value) of cases. Furthermore, since blocks allocation, surgeons and cases are included in the model as data, it is possible to give more or less latitude to the tool when it comes to the choice of cases that should be performed on a given day. This flexibility is interesting because it can give total control over the choice of surgeries to the surgeons, while it can also be used to pick cases from a larger list in order to optimize more global objectives such as minimizing waiting lists, without requiring modifications. Moreover, problems can be solved in real time.

The chapter is organized as follows. In the remainder of this section, we will review previous work on this problem. The methodology and solution approach are then presented in Section 2.2, followed by our results and concluding remarks.

2.1.2 Literature review

Planning of surgeries can be performed at three levels: strategic, tactical and operational. Strategic planning mainly refers to the allocation of time blocks or periods of time to the various surgical specialties. OR hours are usually spread between wards according to historical use but one must be careful not to create undesired disparities between allocated time and usage when demand shifts. Tactical planning covers the building of schedules that maximize the value of surgeries performed while minimizing costs. It includes the assignment of cases to days and/or rooms. Finally, operational planning refers to the scheduling of cases within a given day [11]. It also includes real-time management of delayed surgeries and cancellations. Our tool will focus on tactical and operational planning; however, the proposed simulation tool could be used to analyse different allocation policies, thus, helping at the strategic level.

The problem of surgery planning and scheduling is complex because many constraints must be considered. Authors who attempted to solve this problem usually worked on a simplified version of the problem. Some also divided the problem hierarchically to facilitate solving. Exact methods only work on small instances and are not helpful when it comes to the management of uncertainty. To offset this, a few authors also tried to include uncertainty in their model, or used a simulation tool. The various solution approaches can be classified into three categories: case assignment approaches, scheduling approaches, and approaches that include both assignment and scheduling. Our model belongs to the third category and it also includes a simulation tool.

2.1.2.1 Allocation problem

Strum *et al.* [21] proposed a minimal cost analysis model to determine the optimal allocation of time blocks between surgical services. To evaluate different scenarios, they introduce the concept of under-utilization and over-utilization. They estimate that costs associated with over-utilization increase as usage increases, while costs of under-utilization decrease while usage increases. They also point out that utilization rates can vary greatly from service to service given that average case durations can be widely different (e.g. orthopedic surgery versus ophtalmology), thus questioning the allocation based on historical records.

Ozkarahan *et al.* [18] built a multiple criteria model which allows managers to design schedules based on their desired objectives. Possible decision criteria are: minimization of the variability in day length, minimization of under-utilization and over-utilization per operating room, prioritization of emergencies, or maximization of bed utilization in the intensive care unit (ICU). Their model also takes into account needs for specific rooms.

Santibanez *et al.* [20] developed a mixed integer programming model to evaluate impacts of surgical schedules on bed capacity, surgeons' booking privileges, waiting lists and OR availability at the strategic level in order to help OR managers. They showed that a hospital in British Columbia could handle more cases without increasing its capacity in post-anesthesia care unit (PACU) if it scheduled its specialties differently.

While these models are useful when deciding which cases should be planned, they do not consider the precise scheduling of surgeries within the day. The following section presents models that consider operational planning.

2.1.2.2 Scheduling problems

Goldman *et al.* [9] showed through simulation that scheduling longest cases first and shortest cases at the end of the day, maximizes utilization rate and minimizes overtime. Unfortunately, cancellation rates also increase. When shortest cases are performed first, cancellation rate is minimized but overtime increases.

Marcon and Dexter [16] evaluated the impacts of scheduling on human resource needs in PACU. Assuming that only one surgeon is operating in each room per day, they evaluated seven scheduling strategies. The first three strategies are well-known: *random strategy*, *longest cases first* and *shortest cases first*. The fourth one schedules the shortest case first, followed by longest case, followed by second shortest case... It is called the *mixed strategy*. The next strategy consists in scheduling the shortest case at the beginning of the day, the second shortest at the end of the day, the third shortest case will be performed second... They call it *half increasing duration, half decreasing duration*. *Half decreasing duration, half increasing duration* is the opposite of this strategy. The last strategy considered was *Johnson's* which ranks cases according to their duration in the OR and their estimated lenth of stay in PACU. The shortest of all durations is picked. If it is PACU duration, the case is scheduled at the end of the day. If it is a case duration, it is scheduled at the beginning of the day. The worst strategies are *longest cases first* and *half decreasing, half increasing* because they both create peak periods in PACU. Best strategies are *mixed* and *half increasing, half decreasing*, but they are only slightly better than *random* assignment of the surgeries.

While these models are useful in scheduling cases planned on a given day, they do not consider the choice of surgeries to be performed. The following section presents models that consider both case assignment and operational planning.

2.1.2.3 Models integrating allocation and scheduling

Ogulata and Erol [17] presented a model that maximizes OR usage, balances the distribution of cases between groups of surgeons in terms of duration and blocks assignment, and minimizes waiting times. The problem was subdivided into three parts in order to be solvable in reasonable times. The first step consists in planning cases selected from a waiting list for the following week. At the second step, cases are assigned to a group of surgeons depending on OR capacity and case duration. The precise date and surgeon are determined in the third step. The authors show that short cases have a positive impact on utilization rate, whereas long cases have a negative impact on utilization rate. Medium duration cases have a positive impact on utilization rate if they represent less than 33% of the total number of cases.

Guinet and Chaabane [10] proposed a model which first assigns cases to a day, and then schedules the cases within that day. Their model minimizes the total costs (waiting costs and OR costs) associated with surgery cases. This could mean that at some point, a case could be performed in overtime because it would become less expensive for the hospital. Their model takes into account capacity constraints, such as PACU beds, OR nurses and rooms capacity.

Dulude [7] scheduled the most uncertain cases first and finished the day with the most predictable cases (*decreasing variability*). Her model takes into account needs for specialized equipments and overtime policies. Once the schedule is obtained, she uses simulation to evaluate the robustness of the schedule. A Beta distribution is used to model the duration of each case.

Jebali *et al.* [14] minimized waiting times, under-utilization and over-utilization of available OR rooms in the assignment step. Capacity constraints and overtime policies are taken into account. Then, in the sequencing step, each room is scheduled individually to minimize overtime. Their sequencing strategy allows to exchange cases between rooms if needed.

Testi *et al.* [25] developed a three-phase, hierarchical approach for the weekly scheduling of operating rooms which improves overtime and throughput as well as waiting list reduction. First, they solved a bin packing problem to select the number of sessions to be allocated to each specialty on a weekly basis, then they determined the optimal assignment of specialties to ORs. Lastly, simulation is used to determine the optimal sequencing strategy.

Fei *et al.* [8] designed a two-stage model where they first decide, through a column-generation-based heuristic, on which day a given case will be performed and then they build the schedule with a hybrid genetic algorithm. Their objectives are to maximize utilization of the OR and minimize overtime and idle time between surgical cases.

Tànfani *et al.* [24] proposed a linear model to determine the assignment of wards among ORs and the subset of patients to be operated on each day which minimize the numbers of hospitalizations during the week-end.

Other authors also tried different approaches to help managers understand and solve this problem in the last few years. Many authors have proposed to follow a cyclic master surgical schedule in order to level the utilization of post-anesthesia resources such as PACU nurses, ICU workload and beds utilization [2, 3, 26, 27]. Some authors have also proposed that surgeons operate in two rooms simultaneously to increase number of cases treated [1]. These approaches are beyond the scope of this chapter.

2.1.2.4 Variability

The duration of a case is hard to predict because it can vary widely from one case to another, even for identical procedures. The surgeon performing the surgery, type of anesthesia, gender, age and risks associated with the patient condition are all responsible for part of the uncertainty [23]. Moreover, the difference between the estimated and the real duration causes even more variability. The expected duration is sometimes estimated with historical data. Dexter *et.al* [6] showed with a sample of more than 200,000 cases that at least a million historical data are needed in order to have at least three similar cases 90% of the time. Cases where two or more types of procedures must be performed simultaneously also reduce the probability of having sufficient historical data. Moreover, Zhou *et al.* [28] showed that even with a large quantity of historical data, variability is not reduced significantly. Indeed, when they compared two cases for which they respectively have one and 39 historical data, they only reduced the average lateness from 26 to 22 minutes in one hospital, and from 11 to 9 minutes in the other hospital. In addition, it is not rare that a case is performed only once per year per surgeon (36.5% of cases in the first hospital and 28.6% of cases in the second hospital).

To offset this lack of historical data, some authors use simulation tools to evaluate durations. Hancock *et al.* [12] used a lognormal distribution to estimate the duration of a surgery case. They chose the lognormal distribution because it allows for asymmetric distribution with small variations to the left (slightly shorter cases) but large variations to the right (cases longer than expected). Strum *et al.* [22] also compared normal and lognormal distributions and they found that the lognormal distribution outperforms normal distribution. Estimating the duration of a case at the 60th percentile minimizes costs when overtime costs represent 1.5 times the costs of regular OR hours.

2.2 Materials and methods

2.2.1 Solution approach

OR managers are responsible for managing operating rooms. Depending on the availability of anesthesiologists and OR nurses, they first have to decide how many rooms will be in use. Second, they assign each room to a specialty or to an individual surgeon. Each surgeon then decides which cases he wishes to perform and sends the information to the head of his specialty. The information given usually includes: diagnosis, desired date, expected duration, variability, priority (value), and specialized equipments required. Department heads confirm that the schedules proposed by their surgeons are realistic, and send them to the OR manager, who then makes a final assessment of feasibility of the proposed schedule and makes all necessary adjustments to eliminate specialized equipments' conflicts before approving the resulting overall schedule.

To facilitate the integration of our tool in the hospital, we have decided to mimic the structure of decisions already in place. As many previous authors, we have decided to split the problem into two parts [7, 10, 11, 14, 17]. First, the assignment of surgeries is based on a list of desired cases provided by surgeons. The tool ensures that there are no conflicts for specialized equipments. Second, uncertainty is taken into account implicitly in two ways: *a priori*, through the operating rooms loading level which can be adjusted by the OR manager and, *a posteriori*, through a performance analysis which is completed for each scenario. The OR loading level is defined as the ratio of the expected time of utilization over the operating time available. This parameter can be adjusted to build more or less conservative schedules. Thus, a manager who wishes to maximize utilization of resources (at the planning level) can decide to aim for a loading level of 100%, whereas a manager who wants to avoid overtime will set the loading level lower. This feature of the proposed planning tool allows for flexibility and helps to manage uncertainty. Variability is also covered in the post-optimization analysis. Indeed, each schedule is evaluated through performance ratios that provide feedback on decisions and allow for adjustments.

In the following sections, the different components of the proposed planning approach will be described in details, namely case assignment problem, scheduling strategies and simulation tool.

2.2.2 Case assignment problem

The case assignment problem we propose is based on Dulude's model [7] and can be formulated as a linear integer programming model. The model seeks to maximize the value of cases planned on a given day. The value of a surgery is established by the surgeon based on the priority and the urgency of the case. Surgeries that are not scheduled on the expected date stay on the waiting list and are automatically available for the next operating day. One could argue that the priority of a surgery that cannot be scheduled on the day selected by the surgeon should increase. However, we decided not to implement the model in such a way because the schedules we are constructing cover a short-term horizon, thus, priority will generally not change significantly.

This first step checks for conflicts with specialized equipments. It also integrates constraints on overtime utilization, but, at this stage, we did not authorize overtime. The linear integer problem is defined as follow:

Maximize

$$\sum_{l \in L} \sum_{k \in K} \sum_{j \in J_k} \sum_{i \in I_j} c_{ik} x_{ikl}. \tag{2.1}$$

Subject to:

$$\sum_{k \in K} \sum_{l \in L} x_{ikl} \leq 1, \quad \forall i \in I_j, \forall j \in J_k \tag{2.2}$$

$$y_{ikl} = \sum_{l'=max\{1, l-d_i+1\}} x_{ikl'}, \quad \forall i \in I_j, \forall j \in J_k, \forall k \in K, \forall l \in L \tag{2.3}$$

$$\sum_{i \in I_j} y_{ikl} \leq 1, \quad \forall j \in J_k, \forall k \in K, \forall l \in L \tag{2.4}$$

$$\sum_{j \in J_k} \sum_{i \in I_j} y_{ikl} \leq n_l, \quad \forall k \in K, \forall l \in L' \tag{2.5}$$

$$\sum_{j \in J_k} \sum_{i \in I_j^h} y_{ikl} \leq m_{hk}, \quad \forall k \in K, \forall l \in L, \forall h \in H \tag{2.6}$$

$$x_{ij}^k \in \{0, 1\} \tag{2.7}$$

$$y_{ikl} \in \{0, 1\} \tag{2.8}$$

where I is the set of all cases, J is the set of surgeons, K is the set of all days, and H represents the set of specialized resources. All the cases belonging to surgeon j are defined as I_j. L represents the number of periods during which operating rooms are opened, whereas set L' represents overtime periods available. For each case, two parameters are defined, namely d_i which represents the estimated duration of case i and c_{ik} which is the associated value of case i if it is performed on day k. The value of a case could vary over time since a routine surgery can become urgent if it is not performed within a given time.

As Dulude [7], we work with discrete instead of continuous times in order to decrease computational times. This does not represent a major bias since surgeons rarely estimate surgery durations down to the minute. However, instead of 30-

minutes periods, we used 10-minutes periods to be closer to real duration estimates. The duration of a surgery is thus estimated in number of periods, rounded up.

To respect actual policies in place at our hospital partner, we assume that the number of operating rooms available will always be equal to the number of surgeons performing cases on day k, which are given by set J_k. No case can start before period 1 and no case can be planned outside opening hours, unless otherwise specified. The last period when a surgery i can start is computed as $L-d_i+1$, which is the closing time minus the case duration. Cases' durations always include preparation of the patient in the OR and cleaning time.

In order to establish which surgery will be performed on a given day, at a given period, we need to introduce a decision variable x_{ikl} that can be defined as follows:

$$x_{ikl} = \begin{cases} 1 \text{ if case } i \text{ takes place on day } k \text{ and starts in period } l \\ 0 \text{ otherwise.} \end{cases}$$

x_{ikl} is defined for $l \in (1,\ldots,L-d_i+1)$.

The objective function (2.1) maximizes the value of cases planned for a given planning horizon. When surgeons submit a list of cases I_j, they assign a value c_{ik} to each case. The decision variable x_{ikl} will determine if case i starts in period l on day k. Since x_{ikl} is binary, only the value of selected cases will be included in the calculation of the total value of all cases planned.

Constraints (2.2) ensure that each surgery is performed only once.

The decision variable x_{ikl} indicates the period at which case i starts; it does not reflect the duration of the surgery. Thus, we need to add a constraint (2.3) which ensures that a second case cannot start if the first one is not finished. To achieve this, we added a binary variable y_{ikl} which is equal to 1 if case i starting at period l is still in progress.

Constraints (2.4) ensure that a surgeon does not operate more than one patient at a time, and this, for each period and for each day.

Constraints (2.5) respect overtime policy of our hospital partner in Montreal. For each given period l outside regular hours, a certain quantity of operating rooms are available for overtime. This constraint ensures that only this number of rooms are in service at this period.

Hospitals must work with limited specialized equipments. To address this, constraints (2.6) are added. The number of surgeries requiring some specialized equipment cannot exceed available quantities of that equipment, for any given period. The number of surgeries requiring some special equipment h, $h \in H$, cannot exceed the available quantities of that equipment for any given period k identified by m_{hk}.

Finally, constraints (2.7) and (2.8) define variables x_{ikl} and y_{ikl} as binary variables.

2.2.3 Scheduling strategies

Cases that were previously chosen through the assignment problem are then rescheduled according to eight scheduling strategies. In order to do this, the values corresponding to the selected cases are modified to reflect the desired scheduling strategies. Since the model gives more importance to the cases with the highest value, we need to assign largest values to the cases we wish to see at the beginning of the day. For instance, if we wish to schedule shortest surgeries first, we would give a high value to short surgeries and a low value to long surgeries. However, all surgeries must be scheduled, thus the respect of the scheduling strategy is a secondary objective only. The scheduling strategies considered are:

- *Increasing duration*: Cases are ranked according to their durations. The day starts with the shortest surgery and ends with the longest surgery.
- *Decreasing duration*: Cases are ranked in decreasing order of durations and scheduled in that order.
- *Increasing variability*: Cases are ranked according to their variability rate. The day starts with low variability surgeries and ends with high variability.
- *Decreasing variability*: Cases are ranked according to their variability rate. The day starts with high variability surgeries and ends with low variability.
- *Random.*
- *Half increasing duration, half decreasing duration*: Cases are ranked according to their duration $(d_1, d_2, d_3, \ldots, d_n)$. The day starts with the shortest case d_1. The second shortest surgery d_2 will be performed at the end of the day. We obtain: $d_1, d_3, \ldots, d_n, \ldots, d_4, d_2$ [16].
- *Half decreasing duration, half increasing duration*: Cases are ranked according to their duration $(d_1, d_2, d_3, \ldots, d_n)$. The day starts with the longest case d_n. The second longest surgery d_{n-1} will be performed at the end of the day. We obtain: $d_n, d_{n-2}, \ldots, d_1, \ldots, d_{n-3}, d_{n-1}$ [16].
- *Mixed*: Cases are ranked according to their duration $(d_1, d_2, d_3, \ldots, d_n)$. The day starts with the shortest case d_1 and then, we proceed with the longest case d_n. We obtain: $d_1, d_n, d_2, d_{n-1}, \ldots$ [16].

Since scheduling is a secondary objective, we need to ensure that all cases previously selected will be scheduled, thus, we need to modify slightly our model. Constraint (2.2) becomes:

$$\sum_{k \in K} \sum_{l \in L} x_{ikl} = 1, \quad \forall j \in J_k, \forall i \in I_j. \tag{2.9}$$

The model is then solved for a second time. Constraint (2.9) being equal to 1, each previously selected case will be scheduled in that phase. Each room is rescheduled independently of the other rooms, nevertheless, one must still check for potential conflicts regarding specialized equipments. All constraints that were previously in the model remain, thus, we still ensure that there is no conflict for specialized equipments.

2.2.4 Simulation

To evaluate the robustness of each strategy, we evaluate the impact of simulated durations on the planned schedule. Schedules with simulated durations respect overtime and cancellation policies, and account for potential conflicts regarding specialized equipments. Performance ratios are computed and used to evaluate robustness of each strategy and to help select the best strategy to achieve the hospital's objectives. This secondary objective can be one, or a combination, of the following:

- minimize overtime;
- minimize cancellations;
- minimize costs attributed to overtime;
- minimize waiting times;
- minimize inactivity;
- minimize disparities in rooms' utilization;
- maximize utilization rate.

The performance analysis is performed after 1000 simulations of the cases' real durations to provide more realistic results. The duration is considered as a random variable which is generated from a probability distribution. In the first stage of our study, an approximation of the Beta distribution, known as Beta PERT, was used to simulate durations. This distribution, which is widely used in project management when task durations are not deterministic allows the generation of slightly shorter cases, but also much longer cases (e.g. in case of complications). It also estimates properly variability levels as established in collaboration with our hospital partner. The Beta PERT distribution is based on three parameters: a, the lower bound of the distribution, b, its mode, and c, the upper bound, where a corresponds to the optimistic scenario for the surgery being modeled, b corresponds to the estimated duration (either based on historical data or provided by the surgeon) and c the pessimistic scenario. With the data provided by our hospital partner, surgeries were then classified into three categories, according to their duration and variability:

- if the variability level is low, the potential duration should be between 92.5% and 112.5% of estimated duration;
- if the variability level is medium, the potential duration should be between 92.5% and 125% of estimated duration;
- if the variability level is high, the potential duration should be between 92.5% and 150% of estimated duration.

From there, we generated potential durations for each case, based on the estimation provided by the surgeon.

However since many authors in the literature have used lognormal distributions to simulate real durations, we carried out a second phase of experiments with this distribution. In Section 2.3.5, we will see that lognormal distributions provide similar results to those of the Beta distribution. Finally, one has to note that the lognormal is a distribution that is not bounded to the right and therefore needs to be truncated at some point because surgeries cannot last forever. On the other hand, Beta distribution is defined over a bounded interval, thus avoiding the need to choose an arbitrary cutting point.

2.3 Results and discussion

2.3.1 Test data

One advantage of this tool is that it can build suitable schedules without detailed historical data. Since we did not have proper and complete datasets that could be used to test this tool, we randomly generated data which reflected those previously provided by our hospital partner in Montreal. Datasets include:

- expected surgery date;
- surgeon;
- case number;
- diagnosis type, which includes duration and variability of duration;
- priority of case as established by the surgeon on a scale of 1 to 10, depending on severity of the patient's condition, risks associated with postponement of the surgery, anticipated benefits, time spent on the waiting list... The higher the priority, the higher the chances are that the case will be selected;
- needs for specialized equipments: if specialized equipment is needed for the case, its reference number will be included in the request. This allows to easily add specialized equipments to the system.

Four types of datasets were created to reflect our hospital partner's situation. Two datasets of cases to be scheduled were generated representing a short-term planning horizon of one week (identified by a 5 in the dataset code for the 5 operating days in a week) and a medium-term situation covering one month or a four week planning horizon (identified by a 20). For each horizon, we considered full and partial rooms' availability (respectively 12 rooms and 4 rooms with the corresponding value appearing in the dataset code). Then, for each dataset, four types of scheduling contexts were considered:

- data: the cases among which the tool can choose are only the ones the surgeon would like to perform (Only SC);
- corrige: the cases among which the tool can choose are only the ones the surgeon would like to perform (SC), plus a few desirable cases provided by the surgeon to provide flexibility in the event of a conflict of equipment (X);
- pool: include the waiting lists of all surgeons to choose cases from (WL);
- elective: include one case that the surgeon wants to perform due to high priority (1SC) and then the tool chooses the following cases among the waiting list (WL) of this surgeon.

Overall, a total of 16 distinct datasets were therefore created as described in Table 2.1. For instance dataset data_5_12 corresponds to the dataset for a planning horizon of 5 days with 12 ORs and in a scheduling context where the choice of surgeon over cases to perform is respected. There is a total of 30 different surgeons available and the dataset includes 270 cases, with 2 types of specialized equipments.

The data for the individual cases to be scheduled were generated respecting the types of cases performed at our hospital partner. The three possible categories are:

- Category 1: low variability, short duration of 30 minutes to 2 hours, routine interventions;
- Category 2: medium variability, average duration of 1 to 4 hours, general surgeries, 50% of cases need specialized equipments;
- Category 3: high variability, long duration of 2 to 4 hours, complex cases, 50% of cases need specialized equipments.

2.3.2 Performance Ratios

In order to evaluate each strategy, performance ratios are computed at every step of the solution approach. These ratios demonstrate the efficiency of each strategy to reach secondary objectives, such as the minimization of overtime. These ratios are:

- overtime: number of periods outside regular hours when operating rooms are in service;
- occupation rate: number of periods when surgery rooms are in service including overtime over total availability in regular time;
- under-utilization rate: wasted time divided by number of periods where OR are in service (excluding overtime); it can be computed by surgeon, by day, or for the whole schedule;
- over-utilization rate: overtime divided by number of periods where OR are in service (excluding overtime); it can be computed by surgeon, by day, or for the whole schedule;
- cancellation rate: number of cases cancelled or delayed per day over number of surgeons;
- usage: number of periods where surgery rooms are in service, including overtime; it can be computed by surgeon, by day, or for the whole schedule.

2.3.3 Experimental results

The program was coded in C++ and executed on a Pentium 4 (3GHz) working under Linux. The integer linear program was solved using CPLEX 10.0. Table 2.1 presents a summary of maximum execution times for each instance for the case assignment model and for the scheduling and simulation model. Times are given in seconds of CPU and the second part includes simulation times.

The tool was tested on 16 datasets, for a total of 128 schedules built when considering the 8 scheduling strategies described in Section 2.2.3. Results were obtained after 1000 simulations performed on each of the 128 schedules. The following sections present results for each scheduling strategy.

Table 2.1. Description of datasets and computational times (Legend: SC = Surgeon Choice, X = Extra desirable cases, WL = Waiting List)

	Datasets caracteristics						CPU times (sec)		
Name	*Days*	*Rooms*	*Surgeons*	*Interv.*	*qty. Equip per type*	*Instances Caracteristics*	*Case Assign.*	*Sched. Simul.*	*Total*
data_5_4	5	4	10	95	1	Only SC	0.78	0.62	1.4
data_5_12	5	12	30	270	2	Only SC	2.2	1.72	3.92
data_20_4	20	4	10	370	1	Only SC	7.86	4.49	12.35
data_20_12	20	12	30	1120	2	Only SC	62.26	47.16	109.42
corrige_5_4	5	4	10	155	1	SC + X	0.83	0.85	1.68
corrige_5_12	5	12	30	449	2	SC + X	2.96	6.62	9.58
corrige_20_4	20	4	10	521	1	SC + X	12.12	8.87	20.99
corrige_20_12	20	12	30	1570	2	SC + X	51.78	81.23	133.01
pool_5_4	5	4	10	1844	1	WL	1.52	21.33	22.85
pool_5_12	5	12	30	1844	2	WL	5.54	35.84	41.38
pool_20_4	20	4	10	1844	1	WL	12.73	54.74	67.47
pool_20_12	20	12	30	1844	2	WL	24.07	59.52	83.59
elective_5_4	5	4	10	571	1	1SC + WL	1.46	0.67	2.13
elective_5_12	5	12	30	1664	2	1SC + WL	3.45	2.7	6.15
elective_20_4	20	4	10	629	1	1SC + WL	11.67	7.53	19.2
elective_20_12	20	12	30	1844	2	1SC + WL	47.69	213.7	261.39

Table 2.2. Best strategies per performance indicators (Beta distribution)

	Best strategies for each performance indicators (Beta)							
Simulation type	*Random*	**incr.d.**	**decr.d.**	**incr.v**	*decr.v.*	*h.incr.d*	*h.decr.d.*	*mixed*
Cancellation rate								
Best results	6	8	4	**13**	4	5	5	4
Best and 2nd best results	7	**13**	6	**14**	4	5	5	4
Over-utilization rate								
Best results	1	0	**8**	0	5	0	1	0
Best and 2nd best results	2	0	**12**	1	8	2	5	3
Under-Utilization rate								
Best results	0	1	**8**	0	4	1	0	3
Best and 2nd best results	2	1	**11**	2	6	2	5	4

Table 2.2 presents the best strategies regarding cancellation, over-utilization and under-utilization rates. Cancellation rate is the probability that at least one surgeon must cancel a case, per day. Thus, a cancellation rate of 25% means that one case per day was postponed for a surgery department of four rooms. *Increasing variability* provides best or identical results to other strategies 13 times out of 16. If we take best and second best results, it is the most interesting strategy 14 times out of 16, closely followed by *increasing duration* (13 times out of 16). This is not surprising since longest cases are usually the ones with most variability. No other strategy is within 7% of the best one. Cancellation rate is higher in partial rooms availability schedules because in these instances, we have more category 3 cases (high variability and long duration).

Decreasing duration is the best strategy to minimize over-utilization rate, 8 times out of 16. This is not surprising since cases which will need overtime will be the shortest ones. No other strategy performs closely. At 6% of optimal results, *decreasing variability* is somewhat better than other strategies, but, at this point, *decreasing duration* is part of the best strategies 14 times out of 16.

Under-utilization includes all inactivity periods such as end of the day and waiting times for specialized equipment. *Decreasing duration* minimizes the under-utilization rate, 8 times out of 16. If we look at both best and second best results, this strategy appears 12 times out of 16. This makes sense because in case of a cancellation, inactivity time will be small at the end of the day. Moreover, the probability of doing a case in overtime is higher because most of the time, its duration will not exceed overtime availability.

To see if a schedule is robust, one needs to compare the differences, both positive and negative, between expected usage and simulated usage. The best strategies are the ones closest to 1. The results obtained show that when usage had been underestimated (ratio > 1), differences between the various strategies are small. However, when usage was overestimated (ratio < 1), the strategy that is closest to expected usage is *decreasing duration*.

To summarize, the *decreasing duration* strategy is the one that performs best regarding both under-utilization and over-utilization. If we focus on cancellation rate, the best strategy is *increasing variability*, closely followed by *increasing duration*. These three strategies are kept for the second part of our work where we evaluate impacts of different loading levels on results.

2.3.4 Sensitivity to planning day length

With the results obtained previously, we selected the three most promising strategies: *increasing duration*, *decreasing duration* and *increasing variability*. For each strategy, we evaluate the impact of various loading levels on simulated schedules. Occupation level is defined as the summation of expected duration of all surgeries over opening hours. Since surgeries are planned according to their value, we have no direct influence on occupation level. To influence it, we modify the number of periods during which the cases can be planned. This does not modify real opening hours (480 minutes). We work with days of 450, 460, 470, 480, 490, 500 and 510 minutes. The three first strategies compensate for longer than expected cases. The strategy on 480 minutes uses the full available time. The three last strategies plan cases in overtime, allowing to schedule cases that only need a few more minutes in order to be added to the schedule.

First, we select the cases that should be performed on a given day with our CPLEX model. Second, we schedule these cases with the three selected scheduling strategies. Then, the simulation tool allows to evaluate the impact of variability on each schedule. Finally, we compare the number of cases performed, anticipated utilization rate, overtime, under-utilization and cancellations rate for each loading level and each strategy. Results were computed after 1000 simulations on 8 of the 16 previous datasets and are presented in Table 2.3.

The proportion of cases completed does not necessarily increase with longer planning days. Indeed, even if we plan on more than 8 hours (480 minutes), the real opening time of the block is still 8 hours. Thus, unless cases are shorter than expected or unless we maximize utilization of overtime, we have a higher risk of cancellation. These results are consistent for each dataset, regardless of the strategy. Finally, the total number of cases performed is higher with low loading level and high loading levels. However, this is mainly due to the structure of the datasets. For instance, if many cases take 2.5 hours, it is easier to plan on 7.5 hours than on 8 hours. Thus, the results could be different with other datasets.

In addition, over-utilization rate increases considerably when occupation rate increases, with a steep increase in over-utilization when occupation rate is higher than 95%. Over-utilization rate is obviously at its lowest point when we schedule on shorter days. However, up to a day length of 480 minutes, over-utilization stays fairly low, below 1% in 7 of the 8 datasets, for all scheduling strategies. This basically means that unless a hospital has zero budget for overtime, it should not underbook its schedule. Table 2.3 shows that *decreasing duration* performs slightly better; however, day length has much more impact on the overall over-utilization rate than the scheduling strategy.

On the other hand, under-utilization rate decreases when occupation rate increases. However, when expected occupation rate is too high, under-utilization rises

Table 2.3. This table gives the number of time a strategy provides the best results for a given performance indicator (using Beta distribution). (The total can be higher than 8, since two strategies sometimes provide identical results)

Instance	*Best strategies for each performance indicators (Beta)* *day length (in minutes)*						
	450	460	470	480	490	500	510
Nb. of cases completed							
Increasing Duration	8	4	4	3	1	1	2
Decreasing Duration	4	4	2	3	2	3	1
Increasing Variability	5	8	8	6	5	4	5
Over-utilization rate							
Increasing Duration	1	–	1	–	3	2	3
Decreasing Duration	5	7	6	8	5	6	5
Increasing Variability	2	1	1	–	–	–	–
Under-utilization rate							
Increasing Duration	1	–	–	–	–	–	–
Decreasing Duration	5	7	7	8	7	8	8
Increasing Variability	2	1	1	–	1	–	–
Cancellation rate							
Increasing Duration	8	4	4	3	1	1	2
Decreasing Duration	4	4	2	3	2	3	1
Increasing Variability	5	8	8	6	5	4	5

sharply. It is also worth mentioning that the strategy of *decreasing duration* is the best, especially when the occupation rate is higher than one (490 min and more). This is so because shortest cases are at the end of the day, thus, cancellation risks and inactivity risks are lower.

Cancellation rate increases sharply with day length. Indeed, even the strategy *increasing variability* does not perform so well at a certain point. Cancellation rates are almost at zero when we schedule on days of 450 or 460 minutes. A day of 470 minutes will keep cancellation rate below 2.2% and a day of 480 minutes keeps it below 8.6%, except for *increasing duration* (rate above 15% for two datasets). When day length is more than 480 minutes, we easily achieve cancellation rates higher than 100%, which means that at least one case will have to be cancelled in at least one room.

These results show the importance of the objectives pursued by the OR managers. However, if there is a budget for overtime and if some cancellations are acceptable, planning on a 480 minutes day gives the most balanced schedules.

2.3.5 Study 2 – lognormal distribution

The lognormal distribution with two parameters is the most widely used statistical distribution in the literature to estimate surgical duration [5, 21, 22]. Therefore, we have decided to validate the results previously obtained with the Beta distribution.

Table 2.4. Best strategies per performance indicators (lognormal distribution)

	Best strategies for each performance indicators (Lognormal)							
Simulation type	*Random*	**incr.d.**	**decr.d.**	**incr.v**	*decr.v.*	*h.incr.d*	*h.decr.d.*	*mixed*
Cancellation rate								
Best results	0	2	0	**6**	0	0	0	0
Best and 2nd best results	1	**6**	0	**7**	1	0	0	1
Over-utilization rate								
Best results	0	0	**6**	0	1	0	1	0
Best and 2nd best results	0	0	**7**	0	3	1	5	0
Under-Utilization rate								
Best results	0	0	**6**	2	0	0	0	0
Best and 2nd best results	0	0	**6**	3	0	2	3	2

Table 2.5. This table gives the number of time a strategy provides the best results for a given performance indicator (using lognormal distribution). (The total can be higher than 8, since two strategies sometimes provide identical results)

	Best strategies for each performance indicators (log.)						
Instance	*day length (in minutes)*						
	450	460	470	480	490	500	510
Nb. of cases completed							
Increasing Duration	4	3	2	3	2	–	2
Decreasing Duration	–	–	–	–	–	–	–
Increasing Variability	4	5	6	5	6	8	6
Over-utilization rate							
Increasing Duration	1	–	1	1	–	2	2
Decreasing Duration	6	6	7	7	8	6	5
Increasing Variability	1	1	–	–	–	–	1
Under-utilization rate							
Increasing Duration	–	–	–	–	–	–	–
Decreasing Duration	1	1	6	6	8	8	8
Increasing Variability	7	6	2	2	–	–	–
Cancellation rate							
Increasing Duration	4	3	2	2	2	1	2
Decreasing Duration	–	–	–	–	–	–	1
Increasing Variability	4	4	6	6	6	7	5

A second study was performed focusing on the simulation part. Instead of using the original Beta distribution, we worked with a lognormal distribution. This allowed us to validate that the results were not biased by the type of distribution used. The sample provided by our hospital partner was used to generate means and standard deviations for the three types of cases (low, medium and high variability).

For each case, a random number following the 2-parameter lognormal distribution is generated.

We did the lognormal simulation on the 8 previously selected datasets. Computation times cannot be compared with the previous simulation since a new version of CPLEX was used (version 10.1.1) because of the delays between the two studies.

Results are consistent with what was previously found. *Decreasing duration* provides the best results if one wants to minimize over-utilization. It also gives the best results if under-utilization is to be minimized. On the other hand, if the OR manager wishes to minimize cancellation risks, cases should be ranked in order of variability (*increasing variability*) or in order of duration (*increasing duration).* Those results are similar to what has been found using the Beta distribution, therefore, we still use only these three strategies (*decreasing duration*, *increasing variability*, and *increasing duration*) for the sensitivity analysis phase.

As could be expected given the previous results, smaller loading levels decrease the risk of over-utilization. Moreover, independently of the loading level, *decreasing duration* performs better when it comes to the minimization of overtime.

As was previously demonstrated with the Beta distribution simulation, the under-utilization level is not minimized when one plans on more than a regular day length, trying to squeeze in cases. In fact, once again, the opposite occurs because some cases have to be cancelled. *Decreasing duration* still provides the lowest under-utilization rate, however, with the lognormal simulation, we can see that *increasing variability* outperforms *increasing duration*.

Finally, *increasing variabily* provides the lowest cancellation rate, but it is closely followed by *increasing duration*. Once again, the cancellation rate is minimized when the loading level stays below or at the day length.

To summarize, planning more cases than what the resources can absorb is not a good idea, regardless of the performance ratio looked at.

2.3.6 Discussion

As anticipated, the most promising scheduling strategies depend on the secondary objective pursued. The *decreasing duration* strategy is the one that performs best regarding both under-utilization and over-utilization. If we focus on cancellation rate, the best strategy is *increasing variability*, closely followed by *increasing duration*. It is thus important to line up scheduling strategies with the hospital policies. The choice of day length or loading level is also important to take into consideration if the OR manager wants to achieve specific secondary objectives.

We also found out that over-scheduling has negative impacts not only on overtime and cancellation rate, but more importantly, on the under-utilization rate. Indeed, over-scheduling rarely allows to perform more cases since the hospital must respect certain overtime policies. When remaining time is not enough to cover the expected duration of a case, this room is considered to use overtime. If because of overbooking we have a high number of these cases, most of them will have to be cancelled. The cancellation rate will increase, but so will the under-utilization rate because there will be inactivity at the end of the day due to all those cancelled cases.

2.4 Conclusions

In this chapter, we have proposed a flexible tool which allows for the management of operating rooms, while partially taking into account uncertainty. First, a deterministic integer programming model was designed, using CPLEX, to decide which cases should be performed on a given day. Second, schedules were built according to eight distinct scheduling strategies. A simulation feature was then added to account for uncertainty *a posteriori*. Finally, the different schedules, using simulated results, were compared via different performance criteria. The tool was built to be easily modifiable to fit the hospital's context. Indeed, planning horizon, number of surgeons, opening hours, overtime availability, duration and variability of cases are inputs; they are not built in the tool. It can be used by different type of surgery departments and it can be used in real time. It was tested on 16 datsets which reflected our hospital partner's reality. However, the impacts of day length and anticipated occupation rates have only been tested on 8 of the 16 instances, and only with three scheduling strategies. Further research should replicate this study with real data in order to confirm our results. Testing with real data would help to confirm which distribution is the best fit for case variability between Beta PERT distribution and lognormal distribution. Future works could also assess the utility of this tool when making strategic decisions. Indeed, one could use our model to evaluate the impacts of adding one piece of specific specialized equipment in the long-run. One could also test the impacts of modifications on overtime policies as requested by a workers' union for example. The tool could also be modified to automatically increment priority of a case if it is not performed within a given period of time. Although this work provides a flexible tool to build and to evaluate OR schedules, it does not take into account post-anesthesia care unit (PACU) where resources (beds) are limited. This could mean that cases durations could increase if no beds were available in the PACU because patients would be kept in the operating rooms. A natural extension of this work would take into account patients and material flows.

References

1. Batun, S., Denton, B.T., Huschka, T.R., Schaefer, A.J.: The Benefit of Pooling Operating Rooms and Parallel Surgery Processing under Uncertainty. Working Paper, pp. 1–36 (2010)
2. Belien, J., Demeulemeester, E.: Building cyclic master surgery schedules with leveled resulting bed occupancy. European Journal of Operational Research **176**, 1185–1204 (2007)
3. Belien, J., Demeulemeester, E., Cardoen, B.: A decision support system for cyclic master surgery scheduling with multiple objectives. Journal of Scheduling **12**, 147–161 (2009)
4. Chaabane, S., Guinet, A., Smolski, N., Guiraud, M., Luquet, B., Marcon, E. Viale, J.-P.: La gestion industrielle et la gestion des blocs opératoires. Annales Francaises d'Anesthésie et de Réanimation **22**(10), 904–908 (2003)
5. Dexter, F., Macario, A., Traub, R.D., Hopwood, M., Lubasky, D.A.: An Operating Room Scheduling Strategy to Maximize the Use of Operating Room Block Time: Computer Simulation of Patient Scheduling and Survey of Patients' Preferences for Surgical Waiting Time. Anesthesia & Analgesia **89**, 7–20 (1999)
6. Dexter, F., Traub, R., Fleisher, L.A., Rock, L.A.: What Sample Sizes are Required for Pooling Surgical Case Durations among Facilities to Decrease the Incidence of Procedures with Little

Historical Data? Anesthesiology **96**(5), 1230–1236 (2002)
7. Dulude, M.-C.: La Gestion des Blocs Opératoires dans un Contexte Déterministe. Mémoire de Maîtrise, HEC Montréal (2004)
8. Fei, H., Meskens, N., Chu, C.: A planning and scheduling problem for an operating theatre using an open scheduling strategy. Computers & Industrial Engineering **58**, 221–230 (2010)
9. Goldman, J., Knappenberger, H.A., Shearon, W.T.: A Study of the Variability of Surgical Estimates. Hospital Management **110**(3), 46, 46A, 46D (1970)
10. Guinet, A., Chaabane, S.: Operating Theatre Planning. International Journal of Production Economics **85**(1), 69–81 (2003)
11. Hammami, S.: Aide à la décision dans le pilotage des flux matériels et patients d'un plateau médico-technique. Thèse de Doctorat, Laboratoire d'Automatique de Grenoble INPG/ ENSIEG (2006)
12. Hancock, W.M., Walter, P.F., More, R.A., Glick, N.D.: Operating Room Scheduling Data Base Analysis for Scheduling. Journal of Medical Systems **12**(6), 397–409 (1988)
13. Institut Canadien d'Information sur la Santé: http://qstat.cihi.ca (2004)
14. Jebali, A., Alouane, A.B., Ladet, P.: Operating rooms scheduling. International Journal of Production Economics **99**(1–2), 52–62 (2006)
15. Marcon, E., Kharraja, S., Simonnet, G.: The operating theatre planning by the follow-up of the risk of no realization. International Journal of Production Economics **85**(1), 83–90 (2003)
16. Marcon, E., Dexter, F.: Impact of surgical sequencing on post anesthesia care unit staffing. Health Care Management Science **9**, 87–98 (2006)
17. Ogulata, S.N., Erol, R.: A Hierarchical Multiple Criteria Mathematical Programming Approach for Scheduling General Surgery Operations in Large Hospitals. Journal of Medical Systems **27**(3), 259–270 (2003)
18. Ozkarahan, I.: Allocation of Surgeries to Operating Rooms by Goal Programming. Journal of Medical Systems **24**(6), 339–378 (2000)
19. Santé Canada: Le système des soins de santé du Canada. www.hs-sc.qc.ca (2006)
20. Santibanez, P., Begen, M., Atkins, D.: Surgical block scheduling in a system of hospitals: an application to resource and wait list management in a British Columbia health authority. Health Care Management Science **10**, 269–282 (2007)
21. Strum, D.P., May, J.H., Vargas, L.G.: Modeling the Uncertainty of Surgical Procedure Times: Comparison of Log-normal and Normal Models. Anesthesiology **92**(4), 1160–1167 (2009)
22. Strum, D.P., May, J.H., Sampsom, A.R., Vargas, L.G., Spangler, W.E.: Estimating Times of Surgeries with Two Component Procedures: Comparison of the Lognormal and Normal Models. Anesthesiology **98**(1), 232–240 (2003)
23. Strum, D.P., Sampsom, A.R., May, J.H., Vargas, L.G.: Surgeon and Type of Anesthesia Predict Variability in Surgical Procedure Times. Anesthesiology **92**(5), 1454–1466 (2000)
24. Tànfani, E., Testi, A.: A pre-assignment heuristic algorithm for the Master Surgical Schedule Problem (MSSP). Annals of Operations Research **178**, 105–119 (2010)
25. Testi, A., Tànfani, E., Torre, G.: A three-phase approach for operating theatre schedules. Health Care Management **10**, 163–172 (2007)
26. van Oostrum, J.M., Van Houdenhoven, M., Hurink, J.L., Hans, E.W., Kazemier, G.: A master surgical scheduling approach for cyclic scheduling in operating room departments. OR Spectrum **30**, 355–374 (2008)
27. van Oostrum, J.M., Bredenhoff, E., Hans, E.W. : Suitability and managerial implications of a Master Surgical Scheduling approach. Annals of Operations Research **178**, 91–104 (2010)
28. Zhou, J., Dexter, F., Macario, A., Lubarsky, D.A.: Relying solely on historical surgical times to estimate accurately future surgical times is unlikely to reduce the average length of time cases finish late. Journal of Clinical Anesthesia **11**(7), 601–605 (1999)

Chapter 3

Idealised design and modelling of alternatives to hospital care

Tom Bowen and Paul Forte

Abstract. Alternatives to acute hospital admission and care require new services and corresponding changes to clinical practice and care pathways. Flows of patients into, through and out of hospital are complex and varied and an integrated holistic approach is essential to understand the processes involved. Reducing delays throughout the system, so that work can flow at the appropriate time, is crucial in optimising the use of resources and is also likely to enhance the patient experience and quality of care. Our approach, building on earlier work incorporates transparent presentation of data, multidisciplinary involvement, and idealised design following Ackoff's paradigm of "designing a desirable future and inventing ways of bringing it about". Here we examine a set of linked applications of the approach in the context of the need to reconfigure acute hospital provision in a region in the south-east of England while, at the same time, identifying developmental areas for community services. Overarching the work is the requirement to clarify and agree care pathways and protocols across all clinical and professional groups. The chapter discusses how the case study compares with similar projects, how well the methodology matches up to Ackoff's aspirations, and how it could be further developed in the future.

Keywords: care pathways, whole systems, idealised design, clinicians, managers

---

T. Bowen
The Balance of Care Group, 39a Cleveland Road, London, N1 3ES, UK
e-mail: tom.bowen@balanceofcare.com

P. Forte (✉)
The Balance of Care Group, 39a Cleveland Road, London, N1 3ES, UK
School of Public Policy & Professional Practice, Keele University, Staffordshire, ST5 5BG, UK
e-mail: paul.forte@balanceofcare.com

Tànfani E., Testi A. (Eds.): Advanced Decision Making Methods Applied to Health Care.
International Series in Operations Research & Management Science 173
DOI 10.1007/978-88-470-2321-5_3,

3.1 Introduction and problem addressed

3.1.1 *The search for alternatives to acute hospital care*

The goal of providing good quality healthcare – especially for people with long-term health conditions – is that they should be able to remain in their own homes and communities for as long as possible, feeling safe and competent to do so. The challenge is how to deliver better and cheaper health services which are efficiently organised to enable this to happen. This is what lies at the heart of most service development exercises and is the focus of this chapter.

In many projects for local health economies we have identified alternatives to acute hospital admission and care. Commonly this requires the introduction of a range of new services and corresponding changes to clinical practice and care pathways. An integrated holistic approach is essential and it can be demonstrated that small changes across a range of agendas is likely to have a greater impact than any single large scale initiative.

Exploration of such 'balance of care' issues over many years has highlighted the large potential gains in the overall cost-effectiveness of the system [6, 10, 11]. However some of these gains remain theoretical because the means to articulate the implementation tasks have been difficult to establish and, beyond this, the need to achieve shared commitments to changes in practice are never easy to establish. Success requires not only that the right resources are put in place, but that complementary reengineering of clinical processes occurs. Establishing change across the whole system is far more complex than a single care intervention such as with the introduction of a new drug, whose cost effectiveness will be established, and implementation usually occur, independently of wider changes in care processes.

Since the 1990s, the term patient *care pathway* has become commonplace as a means to describe both the elements of good clinical practice and the interaction between care professionals required to maintain it. If desired pathways can be articulated and agreed by clinicians and other care professionals, it may be possible to identify service volumes along the pathway, the demand in terms of patient numbers, and hence be able to calculate resource requirements. However with the level of complexity this entails, success may be limited to local health economies where charismatic individuals (usually clinicians) champion the changes and ensure the sustainability of developments on a day to day basis [9].

What could happen otherwise? A common experience with apparently excellent deployments of new clinical services is that, rather than provide cost-effective alternatives to existing practice, the new services become complementary and additional to them [16]. This appears to have been commonplace in the UK with the very rapid expansion of new forms of service delivery in the first decade of this century, as a result of the government's decision to rapidly increase public funding levels.

However the evidence in the literature has been limited, possibly reflecting the choice of research topics, with few economic evaluations of new and innovative services. In Balance of Care studies, usually undertaken as consultancies and only occasionally published, we have commonly found that, for example, the introduction of the intermediate care services to provide step-down care after acute hospital stay and for acute admission avoidance may provide enhanced nursing care for patients, but as an addition to the existing care pathway, and hence at additional cost [7]. Such changes may represent valued quality improvements from both clinician and patient perspectives, but miss the opportunity to free up further resource: in the current more constrained financial climate the objective of delivering and maintaining sustained quality gains requires that such issues are now fully addressed.

Because such a large part of healthcare expenditure is devoted to the acute hospital sector it is natural that cost-effectiveness studies should look here for improved quality and efficiency. Interestingly a common finding of such studies (e.g. [5]) is that reduced bed utilisation requires change outside rather than inside the hospital environment and that most of the patients for whom more cost-effective pathways exist are those with long-term conditions. For these patients continuity of care is important, especially at the interface between primary and secondary care.

3.1.2 Developing a new methodology

In the UK there has been substantial agreement between care professionals about the best pathways to develop and these have been set out in a series of *National Strategic Frameworks* (e.g. [8]). However full realisation of all the benefits envisaged remains to be achieved, with the difficulties of investment outlined above affecting outcomes, and further complicated by the numbers of patients, especially the frail elderly, who have multiple pathology.

None of these system features are new, and have been discussed repeatedly over the years by operational researchers working in the field. Rosenhead suggests they have the characteristics of Ackoff's 'messes' [17]. It is possible to develop ever more precise mathematical models that can quantify the potential for change, but again Rosenhead points out that very complex human interactions are needed to deliver these changes. The precision that as modellers we aspire to may be counterproductive if it the resulting complexity of analysis gets in the way of stakeholders' engagement in the change process.

Our response to this dilemma, and the methodology described in this chapter, represents a further development and extension of the Balance of Care modelling approach [10]; incorporating transparent presentation of data, multidisciplinary involvement, and idealised design. In this we are following Ackoff's paradigm of designing a desirable future and inventing ways of bringing it about. Ackoff wrote extensively about the need for whole system approaches, described at that time as 'social ecology'. There was a hazard to be avoided that operational researchers working on complex development projects "could improve part of the system but destroy the whole, by improving the part" [1]. The focus on a single part of the system was tempting if established and quantifiable methodologies were available, but if other parts of the system were ignored, would inevitably fail to address development needs. Ackoff felt that modelling needed to be simplified to allow whole system working, cautioning that perceived complexity may be the result of our inability to handle the situation.

Ackoff proposed an interactive and participative approach to handling these through a process of 'idealised redesign'. "The key to interactive planning is ... the preparation of an *idealised redesign* of the system. [But it must be] technologically feasible ... and operationally viable" [2, p. 191]. In the context of reconfiguring the capacity and clinical processes surrounding acute hospital utilisation, this is a fair challenge, and the evidence base for the work we have undertaken has gradually evolved to encompass more of the relevant dimensions.

3.1.3 Key issues for management

The UK has a National Health Service (NHS) largely funded through general taxation, and most services are free at the point of delivery. The best ways to fund health service provider organisations, in terms of providing the greatest incentives for efficient and high quality healthcare, remain unresolved, despite repeated changes to organisational structures and financial regimes, especially over the last 20 years.

Although it is a national health service, there are some differences in funding (and, increasingly, in policy direction) in Scotland, Wales and Northern Ireland in line with increased devolution of powers to those countries The discussion which follows has general applicability across the UK, but our focus is on the favoured generic approach in England (which accounts for over 80% of the UK population) has been to develop various forms of 'internal market', whereby NHS organisations have been divided into providers (delivering services) and commissioners (purchasing services on behalf of their local populations). There continue to be initiatives to involve clinicians, and especially General Practitioners (GPs), in commissioning: greater involvement of primary care in decisions about alternatives to acute hospital provision should in principle greatly facilitate change, though we note that the involvement of and liaison between provider organisations of all types is essential anyway if a whole system approach is to be adopted successfully.

All commissioning organisations have grappled in different ways with the issues described in this chapter. In some local health economies the historical development of hospital sites has led to financially unsustainable configurations as technology has changed service requirements. For these commissioners the overriding concern is to unlock the resources tied up in these facilities, and redeploy them along the desired new care pathways.

However, even commissioners with satisfactory acute configurations still have the problem of meshing in new service elements: in recent years they have been in a position to pay for the resources needed, but cannot always ensure that new resources are utilised in the manner desired in the purchasing decision. Various financial mechanisms, including the use of specially designed tariffs have been attempted to control implementations. However these have tended to be focussed on the acute hospital (financial mechanisms elsewhere are not sufficiently developed) without incentivising the other organisations. A key role for the OR intervention lies in ensuring that all provider organisations have an equal involvement in the design and implementation of development decisions.

The major expansion in health service funding in England in the last decade has now ended, in part as a response to wider economic recession. At a national level in England the assessment has been made that annual revenue costs need to be reduced by £20billion (€23billion), or about 20% of the current spend. A large part of this will be sought in the acute sector and will require the types of redesign described in this chapter if sustainable savings are to be made without reduction in service quantity or quality. Because our case study relates to a local health economy that was already facing major financial stringency, the issues addressed within the study are likely now to apply to many other parts of the country.

The remainder of this chapter is primarily concerned with a description of our approach in the context of a project undertaken in south-east England. It sets out the general, whole system methodology built around point prevalence studies of hospital and other populations, using clinically acceptable protocols to identify which aspects of current pathways may be amenable to change. It then describes a case study in which this exercise was repeated in all the major acute hospitals and various other key service providers, with involvement from all clinical and care professional groups, and all the various (commissioner and provider) managements.

In the concluding section we discuss the extent to which the approach could potentially be generalised to other healthcare environments in the UK, and to other health systems – especially those in European Union states. We also explore the extent to which this and similar applications match up to Ackoff's aspirations for idealised design, and how the methodology might be further developed.

3.2 Materials and methods

3.2.1 Undertaking a whole system case study

Our methodology for addressing these complex issues is underpinned by a conceptual model of patient flow as set out in Figure 3.1. If, in addition, we focus on the journey of an elderly patient who has had an unscheduled admission for non-surgical reasons, then we are looking at the largest group of hospital inpatients usually to be found in hospital beds on any given day.

Figure 3.1 represents an idealised picture of the patient's progression through the hospital system from a 'pre-admission phase' (i.e. when they are living in the community), through to their eventual discharge from acute hospital care.

Looked at in whole system terms across the entire health and social care environment we are interested in how and why patients end up in this particular care sector and what the potential for alternative care locations might actually be.

There is a variety of drivers which might focus the need for exploring alternatives including: capacity issues in the acute sector (e.g. unscheduled admissions reducing capacity for routine surgery); cost of care provision (acute hospitals are expensive resources); quality of care (e.g. danger from nosocomial infection); patient choice (wanting to be in their home surroundings). We need to consider what might be alternatives to the main processes involved in the patient's hospital journey (the

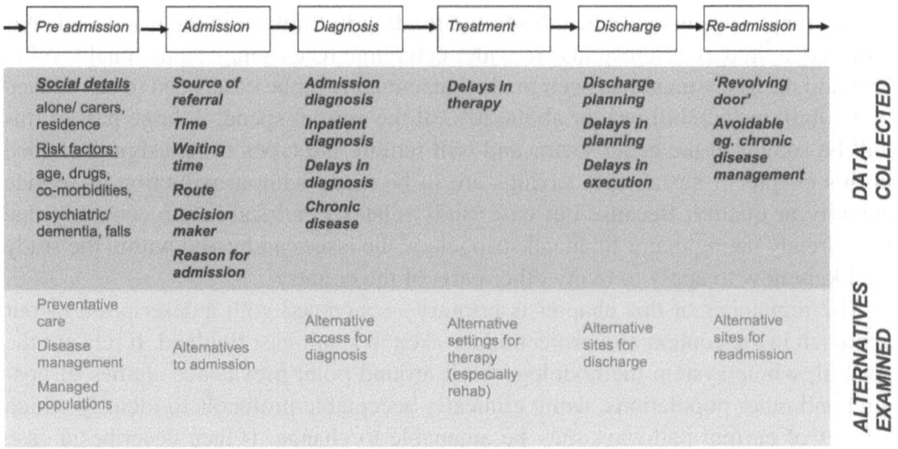

Fig. 3.1. The rich picture of patient flow

bottom row of Figure 3.1) and the data and information required to establish what these alternatives might be and which might provide some indication of the volume of service alternative required (listed under each box on the flow diagram). Of course the diagram is illustrative; more process stages could be considered as could the range of alternatives and information required, but the principle of taking a whole system perspective is clear and is of particular relevance to the type of patients we are considering.

What is also clear from this is the implication that there may be patients currently undergoing acute hospital care who might have potentially avoided the necessity of a hospital admission in the first place, or had a shorter length of stay. The key to understanding what these might be, and the types of patients for whom they might be feasible is information. Knowing what is going on at any one time directly impacts on the ability for managing the entire process: relevant data on the use of beds and the characteristics of patients using them can be used to inform issues about the scope of capacity and future service requirements.

The UK context of the type of whole system of interest described above is usually encapsulated in the idea of a local health and social care economy. This is usually an area of about 300–500,000 people served by a major acute hospital provider (possibly operating across several sites); covered by a single adult services department of a local authority; and by one or two local health commissioning organisations (currently 'primary care trusts' in England) who also manage local non-acute health services. It is at this level where the problems associated with poor configuration and utilisation of services often make themselves most clearly felt as issues over capacity between different organisations and impacts on budgets and joint planning issues become particularly noticeable.

This can often lead to organisations blaming one another for creating problems (as they perceive them) in their own organisation: 'adult services don't provide enough support for people in their own homes'; 'hospital doctors are too ready to discharge people to long-term nursing home care'; 'community clinicians are sending people into hospital in order to get tests carried out more quickly'. What may seem the ideal solution for one organisation can create major operational or financial headaches for another. Clearly, some overview of the impacts is required in order that the interconnectivity of issues, and their potential solutions, can be addressed in a coherent manner. Moreover, this has to be done with the support of the health and social care professionals currently delivering the service or the recognition of the analyses and actions which may need to follow will not be regarded as valid or workable.

However, some organisations in these systems are better provided for with data than others; or data are gathered, but are not available in an easily accessible form. In the UK, for example, there is a wealth of data held in the – mainly paper based – clinical records in hospitals, but they cannot be readily extracted to support exploration of the potential for alternative care settings. The only feasible way to obtain these data is to extract them as part of a bed utilisation survey based on patients' individual care records.

The Balance of Care Group has developed a methodology for obtaining these data and undertaking whole system analyses which has been employed in 25 studies of this nature over the past 10 years in England and Ireland, covering 20,000 patient records. Here we illustrate it with an example based on one acute hospital and its immediate hinterland from an exercise which was undertaken in south-east England. This was driven by the requirement for a reconfiguration of acute services both in that area and in adjacent localities. The overarching question was to scope the potential for shifts in acute service provision both between different acute sites and between acute and community-based health and social care. To do this we first need an objective and clinically acceptable means to identify the size of patient populations for whom alternatives may exist.

3.2.2 Reviewing bed utilisation

A number of instruments have been developed over the past 30 years with significant clinical input, which aim to describe and classify those conditions requiring acute hospital care. The underlying reasons for their development are also similar and remain valid: the requirement to make a connection between resource and clinical utilisation and, in doing so, to have the acceptance and involvement of clinicians in the process.

These tools all have very similar bases and sometimes common starting positions. One long-established instrument is the Appropriateness Evaluation Protocol (AEP). It was developed by Gertman and Restuccia [12], and originated in the USA. It was subsequently the focus of a major pan-European exercise (the 'Biomed project') which established and tested a European version [14]. This was focused more on the appropriateness of hospital use rather than appropriateness of surgical procedures. It has been used in the UK [15] and we have used it widely in many bed utilisation review studies (including the one described in the following section).

The AEP is used to assess a patient's appropriateness for admission to an acute bed, and to their continuing care in that setting. We interpret the term 'appropriateness' here to mean that the care the patient needs is properly provided in an acute hospital setting, and no alternative (e.g. non-acute, ambulatory, community) would be clinically acceptable. There is, moreover, no judgement implied about clinical practice.

Two major groups of criteria, both of which are independent of diagnosis, can be applied to a patient: one group relates to their admission; the other to the care they are receiving on the assessment day (or 'day of care'). Each of these criteria groups is itself sub-divided. There are two subsets of admission criteria (A 'severity of illness' and B 'intensity of service'); and three subsets of 'day of care' criteria (C 'medical services', D 'nursing/ life support services' and E 'patient's condition').

Examples of admission criteria from both subsections are:

A3. Blood Pressure:

a) systolic < 90 or > 200 mm Hg;
b) diastolic < 60 or > 120 mm Hg.

B3. Vital sign monitoring every 2 hours or more often (may include telemetry or bedside cardiac monitor).

Examples of 'day of care' criteria from each of the three subsections are:

C5. biopsy of internal organ that day;
D3. continuous vital signs monitoring (at least every 30 minutes, for at least 4 hours);
E5. coma – unresponsive for at least one hour.

For a patient to fall within AEP criteria for admission they need to meet at least one criterion from either admission subset, while for remaining in acute care requires them to meet at least one criterion from any of the three 'day of care' subsets. In this way, meeting AEP criteria can be regarded as a marker of 'acuity'.

Some argue that clinical judgement (a 'clinical override') should be used in addition to the AEP criteria. However, to do so, introduces subjectivity into what is a retrospective review of 'what actually happened', rather than any attempt to judge what should or might have happened with the benefit of hindsight. So 'clinical override' does not feature in our methodology. (We acknowledge, of course that, at the time, clinical decisions would have been made prospectively).

The criteria are drawn quite widely and tend to include patients within the scope of acuity rather than adopting a very narrow definition. One criterion in particular, relates to the need for the patient to have intravenous drug or fluids therapy, Nowadays, however, for some patients alternative locations are feasible (including patients' homes) if their AEP criteria are solely in connection with intravenous therapy. This can be recognised and accommodated in the application of the AEP and forms a very useful discussion point when reviewing results, as we discuss further below.

To address capacity issues it is not just enough, though, to know that a certain number of patients do not meet admission and/or day of care criteria. It is essential to understand where patients not meeting these criteria might otherwise have received their care – and regardless of whether that care mode actually exists locally or not at that point.

Here we draw on the experience of the surveyors in using their subjective clinical judgment to decide what an alternative type of care might have been in an 'ideal world' irrespective of any resource constraints at all. To develop new capacity requires this perspective; untrammelled by current conditions or it is forever going to be bound by them.

To facilitate the surveyors the survey forms incorporate a wide range of possible alternatives from which they can select an option although they can still define an option of their own if they so wish.

3.2.3 Steps in undertaking a bed utilisation review

As the use of beds in the system is the starting point for understanding how and why processes are operating locally, a bed utilisation review is usually conducted as a point prevalence survey of clinical records at a single point in time (usually on a single day). For the selected sample, using this record, trained surveyors gather data on patient characteristics and their pathway through the hospital system, and can apply the AEP criteria to assess (with hindsight) whether admission criteria were met and whether, at the point of time of the survey, the patient meets 'day of care' acuity criteria. Note that neither patients nor ward staff are themselves interviewed; all data are abstracted from medical, nursing and therapy notes. It is also important to note that the exercise is not a clinical audit – all clinical decisions taken are assumed correct – but a system audit. The basic premise is the reason that patient flow and linkage between different organisations may be not be as ideal as would be wished is down to its systemic development rather than the fault or blame of particular groups of individuals or organisations.

There are several distinct aspects to undertaking a review of this type with many of the steps overlapping with each other or carried out in parallel. We have grouped them under the following headings.

3.2.4 Engaging the key players

This is an important early step and one which requires constant review throughout the exercise because we need these people to be engaged throughout the process from scoping the survey and its objectives, to supporting the data collection process (by facilitating recruitment of surveyors), and bringing their expertise to bear in the analyses and conclusions to be drawn.

The concepts of a bed utilisation review must be clear and acceptable to both clinicians and managers from the outset, and an understanding developed which is about supporting change and best practice. They have to be reassured that it is not about blaming any particular groups of care professionals or organisations and it is not a clinical audit. The value of their input in later stages, particularly in pointing to analyses which are particularly interesting or pertinent and useful is vital to gain local ownership of the exercise, recognise the validity of the data and analyses, and to want to take subsequent action after the review is completed. This can be a time-consuming exercise but is a very necessary one across all of the major organisations involved. This is also the stage where all necessary protocols concerning patient data confidentiality are addressed.

3.2.5 Selection of the sample

This will depend to a large extent on the nature of the questions being asked about the whole system in a given area. We have found that in nearly all of the surveys we have undertaken a fundamental issue to be addressed is that of alternatives to hospital-based bed care, but apart from that there will be local concerns and interests which need to be recognised and accommodated. This will, in turn, influence the scope of the survey; maybe focusing on patients over a particular age, or in particular specialties.

However, within an acute hospital, a common survey scope includes all medical and orthopaedic specialty beds; sometimes all surgical specialties are also included. Specialty exceptions are obstetrics and acute psychiatry (for which the AEP does not apply); likewise paediatrics although there is a variation of the AEP which can accommodate it [18].

Outside the acute hospital we are usually interested in all non-acute hospital beds in community hospitals, for example, or other specially designated 'short-stay' beds in care homes. In these beds the case mix is mainly older patients undergoing some form of rehabilitation prior to returning home or their admission to a long-term care home placement. In the same way that there might be alternative care settings for acute hospital patients, patients in non-acute beds may not require the care provided in that setting any longer. If we do not capture how these beds are being used at the same time as the acute bed survey then this can distort the picture of the requirement for acute bed alternatives later in the analysis – potentially implying that more non-acute beds are needed than is actually the case.

3.2.6 Design of the survey form

The survey form needs to balance several competing needs. On one hand it needs to record those data items which can inform us about the type of patient and how they have entered and are progressing through the hospital system. On the other, the form has to accommodate how – or whether – any of these items are actually recorded in the clinical notes, and also to take on board, where possible, any local interests which might reasonably be met through the survey. Above all the survey form needs brevity and clarity to enable the surveyors to provide good quality data.

Surveys which include non-acute beds require different data forms which do not feature the AEP (as it is not applicable) although many other data items collected are identical to the acute form. Instead of using the AEP surveyors are asked to assess for all patients whether, from the case notes, they still require the care being provided or whether an alternative would be feasible.

In both acute and non-acute survey forms a range of alternative care modes to those where the patient is being surveyed are provided for the convenience of the surveyor.

3.2.7 Recruitment and training of surveyors

This is an important dimension for several reasons. First of all, there is a need to have surveyors with clinical experience completing the survey form: they are familiar with reading and understanding case notes and with deciding what potential care alternatives might be given the patient's circumstances and condition. Secondly, involving a large number of clinical staff – there have been as many as 70 surveyors in some surveys – in an exercise designed to get them to be looking at their own local health and social care system can be both rewarding to them and help to foster a greater understanding of what changes might be possible in the system and how they might be involved in directing and realising them. In this regard the survey can have important immediate effects as well as longer-term consequences after the data have been analysed. On one occasion, by the end of the survey day itself and as a direct result of their participation, several senior nurses decided that changes were needed in the medical notes system and had started to organise how this might be undertaken. A third important aspect concerns patient confidentiality; all care staff will understand inherently these important issues and also be bound to maintaining this by their employment contracts.

While nurses (both hospital and community-based) usually form the backbone of a survey cadre, other care professionals are encouraged to participate and many physiotherapists and occupational therapists usually take part as well. Smaller numbers of social care and medical staff usually become involved too.

Surveyor training is important and a prerequisite of participation in the survey itself. Those taking part need to understand the purpose of the survey as well as how to complete the data form and how different elements on it are defined; not least how to apply the AEP.

Survey logistics on the day can be subject to unexpected events but, in general, a principle we have adopted with success is to ensure that those undertaking the survey do not cover patients who might be in their day-to-day care on a ward. So nurses working in the community survey inside the acute hospital; hospital-based staff might work in a community setting or in a different part of the hospital to their normal location. This brings a fresh eye to particular cases and is often cited in feedback sessions as a rewarding experience for the individual surveyor. The experience also brings different staff together in ways which sometimes translate into useful, ongoing working relationships in their day to day work environments.

3.2.8 Survey feedback

The way in which survey analyses are presented is often as important as the content. It is important that the data are 'owned' by the participating organisations and seen as 'their data' and not that belonging to an external organisation who have collected them.

One way of doing so is to feedback initial results to groups of surveyors – before anyone else – in order to validate them and understand how the surveyors completed the survey forms. This 'reality check' on the data and findings is very important and we can then feel more confident of the messages coming from the analyses when sharing them more widely across the organisations. It is usually also the start of what becomes a continuous cycle of suggestions for analyses which may be of interest to particular organisations or groups of care professionals. In this way the analyses can be developed and led in directions which have authority and commitment from local decision-makers. Involving the surveyors closely in this way also helps to maintain their interest in the outcome of their efforts and contribute to their wider understanding of the whole system issues and professional development.

Following this initial round of analysis others may follow for particular interest groups (e.g. hospital doctors), or for joint planning committees. On each occasion there are usually more requests for additional analyses which are incorporated as far as possible into the final report. A copy of the survey database is also handed over for further local analyses as required beyond the end of our involvement.

3.3 Results and discussion

3.3.1 Overview

With the wealth of data extracted from the patient records there is a large number of potential analyses which can be undertaken exploring the types of patients in the beds including: how they were referred into the hospital system; their clinical characteristics and their home environments. This can often start to raise questions about whether there are aspects of the organisation of care in the community which might contribute to otherwise unnecessary hospital admissions or slow down or restrict the potential for earlier discharge from acute care.

Within the hospital (and in local non-acute beds) there may also be reasons for delays due to internal procedures and processes which start to show up in terms of, for example, delays for assessment.

The results from applying the AEP are central to understanding the types and locations of patients which are affected by these system operations. Across all of the studies we have been involved with in England and Ireland we have found a degree of consistency despite variations in the survey scope of individual surveys. Typically, across medical and orthopaedic specialties we find 12–20% of patients were outside AEP criteria on their admission, and 45–60% outside 'day of care' criteria on the day of the survey.

The results are not entirely surprising. The admission criteria are applied with hindsight to an admission which has already taken place – it is not possible to be absolutely certain at the actual time of admission whether alternatives are appropriate even if they are available. However, these results can still indicate areas where current processes might be improved to reduce unnecessary admissions.

The number of patients outside day of care criteria is also not surprising considering that patients must be technically 'non-acute' before they can leave the hospital. More important than the headline survey day figure is what is revealed by a follow-up analysis 2–3 weeks later when we obtain further data from the hospital information systems to see how many of those patients who were outside day of care criteria on the survey day have been successfully discharged home or moved on to other, non-acute care settings, and how many remain in the hospital.

3.3.2 Implications for bed capacity

Focusing on the acute hospital in our example from south-east England, Figure 3.2 illustrates, for a single acute hospital, those patients who were outside day of care AEP criteria and for whom potential alternatives locations for care had been identified by surveyors. The graph shows the number of days they remained in acute care after the day of the survey. It is clear from this that quite a few people were close to discharge and, within a few days, had successfully done so. More noticeably, however, are those patients who were still in hospital two weeks after the survey and for whom non-acute, bed-based care had been identified as the most appropriate care alternative. Apart from any delays caused by internal hospital processes, the implication is that there is insufficient resource currently available to enable patients to be moved on.

That is not to say, however, that this equates directly with a simple shortage of capacity; rather it is a combination of this and often poor use of existing non-acute capacity. This is why surveys also include non-acute beds so we can understand what is happening in this sector at the same time. A common finding is that, as with acute beds, there are delays in people moving on from these facilities who no longer require them.

We can use these data to calculate a net overall effect of this. Figure 3.3 illustrates this in what we term a 'cascade' diagram showing the potential for change in

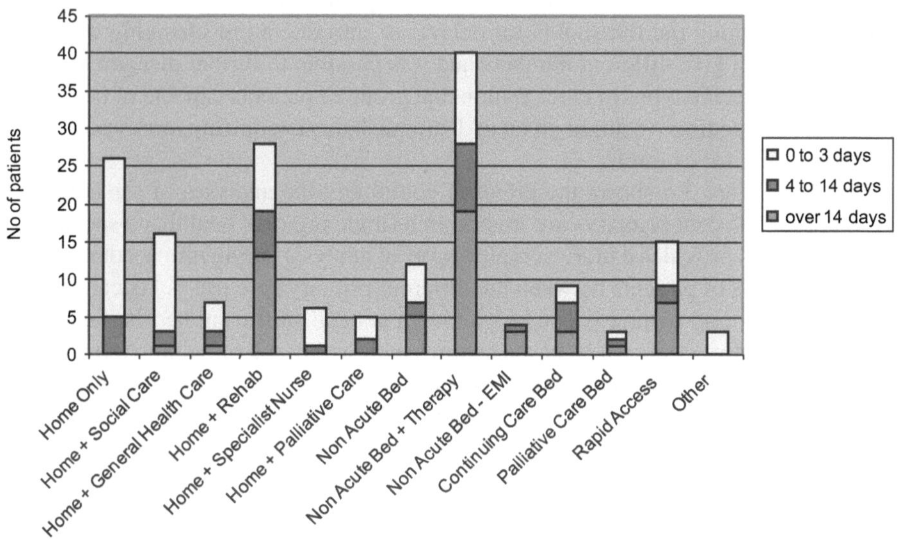

Fig. 3.2. Alternatives in a single acute hospital for patients outside AEP Day of care criteria

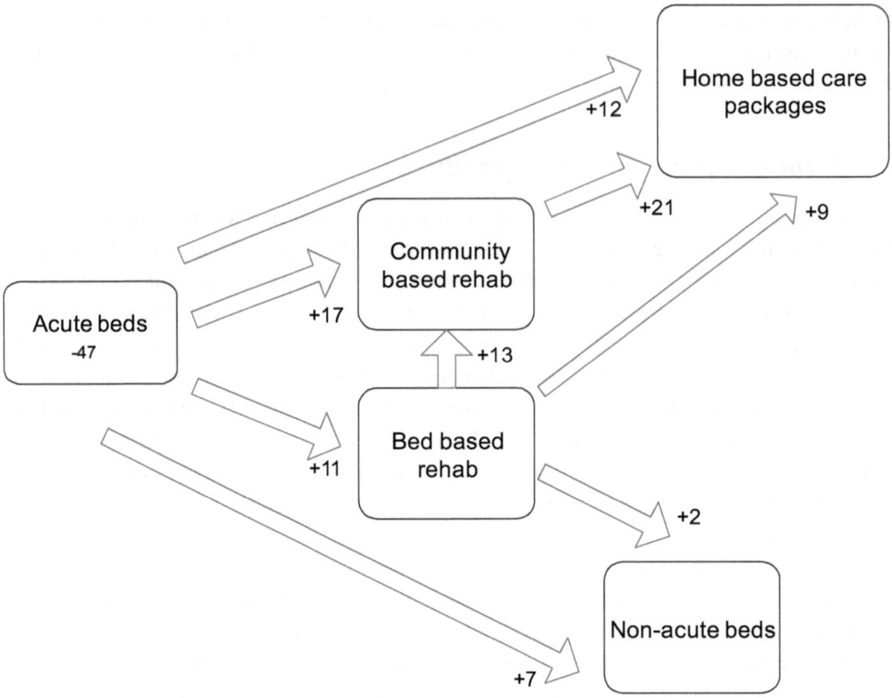

Fig. 3.3. Scenario for potential change in service utilisation for a single hospital and related community services

the number of places (not patients) across the system. Of course, this is only one scenario; changing the thresholds for delays, or introducing or changing other assumptions, will give different numbers and it is possible to further disaggregate the analysis for specific types of care. Within that group of patients capable of being in a non-acute bed setting we might go on to distinguish those requiring more specialised dementia care, for example.

Finally, Figure 3.4 shows the effect of combining the analyses of separate surveys in four adjacent primary care trusts into a single regional health and social care economy. This provides a more complex level of analysis taking into account cross-boundary flows of patients between the different primary care trusts. As can clearly be seen, the overall picture is one of wanting a general shift from bed-based capacity into alternative community-based settings and, within the remaining demand for bed-based care, a shift from acute to non-acute capacity

Simple models of this sort become important tools to support Chief Executives, and others at Board level or similar, to form a view of how the major components of the health and social care system mesh together, and how changes in one part need to relate to those elsewhere. In this way there is a better chance of a clear strategic direction within which clinicians can address changes on the nature and location of care processes.

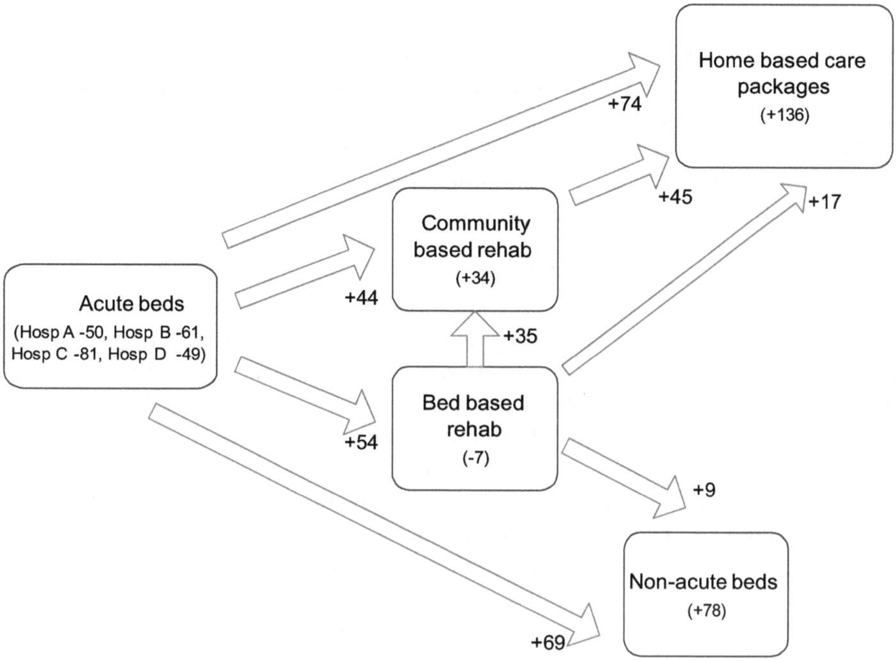

Fig. 3.4. Scenario for potential change in service utilisation across a regional health and social care economy in south-east England

Bed capacity of all types – but particularly in acute hospital settings – is an expensive resource to develop and maintain in any health service and its use should therefore be as efficient and effective as possible. Inevitably issues of overall bed capacity become a significant concern for healthcare organisations, and of major public interest. However, no matter how good day-to-day operational management is, it cannot directly control wider issues outside the hospital but which may still have a major effect on the demand for those beds. This can only be achieved through a more systematic addressing of the whole system – from the pressures and drivers on the admission system, through to the capacity for handling discharged patients and maintaining their continuity of care in non-acute settings.

This, in turn, requires obtaining data on more than just a person's clinical condition; a wider understanding of how they came to be admitted to a bed and non-clinical factors which might affect the length of time and choice of post-acute discharge are also vitally important.

3.3.3 Discussion

We have shown how a carefully designed bed utilisation review process can provide the data needed to examine how the system is operating and point to where the scope lies for action in both the short and long term. Crucially, this process requires local ownership and investment of time and effort into bringing the local stakeholders – particularly clinicians – on board with the process so they can understand it and tailor it as necessary to reflect particular local circumstances and agendas. This sense of control and active input is vital if the information gained is to be acted upon.

The impact of whole system projects such as the case study described is best seen in terms of the changes that are brought about across all levels of the organisations involved. These may not represent acceptance of all aspects of the potential for change, which may not be achievable in a single step anyway. But if operational change within organisations is initiated, coupled with complementary changes in resource and care process across organisations, all within an overall strategic direction adopted at Board level, then gradual progression towards an improved and more cost-effective pattern of service delivery and better outcomes will follow. An important feature here is that all stakeholders have consistent views of the whole system, even if their perspectives may differ: thus chief executives can see the major resource and capacity shifts needed across organisations, clinicians and other care professionals can agree changing roles, referral practice and shared care protocols, finance directors can plan budgets, and so on.

Finally, and more recently, we have found that particular issues arising in the course of local projects have created wider attention, and we have been retained for 'single issue' project work adapting the methodology to provide a new focus, for example to provide case study material for national level initiatives on dementia [3] and on end of life care [4] where findings have been published as a part of national reports.

3.4 Conclusions

This chapter has outlined a developed methodology that has been successfully applied in a number of local health economies in the UK and Ireland. The approach is not specific to those settings, and indeed has been used for a variety of mixes of service provider organisations. The actual reimbursement mechanisms used are not critical to the approach and on this basis there is good reason to suppose that this whole systems approach could be applied in a range of other health system settings.

In particular, the use of a protocol (the AEP) which has been used internationally and validated across Europe suggests that methodology could support widely differing health care systems across Europe, in the same way that the earlier Balance of Care planning model has been applied in other European countries, notably Spain and Italy.

The AEP has provided an adequate instrument to assess the acuity of patients treated as inpatients in acute hospital, and we have not found that developments in clinical practice (especially around intravenous therapies) has limited its use to provide a baseline from which operational and clinical potential for alternative more cost-effective patterns of care. We note however that there appears to be little research on such instruments in other sectors of the healthcare systems, for example in non-acute bed provision where the primary clinical service may be related to rehabilitation, and in community services that aim to support patients with long term conditions by deployment of packages of care services. The benefit of even imperfect instruments is that they allow some objective measure of the appropriateness of service utilisation, and open up the discussion of alternatives to both clinicians, who need to consider how to redesign care pathways and managers, who need to consider how to redesign service configurations recovery.

The approach is focussed around patients who make major use of inpatient medical and surgical services but, as discussed earlier, the majority of such patients, in European hospitals at least, are those with long term conditions and especially frail older people. As well as looking at different service elements, there is potential to extend the approach to other client groups, as mentioned in particular for paediatrics.

In developing the approach we have found ourselves following the recommendations of Ackoff, in particularly the facilitation of interactive planning processes around idealised redesign for the future. The approach is participative and requires organisations to look at where they sit in the wider system, rather than solely focussing on the planning and control of their own organisations. "The principle benefit of planning comes from engaging in it ... [and not from] consumption of the plans it produces" [2].

On these grounds it may not be productive to increase the rigour of analyses by incorporation of more detailed modelling approaches, for example there are many detailed simulation models of patient flow in acute hospitals or particular departments within them. However the reorientation this would create in terms of the focus on internal operational processes could be to the detriment of the whole system methodology, and in particular the participation of such a wide range of stakeholders from different professional backgrounds and organisational interests.

This methodology does of course differ from the more mathematically based models of healthcare processes within more clearly defined organisations and services, and we do believe that there is potential for greater input of the results of whole system approaches into detailed dynamic modelling. For example many models may view the demand for acute hospital as a stochastic variable: however variations in patient presentation for medical emergencies by time of day and day of week are related to GP availability, and models could be extended to explore the implications of changes in GP work patterns and in liaison arrangements.

References

1. Ackoff, R.: Redesigning the Future: A Systems Approach to Societal. Problems. John Wiley & Sons, New York (1974)
2. Ackoff, R.: Resurrecting the Future of Operational Research. Journal of the Operational Research Society **30**, 189–199 (1979)
3. Balance of Care Group: Identifying Alternatives to Hospital for People with Dementia. National Audit Office, London (2007). Obtainable as a free download from www.balanceofcare.com
4. Balance of Care Group: Identifying Alternatives to Hospital for People at the End of Life: Report of Findings. National Audit Office, London (2008). Obtainable as a free download from www.balanceofcare.com

5. Benbassat, J., Taragin, M.: Hospital Readmissions as a Measure of Quality of Health Care: Advantages and Limitations. Arch Intern Med. **160**, 1074–1081 (2000)
6. Boldy, D., Russell, J., Royston, G.: Planning the Balance of Health and Social Services in the United Kingdom. Management Science **28**, 1258–1269 (1982)
7. Bowen, T., Forte, P., Foote, C.: Management and Planning of Services. In: Roe, B., Beech, R. (eds.) Intermediate and Continuing Care, Policy and Practice, pp. 33–49. Blackwell Publishing, Oxford (2005)
8. Department of Health: National Strategic Framework for Coronary Heart Disease. HMSO, London (2000)
9. Foote, C., Stanners, S.: Integrating Care for Older People – New Care for Old – a systems approach. Jessica Kingsley, London (2002)
10. Forte, P., Bowen, T.: Improving the balance of elderly care services. In: Cropper, S., Forte, P. (eds.) Enhancing Health Services Management, pp. 71–85. Open University Press, Milton Keynes (1997)
11. Forte, P., Bowen, T.: Services for Older People: finding a balance. In: Vissers, J., Beech, R. (eds.) Health Operations Management. Patient Flow Logistics in Health Care. Routledge, London (2005)
12. Gertman, P.M., Restuccia, J.D.: The Appropriateness Evaluation Protocol: a technique for assess unnecessary days of hospital care. Med Care **19**, 855–871 (1981)
13. Goddard, M., McDonagh, M., Smith, D., Annex, E.: Avoidable use of beds and cost-effectiveness of care in alternative locations. In: Department of Health, 2000, Shaping the Future NHS: Long Term Planning for Hospitals and Related Services: Consultation Document on the Findings of the National Bed Inquiry – Supporting Analysis. Department of Health, London (2000)
14. Lang, T., Liberati, A., Tampieri, A., Fellin, G., Gonsalves, M., Lorenzo, S., Pearson, M., Beech, R., Santos-Eggiman, B.: A European version of the Appropriateness Evaluation Protocol. Intl. J. Technology Assessment in Health Care **15**, 185–197 (1999)
15. McDonagh, M., Smith, D., Goddard, M.: Measuring appropriate use of acute beds: a systematic review of methods and results. Health Policy **53**, 157–184 (2000)
16. Richardson, G., Maynard, A., Cullum, N., Kindig, D.: Skill mix changes: substitution or service development? Health Policy **45**, 119–132 (1998)
17. Rosenhead, J.: Operational research in health services planning. European Journal of Operational Research **12**, 75–85 (1978)
18. Werneke, U., Smith, H., Smith, I., Taylor, J., MacFaul, R.: Validation of the paediatric appropriateness evaluation protocol in British practice. Arch. Dis. Child. **77**, 294–298 (1997)

Chapter 4

A coordination model for enhancing research on rare diseases

Michela Chessa, Vito Fragnelli, and Stefano Gagliardo

Abstract. Rare diseases affect a great number of patients that suffer of the non existence of effective cures. Medical products for prevention, diagnosis or treatment of this kind of disorders are called orphan drugs and pharmaceutical industries have not a great interest under normal market conditions in developing and marketing products for a small number of patients. The Orphan Drug Act and the Regulation on Orphan Medicinal Products played a relevant role in encouraging the development of new orphan drugs, as in America as in Europe. In this chapter we propose that pharmaceutical industries coordinate their researches in order to avoid that two or more of them study a new molecule for the same disease, with the aim of further enhancing the research on rare diseases.

Keywords: rare disease, orphan drug, multiple knapsack problem, college admissions problem

---

M. Chessa
Department of Mathematics, University of Milano, Via Cesare Saldini 50, 20133 Milano, Italy
e-mail: michela.chessa@unimi.it

V. Fragnelli (✉)
Department of Sciences and Technological Innovation, University of Eastern Piedmont, Viale T. Michel 11, 15121 Alessandria, Italy
e-mail: vito.fragnelli@mfn.unipmn.it

S. Gagliardo
Department of Mathematics, University of Genova, Via Dodecaneso 35, 16146 Genova, Italy
e-mail: gagliardo@dima.unige.it

Tànfani E., Testi A. (Eds.): Advanced Decision Making Methods Applied to Health Care.
International Series in Operations Research & Management Science 173
DOI 10.1007/978-88-470-2321-5_4,

4.1 Introduction and problem addressed

4.1.1 What is a rare disease?

In Europe a disease is considered *rare* when it affects no more than 5 individuals out of 10,000 people (for more information see CNMR [1], EMA [3], Eurordis [5] and Orphan Europe [12]); in the United States the Orphan Drug Act (ODA) [15] and the Rare Diseases Act of 2002 [16] define a rare disease or condition as one that "(A) affects less than 200,000 persons in the United States, or (B) affects more than 200,000 in the United States and for which there is no reasonable expectation that the cost of developing and making available in the United States a drug for such disease or condition will be recovered from sales in the United States of such a drug"; note that the European classification corresponds to 0.05% of the population and classification (A) to 0.07% of the US population. However, the number of patients varies from disease to disease and most of the patients in this field suffer from rare diseases affecting only one in 100,000 people or less, among whom 75% are children, 30% of which die before the age of 5 years.

There are in between 6,000 and 8,000 rare diseases which may affect 30 million of European Union citizens. These numbers show how, even if these diseases are rare, the totality of people suffering from them is not irrelevant and the research on them concerns a large part of the population.

Patients affected by a rare disease suffer a high level of pain because of the non existence of effective cures, being disabled day by day due to the chronic, progressive and degenerative evolution of these diseases. Public opinion is not really involved in such a problem and raising money from humanitarian associations and charity of people is not that easy. An efficient way to fight the indifference of people is to ask a famous personality, possibly affected himself, to be a testimonial for a charity association to catch the attention of the public.

4.1.2 Orphan drugs

Many associations were established to provide assistance to the patients of rare diseases and their families, trying also to influence the public opinion to implement suitable strategies. In fact, medical and scientific knowledge about rare diseases is lacking and less than 1,000 diseases benefit from it. This leads to a deficiency of appropriate quality of health care and, consequently, delays in diagnosis and difficulties in access to treatments.

Medical products for prevention, diagnosis or treatment of this kind of disorders are called *orphan drugs* because the pharmaceutical industry has not a great interest under normal market conditions in developing products intended for a small number of patients and in marketing them. The name refers to the fact that a drug for a rare disease is often not "adopted" by any pharmaceutical industry, but the status of orphan is officially given by a special commission after the drug has been developed, to classify the medicines that may apply for incentives.

The cost of producing a medicine and distributing it on the market can be very high. It normally takes about 10 years to develop a new drug and if the expected sales of the product would not recover the costs, as it often happens when the disease is rare, the companies are advised to pursue orphan drugs only for ethical reasons. This is the reason why diseases affecting much more patients often take priority. It is clear that economic incentives are needed to encourage drug companies to develop medicines for the many rare disease patients, making orphan drugs economically profitable.

4.1.3 Orphan drug designation and incentives

A procedure for the designation of medicinal products as orphan and to provide incentives for the research was established by the ODA in the USA in 1983. It provided incentives on rare disease research and development (R&D), via tax exemption and offering the possibility to be the sole producer of a drug for a period of 7 years. The production of a competing drug is allowed if its clinical superiority for treating the same condition is demonstrated. The benefits of the ODA in encouraging the development of new drugs for rare diseases have been largely studied in the last decade (see, for example, Grabowski [8] and Gites *et al.* [7]). In the first 20 years after the Act, between 1983 and 2003, more than 200 drugs and biological products for rare diseases have been brought to market, while in the decade prior to 1983 less than ten such products came to the market.

Following the example of the USA, in 2000 the *Regulation on Orphan Medicinal Products* [4] was approved by the European Parliament. A specific committee was created to select drugs to qualify as "orphan". The orphan regulation sets up criteria for orphan designation and describes the incentives to encourage the research. As for the ODA, it has yielded to an increase in the number of orphan medicinal products approved [9]. The purpose is "to lay down a Community procedure for the designation of medicinal products as orphan medicinal products and to provide incentives for the research, development and placing on the market". The regulation provides legal and financial incentives, stating that "the Community and the Member States shall not, for a period of 10 years, accept another application for a marketing authorization, or grant a marketing authorization or accept an application to extend an existing marketing authorization, for the same therapeutic indication, in respect of a similar medicinal product". This provides a monopoly, where the holder of the marketing authorization can profit of being the sole producer and seller of a drug or treatment for a special disease, until a "second medicinal product, although similar to the orphan medicinal product already authorized, is safer, more effective or otherwise clinically superior" or until the end of the 10-year long period.

This document guaranteed that the Community and each Member State should have supported research on orphan medicinal products. Member States had to communicate to the Commission detailed information about the strategies to enhance the research on orphan drugs before 22 July 2000 and this information had to be updated regularly.

Orphan drugs were eligible for fee reductions and in 2009 the fee reduction policy has been revised in order to increase support to enterprises and to develop further research. It is always due to the European Commission to design whether a drug is orphan or not. The EMA (European Medicines Agency) founded a committee, called Committee for Orphan Medicinal Products (COMP), which is responsible for this.

A few years ago, it was almost impossible to get a precise diagnosis and this problem brought to patients unnecessary medical interventions and treatments, which worsened their quality of life. Moreover, many children affected by the same kind of illnesses came to life, as it is still difficult to predict the genetic origin of many of them. Diagnosis is now available for about 1,900 diseases and existing drugs, jointly with the study of new drugs and treatments, guarantee a rapid progress in therapies.

All these interventions and incentives increased the interest that pharmaceutical industries deserve to rare diseases, but usually each industry still considers more profitable to invest on common diseases than on a rare one, even if in the first case it has to compete for the market with other incumbent industries, sometimes with well-consolidated drugs.

In this chapter we propose that pharmaceutical industries coordinate their researches in order to avoid that two or more of them study a new molecule for the same disease. In case of common diseases, the lack of coordination makes possible to incur the risk of launching the same drug so that only the first gets the patent, or different drugs with higher advertisement costs and the necessity of further sharing the market, reducing the expected income. In case of rare diseases, if two industries present a new treatment for the same disease, only the first or the best may get the benefits according to the existing normative. Due to the high number of rare diseases and to the small number of R&D projects this matter may seem to happen with a very low probability. The choice of which disease to research on may be influenced by several elements, some of which are the same for all the potential researchers, mainly how much the public opinion speaks about a disease. For instance, in this moment in Europe (and not only) there are some popular retired soccer players affected by amyotrophic lateral sclerosis (ALS), known in the United States and Canada as Lou Gehrig's disease, after the baseball player who first died for it. Consequently, many researchers decided to work on this or other kinds of sclerosis, like multiple sclerosis. The effect of the coordination is that not only the most profitable and/or popular diseases may receive the attention of the pharmaceutical industries.

In the next sections we present a coordination model, which is at first designed and solved as a multiple knapsack problem and then as a college admissions problem. A greedy variation of the second approach is proposed, in order to avoid unfeasibility problems that may occur.

4.2 Materials and methods

In this section, we first introduce what a *R&D assignment problem* is and then we recall the theoretical notions about multiple knapsack problem and college admissions problem we need to develop our models.

4.2.1 R&D assignment problem

We consider a *R&D assignment problem* in which n companies, $f_1, \dots, f_n$, allow a decision-maker coordinating their R&D processes about m diseases, $d_1, \dots, d_m$, assigning the illnesses each firm will research on. We suppose that each company f_i establishes a maximum budget b_i to invest on research on new drugs and that the R&D process on illness d_j has a cost k_j and profit g_j.

Moreover, each company f_i defines a *preference profile* on the set of diseases, denoted with $\succ_i$, $i = 1, \dots, n$, where $d_h \succ_i d_k$ means that disease d_h is preferred to disease d_k for company f_i in its possible R&D program. The preferences are revealed by the companies themselves to the decision-maker and they can be based on the expected profits deriving from a successful R&D process, on a subjective interest in a disease, etc. On the other side, we suppose that also the diseases "define" some preference profiles on the set of the companies, that we denote by $\sqsupset_j$, $j = 1, \dots, m$. To do that, we may assign a curriculum to each pharmaceutical company, given by its historical background (previous researches, technological equipment, human expertise, etc.) and we assume that each disease "prefers" to be studied by the company which has the highest probability of success in the R&D process.

4.2.2 Multiple knapsack problem

Given a set $M = \{1, \dots, m\}$ of items and a set $N = \{1, \dots, n\}$ of knapsacks, with $n \leq m$, let be:

- p_j the *value* of item $j \in M$;
- w_j the *weight* of item $j \in M$;
- a_i the *capacity* of knapsack $i \in N$.

The *0-1 multiple knapsack problem* (*MKP*) [11] consists in assigning the objects to the knapsacks (an object to only one knapsack) without violating capacity constraints and maximizing the total value of the selected items. Formally,

$$\begin{array}{ll} \text{maximize} & z = \sum_{i=1}^{n} \sum_{j=1}^{m} p_j x_{ij} \\ \text{subject to} & \sum_{j=1}^{m} w_j x_{ij} \leq a_i \\ & \sum_{i=1}^{n} x_{ij} \leq 1 \\ & x_{ij} \in \{0,1\} \quad i \in N,\ j \in M \end{array} \tag{4.1}$$

where

$$x_{ij} = \begin{cases} 1 & \text{if item } j \text{ is assigned to knapsack } i \\ 0 & \text{otherwise.} \end{cases}$$

If $n = 1$, the MKP reduces to the classical *knapsack problem* (*KP*), while if $n > m$, the $n - m$ knapsacks of smallest capacity can be eliminated.

In the following, we assume that:

- w_j, p_j, and a_i are positive integer numbers;
- $w_j \leq \max_{i \in N}\{a_i\}$, $j \in M$;
- $a_i \geq \min_{j \in M}\{w_j\}$, $i \in N$;
- $\sum_{j=1}^{m} w_j > a_i$, $i \in N$.

If assumption (4.1) is violated, for non-positive numbers it is sufficient to eliminate all the corresponding knapsacks and items, while rational numbers can be handled multiplying all the numbers by a proper factor. Items violating (4.2) cannot be carried by any of the knapsacks and can be eliminated; the same happens to knapsacks violating (4.3), as they cannot carry any of the items. If a knapsack violates (4.4), then the problem has the trivial solution "assign all the objects to it".

To implement the algorithms we use the standard assumption that the items are sorted so that

$$\frac{p_1}{w_1} \geq \frac{p_2}{w_2} \geq \ldots \geq \frac{p_n}{w_n}.$$

The optimal solution of MKPs is usually obtained by *branch-and-bound* algorithms (*BB*) [13], which are general algorithms for finding optimal solutions of various optimization problems. The reason why BB is preferred to dynamic programming is that the last is impractical for MKPs, both for computational time and storage requirements reasons. Algorithms for solving MKPs are generally oriented to the case of low or high values of the ratio m/n. In general, the R&D assignment deals with the second class. Among the different algorithms presented in literature, we choose the *MTM* algorithm by Martello and Toth [11]. It is a *bound-and-bound* algorithm which differs from common BB as not only upper bounds (UB) are derived at each decision node of the branching process, but also lower bounds (LB). This technique is well suited for problems (like the MKPs) where it is easy to find a fast heuristic solution which yields good LBs, but it is difficult to verify feasibility of UBs. In particular, Martello and Toth derive UBs by solving the surrogate problem, defined considering a unique knapsack of capacity $a = \sum_{i=1}^{n} a_i$, while the LBs are found by solving n individual KPs as follows: the smallest knapsack is optimally filled, the chosen items are removed from the problem and the next knapsack is optimally filled. The process is repeated until all n knapsacks have been optimally filled, one by one, or all the items are assigned to a knapsack. After computing the UB and the LB, the binary branching procedure is implemented, assigning or not an item to a knapsack. The algorithm stops when UB=LB, exploiting feasibility of the LB.

4.2.3 College admissions problem

The *College Admissions Problem* (*CAP*) was introduced by Gale and Shapley in [6]. Given two finite sets $C = \{c_1, \ldots, c_n\}$, the set of colleges, and $S = \{s_1, \ldots, s_m\}$, the set of students, let be q_c the quota of students that college $c \in C$ can admit. When $q_c = 1$ for each $c \in C$, we obtain the *marriage problem*. Each applicant ranks the colleges in the order of her/his preferences, omitting those colleges which s/he would never accept under any circumstances. On the other hand, each college ranks the students who have applied to it according to its preferences, for example by an admission test, eliminating those applicants it would not admit under any circumstances, even not filling its quota. When a student [college] is indifferent between two or more colleges [students], they are nevertheless required to list them in some order (let us assume randomly).

A solution to the problem is given by a *matching* of students to colleges, such that each student is matched to at most one college and each college is matched to at most its quota of students. A student who is not matched to any college is "matched to himself" and a college that has some empty positions is matched to itself in each of those positions.

Following the definition given in [14], for any set X an *unordered family of elements of* X is a collection of elements, not necessarily distinct, in which the order is immaterial. A given element of X may appear more than once in an unordered family of elements of X, differently from a subset of X. A *matching* μ is a function from the set $C \cup S$ into the set of unordered families of elements of $C \cup S$ such that:

- $|\mu(s)| = 1$ for every $s \in S$ and $\mu(s) = s$ if $\mu(s) \notin C$;
- $|\mu(c)| = q_c$ for every $c \in C$ and if $|\mu(c) \cap S| = r < q_c$ then $\mu(c)$ contains $q_c - r$ copies of c;
- $\mu(s) = c$ if and only if s is in $\mu(c)$.

An assignment of applicants to colleges is called *stable* if it does not occur that there are two applicants s and t who are assigned to colleges A and B, respectively, although t prefers A to B and A prefers t to s. A stable assignment is called *optimal* if every applicant is at least as well off under it as under any other stable assignment.

In order to obtain a stable and optimal solution to the CAP, we consider the following procedure (see [6]):

- all students apply to the college they prefer;
- each college $c \in C$ places on its waiting list the q_c applicants it ranks highest, or all applicants it would admit if there are fewer than q_c, and rejects the rest;
- rejected applicants apply to their second best choice and again each college selects the top q_c among the new applicants and those on its waiting list, puts them on its new waiting list, and rejects the rest;
- the procedure terminates when every applicant is either on a waiting list or has been rejected by every college to which s/he is willing and permitted to apply or all the lists of the colleges are filled.

4.3 Results and discussion

In this section we show how MKPs and CAPs can be applied to solve an R&D assignment problem, highlighting the differences in the ideas under them and, consequently, in the solutions they obtain, and we discuss the results on a toy-model based on realistic data.

4.3.1 R&D assignment problem as MKP

The R&D assignment problem can be seen as a MKP in which the companies play the role of the knapsacks, the capacity of each given by the budget, and the diseases the role of the items, the values and weights of each given by the profits and the costs, respectively. We want to stress that this approach does not take into account neither the preferences of the firms nor the ones of the diseases. In fact, from the point of view of the firms the importance of a disease is determined by its expected monetary profit and no subjective parameter is taken into account, leading the preference profiles to be the same for all the firms; from the point of view of the diseases, the firms are "considered" identical, the only important thing being the assignment to one of them.

4.3.2 R&D assignment problem as CAP

Here, we mainly focus our attention on the importance of the preferences, trying to guarantee that the wishes of both the firms and the diseases are respected as much as possible. Defining the preferences of the illnesses according to the historical background of the firms, it is important to look for an allocation which assigns each disease to the company with the best chance of a successful research. In the previous model this aspect is not taken into account. Unfortunately, also this model requires some important simplifications, in particular we have to approximate the costs of the research on a disease with their average cost (so all the costs are equal). Then, the information about the budget of every company is simplified just assigning the number of diseases it can study on (simply dividing the budget by the average cost). With these assumptions we have a classical college admissions problem for which, as we saw, an algorithm to find a stable and optimal solution is available. The pharmaceutical companies play the role of the colleges, while the diseases that of the students: each pharmaceutical company can research on more than one illness, until it reaches its quota, while every disease may be studied by at most one company. It is possible that a company does not want to research on a disease under any circumstances and that a disease never "wants to be studied" by a company (for example if it does not have the technologies for the required R&D process).

A greedy variation of the college admissions problem allows not approximating the costs of the R&D processes. We suppose to keep the information of the costs of the diseases and of the budgets of the companies. We assume to have a marriage problem where we have to couple every company with at most one disease, with the constraint that a company does not rank in its preferences an illness for which it does not have a budget high enough and/or the historical background to deal with the R&D process. We implement the algorithm to find a stable and optimal matching, assigning n illnesses to the n companies. Then we reduce the budget of the companies to their left money and we repeat the algorithm with the other $m-n$ diseases. Such an algorithm, at the end, may not provide a solution with good properties neither of stability nor of optimality, but it works faster and, taking into account the adjusted budgets, allows getting always a feasible solution, differently from applying CAP where we consider average costs.

4.3.3 The toy-model

The R&D process is very long and costly. The probability of success, the costs and the time are very uncertain, as much as the economic returns of new drug introduction. In [8] there is a very exhaustive analysis of the risk that most of the candidates do not reach the market in the development process. Most drug candidates fail and only a few drugs succeed in generating very large returns to the innovating firm.

One of the most important contributions to the new drugs development costs analysis is the research of DiMasi *et al.* [2]. They estimate a pre-tax total cost of $802 million for a generic non-orphan drug, about $250 million of which due to the pre-clinical part, $550 million to the clinical one. The global costs can arrive to $1 billion adding the taxation of 35% and the post-approval costs [7]. Because of the shorter clinical trials and the tax benefits, orphan drugs may have a different cost structure. Many of them, for example, are eligible for a priority review and the trials are done on a much smaller number of patients. Unfortunately, the estimates on the cost of the R&D process for an orphan drug are not that clear and the available data are often contrasting. The conjecture in [8] is that the R&D cost structure of orphan drugs is very different in nature from other drugs. In particular, it is reasonable to conclude that these costs are significantly lower than non-orphan compounds. We assume that the total post-approval costs, including the tax credit, are on average one half, compared with the drugs with non-orphan status. This is reasonable due to the fact that Love [10] gives evidence that pre-clinical costs for an orphan drug are between $11 and $34 million on average (about 10% of the ones for a non-orphan compound). The part of clinical costs is the most difficult one to be discussed: in the literature it can be found that, due to the smaller number of patients and the priority review, the costs for orphan compounds are less than the ones for non-orphan. We estimate them in $400 million. Finally, the orphan status reduces the taxation on clinical costs to 17.5% and put down to zero the post approval costs (see [7]), leading the whole cost to be about $500 million.

Looking at profits, the list of bestselling drugs ranks *Lipitor*, a drug against cholesterol, in the first place, with a total of $14.385 billion of sales in 2006. *Abilify* (anti-depressive – 50th position) earned $1.900 billion, while *Claritin* (allergic rhinitis – 200th position) arrived to earn $418 million.

Data for the orphan drugs are totally different, as most of them have very modest sales: if some of them arrive to be defined as *blockbuster drugs* (i.e. drugs with global annual sales greater than $1 billion), some of the most popular ones arrive to earn only $500 million in their peak year on the market and, going out from the top 10, no more than $10 million.

Speaking about the budget a company can invest on the R&D process, the percentage of the net income invested on R&D varies. For example, in 2000 the top seller company, *Merck and Co. Inc.*, had a revenue of $40.363 billion, but only the 6% has been allocated to R&D, which corresponds to $2.422 billion. *Eli Lilly and Co.*, instead, invested the 19% of its net income of $10.862 billion, corresponding to $2.063 billion. One of the firms that the most invested money in R&D was *Pfitzer Inc.*, which had a net income of $29.574 billion and used the 15%, corresponding to $4.436 billion.

According to this analysis, we consider a toy-model of a R&D assignment problem in which $n = 2$ companies, f_I and f_{II}, with budgets $b_I = \$1650$ and $b_{II} = \$2900$ million, respectively, allow a decision-maker to coordinate their researches on $m = 6$ diseases, 4 of which (d_1 to d_4) are common, the others (d_5 and d_6) are rare. The costs k_j and the profits g_j (in million of \$) of the diseases are in the following table.

Table 4.1. Data for the toy-model of R&D assignment problem

j	k_j	g_j
1	950	55000
2	1050	80000
3	950	10000
4	900	40000
5	450	300
6	650	800

We assume that the preference profiles for the firms are given by

$$f_I : d_2 \succ_I d_1 \succ_I d_4$$
$$f_{II} : d_2 \succ_{II} d_1 \succ_{II} d_4 \succ_{II} d_6 \succ_{II} d_3 \succ_{II} d_5$$

while the ones for the diseases by

$$d_1 : f_{II} \sqsupset_1 f_I \qquad d_4 : f_{II} \sqsupset_4 f_I$$
$$d_2 : f_I \sqsupset_2 f_{II} \qquad d_5 : f_I \sqsupset_5 f_{II}$$
$$d_3 : f_{II} \qquad d_6 : f_{II} \sqsupset_6 f_I.$$

We suppose that f_I is a small firm with a more restricted budget and it bases its preference profile only on the expected profit deriving from a disease, so that it is not interested in the two rare diseases d_5 and d_6 whose profits are really low. Moreover, d_3 excludes f_I from its preference profile, because the firm has not enough technological skills to research on it, so that d_3 does not appear in f_I's preferences. Also firm f_{II} is interested in its profit, but it has some personal reasons to research on d_6 and ranks it higher than d_3. Finally, as it has a higher budget, it would accept to research on each of the diseases.

Following the preferences just defined and without considering coordination among the companies, f_I would decide to research only on d_2 because, adding any other disease it is interested in, the costs greater than its budget, while f_{II} would choose d_2, d_1 and d_4. Then, only three of the six diseases are studied and none of the rare is considered by the firms. In the following, we discuss what happens applying our coordination models to the same example.

4.3.3.1 The MKP solution

We consider a MKP with two knapsacks of capacities $a_I = b_I = 1650$ and $a_{II} = b_{II} = 2900$, respectively, and six items, whose weights and values are $w = k = (950, 1050, 950, 900, 450, 650)$ and $p = g = (55000, 80000, 10000, 40000, 300, 800)$, respectively. The MTM algorithm performs the following steps:

1. Sort the items by decreasing values of the ratio $\frac{p_i}{w_i}$, obtaining $2-1-4-3-6-5$.
2. Compute the UB for the solution, solving the surrogate problem with a single knapsack of capacity $a = a_I + a_{II} = 4550$. We find the optimal solution $(1,1,1,1,0,1)$ (where 1 in the i-th position of the vector means that item i is carried, 0 otherwise) whose value is $U = 185800$.
3. Compute the LB for the solution, filling optimally at first the smallest knapsack (f_I) and then the largest (f_{II}). The optimal solution for the first knapsack is $(0,1,0,0,1,0)$ whose value is 80300, for the second is $(1,0,1,1,0,0)$ with value 105000. Then, the LB is $L = 80300 + 105000 = 185300$.
4. As $L < U$ the branching procedure starts. We consider item d_2 (the first in the ranking) assigned to knapsack f_I:

   - if item d_2 is assigned to knapsack f_I, then nothing changes;
   - if item d_2 is not assigned to knapsack f_I, then the optimal solution for the first knapsack is $(1,0,0,0,0,1)$ with value 55800, for the second is $(0,1,1,1,0,0)$ with value 130000. The new LB is $L = 185800 = U$, so the assignment is optimal for the MKP.

Figure 4.1 reports the branching tree of the algorithm.

The solution assigns the researches on d_1 and d_6 to firm f_I and the researches on d_2, d_3 and d_4 to firm f_{II}. We may remark that the coordination model based on MKP allows researching on five of the diseases instead of three, as it happens in the non-coordination case, including also the rare disease d_6.

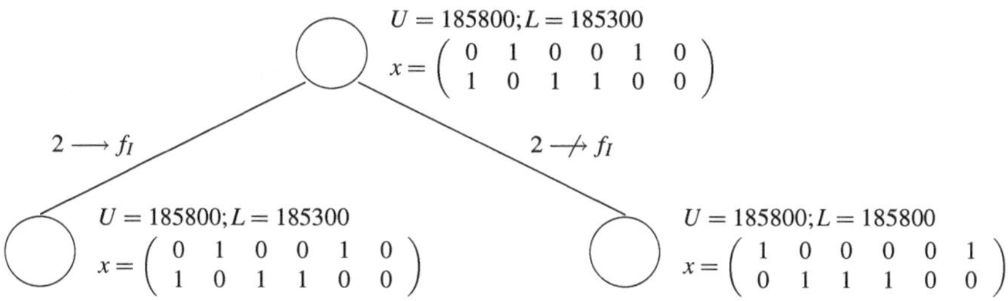

Fig. 4.1. The decisional tree for the MKP algorithm

4.3.3.2 The CAP solution

We consider a CAP in which the set of colleges is represented by the two firms and the set of students by the six diseases. The quotas for the firms are computed on the basis of the average cost of the diseases $\bar{c} = 825$, resulting to be $q_I = 2$ and $q_{II} = 3$. The CAP solution can be found using the following procedure:

1. • d_2 and d_5 "visit" f_I, which could accept both of them but is not interested in d_5, then it chooses to accept only d_2;
   • d_1, d_3, d_4 and d_6 "visit" f_{II}, which could accept no more than 3 of them and accepts d_1, d_4 and d_6 according to its preferences.

   At the end of the first step, the assignment is given by $(0,1,0,0,0,0)$ for f_I and $(1,0,0,1,0,1)$ for f_{II}.
2. • d_3 "visits" f_I, which could accept one more disease but is not interested in d_3, so it decides not to accept it;
   • d_5 "visits" f_{II}, which could accept no more diseases and decide not to change its current assignment because it prefers it to any other containing d_5 (which is its less preferred disease).

   At the end of the second step, the assignment is given by $(0,1,0,0,0,0)$ for f_I and $(1,0,0,1,0,1)$ for f_{II} and the algorithm stops (each non-assigned disease has "visited" all the firms).

The solution assigns d_2 to firm f_I, d_1, d_4 and d_6 to firm f_{II}. We may observe that the constraints given by the preferences of the firms cause the solution to be inefficient, as it assigns four diseases to the two firms while they can potentially research on five (as it happens in the MKP solution). On the other hand, we can notice that without coordination both the firms would have decided to research on three diseases, excluding d_6 from their programs. The coordination gives the possibility of researching also on this rare disease, even if it is not considered a priority by the two firms.

4.3.3.3 The greedy solution

We have just noticed that the CAP approach can lead to inefficient solutions. On the other hand, efficient solutions may cause other problems. Let us think about the same problem, but now let us consider the modified preference profiles for f_I and d_3

$$f_I: \; d_2 \succ_I d_1 \succ_I d_4 \succ_I d_3 \qquad d_3: \; f_{II} \sqsupset_3 f_I.$$

Then, in the second step of the CAP algorithm d_3 is accepted by f_I, so that the final assignment gives both d_2 and d_3 to f_I. But this solution is unfeasible because the total cost of the researches assigned to f_I is $k_2 + k_3 = 2000$ and exceeds the budget of the firm. This problem arises because the budgets of the firms and the costs of the diseases are considered only in computing the quotas for the firms, causing a loss of information. The greedy variation of CAP previously described can help to preserve feasibility as it takes into account all the parameters of the problem. In the following, we describe how it works on the toy model.

1. We solve at first a marriage problem, assigning one disease to each firm:
   - d_2 and d_5 "visit" f_I, which chooses d_2;
   - d_1, d_3, d_4 and d_6 "visit" f_{II}, which chooses d_1;
   - d_3, d_4 and d_6 "visit" f_I, which chooses again d_2;
   - d_5 "visits" f_{II}, which chooses again d_1.

   At the end of the first step:

   - d_2 is assigned to f_I and the budget of the firm is reduced to $a_I \leftarrow a_I - k_2 = 600$;
   - d_1 is assigned to f_{II} and the budget of the firm is reduced to $a_{II} \leftarrow a_{II} - k_1 = 1950$;
   - d_1 and d_2 have been assigned and are not considered anymore in the algorithm;
   - the preferences of f_I on the remaining diseases are $d_4 \succ_I d_3$, but its budget is not enough to study any of the two, that are cancelled from its preference profile;
   - the preferences of f_{II} on the remaining diseases are $d_4 \succ_{II} d_6 \succ_{II} d_3 \succ_{II} d_5$ (the budget is enough for studying each of them).
2. We solve a new marriage problem in which d_1 and d_2 do not appear anymore (as they have been already assigned in the previous step):
   - f_I cannot play anymore as it has not enough budget to study any of its preferred diseases;
   - the remaining diseases are assigned to f_{II} in order of its preferences until its budget is not high enough to cover the costs of any other non-assigned disease.

   At the end of the second step, the assignment is given by $(0,1,0,0,0,0)$ for f_I and $(1,0,0,1,0,1)$ for f_{II} and the algorithm stops.

We may notice that the greedy variation of CAP recovers feasibility, assigning only d_2 to f_I, but it falls again into inefficiency (4 diseases instead of 5).

4.4 Conclusions

The Orphan Drug Act and the Regulation on Orphan Medicinal Products played a relevant role in encouraging the development of new orphan drugs, as in America as in Europe. Despite the benefits they have provided for pharmaceutical firms to conduct this kind of researches and the relevant increase of the investments on rare illnesses, the modest sales of orphan drugs do not always guarantee profitability to the companies. When it is possible to make profit on orphan drugs, the risk to arrive after another company, losing not only the market exclusivity but even the right to sell the medicine, drives away drug developers from investing in rare disease research.

In this chapter we proposed two possible methods for enhancing the research on rare diseases. The former (MKP) is oriented to a situation in which the firms are considered equivalent in their backgrounds (they can research on every disease) and in their objective function (which is unique and based on the profit of the R&D processes). On the other hand, the latter (CAP) allows considering different firms, in background, policy and objectives. Moreover, in the MKP case the decision requires less information about the policies of the firms (only the budgets), while in the CAP one we require to know something more (the preferences on the diseases).

The MKP provides the optimal solution according to the selected objective function, i.e. the value of the items. In our example, it represents the profit due to the selling of a drug, but it could be also the gain of producing and selling the drug or even a social welfare oriented function accounting the number of potential patients, or the number of drugs the firms research on, and possibly a function that assigns larger values to rare diseases. On the other hand, the decision-maker that coordinates the researches of the firms decides with the unique constraint of the budgets and without taking into account the preferences and the characteristics of the companies, being more "powerful": the firms agree in coordinating, but they would maybe prefer to have the possibility to refuse a research program if they do not like it or simply if they do not have the technology to do it.

The CAP method is strongly oriented in the opposite direction, giving the maximal freedom to firms and diseases; in fact, this method is driven towards the solution uniquely by the preferences of the firms and by their characteristics, organization and equipment. A firm not well-equipped for researching on a specific field may be "rejected" by a disease even if the profit from selling it is very high (as it happens when d_3 does not rank f_I in its preference profile). On the other hand, computing the cardinality of the diseases that may be assigned to a firm just on the basis of the average cost, may lead to unfeasible solutions (like when we apply the CAP to the situation in which d_3 can be studied by f_I), requiring the companies to invest more money than planned. If they cannot do such an effort or, simply, they do not want to spend more money, they can refuse one of the diseases (normally, the less preferred one).

Apparently, the greedy algorithm seems to behave very well, but it depends only on the numbers in the example. In fact, a positive feature of this class of algorithms is that they always produce a feasible solution, differently from the CAP, taking into account the preferences of the agents. However, in case of a "bad" choice in one of the first steps, it is possible that the final solution is very far from the best one. Let us think to the following case, in which we want to coordinate the R&D processes of two firms on three diseases, the budgets, costs, profits and preferences of which are given in the following table.

Table 4.2. Data for the comparison of CAP algorithm and its greedy variation

$b_I = 1200$	$q_I = 1$	$I: d_3 \succ_I d_2 \succ_I d_1$
$b_{II} = 1600$	$q_{II} = 2$	$II: d_3 \succ_{II} d_1 \succ_{II} d_2$
$k_1 = 1200$	$g_1 = 10000$	$1: f_I \sqsupset_1 f_{II}$
$k_2 = 800$	$g_2 = 9000$	$2: f_{II} \sqsupset_2 f_I$
$k_3 = 600$	$g_3 = 11000$	$3: f_{II} \sqsupset_3 f_I$

In this case, implementing the CAP algorithm we assign d_1 to f_I and d_2 and d_3 to f_{II}, while implementing the greedy variation we assign d_2 to f_I and d_3 to f_{II} (the adjusted budgets do not allow to assign d_1). Even if both the solutions are feasible, the first one is better because it allows researching on all the diseases.

Future research can focus on a different approach, adopting an auction-like mechanism that allows a firm researching on a specific common disease that is very promising from the point of view of profit, only if the firm commits to research on a rare disease (this mechanism is often used allocating air or railway slots). Another possibility is suggested by the behavior of the first firm in the CAP situation, where it prefers to research on the second disease, even if it requires an investment corresponding to about two thirds of its budget; a company could not accept the corresponding large risk in case of failure. The approach consists in a portfolio-like model in which the probability of success of the research plays the role of the risk of an investment, so the firms may decide to diversify their budget among common and rare diseases.

To conclude, we want to mention the *Stabilimento chimico farmaceutico militare* (the Italian military drug office), a state pharmaceutical firm, that decided to produce orphan drugs, exploiting its no-profit statute in order to favor patients suffering from rare diseases. The preferences of the pharmaceutical companies can also be given, like in this example, by a moral obligation and by the willingness of tackling the health care needs of all individuals. The actual lack of coordination can bring the companies to leave these ethical reasons in favor of the financial ones.

References

1. Centro Nazionale Malattie Rare (National Center for Rare Diseases). http://www.iss.it/cnmr/. Accessed 28 May 2011
2. DiMasi, J.A., Hansen, R.W., Grabowski, H.G.: The Price of Innovation: New Estimates of Drug Development Costs. J. of Health Econ. **22**, 151–185 (2003)
3. European Medicines Agency. http://www.ema.europa.eu/. Accessed 26 May 2011
4. European Parliament and Council: Regulation (EC) NO 141/2000 of the European Parliament and of the Council of 16 December 1999 on Orphan Medicinal Products. Off. J. of the Eur. Communities **43**, 1–5 (2000)
5. Eurordis – Rare Diseases Europe. http://www.eurordis.org/. Accessed 30 May 2011
6. Gale, D., Shapley, L.S.: College Admissions and the Stability of Marriage. The Am. Math. Mon. **69**, 9–15 (1962)
7. Gites, B., Chughtai, M., Chang, J., Philips, I.M.: Benefits of the Orphan Drug Act for Rare Disease Treatments. TuftScope. http://s3.amazonaws.com/tuftscope_exclusives/documents/10/Express_Online_Spring_2010_Gites.pdf (2010). Accessed 25 May 2011
8. Grabowski, H.: Increasing R&D Incentives for Neglected Diseases – Lessons from the Orphan Drug Act. In: International Public Goods, and Transfer of Technology under a globalized Intellectual Property Regime, pp. 457–480. Cambridge University Press, Cambridge (2005)
9. Heemstra, H.E., de Vrueh, R.L.A., van Weely, S., Büller, H.A., Leufkens, H.G.M.: Orphan drug development across Europe: bottlenecks and opportunities. Drug Discov. Today **13**, 670–676 (2008)
10. Love, J.: Evidence Regarding Research and Development Investments in Innovative and Non-Innovative Medicines. Consumer Project on Technology, Washington, DC. http://www.cptech.org/ip/health/rnd/evidenceregardingrnd.pdf (2003). Accessed 24 May 2011

11. Martello, S., Toth, P.: Knapsack Problems: Algorithms and Computer Implementations. John Wiley and Sons, New York (1990)
12. Orphan Europe. http://www.orphan-europe.com/. Accessed 27 May 2011
13. Papadimitriou, C.H., Steiglitz, K.: Combinatorial Optimization: Algorithms and Complexity. Prentice-Hall, New Jersey (1982)
14. Roth, A.E., Sotomayor, M.: The College Admissions Problem Revisited. Econometrica **57**, 559–570 (1989)
15. Senate and House of Representatives of the United States of America: Orphan Drug Act. Public Law 97–414, 97th Congress (1983)
16. Senate and House of Representatives of the United States of America: Rare Diseases Act of 2002. Public Law 107–280, 107th Congress (2002)

Chapter 5

Integrating simulation and risk-based sensitivity analysis methods in hospital emergency department design

Fatah Chetouane and Kash Barker

Abstract. An increasing concern when dealing with critical systems or services design is their preparation for a wide range of potentially uncertain operating conditions. In this chapter a four-step simulation-driven decision making methodology (SDDM) is presented to address sensitivity analysis of candidate designs to uncertainty and extreme operating conditions. The approach accounts for, not only the conventional average system performance metrics, but also (i) upper-tail or extreme values of these metrics, and (ii) performance sensitivity measures to uncertainties in the simulation model. The example used to illustrate the application of this technique is a hospital emergency department design case study wherein different design alternatives are compared using patient time-in-system performance metric under multiple uncertain operating conditions.

Keywords: decision making, simulation, extreme events, sensitivity, hospital department design

5.1 Introduction and problem addressed

One of the challenges most encountered by system and service designers is the capacity to face wide range of unforeseen operating conditions. Specifically, such conditions could be triggered by extreme events such as natural or man-made disasters and accidents, or other events that could lead to fluctuations in assumed system

F. Chetouane (✉)
Faculty of Engineering, Université de Moncton, 18 Ave Antonine-Maillet, Room 122G1, Moncton, New Brunswick, E1A 3E9, Canada
e-mail: fatah.chetouane@umoncton.ca

K. Barker
School of Industrial Engineering, University of Oklahoma, 202 West Boyd Street, Room 124, Norman, Oklahoma, 73019, USA
e-mail: kashbarker@ou.edu

Tànfani E., Testi A. (Eds.): Advanced Decision Making Methods Applied to Health Care.
International Series in Operations Research & Management Science 173
DOI 10.1007/978-88-470-2321-5_5,

models and processes. One technique to understand system behaviors *a priori* and to capture uncertainties originated from their operating environment is simulation. However, decisions which are exclusively based on simulation results are only as good as one's ability to understand and account for the wide spectrum of uncertainties which can hinder the performance of system operations. Usually, prior to simulation and experimentation phases, several steps are required to avoid or reduce bias and uncertainty. A design of experiments (DOE) is often conducted to screen for potentially influencing factors and a validation stage is required to detect model logic and data fitting errors. Since simulation is a means to experiment with various aspects of a system, DOE techniques are commonly used to study the influence between input variables and system responses. However, the distinction between the concepts of *influent factor* (among known model input variables), and *uncertainty* (among other unknown factors), makes DOE techniques less suitable for risk-based analysis than sensitivity analysis methods [13, 17]. Sensitivity analysis is especially important in simulation-based decision making, as underlying uncertainty may skew simulation results. An example of such simulation-based decision making of interest in this chapter is the comparison of design alternatives based on the simulation of system operational behavior. Several approaches for simulation-driven comparison of design alternatives have been reviewed in [4, 10, 12]. With respect to the comparison of alternatives in more extreme operating environments, methods for analyzing simulation-driven metrics, such as mean occurrence frequency for average events and exceedence probabilities for extreme events were discussed in [9].

In this chapter a novel multiobjective approach for simulation-driven decision making (SDDM) is proposed. This approach accounts, not only for the conventional average performance metric, but also for (i) upper-tail, or extreme values of the considered performance metric, and (ii) measures of sensitivity to uncertainties in the model. The proposed approach integrates the Partitioned Multiobjective Risk Method (PMRM) from [2] and the Uncertainty Sensitivity Index Method (USIM) from [11] with a discrete-event simulation model. It can be used as an additional step to add downstream of a simulation project which already integrates DOE analysis in its screening phase for influent factors. Understanding the sensitivity of decisions to underlying uncertainties in the system can improve the decision making process in a number of areas, including: understanding the robustness of an optimal solution, screening for sensitive or important factors, investigating sub-optimal solutions, developing durable recommendations for operating scenarios, comparing simple and complex strategies, and assessing the "riskiness" of a strategy, as enumerated in [16].

The remainder of this chapter is organized as follows. Section 5.2 introduces some design, simulation, risk and sensitivity analysis concepts and terminology prior to the detailed presentation and discussion of the proposed method. In Section 5.3, the proposed approach is applied to a hospital emergency department (ED) service design case study. The efficient operation of a hospital ED should incorporate a potentially uncertain and wide range of operating conditions. The proposed approach is deployed to measure the sensitivity of average and upper-tail times in the ED under a stochastic patient arrival process. These measures are ultimately used to compare different ED system designs towards providing reliable performance under multiple operating conditions. In Section 5.4 a summary and conclusions are provided.

5.2 Materials and methods

Service operations design is an important use of simulation. Service systems such as hospitals, airports, and post offices are complex systems which involve multiple personnel and equipment and where timely service delivery is an important quality for their efficient functioning. The use of simulation requires an identification of simulation model inputs (variables) and outputs (responses or performance metrics) prior to model logic programming. For example in a healthcare service, several inputs may be encountered such as the number of healthcare personnel, patient arrival rate, service times required for different operations, size of patient waiting area, personnel work schedules, number of examination rooms, availability of transportation services, and patient priority assignment rule, among many others. For the healthcare service case, model outputs could include patient time-in-system, system throughput, number waiting, and personnel idle time. Simulation outputs are usually produced with mean and variance values based on a selected number of runs and simulation horizon length. When simulation is used to find an optimal design or to enhance existing one, alternative candidate designs are evaluated based on the selected output using a what-if analysis approach. For candidate design simulation-based sensitivity and risk analysis, the selected output must include sensitivity metric with regards to uncertain factors (risk). The concept of factor is not limited only to model input variables, it can also represent, a logical module or a physical parameter of the model, or any independent variable external to the simulation model.

5.2.1 Methodological background

The approach discussed in this chapter makes use of two approaches for determining sensitivity metric: the Partitioned Multiobjective Risk Method (PMRM), which quantifies high consequence risk events of lower probability of occurrence, and the Uncertainty Sensitivity Index Method (USIM), which addresses the sensitivity of model response to errors in model factors based on a multiobjective formulation. These methods are first described in the following paragraphs before their integration in the simulation-based approach for risk analysis proposed in this chapter.

When comparing among a set of alternative candidate designs using a simulation output X, decision makers often rely on the output's expected value $E[X]$. However, the expected value may not represent a wide range of operating conditions under which the chosen design is expected to perform efficiently, particularly with respect to risk avoidance and operating conditions of low likelihood but high adverse events. To address these concerns, PMRM was developed to enhance the decision making process by complementing the conditional expected value measure with the conditional expected value under extreme adverse conditions in a multiobjective frame-

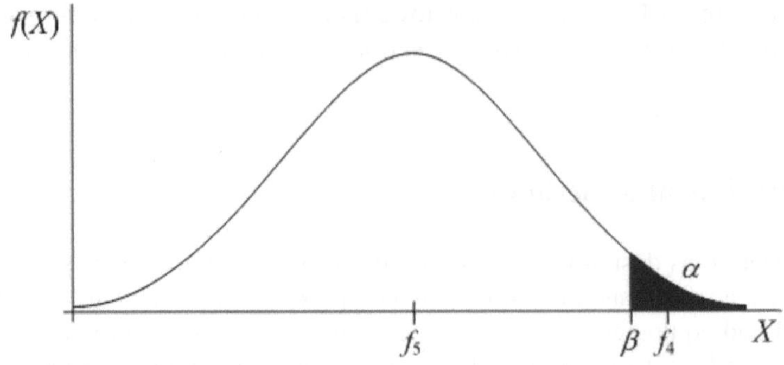

Fig. 5.1. Average and upper tail values of a random variable X, where the upper-tail value is defined by $X = \beta$ or $P(X > \beta) = \alpha$

work. The expected value, or average value denoted f_5, and the conditional expected value, or upper tail value denoted f_4, are illustrated in Figure 5.1. As the PMRM is typically applied in a risk context, the conditional expected value describes the upper tail of the risk or damage probability distribution function. The upper tail value is analogous to the conditional value-at-risk found in many finance applications [14], but also recently applied to the waiting time metric for the analysis of a hospital surgical unit [6]. The upper-tail value is $E[X \mid X > \beta]$, where β defines the X value encountered under extreme operating conditions. Alternatively, β can be selected equal to the probability α $(0 \leq \alpha \leq 1)$ of occurrence of extreme operating conditions, such that $P(X > \beta) = \alpha$. The calculation of f_5 and f_4 are found in Eqs. (5.1) and (5.2) respectively:

$$f_5(\cdot) = E[X] = \frac{\int_{-\infty}^{\infty} x f(x)\, dx}{\int_{-\infty}^{\infty} f(x)\, dx} = \int_{-\infty}^{\infty} x f(x)\, dx \tag{5.1}$$

$$f_4(\cdot) = E[X \mid X > \beta] = \frac{\int_{\beta}^{\infty} x f(x)\, dx}{\int_{\beta}^{\infty} f(x)\, dx}. \tag{5.2}$$

Assuming a valid simulation model and no clustered data (e.g., arrival times between entities in a simulation model are iid), the upper-tail area represents the likelihood of obtaining an extreme event value equal at least to β. This information is valuable when designing critical systems which may be subjected to extreme operating conditions. For example, healthcare service designer may be concerned with extreme values of patient waiting time in disaster situations such as epidemic, and natural or man-made disasters. Traditional expected values and upper tail values of patient waiting times (X) can be used to determine how each candidate design behaves under average and extreme adverse conditions. The PMRM formulation trades off two or more objectives, such as cost versus risk, where average and upper-tail risks are examined.

When system models do not represent the current state of the system (e.g., during extreme events), decision making can suffer. Often, the utility of risk-based decision making is not necessarily to select the "best" design, but rather to avoid the least desirable designs. One such undesirable quality of a design is its sensitivity to changes in operating conditions or its sensitivity to model parameter fluctuations. The proposed methodology makes use of a simple sensitivity metric from the USIM method, which addresses the sensitivity of optimal model response to errors in model parameters based on a multiobjective framework. The USIM method assumes that $f(\mathbf{u},\lambda)$ is an objective function representing a performance metric (e.g., a simulation response variable) to be minimized. Vector **u** represents a set of decision variables, and λ is a potentially uncertain model factor in $f(\cdot)$. The sensitivity metric $\psi(\cdot)$ in Eq. (5.3) below represents the sensitivity of $f(\cdot)$ to uncertainty in the factor λ, calculated as the squared partial derivative of $f(\cdot)$ with respect to λ. The multiobjective framework is to minimize $\psi(\cdot)$ while optimizing $f(\cdot)$. Several extensions to the USIM method are also provided in [15].

$$\psi(\mathbf{u},\lambda) = \left[\frac{\partial}{\partial \lambda} f(\mathbf{u},\lambda)\right]^2. \tag{5.3}$$

The function $f(\cdot)$ can be obtained by mathematical derivation when system equations are available and simple to manipulate or by combining DOE methods and simulation to determine a metamodel (e.g., an input output transformation) of the underlying simulation model using regression or multivariate regression analysis if several response variables are considered. The sensitivity metric $\psi(\cdot)$ provides a metric to assess response changes with regards to uncertainty on λ factors, including input variables, simulation model and statistical distribution parameters such as arrival rate or processing time distributions.

5.2.2 Proposed integration of methods

Based on the integration of extreme event and sensitivity analysis methods with discrete-event simulation, a simulation-driven decision making methodology (SDDM) is proposed to perform a multiobjective comparison of several candidate designs, where the metrics quantifying the efficiency of each design are determined using discrete event simulation. The four main steps of the proposed SDDM methodology are illustrated in Figure 5.2. Note the feedback loop from Step 3 to Step 1, suggesting that information gained from Steps 1 through 3 can be used to improve candidate designs prior to their comparison in Step 4.

5.2.2.1 Step 1. Discrete event simulation of a candidate design

The SDDM methodology is based on discrete-event simulation of candidate designs (Step 1 of Fig. 5.2). A discrete-event simulation model of a candidate design is con-

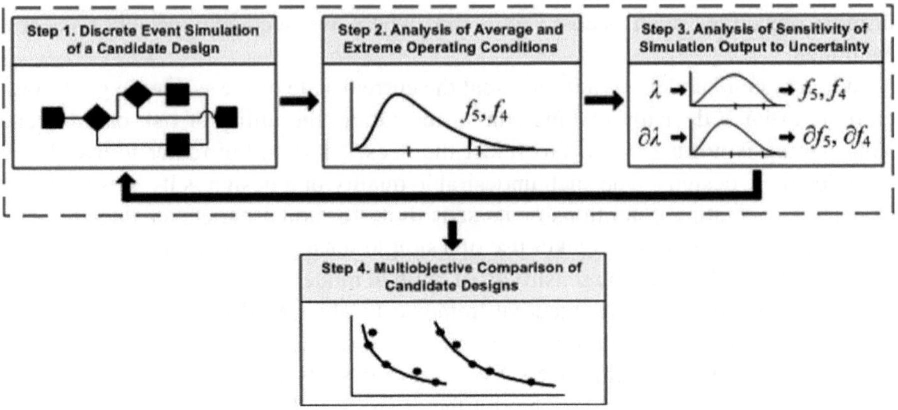

Fig. 5.2. Main steps of the simulation-driven decision making methodology

structed based on system layout and operation characteristics. The model building process can be resumed through the following steps:

- *Step 1.1.* Convert candidate design goals and objectives to a set of performance metrics.
- *Step 1.2.* Determine the group of decision variables influencing these performances.
- *Step 1.3.* Build a conceptual model of the system based on Step 1.1.
- *Step 1.4.* Collect data, perform statistical analysis and representation.
- *Step 1.5.* Code model using computer simulation program.
- *Step 1.6.* Test model and debug errors.
- *Step 1.7.* Validate model with regards to design goals being modeled (Step 1.1).

5.2.2.2 Step 2. Analysis of average and extreme operating conditions

The PMRM calculations of expected value f_5 and conditional expected value f_4 are naturally extended to the discrete event simulation environment for our methodology. Several simulation runs will generate a distribution for a desired performance metric similar to that in Figure 5.1. The arithmetical mean of all simulation runs constitutes f_5, and the average of the upper (or lower, depending on the metric) values X_i such that $X_i \geq \beta$ with a probability α constitutes f_4. To analyze average and extreme operating conditions (Step 2 of Fig. 5.2), the PMRM is integrated in the discrete-event simulation environment according to the following steps:

- *Step 2.1.* A set of n discrete observations X_i of the performance metric X are collected.
- *Step 2.2.* The set $\{X_i,\ i = 1,\ldots, n\}$ is divided into m intervals (cells) of a fixed width d.
- *Step 2.3.* The number of observations falling into a cell j is its absolute frequency a_j.

- *Step 2.4.* Cell j absolute frequency is divided by n to obtain the relative frequency r_j.

Cell frequencies and relative cumulative frequencies are used to compute the expected value f_5 and the conditional expected value f_4 of using the following Eq. (5.4) and Eq. (5.5). The value β is determined with Eq. (5.6).

$$f_5 = \sum_{j=1}^{m} \left(\frac{2j-1}{2}\right) \cdot d \cdot r_j \tag{5.4}$$

$$f_4 = \sum_{j \geq \beta/d} \left(\frac{2j-1}{2}\right) \cdot d \cdot r_j \tag{5.5}$$

$$\sum_{j \leq \beta/d} r_j = 1 - \alpha. \tag{5.6}$$

The value of α represents the frequency of occurrence of extreme operating conditions. In Eqs. (5.4) and (5.5), class values are represented by the mean value of the cells. This can be replaced by the greatest possible or least possible mean values by substituting the factor $(2j-1)/2$ by $(j-1)$ or j, respectively. Furthermore, the number and width of cells can be determined using different empirical formulas; in our case Sturges' rule is used keeping number of observations (number of simulation replications performed in Step 1) greater than 30. The fast Fourier transform approach may also be used to extract probability distribution functions (pdfs) based on the set $\{X_i, i = 1, \ldots, n\}$, as used in [5].

5.2.2.3 Step 3. Analysis of simulation output sensitivity to uncertainty

To perform sensitivity analysis of simulation output to an uncertain factor λ (Step 3 of Fig. 5.2), several operating conditions may be simulated for different values of factor λ to be expected under extreme conditions. At this step, the USIM method is used to calculate sensitivity metrics ψ_{f_5} and $\psi_{f_4}$of the expected value f_5 and the conditional expected value $f_4$to uncertainty in the underlying parameter λ using a discrete approximation of Eq. (5.3) above. For example, assuming a λ factor with four-level: $\lambda + 2$, $\lambda + 1$, $\lambda - 1$, and $\lambda - 2$, sensitivity metrics to uncertainty in λ, are calculated using the numerical five-point derivative method, provided in the following Eq. (5.7) for each set of decision variables (model input variables) represented by a vector $\mathbf{u}$ (independent from λ). Parameter h refers to the step size between two neighboring points.

$$\psi = \left[\frac{\partial f(\lambda)}{\partial \lambda}\right]^2 \approx \left[\frac{-f(\lambda+2h) + 8f(\lambda+1h) - 8f(\lambda-1h) + f(\lambda-2h)}{12h}\right]^2. \tag{5.7}$$

5.2.2.4 Step 4. Multiobjective comparison of candidate designs

These values are computed in Step 4 of the proposed methodology, a multiobjective framework is discussed to minimize $\psi(\cdot)$ while optimizing $f(\cdot)$. Subsequent to the evaluation of f_5 and f_4 sensitivity to uncertainty in an underlying design factor λ, step 4 culminates with the decision maker being provided with a powerful

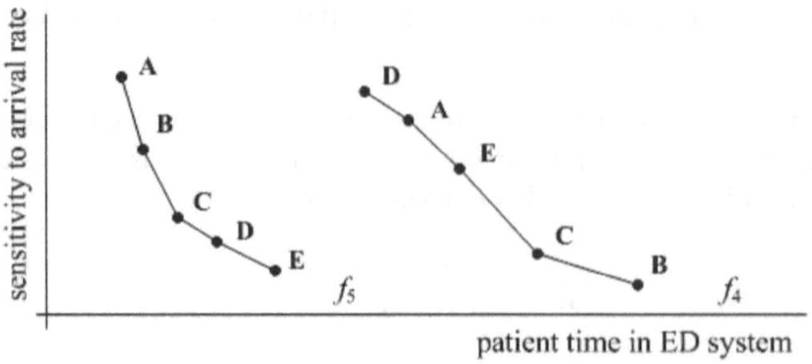

Fig. 5.3. Pareto-optimal frontiers depicting average and upper-tail risks

multiobjective comparison framework that considers both average and extreme operating conditions performance of each design with their sensitivity measures to uncertainty. The goal is to choose a candidate design that provides the best tradeoff between these four objectives, as shown in Eq. (5.11), where optimal values of each are sought. Vector **u**, extended to a discrete event simulation sense, represents "decisions" made about each candidate design (e.g., different facility layouts, different service time parameters), and $\hat{\lambda}$ represents the nominal or presumed value of uncertain factor λ.

$$\begin{aligned} \min_{\mathbf{u}} \; & f_5\left(\mathbf{u},\hat{\lambda}\right) \\ & \psi_{f_5}\left(\mathbf{u},\hat{\lambda}\right) \\ & f_4\left(\mathbf{u},\hat{\lambda}\right) \\ & \psi_{f_4}\left(\mathbf{u},\hat{\lambda}\right). \end{aligned} \tag{5.8}$$

The usefulness of this integration of PMRM and USIM approaches in decision making is illustrated in Figure 5.3, where five ED design alternatives (designs A, B, C, D, E) are compared according to their resulting patient time-in-system average and upper-tail metrics, and their sensitivity to uncertainty in the underlying patients arrival rate factor. These five design alternatives represent noninferior (Pareto-optimal) solutions, where opting for an alternative improves the value of one objective (in this case time-in-system) only at the expense of another objective (in this case sensitivity to uncertainty on arrival rate). The tradeoff curve among these five designs is referred to as the Pareto-optimal frontier (or the Pareto-optimal set). Figure 5.3 provides decision makers with a representation of the time-sensitivity tradeoff under normal (f_5 values) and extreme operating conditions (f_4 values). Note that tradeoffs may be different under the operating conditions, and some options may be inferior in certain operating conditions.

Based on Figure 5.3, alternative B represents a design that is a bit more sensitive to fluctuations in the underlying patients arrival rate under average operating conditions, but a design which is much more robust under extreme operating conditions, though with a time-in-system performance metric far greater than the other designs. Alternative A, while perhaps the least robust of all designs, has fairly low time-in-system under average and extreme operating conditions. Multiobjective design problems may have many solutions, which lead to several design alternatives. The Pareto frontier represents the set of optimal designs, in the sense that there are no other designs which are superior in all objectives. Pareto frontier depicts the trade-offs between objectives, so the best design can be selected. The difficulties in using Pareto frontier for best design selection include: computing the Pareto frontier for multiobjective problems, determining the set of solutions representing the frontier, and performing a sensitivity analysis of the frontier. Due to these difficulties, simulation-based design methods are usually preferred because of their inherent capability to program uncertainty and perform sensitivity analysis during simulation experiments.

5.3 Results and discussion

The proposed four-step simulation-driven decision making (SDDM) methodology with sensitivity analysis capability, outlined in Figure 5.2, is applied herein on a case study involving an ED service design at a regional hospital in the province of New Brunswick, in Canada. The objective of this case study, which is derived from [7], is to employ discrete-event simulation to compare ED operational characteristic, namely time-in-system, among several candidate designs, with its sensitivity to arrival rate parameter under average and extreme operating conditions.

5.3.1 Step 1 application. Discrete-event simulation of candidate ED designs

The candidate ED design provided here is intimately linked to the high impact of humans. The effectiveness of the ED design is defined by the variability of patients, personnel, and other actors passing through the system. The performance metric selected here is the total time spent in the system by the patient. The groups of decision variables influencing this performance are resources (physicians, nurses, additional rooms) and work shifts. Several alternatives are constructed based on these decision variables and all of these alternatives are tested under varying patient arrivals rate. Patient arrival rates to the ED are given in Table 5.1 at different week days. Arrival rates correspond to the data collected from the system.

Table 5.1. Distribution of patient interarrival times for different days of the week

Week day	*Patient interarrival time (minutes)*
Monday	EXPO(7)
Tuesday	EXPO(9.5)
Wednesday/Thursday/Friday	EXPO(10)

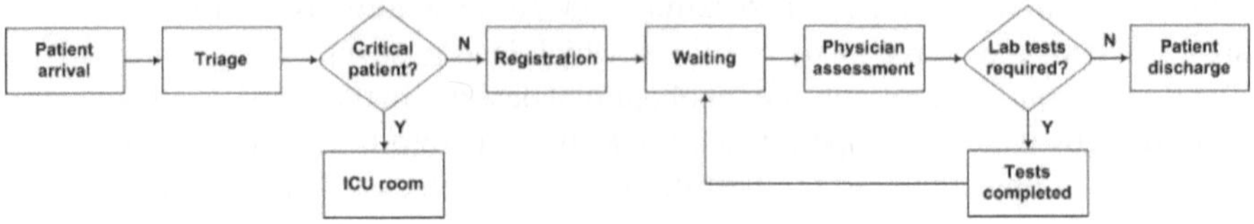

Fig. 5.4. Process flow in the emergency department

In the baseline design of the 24-hour operation ED system, we are interested in the operation between 8:00 AM and 8:00 PM. There are eight general examination rooms, but it operates only on five. There is one nurse at triage and one nurse at registration during all operation hours. There are five physicians: three with twelve-hour shift starting at 8:00 am, and two with ten-hour shifts starting, at 10:00 am. Examination room nurses work in conjunction with physicians and share similar shifts. An arriving patient picks a number and remains in a waiting area until the number is called. A triage nurse assesses the patient based on an emergency severity metric list and assigns a triage code to the patient. Patients assigned Code 1 undergo zero waiting time (critical condition), and patients with Codes 2, 3, 4, and 5 should not wait more than 15, 30, 60, and 120 minutes, respectively. Patient flow is dispatched by the triage service according to the following rates (based on collected data): 18% Code 3, 54% Code 4, 20% Code 5, and less than 7% for Codes 1 and 2. Registered patients with a triage code wait for physician assessment. The waiting period depends on physician and examination room availabilities. Based on the collected data, 23% of patients are required to undertake lab tests. For these patients a second assessment is needed with the same physician ordering the tests. After passing through the ED system, a patient is either discharged or admitted to the hospital. A simulation model was developed from the flow chart given in Figure 5.4. Additional data for assessment, triage, registration and lab test durations are provided in Table 5.2. TRIA, POIS, and EXPO are abbreviations for triangular, Poisson, and exponential distributions, respectively.

The baseline design is referred to as Alternative 0 (no additional resources). Five other alternatives were designed with different parameters shown in Table 5.3, which represent additional physicians, nurses, and ED rooms.

Table 5.2. Distribution and parameters describing the length of ED activities, in minutes

Triage	*Registration*	*1st assessment*	*Lab tests*	*2nd assessment by code*
POIS(6)	TRIA(3,5,7)	TRIA(25,30,40)	TRIA(30,45,60)	TRIA(10,12,15), code 3
				TRIA(8,10,12), code 4
				TRIA(6,7.5,9), code 5

Table 5.3. Alternatives and their corresponding control variable settings

	Control variable settings		
ED designs	*additional physician, shift*	*additional nurse, shift*	*additional room*
Alternative 0	0	0	0
Alternative 1	1 physician, [0800h, 1600h]	1 nurse, [0800h, 1600h]	0
Alternative 2	1 physician, [0800h, 1600h]	1 nurse, [0800h, 1600h]	1
Alternative 3	1 physician, [1000h, 1700h]	1 nurse, [1000h, 1700h]	0
Alternative 4	1 physician, [1000h, 1700h]	1 nurse, [1000h, 1700h]	1
Alternative 5	1 physician, [0800h, 2000h]	1 nurse, [0800h, 2000h]	0

5.3.2 Step 2 application. Analysis of average and extreme ED operating conditions

The random flow of patients has three main characteristics. First, it is driven by seasonal illness or incident: in winter most patients are admitted for cold, lung infection illness, and flu viruses and summer admissions are often related to outdoor incidents and allergies. Extreme events of low probability and high consequence (e.g., large-scale incidents) may also occur. Second, patient flow fluctuates considerably depending on days of the week: more arrivals are observed on Mondays and Fridays than the rest of the week (this may be due to fatigue appearing usually in the end of the week). Third, patient arrivals increase between 8:00 am and 8:00 pm of a given day.

To capture the uncertainty associated with varying ED operating conditions, the arrival rates shown in Table 5.1 were perturbed by a disturbance parameter λ. That is, Monday's interarrival times were modeled as EXPO($7+\lambda$), Tuesday's as EXPO($9.5+\lambda$), and the interarrival times on Wednesday, Thursday, and Friday as EXPO($10+\lambda$). In general, for an interarrival time distribution EXPO(a) under normal operating conditions (a $=7$, 9.5 and 10 in our case), a disturbance λ on the arrival rate will cause the total number of patients arriving to the ED, to increase by $(\lambda/a-\lambda)100\%$, or to decrease by $(\lambda/a+\lambda)100\%$, for a negative, or a positive λ value respectively.

Each alternative in Table 5.3 is simulated using 10 replications of 12 hour lengths, for each day with different value of parameter λ (-2, -1, 0, $+1$, $+2$) as suggested by Eq. (5.7). This means, each alternative generated 25 different simulations. A total of 125 simulations were conducted. Statistics regarding the patient's total time spent in the ED were collected and input to the SDDM algorithm to compute the expected value f_5 and conditional expected value f_4 of the total time spent in the ED using Eqs. (5.1) and (5.2) respectively. These calculations are found in Table 5.4 for each alternative corresponding to the different week days of operation. Table 5.4 provides some interesting results, bringing about potential differences in the alternatives that may not be seen with the traditional expected time in the ED service

Table 5.4. Expected and conditional expected time in the ED across all week days for the baseline and five alternatives, in minutes, for the $\lambda = 0$

ED designs	*Monday*		*Tuesday*		*Wed./Thurs./Fri.*	
	f_5	f_4	f_5	f_4	f_5	f_4
Alternative 0	107.00	214.54	76.70	169.73	71.10	150.69
Alternative 1	98.60	209.49	76.00	149.45	69.50	150.22
Alternative 2	88.00	189.03	72.80	158.43	68.80	136.56
Alternative 3	101.00	224.02	75.40	161.40	71.80	160.90
Alternative 4	88.70	198.26	71.40	156.24	69.50	152.57
Alternative 5	98.60	209.49	76.00	149.45	69.50	150.22

system alone. For example, for the Wednesday/Thursday/Friday scenario, no alternatives stand out as particularly advantageous when considering only the expected value, though Alternative 2 requires considerably less time in the system when extreme operating conditions are examined on average based only on nominal arrival rate values ($\lambda = 0$).

5.3.3 Step 3 application. Sensitivity of ED system metrics to uncertainty in arrival times

Step 3 allows us to account for how varied the time-in-system calculations become under average and extreme operating conditions when the underlying interarrival time parameter differ from the nominal value in normal operation conditions. That is, f_5 and f_4 can vary depending on the value of λ. Sensitivity metrics ψ_{f_5} and ψ_{f_4} for the different alternatives and for different week days are found in Table 5.5, calculated from Eq. (5.7). It appears that time-in-system for Monday is highly affected by interarrival time fluctuations, far more so than any other week day. Further, the conditional expected value is generally more sensitive to changes in interarrival time, though the extent of that sensitivity is not necessarily consistent (e.g., a more sensitive expected value of time in the ED system does not necessarily beget a more sensitivity conditional expected value).

5.3.4 Step 4 application. Multiobjective comparison of candidate ED system designs

In Step 4, the average and upper-tail values for the time in the system are plotted with respect to their sensitivity to uncertainty in patient arrival rate, ψ_{f_5} and ψ_{f_4} for different week days, as shown in Figure 5.5. Black square plotted points represent sensitivity to f_5 versus f_5 time in the system, and gray diamond points represent sensitivity to f_4 versus f_4 time in the system. Noninferior design alternatives are labeled in bold font. This provides decision makers with a representation of the time-sensitivity tradeoff under normal (f_5 values) and extreme operating conditions (f_4

Table 5.5. Sensitivity metrics for expected and conditional expected time in the ED across all week days for the baseline and five alternatives

ED designs	*Monday*		*Tuesday*		*Wed./Thurs./Fri.*	
	ψ_{f_5}	ψ_{f_4}	ψ_{f_5}	ψ_{f_4}	ψ_{f_5}	ψ_{f_4}
Alternative 0	460.10	600.74	19.01	146.65	0.62	22.56
Alternative 1	576.96	1468.42	0.06	1.82	30.80	193.49
Alternative 2	168.22	500.86	9.86	29.48	10.89	4.24
Alternative 3	349.69	130.64	6.60	58.06	7.62	261.47
Alternative 4	258.57	692.74	33.64	223.20	5.90	32.04
Alternative 5	572.64	1536.64	0.06	3.03	30.80	203.92

values), in their attempt to minimize the expected and upper-tail values of time in the system for a given amount of risk measured by the sensitivity of these values to fluctuations in the arrival process. ED system service design alternatives can be carefully selected by reducing their sensitivity to external disturbances.

Based on Figure 5.5, alternatives simultaneously showing the best time-sensitivity tradeoff on both plots (f_5, ψ_{f_5}) and (f_4, ψ_{f_4}), are the ones to be selected for minimizing time in the system (average and upper-tail average) with capacity to account for fluctuations in patients arrival rate. As f_5 and f_4 values have units of time and their sensitivity metrics are dimensionless, these four objectives are noncommensurable, and therefore cannot be easily combined into a single metric. One basic approach is to enumerate the noninferior designs for each week day, as shown in Table 5.6, and look to find alternatives that are common to all week days. Alternative 2 is Pareto-optimal for all week days except for the extreme condition average and sensitivity comparison for Tuesday, making Alternative 2 fairly robust to different operating conditions and different interarrival rates for most days of the week. One could also develop a weighting scheme for the different days of the week, adding importance to system performance for certain days, and include the cost of implementation as an objective, as each alternative would incur different cost requirements to employee various personnel.

Table 5.6. Noninferior design alternatives for the comparison of sensitivity and average/upper-tail average time in the ED system for each week day

Monday		*Tuesday*		*Wed./Thurs./Fri.*	
ψ_{f_5} vs. f_5	ψ_{f_4} vs. f_4	ψ_{f_5} vs. f_5	ψ_{f_4} vs. f_4	ψ_{f_5} vs. f_5	ψ_{f_4} vs. f_4
Alternative 2	Alternative 2	Alternative 1	Alternative 1	Alternative 0	Alternative 2
	Alternative 3	Alternative 2	Alternative 5	Alternative 2	
		Alternative 3		Alternative 4	
		Alternative 4			
		Alternative 5			

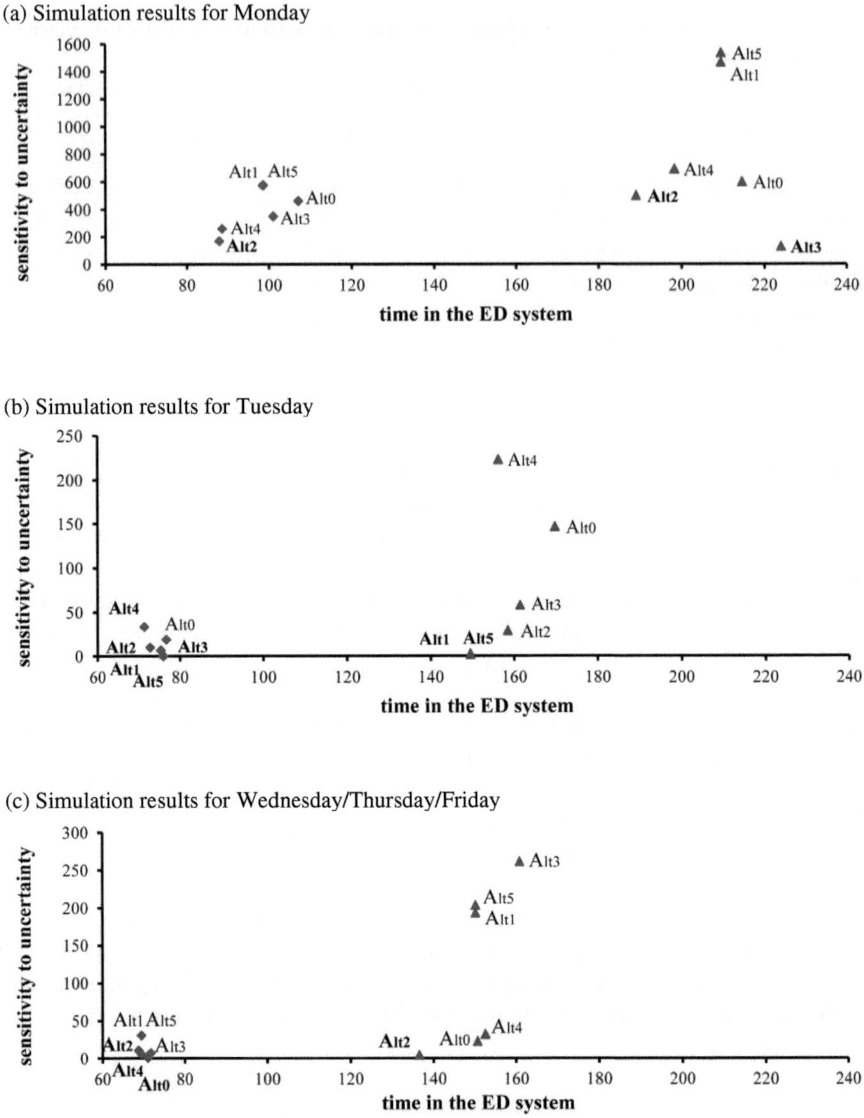

Fig. 5.5. Sensitivity of time in the system to changes in arrival rate versus time in the system for ED design alternatives, by day of the week (time in minutes, sensitivity dimensionless)

Recommended alternatives with risk and uncertainty on patient arrivals rate parameter, taking into consideration are Alternatives 2 and 3. Even if Alternative 4 performs better than Alternative 3, when only expected value is considered, the drawback of implementing Alternative 4 is when extreme operating conditions arise ($\alpha =$ 0.10 in this study), under such consequences users will find that the baseline design (Alternative 0) would perform better.

5.4 Conclusions

A concern of decision making in choosing system design alternatives is that such decisions be robust to a wide range of uncertain operating conditions, establishing a balance between achieving current goals and flexibility in the future. This chapter provides a systematic approach to perform candidate design sensitivity analysis based on discrete-event simulation modeling, under both average and extreme operating conditions. The purpose of this novel approach, the simulation-driven decision making (SDDM) methodology, is to perform a multiobjective comparison of several candidate layout and operational designs, where the metrics quantifying the efficacy of each design are found through discrete-event simulation. The SDDM, whose framework is depicted graphically in Figure 5.2, integrates the Partitioned Multiobjective Risk Method (PMRM) with the Uncertainty Sensitivity Index Method (USIM), extending the work of [3] specifically for decision making driven by simulation models.

The SDDM is applied to risk analysis in health care facility service design. Health care delivery, especially in emergency conditions, is intrinsically uncertain and yet is expected to operate under a number of conditions. Patient time in the emergency department system was the simulation metric used here, though others could be explored.

While illustrated with emergency department design, such a methodology can be applied to other critical systems and infrastructures where the consideration of average and extreme operating conditions are important, e.g., transportation network design, evacuation planning, vehicle routing. Even more generally, facility layout and operational design are discussed, though this approach could be used in a number of applications of simulation-driven comparisons of candidate options.

References

1. Arsham, H.: Algorithms for sensitivity information in discrete-event systems simulation. Simulation Practice and Theory **6**, 1–22 (1998).
2. Asbeck, E., Haimes, Y.Y.: The partitioned multiobjective risk method. Large Scale Systems **6**, 13–38 (1984)
3. Barker, K., Haimes, Y.Y.: Assessing uncertainty in extreme events: applications to risk-based decision making in interdependent infrastructure sectors. Reliability Engineering and System Safety **94**, 819–829 (2009)

4. Bechhofer, R.E., Santner, T.J., Goldsman, D.: Design and analysis for statistical selection, screening, and multiple comparisons. John Wiley and Sons, New York (1995)
5. Chetouane, F.: Risk theory approach to design buffer capacity in recycling plant environment. Proceedings of the 4th IFAC Conference on Management and Control of Production and Logistics, Romania, 27–30 September 2007
6. Dehlendorff, C., Kulahci, M., Merser, S., Andersen, K.K.: Conditional value at risk as a measure for waiting time in simulations of hospital units. Quality Technology and Quantitative Management **7**, 321–336 (2010)
7. Duguay, C., Chetouane, F.: Modeling and improving emergency department systems using discrete simulation. Simulation 83, 311–320 (2007)
8. Ehrgott, M.: Multicriteria optimization. Springer, Berlin (2005)
9. Fishman, G.S.: Discrete-event simulation: modeling, programming, and analysis. Springer-Verlag, Berlin (2001)
10. Goldsman, D., Nelson, B.L.: Comparing systems via simulation. Handbook of simulation: principles, methodology, advances, applications, and practice. John Wiley, New York (1998)
11. Haimes, Y.Y., Hall, W.A.: Sensitivity, responsivity, stability, and irreversibility as multiobjectives in civil systems. Advances in Water Resources **1**, 71–81 (1977)
12. Kim, S.H., Nelson, B.L.: Selecting the best system. Handbooks in operations research and management science. Elsevier, New York (2006)
13. Kleijnen, J.P.C.: Sensitivity analysis and related analyses: a review of some statistical techniques. Journal of Statistical Computation and Simulation **57**, 111–142 (1997)
14. Krokhmal, P., Palmquist, J., Uryasev, S.P.: Portfolio optimization with conditional value-at-risk objective and constraints. The Journal of Risk **4**, 11–27 (2002)
15. Li, D., Haimes, Y.Y.: The uncertainty sensitivity index method (USIM) and its extension. Naval Research Logistics **35**, 655–672 (1988)
16. Pannell, D.J.: Sensitivity analysis of normative economic models: theoretical framework and practical strategies. Agricultural Economics **16**, 139–152 (1997)
17. Saltelli, A., Tarantola, S., Campolongo, F., Ratto, M.: Sensitivity analysis in practice: a guide to assessing scientific models. John Wiley and Sons, Hoboken, New Jersey (2004)

Chapter 6

Technical and scale efficiencies of Catholic hospitals: Does a system value of stewardship matter?

Tiang-Hong Chou, Yasar A. Ozcan, and Kenneth R. White

Abstract. Applying data envelopment analyses and relevant multivariate regression techniques, this study explores the relationship between the efficiency of Catholic system-affiliated hospitals and certain organizational and market characteristics. Results show the system value of stewardship did not have a significant impact on Catholic hospital efficiency in the study period between 2005 and 2007. However, the diocesan model of organizational governance, with a value of stewardship, demonstrated a positive relationship with efficiency. This study also shows that organizational and market characteristics such as the proportion of Medicaid patients, rural location, market competition, and for-profit penetration are important determinants of Catholic hospital efficiency. Explanations, implications, and limitations of the findings as well as directions for future research are discussed and proposed.

Keywords: hospitals, catholic health systems, system value, stewardship, technical and scale efficiency, data envelopment analysis

6.1 Introduction and problem addressed

Catholic health care is provided by the largest group of nonprofit providers, systems, and facilities in the United States [3]. In 2006, U.S. Catholic hospitals ac-

T.-H. Chou
Mennonite Christian Hospital, 44 Min-chuan Rd., Hualien City, 970, Taiwan
e-mail: thchoutw@gmail.com

Y.A. Ozcan (✉)
Department of Health Administration, Virginia Commonwealth University, P.O. Box 980203, Richmond, VA 23298-0203, USA
e-mail: ozcan@vcu.edu

K.R. White
Department of Health Administration, Virginia Commonwealth University, P.O. Box 980203, Richmond, VA 23298-0203, USA
e-mail: krwhite@vcu.edu

Tànfani E., Testi A. (Eds.): Advanced Decision Making Methods Applied to Health Care.
International Series in Operations Research & Management Science 173
DOI 10.1007/978-88-470-2321-5_6,

counted for: beds, 15.1%; admission,15.6%; Medicare discharges, 16.7%; and Medicaid discharges,13.6% among all U.S. community hospitals [4]. Approximately one in six patients in the U.S. is cared for in Catholic hospitals each year. Catholic hospitals shared more than 20% of admissions in 21 states and the District of Columbia, usually providing a critical safety net to many uninsured patients in the communities they serve. One could reasonably imagine that the landscape of the U.S. health care system would be significantly different and weakened without the presence of Catholic hospitals [38].

Compared to hospitals of other ownership types, Catholic hospitals are unique in terms of their governance, mission, values, ethical principles, and system affiliation. First, they are all under the authority of the Roman Catholic Church. The ultimate legitimacy of being a Catholic hospital comes from the Church and its designated authority, i.e., a local bishop in the area where the hospital operates. Catholic hospitals have identical ecclesiastical identity with various governance authority, including religious orders of women or men, diocesan (reporting directly to the local bishop), or newer mixed models of religious and lay sponsors. Catholic hospitals exist as a social ministry based on common beliefs and similar mission orientations, originally established to provide necessary care to the poor and marginalized people within their local parish locations [22]. The Catholic Health Association clearly states that "Catholic health care is committed to improving the health status of communities and creating quality and compassionate heath care that works for everyone, especially the vulnerable" [3].

Catholic hospitals are also unique in terms of their core values, namely: respect, justice, compassion, stewardship, and excellence, among others [38]. Moreover, Catholic hospitals conduct services based on uniform ethical principles codified in the Ethical and Religious Directives (ERD) for Catholic Health Care Services [33]. In consequence, Catholic hospitals are more likely than their secular ownership counterparts to provide certain types of services, such as end-of-life care [40]. Catholic hospitals also distinguish themselves from other hospitals by not providing certain types of services such as abortion and reproductive services prohibited by the ERD. Finally, in 2007, there were 624 Catholic hospitals and 60 Catholic health systems operating in the U.S [4]. Among the 624 Catholic hospitals, more than 560 hospitals are members of the Catholic health systems. These commonalities in size, mission, and systemness make Catholic hospitals a distinct group from other not-for-profit, public, and investor-owned hospitals.

Efficient operation of Catholic hospitals is critical not only to Catholic hospitals but also to the whole U.S. health care system. First, Catholic hospitals need to be efficient enough to be sustainable in a highly competitive healthcare market. As mentioned earlier, most Catholic hospitals are committed to serving the vulnerable populations in the community, which is increasingly difficult with reduced reimbursement rates. Hospitals are facing greater challenges in offering charitable care or community benefits. Operational efficiency would make Catholic hospitals more capable of providing charitable or uncompensated services to meet the health care needs of vulnerable populations, such as more services by employing the same amount of resources available under budget constraints [15]. Moreover, if Catholic hospitals operate efficiently, they may contribute significantly to the improvement of overall healthcare value and cost control in the U.S. One could reasonably expect that the efficient practices employed by Catholic hospitals would influence their counterparts in other ownership forms either through the mechanism of market competition or transfer of best practice. As mentioned earlier, the majority of Catholic hospitals are members of multi-hospital systems in response to the market's requirement for efficient operations. System membership is widely thought to be an effective strategy for hospitals to share relevant resources and information, enhance economies of scale, or/and deepen specialization which together may contribute to the improvement of hospital efficiency and competitive advantage. However, the factors within a health system associated with hospital operational efficiency are examined. Thus, this study will shorten the gap in the literature by exploring the relationship of a system value of stewardship in determining the technical and scale efficiencies of the hospitals in the system. Stewardship is a common value chosen by Catholic health systems and hospitals to represent the efficient use of resources and operational and scale efficiencies.

The objective of this study is to see which Catholic hospitals are efficient relative to the association of a system value of stewardship. Specifically, the aim is to answer the following questions: (1) Is a system value of stewardship positively associated with the operational and scale efficiencies of Catholic system-affiliated hospitals? (2) Is the system value of stewardship associated with the improvement of operational and scale efficiencies of Catholic system-affiliated hospitals over the study period (2005–2007)? and (3) What are other factors associated with the operational and scale efficiencies of Catholic hospitals in multi-hospital systems? The answers to these questions have several important implications. In learning more about hospital ownership it is useful for researchers and policy makers to examine the relationship of system mission and values to operational efficiency of system hospitals. This study sheds light on the relationship of interest by empirically exploring a group of homogeneous hospitals with a high rate of system membership. The aspect of homogeneity contributes to the internal validity of the finding by reducing the possibility of the existence of uncontrollable major confounding factors.

In addition, policy makers should be interested in the finding of this study because – as the uninsured population and health care expenditures continue to rise and hospital costs account for a significant portion of the total expenditure – it is important to know whether health systems or which aspects of the health system make a difference in enhancing hospital operational efficiency. The result of this study provides policy makers with empirical evidence regarding the black box of multi-hospital systems that have become increasingly dominant in the U.S. health care system.

Finally, there are anecdotal and theoretical discussions suggesting that organizational values are critical to the success of the organization [21, 27]. Griffith and White [14] provide case studies on a number of successful Catholic hospitals in a health system and emphasize the importance of values as a governance mechanism. However, empirical evidence of the linkage between the health system-related values and factors and hospital performance is limited. Thus, this study advances knowledge of the relationship of values and efficiency in the hospital sector.

6.1.1 Conceptual framework

The relationship between health system characteristics and performance has long been of interest to researchers. The expectation is that system structures would have degrees of impact on subsystems or institutions comprised by the system. Bazzoli *et al.* [2] found that hospitals in moderately centralized systems performed better financially compared with those in highly centralized systems. In addition, by using the Battese/Coelli simultaneous stochastic frontier analysis (SFA) technique, Rosko and others [29] found that membership in different types of systems was associated with differences in cost-inefficiency. The specific interest of this study is to find out whether there is any association between the Catholic health system value of stewardship and the efficiency of the hospitals in the systems. However, organizational scholars also recognize that organizations have diverse goals. Organizational goals may serve cognitive, motivational, symbolic, or justification purposes [32]. In some cases, these goals may be competing within an organization. More specifically, Daft [10] distinguishes official goals (e.g., mission statements) from operative goals. By operative goals, Daft refers to organizational performance (e.g., profitability, growth, and output volume), resources (i.e., acquisition of needed material and financial resources from the environment), market share, employee development, innovation, and productivity/efficiency. While official goals provide legitimacy (symbolic functions), operative goals provide decision guidelines and criteria of performance (cognitive functions), employee development (motivational functions) [10], and explanation and defense of organizational decisions and behaviors (justification functions) [35].Core values of an organization may reflect both the organization's official and operative goals. If an organization views its officially stated values as operation-guiding principles, these values may indeed affect its operation. However, if core values is stated for obtaining legitimacy, these values may not be related to its operation. This study assumes that Catholic systems and their members are committed to their core values publicly presented. Thus, those values are actually the guiding principles for the operation of Catholic systems and their member hospitals. This study employs the argument of organizational integrity as a conceptual framework to guide the development of hypotheses. Organizational integrity is a construct used to describe the alignment of mission, values, and efforts/directions of Catholic hospitals [20]. The choice of hospital strategic efforts and directions would be a logical outgrowth of the health system and hospitals' values, which in turn emanates from the mission statement. Mission is the ultimate and unchanging purpose of the organization. It describes what the organization is and why it exists, operates, and develops. Values are the basic beliefs, principles, and directions of the organization, derived from the mission. In other words, mission leads to values. Core values are the foundation on which the organization operates and grows. Therefore, they determine what effort is needed to move the organization ahead. The operation and development of an organization ideally would reflect its values, thus fulfilling its mission.

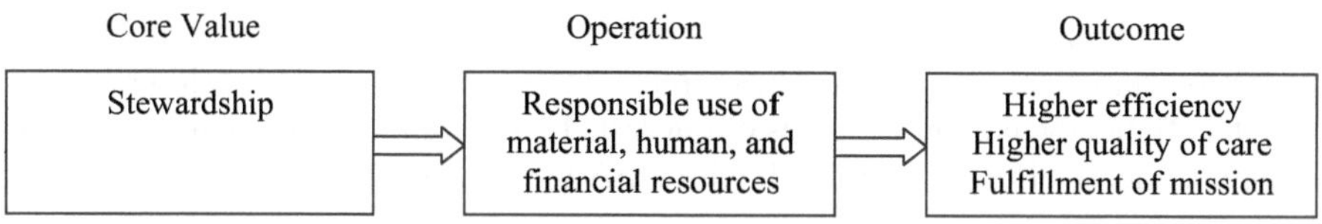

Fig. 6.1. Hospital Outcome

Welbig [36] defines stewardship as "the way the ministry shepherds its material, human, political and spiritual resources in order to create and sustain healthy, well-ordered communities that foster the human dignity of all their members." Stewardship has two aspects: (1) internal stewardship which includes (a) high-quality patient care, concern for patient rights, transparency, clinical and economic integrity, and hospitality toward those who need care; (b) good work environment and schedule, just financial remuneration and benefits, respect for the dignity of each employee, space for human spirit to grow and develop; (c) responsible, accountable distribution and use of material resources, budgets, strategic plans, and benchmarking protocols; and (2) external stewardship which refers to efforts to promote a community's health including not only clinical care, but also employment, education, housing, safety, and the environment [36]. Property rights theory suggests that efficiency would be greater in investor-owned hospitals than in Catholic hospitals where the claims to residuals (profits) are attenuated [29]. Among Catholic hospitals, the presence of the value of stewardship at the system level may compensate for the absence of the motivation to profit claiming. Thus, it is hypothesized that Catholic hospitals with a system value of stewardship are more efficient than Catholic hospitals without a system value of stewardship. According to the argument presented above, a conceptual framework of Catholic stewardship is proposed. As shown in Figure 6.1, the value of stewardship is a guiding principle that requires Catholic hospitals to be accountable for the use of resources in operations, which would lead to better performance including higher efficiency and quality, and the ultimate fulfillment of the mission.

Based on the discussion, the following hypotheses are proposed:

- Catholic hospitals in a system with a system value of stewardship would be more efficient than those in a system without the value;
- the improvement of technical efficiency would be greater for the Catholic hospitals in a system with a system value of stewardship than for those in a system without the value.

6.2 Materials and methods

6.2.1 Study design

This study will apply a longitudinal approach to examine the efficiency of system-affiliated Catholic hospitals in 2005, 2006, and 2007. This analysis has two-stages. First, data envelopment analysis (DEA) will be used to compute the efficiency scores for each Catholic system-affiliated hospital in the three years. Next, multivariate regression statistical analyses will be employed to examine the relationship between hospital efficiency and the variables of interest. This combined approach is common in the healthcare efficiency research with DEA worldwide [16].

6.2.2 The DEA model

DEA is a non-parametric approach to the estimation of individual or organizational performance (i.e., efficiency, productivity, quality, effectiveness) taking into consideration of multiple inputs and outputs. This gives DEA an advantageous position over a single ratio analysis because DEA can provide a comprehensive evaluation the performance of interest [28]. DEA identifies best performers (benchmarks) by maximizing the combination of the outputs given the combination of the inputs. Thus, DEA is able to provide performance frontier/benchmarking condition for a group of decision making units (DMUs).

In carrying out a DEA, researchers will need to select from either an input-oriented or an output-oriented model as well as from a constant return to scale (CRS) or a variable return to scale (VRS) model. An input-oriented model is appropriate when the DMUs have control over the inputs but not the outputs. In contrast, an output-oriented model is preferred if the DMUs can change their outputs based on their goals or strategies. In addition, a CRS model is applied in the situation that the returns of the inputs to the outputs are constant across all DMUs. If this is not the case, i.e., the returns are either increasing or decreasing, or mixed, a VRS model is preferred.

This study applies an input-oriented model because Catholic hospitals may not be able to control outputs (i.e., services volume or cases) in highly competitive healthcare markets. However, they are able to manage their inputs such as expenses, personnel, service mix to certain extent. In terms of which return to scale model should be used, this study employs VRS models to compute efficiency scores because a CRS model may be too restricted given the diverse aspects of Catholic hospitals mentioned earlier.

Following Cooper *et al.* [9], a scale efficiency score for each DMU is calculated by dividing the CRS efficiency score by VRS efficiency score of the DMU. The DMUs in this analysis are individual Catholic hospitals in a particular year. In other words, this study applies an approach similar to the window analysis introduced by Cooper *et al.* [9] to trace the trend of Catholic hospital efficiencies in the three-year period.

Following previous research applying DEA to study hospital efficiency [5, 34], the input and output variables are selected to conduct the DEA analyses. Input (e.g., labor, capital investment, and other operating expenses) and output categories (e.g., adjusted admissions, outpatient visits, and teaching) have been widely applied and are standards for hospital DEA research [26, 28]. The measures of these inputs and outputs will be described later (see Table 6.1 for a brief description).

It is worth noting that Medicare case-mix adjusted cases rather than a direct count of cases treated by a hospital should better reflect the output of the hospital. A case-mix adjusted approach takes into account the severity of patients treated in a hospital. It takes more efforts and resources to care a more severe patient than to take care of a less severe patient. Annually, a hospital's Medicare case-mix index (CMI) is computed and provided by CMS, based on the DRG diagnosis history of the hospital. Medicare case-mix index has been widely used as a relative severity of inpatient patients treated in a U.S. hospital. Medicare CMI and all-payer CMIs tend to be highly correlated and so the use of the MCMI has become standard practice.

However, there is no case-mix index currently available for adjusting/weighting hospital outpatient cases. Therefore, this study applies three major types of outpatient services provided by hospitals including general outpatient service, emergency services, and outpatient surgical services. There should be significant variations in resource utilization and the nature of medical conditions treated among these three types of services. Thus, it would be better to include them separately in the DEA model than to bundle them together.

6.2.3 The post hoc analysis

The second stage of the analysis is applying multivariate regression to examining the relationship of interest. Specifically, a tobit model is used for the post hoc analysis. Tobit statistical modeling has been employed by researchers to regress efficiency scores from the DEA on relevant factors [6, 25].

These multivariate regression analyses will apply the approach of independently pooled cross-sections across time. The general models are specified as follows:

$$\begin{aligned}\text{ineff}_{\text{i, year}} = \pi[\beta_0 + \beta_1(\text{stewardship}_\text{i} + \beta_2\text{yr}_{06} + \beta_3\text{yr}_{07} + \beta_4(\text{stewardship}_\text{i} \times \text{yr}_{06})\\ + \beta_5(\text{stewardship}_\text{i} \times \text{yr}_{07}) + \text{B}_6\text{X}_{4\text{i, year}} + \text{B}_7\text{X}_{5\text{i, year}}] + \varepsilon_{1\text{i, year}}.\end{aligned}$$

$\pi(\mathrm{x})$ is a tobit function with a lower limit of 0.
$\text{ineff}_{\text{i, year}} = (1/\text{technical or scale efficiency score}) - 1$.
In this case, however, the greater the $\text{ineff}_{\text{i,year}}$, the less efficient is the DMU.

In the equation, stewardship$_i$, is a dummy variable indicating whether a Catholic hospital had a system value of stewardship during the study years. yr_{06} is a dummy variable which equals 1 for the year 2006 and 0 otherwise. yr_{07} is a dummy variable which equals 1 for the year 2007 and 0 otherwise. $\text{X}_{4\text{i, year}}$ is a vector of organizational (i.e., hospital and system) characteristics in a particular year. $\text{X}_{5\text{i, year}}$ is a vector of market characteristics in a particular year. $\varepsilon_{\text{i, year}}$ is the error term of the model.

6.2.4 Data source and sample

The sample is composed of all Catholic short-term general (non-specialty) hospitals which were affiliated with Catholic multiple-hospital systems and reported data to the American Hospital Association annual surveys in the three years. Catholic hospital systems that are comprised of predominantly long-term care facilities are excluded from this study. White and Dandi [38] have identified 50 Catholic multiple-hospital systems in the U.S with a focus of acute care hospitals, which will be used in this study. The hospitals in the sample represent 87% of total Catholic hospitals identified in the American Hospital Association dataset.

The data come from three major datasets as well as websites of the related Catholic health systems. These datasets include the American Hospital Association (AHA) annual survey files, Centers for Medicare and Medicaid Services (CMS) case-mix index files, and Area Resource Files (ARF). The three datasets have been widely used in health services research. The data regarding the value of stewardship of the Catholic health systems were retrieved from the websites of these systems in 2007.

6.2.5 Variables and measures

6.2.5.1 DEA input and output variables

The variables, measures, and their corresponding data sources are summarized in Table 6.1. As mentioned earlier, inputs for the DEA include hospital size, service complexity, labor, and supplies. Hospital size is measured by the number of operational beds in a hospital in a particular year. Labor is measured by the number of non-physician full-time equivalent (FTE) employed by a hospital in a year. The rationale for excluding physician FTEs is that typical physicians are not employees of hospitals. Instead, most physicians in the U.S. are granted privileges to treat and take care of their patients in the hospital. Hospital supplies variable is measured by subtracting payroll and capital expenses from the operating expenses. Payroll and capital expenses are excluded to avoid double enumeration because labor and hospital service complexity have been considered as individual input items.

However, the service-mix variable, which measures as a simple count of available diagnostic and special services, provides no weighting for service complexity. Thus, while many published papers have used unweighted counts of service mix measures based on correlations of such counts with actual measurement of service inputs, such measures may not capture adequately the great diversity and levels of input mix across hospitals.

Therefore, in order to provide some relative weighting, we ranked the services from 1 to 3, based on relative clinical and investment intensities, and applied these weights in calculating a service mix index. To do this, we asked three expert raters (one from academia and two with hospital administration and academic backgrounds) to rate each of the services reported in the AHA Annual Survey. They scored the services based on two dimensions: 1) clinical intensity and 2) investment intensity. We used these scores (clinical and investment) to generate a weighted service-mix index, with scores ranging from 1 to 9 and assigned these weights to each hospital's reported services. We used a nominal group process to reach full agreement among the raters, which they achieved after three rounds of scoring. We then summed these across services, thereby producing a weighted service-mix score for each hospital.

With respect to the outputs used in the DEA, treated cases are a result of multiplying inpatient admissions by the CMI of the hospital in a year. Outpatient surgeries

Table 6.1. Variables and measures of this study

Variable type	*Variable name*	*Operational definition*	*Source*
DEA- input	Hospital size	# of operational hospital beds in 2005, 2006, & 2007	AHA
	Hospital service complexity	# of diagnostic and special services	AHA
	Labor	# of non-physician FTEs employed	AHA
	Supplies	Operating expenses less payroll and capital expenses	AHA
DEA- output	Treated cases	Inpatient discharges* CMI (Medicare case-mix adjusted)	AHA+CMS
	Outpatient visits	# of visits to outpatient facilities less outpatient surgeries and ER visits	AHA
	Outpatient surgeries	# of outpatient surgeries	AHA
	Emergency visits	# of emergency department visits	AHA
	Teaching FTEs	Weighted sum of trainees (medical, dental, nurses, physical therapists, etc.), FT = 1, PT = 0.5	AHA
Dependent	Technical efficiency	= (1/Technical efficiency score)-1	From DEA
	Scale efficiency	= (1/Scale efficiency score)-1 CRS technical efficiency score = VRS technical score/CRS technical score	From DEA
Independent variable	System value-stewardship	"1" if a system value of stewardship is present for a hospital and "0" otherwise	Catholic system websites
	Year06	"1" if the observation/DMU is in year 2006, and "0" otherwise (Base: year 2005)	AHA
	Year07	"1" if the observation/DMU is in year 2007, and "0" otherwise (Base: year 2005)	AHA
Organizational factors	Hospital size	# hospital beds set up and staffed in 2005, 2006, & 2007, in natural logarithm	AHA
	System size	= # total beds in the system, in natural logarithm	AHA
	Sponsor type-multiple sponsor	"1" if a hospital belongs to a system with multiple sponsors and "0" otherwise (Base: single sponsor)	System websites
	Sponsor type-diocese	"1" if a hospital belongs to a system sponsored by a diocese and "0" otherwise (Base: single sponsor)	
	Medicare %	% of Medicare patients in a hospital in a particular year	AHA
	Medicaid %	% of Medicaid patients in a hospital in a particular year	AHA
Market factors	Rural	"1" if a hospital is located in a rural area and "0" otherwise	AHA
	Competition	=1/ Herfindahl-Hirschman Index	ARF
	% for-profit in the market	=(# for-profit hospitals)/(# total beds) in a county	AHA

are the number of outpatient operations undergone in a hospital in a particular year. Emergency visits are the number of emergency department visits. Outpatient visits are calculated by deducting outpatient surgeries and ER visits from the total visits to outpatient facilities in a hospital in a particular year. Finally, teaching FTEs is a measure of the hospital output of medical education activities. It is measured by the weighted sum of trainees (medical, dental, nurses, physical therapists, etc.). The weight is 1 for full-time trainees and is 0.5 for part-time trainees.

6.2.5.2 Independent variable

The key independent variable of interest is the system value of stewardship. The data regarding Catholic health system values including justice, compassion, stewardship, respect, and excellence are based on the works of past research [37,38]. From a directory on the CHA website listing member health systems, they scanned the websites of each system to collect data regarding the values held by each Catholic health system. They extracted the presence or absence of the word "stewardship" as a system value that would apply to all member hospitals. Two types of software were used to standardize the words and combine them to increase reliability and validity [38]. If individual websites did not contain explicit values, phone calls and email communication yielded a set of core values for each health system between February and April 2007. Each health system had information about its mission statement, core values and related descriptions on the website. A table of Catholic health system values was then created based on the system data documented by the authors mentioned above. This study, however, only uses the system value of stewardship. Ideally, the information about the system value should be collected during 2005, 2006, and 2007 in accordance to the period of this study. Since the aforementioned studies started around 2007, it is not possible to retrieve the information before 2007. Nevertheless, it should be reasonable to expect that system values are a stable characteristic of healthcare organizations. Thus, it is assumed that the existence of the value of stewardship for each Catholic system studied remained the same in the years 2005 through 2007. The variable of stewardship is coded as "1" if a hospital belonged to a system with a value of stewardship in a particular year, and otherwise coded as "0."

6.2.5.3 Control variables

This section will describe the control variables employed in the post hoc analysis. The first group of control variables comprises certain organizational characteristics related to hospital efficiency, including hospital and system sizes, system sponsorship type, and hospital payer mix. First, hospital size and system size are assumed to have positive impacts on hospital efficiency if economies of scale or scope are present. System size is measured the number of total beds in a system in a particular year. Following the work of LeBlanc and Hurley [24] and White *et al.* [39], a natural logarithm transformation is calculated for the two measures.

Three types of sponsorship models in U.S. Catholic health systems are analyzed in this study, including single-sponsor religious institutes, multiple-sponsor religious institutes, and diocesan (direct report to the local bishop without a religious institute). It is assumed that the single sponsorship model is the most cohesive and consistent in terms of system mission, values, decision making and management direction in a system, thus contributing to the likelihood of fulfilling its values. Two dummy variables indicate whether a Catholic hospital belonged to a system with multiple sponsors or a diocesan sponsorship, while single sponsorship is the base group. Moreover, hospital payer mix is a control variable in the analysis. It is believed that payer mix has an impact on hospital efficiency. For example, Medicaid reimbursement payments generally are the lowest compared to Medicare and private payers. If a hospital relies heavily on Medicaid, it would face more tightened revenues. Hospitals in this situation have to be more efficient in order to survive. In order to isolate the effect of payer mix, both the proportions of total discharges contributed by Medicare and Medicaid patients in the hospital in a particular year are included in the analytical model. The market factors controlled include rural area, market competition, and for-profit hospitals located in a market. Rural and urban areas are different environments where hospitals operate. The expectation is that hospitals in rural areas would have a smaller population to serve, thus generating fewer outputs. In addition, market competition could affect hospital efficiency at least in three ways. First, competition may drive up efficiency. Second, researchers have reported that in mixed ownership markets such as hospital markets, competition could shift demand curve faced by for-profit hospitals downward, resulting in excess capacity and relatively high fixed costs [1,8]. This implies that competition in a mixed ownership market may increase the demand for not-for-profit hospitals, and may lead to a higher utilization rate of hospital facilities and resulting efficiency. Third, economists and researchers have pointed out that health care competition involves non-price competition [11, 13]. One type of non-price competition commonly observed termed the "medical arms race," (MAR) in which hospitals try to attract patients by adopting the most advanced medical equipment. This state-of-the-art equipment is usually very expensive, thus driving up the costs of hospitals. MAR can lead to the reduction of hospital efficiency because it often produces excessive capacities. In this study, market competition is measured by the Herfindahl-Hirschman Index (HHI), a widely used measure of market competition.

Finally, the model specifies a variable representing the degree of market domination by for-profit hospitals. Researchers have reported empirical evidence showing the association between the presence of for-profit hospitals in a market and hospitals' responsiveness to financial incentives among nonprofits in the same market [18]. Not-for-profit hospitals located in markets with greater for-profit hospital penetration are more likely than those in less for-profit dominated markets to provide profitable services [17, 19], to avoid unprofitable services [31], and to spend less on admitted cardiac patients [12,23]. From the perspective of institutional isomorphism, it is plausible that a nonprofit hospital surrounded by influential for-profit hospitals can be isomorphic to their for-profit neighbors by adopting more efficient practices.

6.3 Results and discussion

As shown in the descriptive summary table, Table 6.2, the mean of the technical efficiency scores for all DMUs is 0.69. After excluding the benchmark DMUs, the mean of the technical efficiencies for the inefficient DMUs is 0.664. This finding suggests that the overall inefficient Catholic hospitals can improve their technical

Table 6.2. Summary statistics of the variables

Variable	*Mean*	*Stand. Dev.*	*Min*	*Max*
# Hospital bed	193	173	6	1,584
Labor (FTEs)	976	971	22	7,195
Supply-Total expenses less payroll and capital expenses (in 1000)	63,970	57,647	28	383,000
Service complexity (# weight services)	203	87	0	531
Outpatient visits (in 1,000)	117	167	0	2,310
Emergency visits (in 1,000)	27	23	0	230
Outpatient surgeries (in 100)	39	40	0	316
Case-mix adjusted admissions (in 100)	133.8	146.0	0.2	1,054
Teaching FTEs	12	37	0	593
Technical efficiency score	0.69	0.18	0.14	1
Technical efficiency dummy	0.07	0.25	0	1
Technical efficiency score (inverse-1)	0.58	0.56	0	6.32
Scale efficiency score	0.93	0.14	0.14	1
Scale efficiency dummy	0.04	0.20	0	1
Scale efficiency score (inverse-1)	0.13	0.40	0	6.10
Stewardship	0.47	0.50	0	1
Year 2005	0.34	0.47	0	1
Year 2006	0.33	0.47	0	1
Year 2007	0.33	0.47	0	1
# System beds	5,638	4,088	267	14,270
Sponsor-single	0.38	0.48	0	1
Sponsor-multiple	0.59	0.49	0	1
Sponsor-diocese	0.03	0.17	0	1
Medicare %	0.49	0.14	0	0.98
Medicaid %	0.15	0.09	0	0.74
Rural area	0.18	0.38	0	1
HHI	0.36	0.39	0.00	1
Competition (ln(1/HHI))	2.17	1.96	0	10.31
For-profit market	0.08	0.14	0	1

efficiency by 33% $(1-0.664=0.33)$ to be as efficient as their benchmarks. Reviews of the descriptive statistics shown in Table 6.2 reveal no unreasonable values or outliers existing in the data.

6.3.1 Bivariate analysis

First, technical and scale efficiency scores between the hospitals with a system value of stewardship and those without the value are compared. As shown in Table 6.3, these two groups of Catholic hospitals differed in their efficiencies measured by technical and scale efficiency scores. However, the direction is contrary to our expectation. Catholic hospitals without a system value of stewardship generally were more efficient than their peer hospitals with this value in terms of both technical and scale efficiencies. For example, the mean of the technical efficiency scores is 0.698

Table 6.3. Comparison of the efficiency scores between Catholic hospitals with and without a system value of stewardship

Hospitals	*N*	*Efficiency*	
		Technical	*Scale*
With stewardship	785	67.50%	92.19%
Without stewardship	900	69.78%	93.20%
Total	1685	68.72%	92.73%
Difference		−2.29%	−1.02%
z-value (Mann-Whitney two-sample test)		0.587	1.021
p-value		0.5575	0.3071

for Catholic hospitals without the value of stewardship and 0.675 for those with the value of stewardship, a difference of 0.023. A further examination of the difference using a Mann-Whitney two-sample test – a non-parametric t test of equal means – reveals that there is no significant difference between the two groups for technical and scale efficiencies. These results provide preliminary evidence that the first hypothesis indicates that the presence of a system value of stewardship is positively associated with Catholic hospital efficiency is not supported.

We then examine whether the overall Catholic hospitals improved efficiency in the study period between 2005 and 2007. The related crosstab is shown in Table 6.4. Although the number and proportion of efficient Catholic hospitals (benchmark hospitals) increases for both technical and scale efficiencies from 2005 to 2007, the changes are not significantly different from zero (test statistics are not reported here). The result is also insignificant even if efficiency scores are used for the comparison. In short, Catholic system-affiliated hospitals did not improve efficiency in the study period.

Table 6.4. Comparison of the efficient and inefficient DMUs across the three years

Efficiency type	*Hospital*	*2005*	*2006*	*2007*	*Total*				
		#	%	#	%	#	%	#	%
	Inefficient	534	94.5%	518	92.5%	517	92.3%	1,569	93.1%
Technical efficiency	Efficient	31	5.5%	42	7.5%	43	7.7%	116	6.9%
	Total	565	100.0%	560	100.0%	560	100.0%	1,685	100.0%
	Inefficient	544	96.3%	536	95.7%	536	95.7%	1,616	95.9%
Scale efficiency	Efficient	21	3.7%	24	4.3%	24	4.3%	69	4.1%
	Total	565	100.0%	560	100.0%	560	100.0%	1,685	100.0%

6.3.2 Multivariate analysis

Results from the multivariate regression analyses are presented in Table 6.5. The coefficient of stewardship is not significantly different from zero at the 95% confidence level. Consistent with the finding from the bivariate analysis, the presence of the system value of stewardship has no impact on Catholic hospital technical efficiency, holding other things equal. In addition, the coefficients for the years 2006 and 2007 are also not significant at the conventional level of significance. These results suggest Catholic system-affiliated hospitals did not differ in both technical and scale efficiencies across time in the study period. Furthermore, the coefficients of the cross terms of stewardship and years are not significantly different from zero, either. Therefore, none of these relative changes in efficiency are significantly different from zero at the 5% significance level. Therefore, both hypotheses are not supported.

Table 6.5. Results from the multivariate regression analyses of the technical and scale inefficiencies of Catholic system-affiliated hospitals

Variable	*Technical inefficiency*	*Scale inefficiency*				
	β	*Stand. Error*	*β*	*Stand. Error*		
Stewardship	0.022		0.045	0.015		0.037
Year 2006	0.041		0.047	−0.042		0.032
Year 2007	0.010		0.047	−0.041		0.036
Stewardship × Year 2006	−0.045		0.069	0.017		0.046
Stewardship × Year 2007	0.012		0.067	0.021		0.047
ln(# hospital bed)	0.024		0.017	−0.091	***	0.013
ln(# system beds)	−0.062	*	0.025	−0.016		0.016
Sponsor-multiple	0.005		0.040	0.082	***	0.021
Sponsor-diocese	−0.309	***	0.063	−0.075	**	0.026
Medicare %	0.110		0.196	0.260		0.156
Medicaid %	0.209		0.210	−0.480	***	0.120
Rural area	0.240	***	0.050	0.160	***	0.033
Competition (ln(1/HHI))	0.010		0.013	0.052	***	0.011
For-profit market	−0.303	**	0.115	−0.144	*	0.064
Constant	0.816	***	0.247	0.466	**	0.176
F statistics	F(14, 1671) = 5.47	F(14, 1671) = 13.07				
Prob > F	< 0.0001	< 0.0001				
Pseudo-R^2	0.0251	0.2186				
N	1685	1685				

* p<0.05; ** p<0.01; *** p<0.001

It is noteworthy that most of the organizational and market factors had certain impacts on the technical and scale efficiencies of Catholic hospitals. Larger Catholic hospitals tended to be significantly more scale efficient while hospitals in larger Catholic health systems tended to be more technically efficient. As expected, a multiple sponsorship, as contrast to a single sponsorship, was negatively associated with Catholic hospital scale efficiency. However, hospitals with a diocesan sponsorship was significantly more likely than those with a single sponsorship to be more scale and technically efficient. Additionally, Catholic hospitals serving higher proportions of Medicaid patients tended to be more scale efficient. This is consistent with the notion that hospitals serving more Medicaid patients and thus are reimbursed lower have to be efficient enough in order to survive. Further, consistent with expectation, rural hospitals had lower likelihood to be operating as efficiently as their urban counterparts. Moreover, market competition was negatively associated with Catholic hospitals' likelihood of being scale efficient. This finding supports the finding by Chirikos and Sear [7] that hospital inefficiency ratings were associated with the competitive conditions of local health care markets. Finally, the degree to which for-profit hospitals penetrated a market increased Catholic hospitals' likelihood of being scale and technically efficient. This finding is consistent with the evidence reported by Kessler and McClellan [23] that for-profit hospitals have spillover effects for medical productivity.

A sensitivity analysis was conducted to examine the robustness of the results by comparing the results from three regression models commonly used following the DEA estimation of efficiency scores. The first model is reported here. The second mode is a logit model using a binary dependent variable which is coded as 1 if a hospital's efficiency score is 1.000 and as 0 otherwise. The third model is a two-limit tobit model directly applying the efficiency scores as the values of its dependent variable. The independent variables in these three models are the same. The three models yield similar results. Among these factors, a diocesan sponsorship and a rural location are the most consistent predictors of Catholic hospital technical efficiency across the three models. Hospital size, market competition and for-profit market are consistent and significant predictors in the two tobit models.

6.4 Conclusions

As the Iltis [20] conceptual framework would have suggested, the data do not support the notion that a value of stewardship would be positively associated with technical and scale efficiency. This study does not find a significant relationship between the presence of a Catholic health system value of stewardship and technical or scale efficiencies of their member hospitals. Further, the efficiency of Catholic system affiliated hospitals did not improve over the three-year period.

However, the interpretation of this result should not be construed as evidence indicating Catholic hospitals' poor performance in terms of operational and scale efficiencies. As mentioned earlier, efficiency scores calculated from DEA are indicators of relative performance rather than true or absolute performance. One should keep this notion in mind when interpreting the results. There is no intention to compare efficiency between Catholic hospitals to hospitals of other ownership types.

There may be several explanations for this finding. First, Catholic hospitals in general may have been relatively homogenous in terms of operations regardless of the difference in espoused values. This is plausible because the sample hospitals are guided and directed by Roman Catholic Church traditions and rules. The authoritative or coercive pressures from the Church may have made Catholic hospitals operationally isomorphic with each other.

The second explanation relates to the indirect role that health system values play on the overall operation of individual Catholic hospitals. For individual hospitals, their own core values and mission statements may play a more direct role in guiding their operations and daily decision making processes. The values of Catholic health systems may thus have a distant and weak impact on the operations of their member hospitals.

The third potential explanation comes from the nature of organizational goals. As discussed earlier, like other organizations, Catholic hospitals and systems may have different views regarding their official goals (e.g., mission statement) and principles (e.g., core values). If system core values serve only as stated goals or guidelines for the purpose of legitimacy, they may not have the real impact on organizational operations.

This study has several important implications for organizational researchers. First, using the efficient Catholic hospitals as benchmarks, the inefficient Catholic hospitals can improve their operational efficiency significantly. Overall, there is a 33% efficiency gap between the efficient and inefficient Catholic hospitals (set efficient hospitals as 100%). If the inefficient Catholic hospitals can make up the gap by reducing the relevant inputs, there can be a huge cost saving and a big jump of competitiveness. This also implies that these inefficient Catholic hospitals have slack resources that can be used to provide more uncompensated or charity care without additional costs if they can be as operationally efficient as their efficient counterparts.

Second, this study reveals that the system value of stewardship may not be an effective determinant of the efficiency of Catholic hospitals. A previous study by White *et al.* [37] also found that, in general, there is no clear pattern in the relationship between the Catholic system values of justice and compassion and the provision of services that are operationally defined to represent those values. This may suggest a need for Catholic health systems to examine the linkage between their core values and the operations of their member hospitals. Since the exploration of the relationship of core values and hospital operations is budding, more empirical studies are needed that examine the relationship between health systems of other or mixed ownership forms in order to better understand the phenomena.

Third, this study demonstrates that a diocesan sponsorship is a significant, consistent, and positive predictor of Catholic hospital efficiency. Hospitals in Catholic systems with the diocesan model of governance appear to be more likely than those systems governed by religious congregation sponsors to be more efficient. Further investigations would be helpful to understand better the mechanism behind this finding. This study also adds empirical evidence into the literature that market competition may have a negative impact on hospital efficiency, implying that non-price competition may be present in the hospital market. Further, consistent with previous findings, the presence of for-profit hospitals have a positive effect on the efficiency of Catholic hospitals.

There are several noteworthy limitations to this study to consider. First, the year (2007) of information collection on system core values is two years later than the beginning year (2005) of the study period, potentially causing non-alignment between the dependent and independent variables. However, this problem may be minor because system values usually do not change frequently over time. Second, there may be omitted variable biases. For example, the number of years a Catholic hospital had been affiliated with a health system should have certain effects on the realization of system values in the hospital's operation. Ideally, a control variable would be added to the analytical model for years in the system, but there is no complete public data available for this measure. Third, this study focuses on Catholic hospital system-affiliated hospitals only. The finding of this study thus cannot be generalized to other non system-affiliated Catholic hospitals as well as hospitals in other religious denominations or ownership forms. Last, the study period may be too short to detect the difference and the change of the efficiency of Catholic system-affiliated hospitals. Thus, the continuation of this stream of study in a longer time could be promising. This not only provides an extended period to examine the relationship of interest, but also attenuates the problem of the time lag between the data collecting point of the independent variable (i.e., system value of stewardship collected in 2007) and the study period of the dependent variable (i.e., operational efficiencies in 2005 through 2007).

In conclusion, applying DEA and relevant multivariate regression techniques, this study was able to explore the relationship between the efficiency of Catholic system-affiliated hospitals and certain organizational and market characteristics. Although the system value of stewardship was not found to have a significant impact on Catholic hospital efficiency, a diocesan governance model was demonstrated to be a positive determinant. This study also shows that organizational and market characteristics such as the proportion of Medicaid patients, rural location, market competition, and for-profit penetration are important determinants of Catholic hospital efficiency.

References

1. Banks, D.A., Paterson, M., Wendel, J.: Uncompensated hospital care: Charitable mission or profitable business decision? Health Economics **6**(2), 133–143 (1997)
2. Bazzoli, G.J., Chan, B., Shortell, S.M., D'Aunno, T.: The financial performance of hospitals belonging to health networks and systems. Inquiry **37**(3), 234–52 (2000)
3. Catholic Health Association of the United States: The healing ministry of catholic health care. Retrieved 10/02/2008, from http://www.chausa.org/Pub/MainNav/AboutCHA/ overview.htm (2008)
4. Catholic Health Association of the United States: Catholic health care in the United States. Retrieved 05/04/2009, from http://www.chausa.org/NR/rdonlyres/68B7C0E5-F9AA-4106-B182-7DF0FC30A1CA/0/FACTSHEET.pdf (2009)

5. Chang, H.H.: Determinants of hospital efficiency: The case of central government-owned hospitals in Taiwan. Omega **26**(2), 307–318 (1998)
6. Chilingerian, J.A.: Evaluating physician efficiency in hospitals: A multivariate analysis of best practices. European Journal of Operational Research **80**(3), 548–574 (1995)
7. Chirikos, T.N., Sear, A.M.: Technical efficiency and the competitive behavior of hospitals. Socioeconomic Planning Sciences **28**(4), 219–227 (1994)
8. Clement, J.P., White, K.R., Valdmanis, V.: Charity care: Do not-for-profits influence for-profits? Medical Care Research and Review **59**(1), 59–78 (2002)
9. Cooper, W.W., Seiford, L.M., Tone, K.: Data envelopment analysis: A comprehensive text with models, applications, references and DEA-solver software. Springer, New York (2007)
10. Daft, R.L.: Organization theory and design. South-Western College Pub., Cincinnati, OH (2001)
11. Devers, K.J., Brewster, L.R., Casalino, L.P.: Changes in hospital competitive strategy: A new medical arms race? Health Services Research **38**(1), 447–469 (2003)
12. Ettner, S.L., Hermann, R.C.: The role of profit status under imperfect information: Evidence from the treatment patterns of elderly Medicare beneficiaries hospitalized for psychiatric diagnoses. Journal of Health Economics **20**(1), 23–49 (2001)
13. Folland, S., Stano, M., Goodman, A.C.: The economics of health and health care, 4th ed. Pearson/Prentice Hall, Upper Saddle River, NJ (2004)
14. Griffith J.R., White K.R.: The well-managed healthcare organization. Health Administration Press, Chicago (2007)
15. Harrison, J.P., Sexton, C.: The improving efficiency frontier of religious not-for-profit hospitals. Hospital Topics **84**(1), 2–10 (2006)
16. Hollingsworth, B.: The measurement of efficiency and productivity of health care delivery. Health Economics **17**(10), 1107–1128 (2008)
17. Horwitz, J.R.: Does nonprofit ownership matter? Yale Journal on Regulation **24**(1), 139–199 (2007)
18. Horwitz, J.R., Nichols, A.: What do nonprofits maximize? nonprofit hospital service provision and market ownership mix. National Bureau of Economic Research (2007)
19. Hughes, R.G., Luft, H.S.: Keeping up with the joneses: The influence of public and proprietary neighbors on voluntary hospitals. Health Services Management Research **3**(3), 173–181 (1990)
20. Iltis, A.S.: Institutional integrity in Roman Catholic health care institutions. Christian Bioethics **7**(1), 95–103 (2001)
21. Jones, G.R.: Organizational theory: Text and cases. Prentice Hall, Upper Saddle River, NJ (2001)
22. Kauffman, C.J.: Ministry and meaning: A religious history of Catholic health care in the united states. Crossroad, New York (1995)
23. Kessler, D.P., McClellan, M.B.: The effects of hospital ownership on medical productivity. The Rand Journal of Economics **33**(3), 488–506 (2002)
24. LeBlanc, A.J., Hurley, R.E.: Adoption of HIV-related services among urban US hospitals: 1988 and 1991. Medical Care **33**(9), 881–891 (1995)
25. Mobley, L.R.: Effects of selective contracting on hospital efficiency, costs and accessibility. Health Economics **7**(3), 247–261 (1998)
26. O'Neill, L., Rauner, M., Heidenberger, K., Kraus, M.: A cross-national comparison and taxonomy of DEA-based hospital efficiency studies. Socioeconomic Planning Sciences **42**(3), 158–189 (2008)
27. O'Reilly, C.A., Pfeffer, J.: Hidden value: How great companies achieve extraordinary results with ordinary people. Harvard Business School Press, Boston (2000)
28. Ozcan, Y.A.: Health care benchmarking and performance evaluation an assessment using data envelopment analysis (DEA). Springer, New York (2008)
29. Rosko, M.D.: Impact of HMO Penetration and Other Environmental Factors on Hospital X-Inefficiency. Medical Care Research and Review **58**: 430–454 (2001)
30. Rosko, M.D., Proenca, J., Zinn, J.S., Bazzoli, G.J.: Hospital Inefficiency: What is the Impact of Membership in Different Types of Systems? Inquiry **44**(3): 335–349 (2007)

31. Schlesinger, M., Dorwart, R., Hoover, C., Epstein, S.: Competition, ownership, and access to hospital services: evidence from psychiatric hospitals. Medical Care **35**(9), 974–992 (1997)
32. Scott, W.R., Davis, G.F.: Organizations and organizing: Rational, natural, and open system perspectives. Pearson Prentice Hall, Upper Saddle River, NJ (2007)
33. United States Conference of Catholic Bishops: Ethical and Religious Directives for Catholic Health Care Services, 4th ed. (2001). Retrieved 07/01/2010, from http://www.nccbuscc.org/bishops/directives.shtml
34. Wang, B.B., Ozcan, Y.A., Wan, T.T., Harrison, J.: Trends in hospital efficiency among metropolitan markets. Journal of Medical Systems **23**(2), 83–97 (1999)
35. Weick, K.: The social psychology of organizing. Addison-Wesley, Reading, MA (1969)
36. Welbig, L.M.: Our defined social purpose. Catholic hospitals have organic relationships with communities. Health Progress **89**(1), 48–50 (2008)
37. White, K.R., Chou, T.H., Dandi, R.: Catholic hospital services for vulnerable populations: Are system values sufficient determinants? Health Care Management Review **35**(2), 175–186 (2010)
38. White, K.R., Dandi, R.: Intrasectoral variation in mission and values: The case of the Catholic health systems. Health Care Management Review **34**(1), 68–79 (2009)
39. White, K.R., Begun, J.W., Tian, W.: Hospital service offerings: Does Catholic ownership matter? Health Care Management Review **31**(2), 99–108 (2006)
40. White, K.R., Cochran, C.E., Patel, U.B.: Hospital provision of end-of-life services: Who, what, and where? Medical Care **40**(1), 17–25 (2002)

Chapter 7

Optimal allocation of urban nuclei to hospital birth centres in a geographical region

Paola Facchin, Anna Ferrante, Elena Rizzato, Giorgio Romanin-Jacur, and Laura Salmaso

Abstract. We consider a geographical region with a three-tiered neonatal care network, which includes birth centres for supplying basic assistance for delivery, neonatal care and neonatal intensive care, with a design such that all higher-level centres also provide the lower levels of assistance. The region's population is distributed in urban nuclei, the needs of which – in terms of assistance related to birth and newborn – are established on the basis of statistical analyses. Every mother-to-be is admitted to a birth centre serving the level corresponding to the needs of her pregnancy. Newborn transfers from a lower- to a higher-level centre are feasible in the event of unforeseen health issues. In this chapter we allocate urban nuclei to birth centres for what concerns all-level admissions, also allocating lower-level centres to suitable upper-level centres for any transfers, with a view to minimising the incon-

P. Facchin
Epidemiology and Community Medicine Unit, Department of Paediatrics, University of Padova, Via Giustiniani 3, 35128 Padova, Italy
e-mail: facchin@pediatria.unipd.it

A. Ferrante
Epidemiology and Community Medicine Unit, Department of Paediatrics, University of Padova, Via Giustiniani 3, 35128 Padova, Italy
e-mail: ferrante@pediatria.unipd.it

E. Rizzato
Epidemiology and Community Medicine Unit, Department of Paediatrics, University of Padova, Via Giustiniani 3, 35128 Padova, Italy
e-mail: erizzato@libero.it

G. Romanin-Jacur (✉)
Department of Management and Engineering, University of Padova, Stradella San Nicola 3, 36100 Vicenza, Italy
e-mail: romjac@dei.unipd.it

L. Salmaso
Epidemiology and Community Medicine Unit, Department of Paediatrics, University of Padova, Via Giustiniani 3, 35128 Padova, Italy
e-mail: salmaso@pediatria.unipd.it

Tànfani E., Testi A. (Eds.): Advanced Decision Making Methods Applied to Health Care.
International Series in Operations Research & Management Science 173
DOI 10.1007/978-88-470-2321-5_7,

venience due to the distances involved without overloading any centres; we use the results obtained for suitably resizing the network to further improve its efficiency. The allocation model is a linear program solved using GAMS algebraic language and Cplex solver. An actual application was considered.

Keywords: perinatal assistance network, decision support, linear programming

7.1 Introduction and problem addressed

7.1.1 Introduction

In recent years, numerous clinical and technological advances have brought about dramatic changes in neonatal care, enabling even the small numbers of newborns that are severely premature or born in critical conditions and requiring intensive care to be supported and kept alive. The medical specialization and instruments consequently required for neonatal intensive care make it necessary to link large catchment areas to a few suitable facilities. Alongside this restricted group of patients, there is a large group of newborns coming into the world in physiological or mildly pathological conditions, who can be cared for at less specialized facilities and by less expert staff. It is more convenient to organise a more capillary distribution of the healthcare network for such newborns, with facilities serving smaller catchment areas, so as to contain the distances between the facilities and the urban nuclei they serve. To satisfy all the above requirements demands the creation of birth assistance networks with facilities on different levels, and to allow for any transfers needed from lower-level facilities to higher-level facilities for patients whose initial conditions deteriorate.

Three-tiered perinatal care networks have been planned in Europe and the USA ever since the '80s, as reported in [9, 23, 44]. The three levels correspond to basic neonatal care on the first level, intermediate care for neonatal diseases on the second, and neonatal intensive care on the third.

Each perinatal care network has to be accurately planned in logistic terms, providing suitably sized and connected facilities for ensuring the maximum efficiency of each level of care. Local governments generally follow guidelines such as those described in [43], which establish standard relationships between the resident populations and the sizing of facilities, but without giving any indications on the location of these facilities or how to allocate patients to a given facility. Suitable models are needed to solve problems concerning facility location and patient allocation.

In this chapter, we assume that the women and babies needing these services live in urban nuclei dotted all over a given territory. Each urban nucleus has a certain demand for each of the three perinatal care levels previously mentioned. Within the territory considered, there is a service network that includes facilities for each level of neonatal care, and a characteristic of the network lies in that every higher-level care facility also provides the lower-levels of care. Each facility is characterized by a capacity, i.e., the amount of assistance it can provide. The aim of this study can be divided into two successive stages: in a first step, we allocate patients to the existing facilities, also establishing any transfers from lower- to upper-level facilities with a view to minimising the inconvenience due to the distances involved; in a second step, we resize the existing facilities (adapting their capacity) so to improve the global efficiency of the network. In the first step, a given urban nucleus may be divided and allocated to more than one facility. The problem is studied both assuming stable demand trends and in the event of short- and medium-term variability.

The service location-allocation problem has been widely studied in the literature since the '70s, e.g. [8,42]. Numerous review papers have considered general services [33, 36, 37], general health services [18], specific ambulance services [4], all using deterministic models, and general services described by stochastic models [5, 31].

Based on such reviews, the model adopted in the present chapter can be classified as a hierarchical, multi-level, multi-flow, capacitated, nested, referral, non-coherent model, which seeks the p-median to allocate customers to services, although we consider the possible addition of compatibility and/or compulsory assignment constraints, which make ours more similar to the coverage model.

The model is hierarchical because the services provided are of three different types, with an increasing degree of specialization and mutually interact; it is multi-level because the types of service offer different levels of care; it is multi-flow in that requests for assistance are classified on three distinct levels and originate independently from the territory served; it is capacitated because each facility is associated with a given capacity to provide assistance; it is nested in that a higher-level facility implicitly also contains the lower levels; it is a referral model because patients requiring a higher level of care can be transferred from a lower-level facility to a higher-level facility; and it is non-coherent because patients needing a higher level of care may be transferred to a facility elsewhere. Unlike all the other papers in the literature, in this study any referral from a lower level to a higher-level facility is not established *a priori*, but is a part of the problem to solve. Finally, the model adopted differs from traditional location-allocation models in that our aim was not to choose which facilities to reinforce (or close) from a candidate set, but to achieve an optimal allocation of the users to the existing facilities, and establish any consequent facility resizing needs.

The model we adopted is deterministic since we study a short- and medium-term planning action to respond to a typical demand, so we felt that a stochastic model would add to the complexity of the problem without having any advantage in terms of the results obtained. We do not impose integer allocation for every urban nucleus to a single facility for each level, because this might entail solutions that would be inefficient in practice. For instance, this can happen in the case of urban nuclei with a low demand, that consequently risk being allocated to facilities far away, or in the case of urban nuclei with a high demand that are close to low-capacity facilities.

The facility location-allocation problem was first introduced in [8, 42] and described by a coverage model: a network was considered where customers were located in a number of nodes, while all other nodes were candidate locations for the set-up of new facilities. A maximum radius (i.e., the maximum acceptable distance between facility and customer) was chosen and then the minimum number of facilities needed was established, imposing the constraint that all users had to be covered (i.e., for every user there had to be an active facility within the specified maximum distance). The problem here is uncapacitated so the workload of the facilities activated is a consequence of their location. Such a choice may be convenient in the case of new facilities to set up in areas that have yet to be served, but it not practical in a situation where the set-up of new facilities is expensive and takes too long.

The original model was extended in [10] to describe a system including facilities in a hierarchy and applied to the planning of services in a region in Honduras, and also in [3], where multi-level models are presented. A generalisation enabling different degrees of coverage at different costs is studied in [2], and a further extension of the model with a variable-radius coverage at a minimum total coverage cost is discussed in [41].

A recent interesting paper [21] presents a hierarchical model with referral and minimum and maximum capacity constraints for candidate facilities. Many alternative constraints relating to the customer-facility paths are considered. Real world applications concerned different planning levels for the school network in Portugal. The opening of new facilities and closing of existing ones is also considered in [21], whereas we restrict ourselves in the present chapter to suggesting any resizing of existing facilities.

All the above-mentioned papers deal with deterministic models, but there are also many publications discussing facility networks that are either single or multiple server queues. The main constraint in such papers imposes the maximum allowable probability of having to wait for a given service, while the goal consists in minimising the number or the cost of the available facilities. Emergency situations are considered in [7, 24–28, 32, 39, 45], where urgent admission is essential. It is worth noting that a queuing model includes non-linear equations and therefore makes the solution more difficult. In the present chapter, moreover, considering a congested system would lead to a model which does not fit in with the real world.

As for specific applications to health care service planning, the problem of the location-allocation of facilities was discussed in [40,42], using single-level coverage models. For [38] paediatric emergency centres, location-allocation was considered using models aiming to minimise the mean or the maximum distance of the user from the facility. In [30], hierarchical mini-sum models were used to plan blood services in Turkey. A non-hierarchical model is adopted in [34], with a non-uniform maximum capacity for all the facilities to locate, a bi-objective function including the sum of the distances between patients and facilities (hospitals and health centres), and an index of fair facility distribution. An extension of the hierarchical maximum coverage model described in [10] is suggested, and applied to the location of medical facilities in Pakistan [20].

Among the above papers, only [34] considers the maximum capacity of existing or candidate facilities as a constraint. Only some papers consider a hierarchical facility system, and only [30] considers a hierarchical system with referral. In the present chapter, we consider a hierarchical model with referral, where the capacities of existing facilities impose a system constraint.

As for the study of location-allocation problems using stochastic models in the health care field, facility planning in Great Britain is discussed in [22], and the location of ambulances on highways is optimised in [35] by minimising ambulance response time and workload unbalance.

The problem of how to optimally allocate patients and resources to hospitals that are expected to be built or enlarged is studied in [13]; and optimal resource allocation amongst different facilities (hospitals and primary care centres) is considered in [15]. In the present chapter, on the other hand, we discuss the optimal allocation of patients to existing facilities, and we do not consider optimal resource allocation.

Specific territorial perinatal service planning was studied in [6,12,16,17], where an integer location-allocation problem with a multi-level, hierarchical model with a fixed referral was applied to a developing region of Brazil. The models are uncapacitated, i.e., the planned facilities theoretically have an infinite capacity, in all the above papers except for [12], where a common maximal capacity is stated for all the facilities to locate.

Compared with all the above papers, the main advantages of the present study lie in that: we take the capacity of existing facilities into account, so we never assign an excessive workload to any of them; the non-integer allocation of urban nuclei to facilities enables us to avoid model rigidity and difficulties in finding the solution, which could be done using a widely-available, inexpensive software. The model adopted is a linear program coded in GAMS language and solved precisely and speedily using Cplex software on a personal computer (within a few minutes for real problems).

This chapter is organised as follows. Section 7.1.2 is devoted to describing the perinatal and neonatal care services, focusing on the different levels of care and the characteristics of the corresponding birth centres. Section 7.1.3 introduces the specific problem in detail, providing the data and the decision variables, objective function and constraints. Section 7.2 discusses the linear programming mathematical model, which was constructed to formally describe the actual problem. Section 7.3 presents the computer implementation and some practical results. The final conclusions are given in Section 7.4.

7.1.2 Birth assistance and birth centres

Pregnancy may take a physiological or a pathological course. Complications in pregnancy may include gestational diabetes, infections, foetal malformations, and so on. Such complications may cause problems during delivery and/or in the neonatal period, so a higher level of care should preferably be chosen in advance for such cases [23,29,46].

Birth may take a physiological or a pathological course too. Some complications, such as those due to foetal-pelvic disproportion, placental deformity, etc., may be foreseen, so a higher level of care can be planned. Others, e.g. foetal distress, haemorrhage, premature birth, etc., may be unexpected and require prompt referral to a higher level of care.

Mothers are assisted during delivery by a gynaecological-obstetric team and the newborn by a paediatric-neonatology team. The care provided is generally classified on three levels, i.e. neonatal basic care, intermediate care for neonatal diseases and neonatal intensive care. Such a classification is widely accepted in Europe and the USA, as reported in [9, 11, 19, 23, 44]. The main characteristics of each level of care are recalled below:

- the first level of care is provided in the case of uncomplicated pregnancies and is characterized by the following capabilities:
  - assistance for the mother: continuous specialist assistance can be provided;
  - assistance for the newborn: continuous neonatological assistance can be provided, a neonatological unit can be used for primary resuscitation;
- the second level of care is provided in the event of pregnancies and births at low risk and/or involving mild prematurity (pregnancies shorter than 30 weeks or a birth weight below 1.5 kg), and is characterized by the following capabilities:
  - assistance for the mother: continuous specialist assistance can be provided, specialist monitoring equipment may be used during labour;
  - assistance for the newborn: continuous neonatological assistance can be provided, a neonatological unit can be used for resuscitation, and incubators may be used;
- the third level of care is provided in the case of higher-risk pregnancies and/or severely premature births (before 28 weeks of gestation, or birth weights below 1.0 kg), and is characterized by the following capabilities:
  - assistance for the mother: continuous specialist assistance, with anaesthesiological, intensive care and other specialist consultants available; specialist monitoring apparatus can be used during labour;
  - assistance for the newborn: continuous neonatological assistance, intensive care with artificial ventilation, and specialist consultants available; a neonatal intensive care ward may be used.

Each birth centre may be associated with various levels of care. Most centres provide only basic care, while a few specialist centres provide both first and second levels of care, and only a very few highly-specialized centres provide all levels of care. Clearly, every pregnant woman should generally be admitted to a birth centre where the level of care is appropriate for any expected birth complications; in other words, a "level requirement" may be defined.

7.1.3 The problem

Let us consider a birth centre and all the levels of care it can provide, bearing in mind that there are three levels of neonatal care and, for each of these, the capacity in terms of births per year can be established from the distribution of the duration of the users' stay. More precisely, the capacity related to all care levels combined emerges from the number of beds available for mothers in the obstetric ward. In addition, the capacity of the third level of care is limited by the number of artificially-ventilated incubators available and the capacity of the second level by the number of incubators, while for the first level of care there are no such structural limitations. The site and size of the birth centres are fixed *a priori*. Recommendations for adjusting the size of a given centre may emerge from the solution of the model.

Let us consider an urban nucleus [14], i.e., a homogeneous built-up area that can be seen as a point in relation to distances; it may be a district, a town or a group of towns lying close to one another. For each nucleus and each level of care, we define the corresponding demand in terms of births per year (this demand can be extrapolated from the statistics for previous years).

As seen in the previous section, a pregnant woman should be admitted to a centre and occupy a place on a level appropriate to her needs. Let us consider a situation where she has occupied a place where first- or second-level care is provided but her newborn presents unexpected complications and requires urgent transfer to a centre providing a higher level of care, at the same location or elsewhere, depending on the availability of levels of care and vacant places. In such a case, the newborn is transferred while the mother remains at the centre where she gave birth. Lower-level birth centres may thus become a source of further requests for the admission of newborn, adding to the above-mentioned requests coming directly from the urban nuclei.

The sum of all the admissions associated with births and any transfers constitutes the workload of a given centre for each level of care. The ratio between workload and capacity gives us the centre's saturation point for a given level. Of course, the overall workload on a given level is well balanced if all the centres have much the same saturation point. If the saturation range for a given level is defined as the difference between the maximum and the minimum centre saturation, then such a range is an index of the workload imbalance.

Whenever an urban nucleus is allocated to a birth centre for a given level (so mothers-to-be living in the area are admitted to the said centre), then an associated cost depending on their distance can be established. Much the same consideration applies to the process of allocation to centres providing a higher level of care for newborn transfers. If all urban nuclei are allocated to birth centres for admissions and all lower-level centres are allocated to higher-level centres for any transfers, then an overall cost associated with the distances involved can be established.

Let us consider the following optimal allocation problem: urban nuclei are allocated to birth centres for admissions, and lower-level birth centres are allocated to higher-level centres for transfers so as to minimise the weighted sum of the overall cost of the distances and of the workload imbalance index.

Allocation is not necessarily integer, i.e. the allocation of a given urban nucleus or birth centre may be fractionated. Optimal allocation is when the users' choices coincide with minimum overall inconvenience, so it represents a useful indicator of the current situation for care system managers and helps them to forecast future situations. Whenever it reveals any imbalance in the birth centres' workload, it indicates centre sizing and/or location errors, and it may point to appropriate corrective mea-

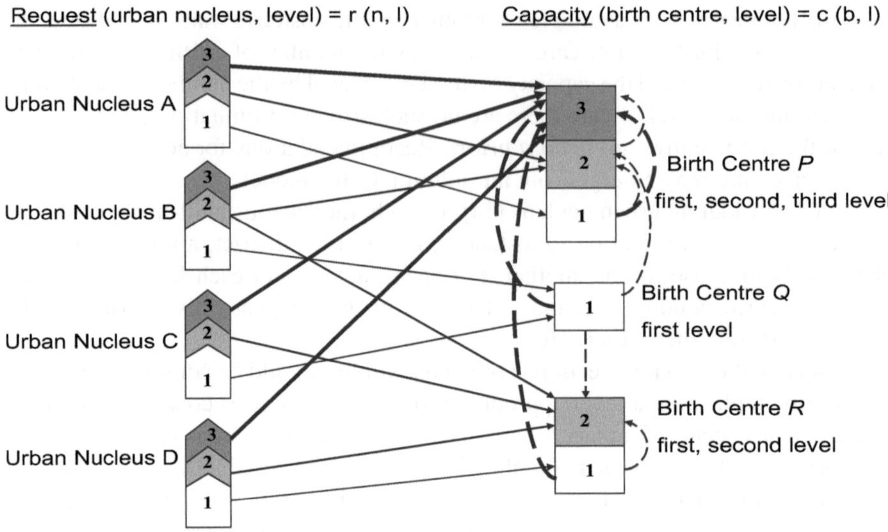

Fig. 7.1. An example of admission and transfer allocations

sures. To give a simple example, let us look at Figure 7.1, which shows a possible allocation layout. Nuclei A, B, C and D present requests for the three levels of care; centre P provides assistance on all levels, centre R on the first and second levels, and centre Q on basic care. For admissions to all levels of care, all the urban nuclei may be allocated entirely to one centre or their allocation may be divided between more than one centre, as represented by the arrows. For transfers, every birth centre providing first- or second-level care may be allocated (referred) to one or more birth centres providing higher levels of care, at the same or different locations.

7.2 Materials and methods

The formal model is presented below, with a detailed discussion of the related data, variables, objectives and constraints.

7.2.1 Model data

Let us consider:

- the set ν of urban nuclei indexed by n, $n = 1,2,\ldots,N$;
- the set β of birth centres indexed by b, $b = 1,2,\ldots,B$;
- the set λ of levels of care indexed by l, $l = 1,2,3$.

Let us then consider the following essential data:

- the capacity $c(b,l)$ of centre b for level l, in births/year, $\forall\, b = 1,2,\ldots,B, \forall\, l = 2,3$;

- the total capacity $c(b,0)$ of centre b for all levels 1, 2, 3 together, in births/year $\forall$ $b = 1,2,\ldots,B$;
- the requests r(n,l) from the nucleus n for level l, in births/year $\forall\ n = 1,2,\ldots,N$, $\forall\ l = 1,2,3$;
- the transfer ratio $t(l1,l)$ from level $l1$ to level l for any centre, $\forall\ (l1,l) \in \{(1,2),(1,3),(2,3)\}$;
- the inconvenience $f(n,b,l)$ deriving from allocating the nucleus n to the centre b for level l, $\forall\ n = 1,2,\ldots,N$, $\forall\ b = 1,2,\ldots,B$, $\forall\ l = 1,2,3; f(n,b,l)$ is a suitable convex function of the transit time;
- the inconvenience $g(b1,b,l1,l)$ deriving from transfers from the centre $b1$ to the centre b for a higher level of care, from $l1$ to l, $\forall\ b1,b = 1,2,\ldots, B$, $b1 \neq b$, and $\forall\ (l1,l) \in \{(1,2),(1,3),(2,3)\}$; $g(b1,b,l1,l)$ is a suitable convex function of the transit time;
- the weight $k(l)$, which is the imbalance multiplier relating to level l in the objective function $\forall\ l = 1,2,3$.

In the general problem, every (n,b,l) triple is allowed for allocation and every $(b1,b,l1,l)$ fortuple is allowed for transfer. In practice, some of these may be forbidden or imposed by technical considerations and/or matters of convenience. We can thus use the following optional data:

- allocation compatibility $ac(n,b,l) \in \{0,1\}$ $\forall\ n = 1,2,\ldots,N$, $\forall\ b = 1,2,\ldots,B$, $\forall$ $l = 1,2,3$;
- transfer compatibility $tc(b1,b,l1,l) \in \{0,1\}$ $\forall\ b1,b = 1,2,\ldots,B$, $b1 \neq b$, and $\forall$ $(l1,l) \in \{(1,2),(1,3),(2,3)\}$,
- compulsory allocation $ca(n,b,l) \in \{0,1\}$ $\forall\ n = 1,2,\ldots,N$, $\forall\ b = 1,2,\ldots,B$, $\forall$ $l = 1,2,3$;
- compulsory transfer $ct(b1,b,l1,l) \in \{0,1\}$ $\forall\ b1,b = 1,2,\ldots,B$, $b1 \neq b$, and $\forall$ $(l1,l) \in \{(1,2),(1,3),(2,3)\}$;

7.2.2 Model variables

We consider the following decision variables:

- allocation $x(n,b,l)$ in births/year of nucleus n to centre b for level l, $\forall\ n = 1,2,\ldots,N$, $\forall\ b = 1,2,\ldots,B$, $\forall\ l = 1,2,3$;
- transfer $y(b1,b,l1,l)$ in births/year from centre $b1$ to centre b for a level increase from $l1$ to l, $\forall\ b1,b = 1,2,\ldots,B$, $b1 \neq b$, and $\forall\ (l1,l) \in \{(1,2),(1,3),(2,3)\}$.

To make the model easier to understand, we introduce the following auxiliary variables:

- birth centre saturation, $sat(b,l)$, i.e. the ratio between the total workload of centre b and its capacity on each level, $\forall\ b = 1,2,\ldots,B$, $\forall\ l = 1,2,3$;
- saturation range, $ra(l)$, i.e. the difference between the maximum and the minimum saturation points for all centres, related to level l, $\forall\ l = 1,2,3$.

All above variables are obviously non-negative.

7.2.3 Model objective

The objective is to minimize the sum of the total allocation costs, the total transfer costs, and the weighted sum of the saturation ranges on all levels:

$$\begin{aligned} MINz: z = {} & \Sigma(f(n,b,l) * x(n,b,l) | n = 1,2,\ldots,N; b = 1,2,\ldots,B; l = 1,2,3) \\ & + \Sigma(g(b1,b,l1,l) * y(b1,b,l1,l) | b1, b = 1,2,\ldots,B; b1 \neq b; \\ & (l1,l) = (1,2),(1,3),(2,3)) + \Sigma(k(l) * ra(l)) | l = 1,2,3). \end{aligned} \tag{7.1}$$

Weights $k(l)$ are chosen by the manager to graduate the impact of any workload imbalance on the total costs.

7.2.4 Model constraints

Model constraints may be classified as essential (listed first) and optional.

Because of the beds assigned to the mothers, the sum of the allocations for every centre and for all levels is less than the full capacity:

$$\Sigma(x(n,b,l) | n = 1,2,\ldots,N; l = 1,2,3) \leq c(b,0) \qquad \forall b = 1,2,\ldots,B. \tag{7.2}$$

Moreover, for every second- or third-level centre, the sum of the allocations and transfers is less than their respective capacities for each level:

$$\begin{aligned} & \Sigma(x(n,b,l) | n = 1,2,\ldots,N) + \Sigma(y(b1,b,l1,l) l b1 = 1,2,\ldots,B, b1 \neq b; l1 = 1,l) \\ & \quad \leq c(b,l) \qquad \forall b = 1,2,\ldots,B \quad \forall l = 2,3. \end{aligned} \tag{7.3}$$

Every request from an urban nucleus shall be satisfied for each level:

$$\Sigma(x(n,b,l) | b = 1,2,\ldots,B) = r(n,l) \qquad \forall n = 1,2,\ldots,N \quad \forall l = 1,2,3. \tag{7.4}$$

The number of transfers from one centre to another affording a higher level of care is a known ratio of the demand allocated to the same centre at the lower level:

$$\begin{aligned} & y(b1,b,l1,l) = t(l1,l) * \Sigma(x(n,b1,l1) | n = 1,2,\ldots,N) \\ & \forall b1, b = 1,2,\ldots,B; b1 \neq b; \forall (l1,l) = (1,2),(1,3),(2,3). \end{aligned} \tag{7.5}$$

The saturation of obstetric ward beds at a given centre is the ratio between the total admissions of mothers for the three levels and the centre's total obstetric ward capacity; for uniformity, this will be referred to as the level 1 saturation:

$$\begin{aligned} & sat(b,1) = [\Sigma(x(n,b,l) | n = 1,2,\ldots,N; l = 1,2,3)] / c(b,0) \\ & \forall b = 1,2,\ldots,B. \end{aligned} \tag{7.6}$$

The saturation of the incubators at a level 2 or 3 centre is the ratio between the total newborn workload (birth admissions plus transfers) and the centre's capacity for the same level:

$$sat(b,l) = [\Sigma(x(n,b,l)|n = 1,2,\ldots,N) + \Sigma(y(b1,b)|b1 = 1,2,\ldots,B)]/c(b,l)$$
$$\forall b = 1,2,\ldots,B \quad \forall l = 2,3. \tag{7.7}$$

The saturation range for level l is given by the difference between the maximum and minimum saturation points for all centres:

$$ra(l) = max\{sat(b)|b = 1,2,\ldots,B\} - min\{sat(b)|b = 1,2,\ldots,B\} \tag{7.8}$$
$$\forall l = 1,2,3.$$

Optional constraints concern any compatibility and compulsory nature of allocations and transfers.

The nucleus-to-centre allocation compatibility for each centre and each level is:

$$x(n,b,l) \leq ac(n,b,l) * r(n,l) \tag{7.9}$$
$$\forall n = 1,2,\ldots,N \quad \forall b = 1,2,\ldots,B \quad \forall l = 1,2,3.$$

The centre-to-centre transfer compatibility for each increase in level is:

$$y(b1,b,l1,l) \leq tc(b1,b,l1,l) * \Sigma(x(n,b1,l1)|n = 1,2,\ldots,N) \tag{7.10}$$
$$\forall \mathrm{b1,2,\ldots,B = 1,2,\ldots,B;\ \ b1 \neq b;} \quad \forall \mathrm{(l1,l) = (1,2),(1,3),(2,3).}$$

The compulsory nature of the nucleus-to-centre allocation for each centre and each level is:

$$x(n,b,l) \geq ca(n,b,l) * r(n,l) \tag{7.11}$$
$$\forall n = 1,2,\ldots,N \quad \forall b = 1,2,\ldots,B \quad \forall l = 1,2,3.$$

and the compulsory nature of the centre-to-centre transfer for each increase in level is:

$$y(b1,b,l1,l) \geq ct(b1,b,l1,l) * \Sigma(x(n,b1,l1)|n = 1,2,\ldots,N) \tag{7.12}$$
$$\forall \mathrm{b1,2,\ldots,B = 1,2,\ldots,B; b1 \neq b;} \quad \forall \mathrm{(l1,l) = (1,2),(1,3),(2,3).}$$

7.2.5 Model formulation

The whole Linear Programming model is given below:

$$MIN\Sigma(f(n,b,l) * x(n,b,l)|n = 1,2,\ldots,N; \quad b = 1,2,\ldots,B; \quad l = 1,2,3)$$
$$+\Sigma(g(b1,b,l1,l) * y(b1,b,l1,l)|b1,b = 1,2,\ldots,B; \quad b1 \neq b; (l1,l)$$
$$= (1,2),(1,3),(2,3) + \Sigma(k(l) * ra(l))|l = 1,2,3), \tag{7.1}$$

subject to:

$$\Sigma(x(n,b,l)|n = 1,2,\ldots,N; \quad l = 1,2,3) \leq c(b,0) \qquad \forall b = 1,2,\ldots,B \tag{7.2}$$

$$\Sigma(x(n,b,l)|n=1,2,\ldots,N)+\Sigma(y(b1,b,l1,l)|b1=1,2,\ldots,B;\ b1\neq b;\ l1=1,l)$$
$$\leq \mathrm{c(b,l)} \qquad \forall \mathrm{b}=1,2,\ldots,\mathrm{B} \quad \forall \mathrm{l}=2,3 \tag{7.3}$$

$$\Sigma(x(n,b,l)|b=1,2,\ldots,B)=r(n,l) \qquad \forall n=1,2,\ldots, \qquad \forall l=1,2,3 \tag{7.4}$$

$$y(b1,b,l1,l)=t(l1,l)*\Sigma(x(n,b1,l1)|n=1,2,\ldots,N)$$
$$\forall b1,b=1,2,\ldots,B;b1\neq b; \quad \forall(l1,l)=(1,2),(1,3),(2,3) \tag{7.5}$$

$$sat(b,1)=[\Sigma(x(n,b,l)|n=1,2,\ldots,N;\ l=1,2,3)]/c(b,0)$$
$$\forall b=1,2,\ldots,B \tag{7.6}$$

$$sat(b,l)=[\Sigma(x(n,b,l)|n=1,2,\ldots,N)+\Sigma(y(b1,b)|b1=1,2,\ldots,B)]/c(b,l)$$
$$\forall b=1,2,\ldots,B\forall l=2,3 \tag{7.7}$$

$$ra(l)=max\{sat(b)|b=1,2,\ldots,B\}-min\{sat(b)|b=1,2,\ldots,B\}$$
$$\forall l=1,2,3 \tag{7.8}$$

$$x(n,b,l)\leq ac(n,b,l)*r(n,l)$$
$$\forall n=1,2,\ldots,N \quad \forall b=1,2,\ldots,B\forall l=1,2,3 \tag{7.9}$$

$$y(b1,b,l1,l)\leq tc(b1,b,l1,l)*\Sigma(x(n,b1,l1)|n=1,2,\ldots,N)$$
$$\forall b1,b=1,2,\ldots,B;b1\neq b; \quad \forall(l1,l)=(1,2),(1,3),(2,3) \tag{7.10}$$

$$x(n,b,l)\geq ca(n,b,l)*r(n,l)\forall n=1,2,\ldots,N$$
$$\forall b=1,2,\ldots,B \quad \forall l=1,2,3 \tag{7.11}$$

$$y(b1,b,l1,l)\geq ct(b1,b,l1,l)*\Sigma(x(n,b1,l1)|n=1,2,\ldots,N)$$
$$\forall b1,b=1,2,\ldots,B;b1\neq b; \quad \forall(l1,l)=(1,2),(1,3),(2,3) \tag{7.12}$$

$$x(n,b,l)\geq 0$$
$$\forall \mathrm{n}=1,2,\ldots,\mathrm{N} \quad \forall \mathrm{b}=1,2,\ldots,\mathrm{B} \quad \forall \mathrm{l}=1,2,3 \tag{7.13}$$

$$y(b1,b,l1,l)\geq 0$$
$$\forall \mathrm{b1,b}=1,2,\ldots,\mathrm{B;b1}\neq \mathrm{b}; \quad \forall(\mathrm{l1,l})=(1,2),(1,3),(2,3) \tag{7.14}$$

$$sat(b,l)>0 \qquad \forall b=1,2,\ldots,B \quad \forall l=1,2,3 \tag{7.15}$$

$$ra(l)>0 \qquad \forall l=1,2,3 \tag{7.16}$$

(constraints from (7.9) to (7.12) are optional and may be omitted if considered unnecessary).

7.3 Results and discussion

The model discussed above was implemented and solved using the GAMS model generator and the Cplex solver.

Let us consider an actual application, relating to the Veneto region (north-eastern Italy, with a population of about 4 700 000, and about 47 000 newborns per year),

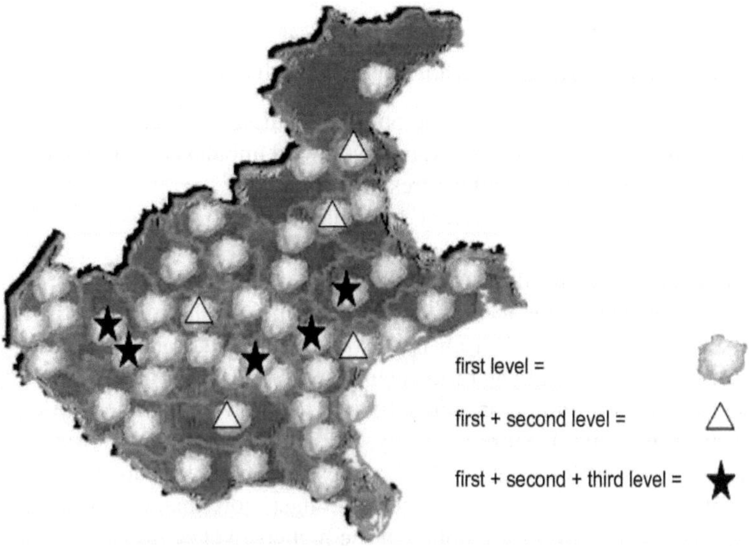

Fig. 7.2. Birth centre locations in the Veneto region

which includes 581 urban nuclei (municipal districts) and 41 birth centres (at hospitals and university clinics). A dramatic change relating to births has taken place in this region, i.e. in a decade, the number of births has increased by one third and the mean age of the mothers at delivery has increased by ten years. The diseases seen in the newborn have consequently changed too, with an increase in the ratio of newborns requiring second and third levels of care. Figure 7.2 shows a map of the region, where first-level birth centres are represented by cauliflowers, the second-level centres by triangles, and the third-level centres by stars.

For the optimal allocation model we have the following data:

- for each of the 581 urban nuclei, the demand for each level of care in births per year;
- for each of the 41 birth centres, the capacity per level of care in admissions per year;
- for each urban nucleus / birth centre / care level triple, the distance and the possible compatibility and compulsory allocation issues;
- for each birth centre / birth centre / level / level fortuple, the distance and the possible compatibility and compulsory allocation issues;
- birth allocation cost function parameters and transfer allocation cost function parameters (in the application considered, we adopt linear piecewise functions);
- the weight coefficient for costs of any imbalance;

and we have the following variables:

- about 60,000 variables are nucleus-to-centre allocations;
- about 5,000 are centre-to-centre allocations;
- the remaining 5,000 concern centre saturation and saturation range;

and the following equations:

- about 150,000 in 12 groups as seen in the model listing.

The direct results of the model include optimal admission allocations x*(n,b,l), optimal transfer allocations y*(b1,b,l1,l) and workload unbalance ra(l); the derived results include the workloads of all centres on each level.

The model was solved for different data sets relating to various conditions in the demand for care.

First of all, we consider the current situation: in the solution, most urban nuclei are allocated for admissions to only one birth centre, while a few are fractionated between several birth centres for all levels; this latter situation is often the case of municipal districts containing no birth centre, or districts that contain several centres, the single capacities of which are not sufficient for the whole nucleus (e.g. the municipal district of Venice). More precisely, 6% of the allocations to first-level care, 2% of those for second-level care and 1% of those to third-level care are fractionated.

About 50% of transfers are fractionated amongst more than one birth centre due to the scarcity and the saturation points of the higher-level centres.

Figure 7.3 shows the total admissions allocated to each centre alongside the centre's capacity, which depends on the number of beds in the obstetric ward.

Some centres appear to be oversized while others are totally saturated. Clearly, if the trend of the demand for care remains stable, a non-negligible subset of existing centres could be reduced without any negative consequences on the service being provided or correlated inconvenience concerning the distance mothers have to travel.

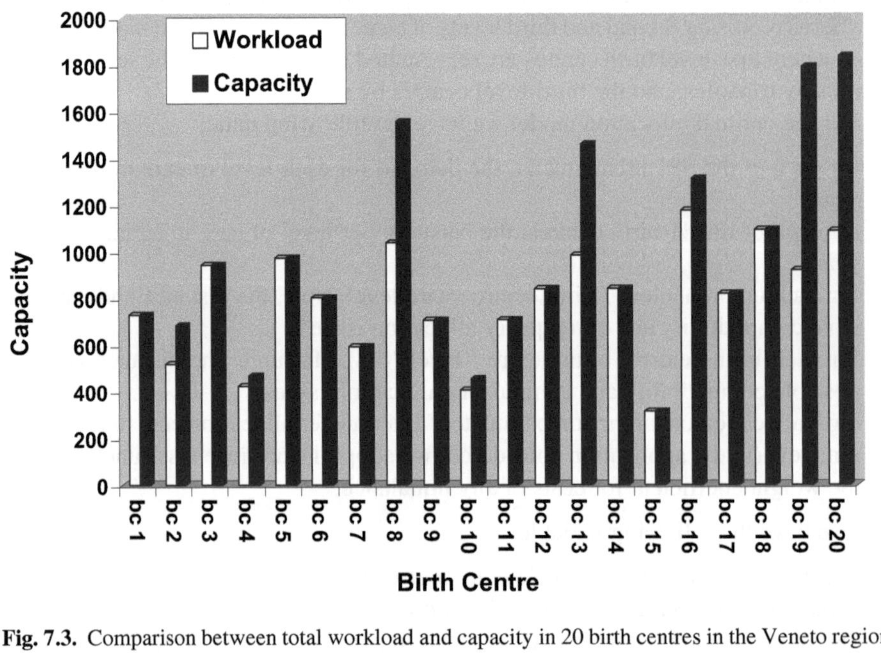

Fig. 7.3. Comparison between total workload and capacity in 20 birth centres in the Veneto region

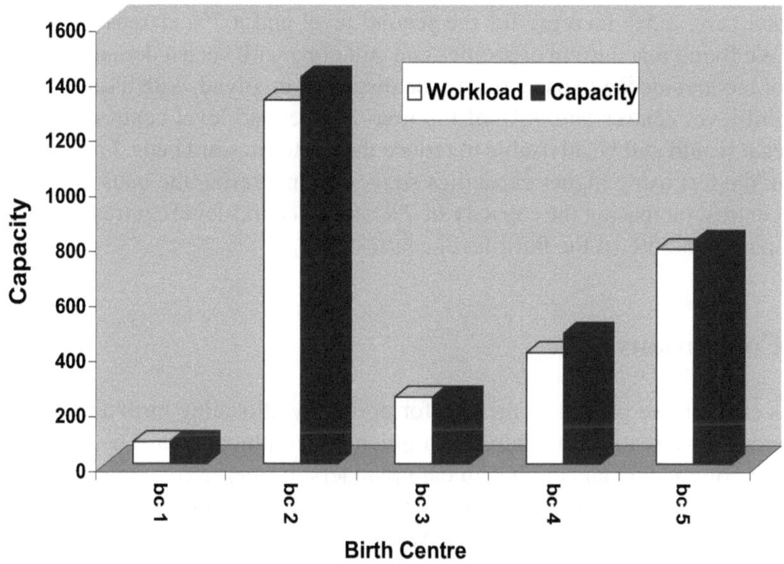

Fig. 7.4. Comparison between third-level workload and capacity in birth centres in the Veneto region

Figure 7.4 shows the third-level workload, i.e. admissions plus transfers, at all third-level centres alongside their third-level capacities. All the centres are heavily saturated, meaning that the service provided is falling short of the demand.

If we increase the weight of the cost of imbalance in the cost function, negligible variations emerge: this means that, because of the distance factor, both saturated and oversized centres remain the same. A capacity adaptation would consequently prove useful to reduce the total inconvenience. To establish where to increase the capacity of which centres, we can run the model after strongly increasing all the capacities, so that all the centres for which the optimal solution indicates a higher workload can be enlarged while all those for which it chooses a lower workload can be reduced to achieve a lower total inconvenience. In our experiment, we found that the capacity of almost all the centres warranted adaptation measures: in particular, 60% of the basic level centres could be reduced while the other 40% should be enlarged.

A second scenario was tested to establish the maximum increase in demand that the system of care considered could tolerate. We found that the system is still able to provide all the assistance required for all levels of care if the demand increases by 5% with respect to the current situation. This means that, in its current state, the system can cope with such an increase in demand if the population grows and the type of demand remains the same, even if the system is not well balanced.

Recent studies have shown that the trend of the demand for neonatal care in the Veneto region will not remain the same, however, in years to come. More precisely, the demand for higher-level care is expected to increase more substantially. We consequently studied a scenario in which we had a 3% increase in the demand for basic neonatal care, a 5% increase for the second level and a 7% increase for intensive care. We found that current capacities can still cope with such a demand, albeit with a lot of inconvenience to users due to the distances involved, with a saturation of all the third-level centres and 90% of the first- and second-level centres, so for some centres it would still be advisable to reduce the obstetric ward beds. For this new situation, the test using higher capacities suggested increasing the beds in 44% of the birth centres, increasing the capacity of 7% of the second-level centres, and increase the capacity of 55% of the third-level centres.

7.4 Conclusions

In this chapter, we propose a method for optimally allocating birth admissions and newborn transfers to birth centres in a given geographical area. The results of our optimization model can help health care planners to steer users towards a choice of centre that minimizes the total inconvenience relating to distance. Our results also pinpoint any workload imbalance between birth centres and unevenly distributed services in the territory considered. A poorly distributed service network causes inconvenience to users by obliging them to travel excessive distances, so it is useful to have suggestions on suitable adjustments to the sizing of the centres involved.

An actual application of our model relating to the Veneto region is discussed. The model can be usefully applied to other situations by adapting the specific data input, with no need for any structural changes, and it is suitable for use in both stable and dynamically evolving situations.

References

1. Barella, A., Facchin, P., Romanin Jacur, G.: Pregnancy-birth course in Veneto Region: development of a flexible simulation model for description and forecasting. ISC 2008 **1**, 348–352 (2008)
2. Berman, O., Drezner, Z., Krass, D., Wesolowsky, G.O.: The variable radius covering problem. European Journal of Operational Research **196**, 516–525 (2009)
3. Berman, O., Krass, D.: The generalized maximal covering location problem. Computers & Operations Research **29**, 563–581 (2002)
4. Berman, O., Larson, C.L., Odoni A.R.: Developments in network location with mobile and congested facilities. European Journal of Operational Research **6**(2), 104–116 (1981)
5. Boffey, B., Galvao, R., Espejo, L.: A review of congestion models in the location of facilities with immobile servers. European Journal of Operational Research **178**, 643–662 (2007)
6. Boffey, B., Yates, D., Galvão, R.D.: An algorithm to locate perinatal facilites in the municipality of Rio de Janeiro. Journal of the Operational Research Society **54**, 21–31 (2003)
7. Branas, C.C., MacKenzie, E.J., ReVelle, C.S.: A trauma resource allocation model for ambulances and hospitals. Health Services Research **35**(2), 489–507 (2000)
8. Brandeau, M.L., Chiu, S.: An overview of representative problems in location research. Management Science **35**(6), 645–674 (1989)
9. Brann, A.W., Hall, R.T. Harper, R.G., Maisels, J., Poland, R.L., Rhodes, P.G. *et al.*: Level II neonatal units. Pediatrics **66**(5), 810–1 (1980)
10. Church, R., Gerrard, R.A.: The multi-level location set covering model. Geographical Analysis **35**(4) (2003)

11. Committee of fetus and newborn: Levels of neonatal care. Pediatrics **114**, 1341–1347 (2004)
12. Eberhard, A., Wenzlaff, P., Lack, N., Misselwitz, B., Kaiser, A., Bartels, D.B.: Federal admission criteria for levels of perinatal care: definition, interpretation and first conclusions. Zeitschift fur Geburtshilfe und Neonatologie **212**(3), 100–108 (2008)
13. Flessa, S.: Where efficiency saves lives: a linear programme for the optimal allocation of health care resources in developing countries. Health Care Management Science **3**, 249–267 (2000)
14. Gallego, F.J.: Mapping rural/urban areas from population density grids. Institute for Environment and Sustainability, JRC – EC, ISPRA, Italy (2004)
15. Galvão, R.D., Espejo, L.G.A., Boffey, B.: A hierarchical model for the location of perinatal facilities in the municipality of Rio de Janeiro. European Journal of Operational Research **138**, 495–517 (2002)
16. Galvão, R.D., Espejo, L.G.A., Boffey, B.: Practical aspects associated with location planning for maternal and perinatal assistance. Ann. Oper. Res. **143**, 31–44 (2006)
17. Galvão, R.D., Espejo, L.G.A., Boffey, B., Yates, D.: Load balancing and capacity constraints in a hierarchical location model. European Journal of Operational Research **172**, 631–646 (2006)
18. Goldberg, J.B.: Operations research models for the deployment of emergency services vehicles. EMS Management Journal **1**(2), 20–39 (2004)
19. Gonzalez, R.R., Medina, J.S.: Theories, Models and urban realities. From New York to Kathmandu. Dela **21**, 69–81 (2004)
20. Harper, P.R., Shahani, A.K., Gallagher, J.E., Bowie, C.: Planning health services with explicit geographical considerations: a stochastic location – allocation approach. Omega **33**, 141–152 (2005)
21. Hogan, K., ReVelle, C.: Concepts and applications of backup coverage. Management Science **32**(11), 1434–1444 (1986)
22. Iannoni, A.P., Morabito, R., Saydam, C.: An optimization approach for ambulance location and the districting of the response segments on highways. European Journal of Operational Research **195**, 528–542 (2009)
23. Le Roy, C., Carayol, M., Zeitlin, J., Breart, G., Goffinet, F.: Level of perinatal care of the maternity unit and rate of cesarean in low risk nulliparas. Obstetrics & Gynecology **107**(6), 1269–1277 (2006)
24. Marainov, V., ReVelle, C.: The queuing probabilistic set covering problem and some extensions. Socio-Economic Planning Sciences **28**(3), 167–178 (1994)
25. Marianov, V., ReVelle, C.: The queueing maximal availability location problem: a model for the siting of emergency vehicles. European Journal of Operational Research **93**, 110–120 (1996)
26. Marianov, V., Serra, D.: Probabilistic maximal covering location-allocation models with constrained waiting time or queue length for congested systems. Social Science Research Network (1997)
27. Marianov, V., Serra, D.: Hierarchical location-allocation models for congested systems. European Journal of Operational Research **135**, 195–208 (2001)
28. Marianov, V., Serra, D.: Location-allocation of multiple-server service centres with constrained queues or waiting times. Annals of Operations Research **111**, 335–350 (2002)
29. Mayfield, J.A., Rosenblatt, R.A., Boldwin, L.M., Chu, J., Logerfo, J.P.: The relation of obstetrical volume and nursery level to perinatal mortality. American Journal of Public Health **80**(7), 819–823 (1990)
30. Mitropoulos, P., Mitropoulos, I., Giannikos, I., Sissouras, A.: A biobjective model for the locational planning of hospitals and health centers. Health Care and Management Science **9**, 171–179 (2006)
31. Moore, G.C., ReVelle, C.: The hierarchical service location problem. Management Science **28**(7), 775–780 (1982)
32. Morabito, R., Chiyoshi, F., Galvao, R.D.: Non-homogeneous servers in emergency medical systems: practical applications using the hypercube queueing model. Socio-Economic Planning Sciences **42**, 255–270 (2008)

33. Rahman, S., Smith, D.K.: Use of location – allocation models in health service development planning in developing nations. European Journal of Operational Research **123**, 437–452 (2000)
34. Ratick, S., Osleeb, J.P., Hozumi, D.: Application and extension of the Moore and ReVelle hierarchical maximal covering model. Socio-Economic Planning Sciences **30**, 1–10 (2008)
35. Rauner, M.S., Schneider, G., Heidenberger, K.: Reimbursement system and regional inpatient allocation: a non-linear optimisation model. IMA Journal of Management Mathematics **16**(3), 217–37 (2005)
36. ReVelle, C.S., Eiselt, H.A.: Location analysis: a synthesis and survey. European Journal of Operational Research **165**, 1–19 (2005)
37. Sahin, G., Sural, H.: A review of hierarchical facility location models. Computers & Operations Research **34**, 2310–2331 (2007)
38. Sahin, G., Sural, H., Meral, S.: Locational analysis for regionalization of Turkish red crescent blood services. Computers & Operations Research **34**, 692–704 (2007)
39. Syam, S.: A multiple server location-allocation model for service system design. Computers & Operations Research **35**, 2248–2265 (2008)
40. Tanikawa, T., Ohba, H., Terashita, T., Uesugu, M., Jiang, G., Ogasawara, K., Sakurai, T.: Model analysis for optimal allocation of pediatric emergency center. AMIA Annual Symposium Proceeding **1115** (2006)
41. Texeira, J.C., Antunes, A.P.: A hierarchical location model for public facility planning. European Journal of Operational Research **185**, 92–104 (2008)
42. Toregas, C., ReVelle, C.: Optimal location under time or distance constraints. Operations Research **28**(2), 133–142 (1972)
43. Toregas, C., Swain, R., ReVelle, C., Bergman, L.: The location of emergency service facilities. Operations Research **19**(6), 1363–1373 (1971)
44. Van Reempts, P., Gortner, L., Milligan, D. *et al.*: Characteristics of neonatal units that care for very preterm infants in Europe: result from the Mosaic study. Pediatrics **120**(4), 815–825 (2007)
45. Wang, Q., Batta, R., Rump, C.M.: Algorithms for a facility location problem with stochastic customer demand and immobile servers. Annals of Operations Research **111**, 17–34 (2002)
46. Zeitlin, J., Papiernik, E., Breart, G., the Europet group: Regionalization of perinatal care in Europe. Seminars in Neonatology **9**, 99–110 (2004)

Chapter 8

The nurse-to-patient assignment problem in Home Care services

Ettore Lanzarone and Andrea Matta

Abstract. The nurse-to-patient assignment problem in Home Care (HC) under continuity of care consists of allocating each newly admitted patient to only one reference nurse, without changing the assignment for a long period. The reference nurse of the new patient is chosen among a set of compatible ones, with the main goal of balancing the workloads among the nurses. In the literature, the assignment problem is usually solved with numerical approaches based on mathematical programming. In this chapter, we present a set of structural policies for solving the problem in the HC context. They take into account the randomness related to the patients' demands and to the workloads already assigned to nurses. The goal is to minimize a stochastic cost function based on the time for visits provided by the nurses above their capacities. A comparison with the current practice of HC providers that assign the new patient to the nurse with the highest expected available capacity is also presented. To apply the policies, an estimation of patient requirements in the planning period is needed. For this purpose, this chapter also presents a patient stochastic model to describe the patient's care pathway and his/her demands for visits over time. Finally, the application to a relevant real case is described, and the benefits deriving from implementing the proposed approach are shown.

Keywords: Home Care, human resource planning, nurse-to-patient assignment, continuity of care, structural policies, patient stochastic model

---

E. Lanzarone (✉)
Department of Mechanics, Politecnico di Milano, Via La Masa 1, 20156 Milano, Italy
e-mail: ettore.lanzarone@polimi.it

A. Matta
Department of Mechanics, Politecnico di Milano, Via La Masa 1, 20156 Milano, Italy
e-mail: andrea.matta@polimi.it

Tànfani E., Testi A. (Eds.): Advanced Decision Making Methods Applied to Health Care.
International Series in Operations Research & Management Science 173
DOI 10.1007/978-88-470-2321-5_8, © Springer-Verlag Italia 2012

8.1 Introduction and problem addressed

8.1.1 Home Care service

Home Care (HC) includes medical, paramedical and social services that are delivered to patients in their homes. The purpose of HC is to alleviate the pain of the assisted patients and to improve or sustain their health and quality of life. The main benefit of HC is a decrease in the hospitalization rate, leading to both significant increases in the quality of life for patients and relevant cost savings in the health care system [16].

This service is a relevant and growing sector in the healthcare domain of western countries because of the ageing of the population, the increase in chronic pathologies, the introduction of innovative technologies and the continuous pressure of governments to contain healthcare costs. HC is an important sector in Europe, Canada and Australia [18]. In the US, in 2009, more than 11,400 organizations delivered HC services to 3.3 million patients, with a total spending of 19 billion dollars [37]. Moreover, the number of elderly people in the US who potentially require HC is continuously increasing [3].

Many resources are involved in service delivery, including different categories of operators (e.g., nurses, physicians, physiotherapists, social assistants and psychologists), support staff and material resources. Patients are classified into different categories (usually, they are divided into palliative and non-palliative patients), and each category includes a certain number of Care Profiles (CPs) based on specific needs, the level of requirement and the costs associated with the provided services. Patients need to be cared for by different categories of operators: they are always under the charge of the nurses and, in some cases, of other operators. Within each category, operators are divided into *districts*: they take care of patients belonging to CPs that they are skilled for and, in large HC providers, they are divided into territorial groups and take care (only or preferably, according to the provider policy) of patients who are resident in their territory [16].

Some HC providers pursue the continuity of care, i.e., patients are assigned to only one operator for each category, named *reference operator*, who follows the entire patient care pathway and preferably provides all of the visits that are pertinent to his/her category. The continuity of care is an important quality indicator of the HC service because the quality perceived by the patient is preserved when he/she receives care from the same person and, thus, he/she does not have to continuously change his/her relationship with a new operator [45].

8.1.2 Human resources planning in HC

The main issues in HC human resource planning are the dimensioning, the partitioning of a territory into districts, the assignment of visits to operators and the routing problem. These issues involve three different levels of planning:

- *Middle-term planning* (6–24 months): This level concerns the dimensioning of the provider, including the division into districts and the choice of the number and typology of operators to assign to each district.

- *Short-term planning* (1–3 months): This level concerns the assignment of visits to the operators. When the provider adopts continuity of care, patients (and not visits) are assigned to the operators; nurses are usually assigned in this manner.
- *Very-short-term planning* (1 week): Once the human resources that are allocated to each visit are determined, this level includes the definition of the weekly plan with the sequence of visits for each operator. In providers with large districts, short-term planning and very-short-term planning are determined together.

All of these levels need robust planning to avoid process inefficiencies, treatment delays and a low quality of service. Unfortunately, planning in the HC context is quite complex because of the large number of assisted patients, the synchronization of many resources and the service delivery often encompassing a vast territory. Planning is also challenging because it requires assigning and scheduling different resources to a large number of patients who live in different locations of a geographical area. In addition, random events affect service delivery (e.g., variations in patients' conditions, resource unavailability and the duration of operator transfers in a territory), increasing the complexity of the planning problem and mining the feasibility of plans. The most critical issue is that the amount of service required by the patients is intrinsically random [16]. Finally, the existence of some constraints, such as the continuity of care and the risk of incurring a burnout of operators [20], makes the HC resource planning peculiar and different from planning problems that are encountered in other production and service systems.

In the majority of HC providers, the complexity of human resource planning is not counterbalanced by suitable skills, methodologies and tools for managing logistics and organizational activities to support the care delivery. HC providers typically suffer from a lack of adequate competencies in their staff. Hence, the possibility of implementing adequate planning models in the HC context could improve the robustness of their plans with a limited investment of support staff sustained by HC providers. In detail, models for dimensioning the operators to be inserted into the organic (type and district) are requested for middle-term planning; assignment models, taking into account the compatibility of the patient-operator pair and the continuity of care where pursued, are requested for short-term planning; and routing and scheduling models of the visits, for minimizing the distances travelled, are requested for very-short-term planning.

Under continuity of care, short-term planning (the assignment problem) plays a crucial role in maintaining a high quality of the provided service. In fact, the assignment influences the scheduling of visits and is the driver for defining the districting of the provider.

8.1.3 Topic of the chapter

This chapter focuses on the patient assignment problem under continuity of care. Specifically, the assignment of the *reference nurse* to the HC patients is analyzed. Nurses are chosen because they provide the largest number of visits to the HC patients, and they manage the emergencies and the variations in demand with a high uncertainty of the workload amount.

We describe a set of structural policies for solving the nurse-to-patient assignment problem, with the main goal of balancing the workload amount among the nurses, under the constraint of satisfying the care volume necessary to the patients under the charge and preserving the continuity of care.

The policies presented here, as well as each alternative approach for evaluating the impact of an assignment, require an estimate of the demand from the patients under the charge during the planning period. For this purpose, we also present an approach for developing a stochastic model that can describe the evolution of a patient's conditions and provide estimates on the amount of visits required during his/her stay.

Finally, a practical application of the proposed methodology in real cases is considered to be crucially important, for validation of the model and because only a small percentage of the models in the literature have been implemented in practice [26]. Hence, the approaches developed here are applied to the real case of one of the largest Italian public HC providers. Data from this provider are used to develop and validate the models, and a software application containing them is currently used by the provider to assign workloads to the operators. This HC provider is representative of a general class of providers in terms of organization and resource planning; therefore, the results obtained can be considered general and applicable to other similar structures.

8.1.4 Literature review

The literature on human resource planning in HC addresses four main issues: the partitioning of a territory into a given number of districts; the human resource dimensioning in each district; the assignment of visits to the operators or, alternatively, of patients to the operators under continuity of care; and the scheduling and routing problem. Among these issues, the assignment and the scheduling-routing represent the most important target of existing investigations.

In the HC context, several studies address human resource planning without continuity of care or with a partial continuity of care [2, 10, 11, 16, 22, 23, 42], without including the uncertainty of demands.

However, a few papers consider the importance of the continuity of care constraint. Borsani *et al.* study the scheduling of visits in two HC organizations operating under continuity of care. They propose an assignment model coupled to a scheduling model. The objective of the assignment is to ensure a workload balance among the operators while respecting qualification requirements and geographical coherence constraints [12]. Ben Bachouch *et al.* develop a mixed-integer linear programming model to minimize the total distance that is travelled by nurses. This model is subject to several constraints: visits' and nurses' time windows, nurses' meal breaks, continuity of care, the beginning and ending of each nurse's route at the HC facility and a limited maximum distance between two consecutive visits by the same nurse [9]. Hertz and Lahrichi propose two mixed programming models for allocating HC nurses to patients. One model consists of linear constraints and a quadratic objective function, while the other model includes nonlinear constraints and is solved by a Tabu search heuristic. Constraints related to maximum acceptable workloads and the assignment of each patient to exactly one nurse of each type are imposed. The objective of the assignment is to balance the nurses' workloads by minimizing a weighted sum of the number of visits provided, the assigned patients and the distances travelled. The possibility of assigning a patient to a nurse who does not work within the patient's district is considered [25]. Lanzarone *et al.* propose a set of linear programming models to balance the workloads of the operators; these models consider the distinctiveness of the HC services, such as the continuity of care, the skills of the operators and the geographical areas that patients and operators belong to [29]. In this last study, the uncertainty in the patients' demands is taken into account by means of different scenarios.

The importance of this research topic is also acknowledged by the large number of papers that propose solutions to the assignment and scheduling of nurses and medical staff in hospitals.

A bibliographic survey of the models and methodologies available to solve the nurse rostering problem is reported in Cheang *et al.* [17]. Burke *et al.* propose another literature review of the problem, discuss the strengths and weaknesses of the literature on the nurse rostering problem and outline the key issues to be addressed in the research [15]. Aickelin and White solve the nurse scheduling problem with an integer programming formulation and evolutionary algorithms. They also detail a statistical method for comparing and building better scheduling algorithms by identifying successful algorithm modifications [1]. Topaloglu present a goal programming model for scheduling emergency medicine residents that accommodates both hard and soft constraints with a monthly planning horizon [44]. Bard and Purnomo propose different methods for scheduling nurses: integer programming solved with a branch-and-price algorithm, a column generation approach that combines integer programming and heuristics, and integer programming decomposed using Lagrangian relaxation [5,6,38]. Belien and Demeulemeester present a model that integrates the scheduling of nurses and operating rooms; they also show how the column generation technique can easily address this model extension [8]. Punnakitikashem *et al.* develop a stochastic integer programming model for nurse assignments, including variability in the demands. This model is solved by a Benders' decomposition approach, with a greedy algorithm to solve the recourse subproblem [43]. De Grano *et al.* propose a two-stage approach for nurse scheduling that considers both nurse preferences and hospital constraints. At the auction stage, nurses bid for their preferred shifts and rest days, and an optimization model allocates shifts while taking into account preferences and hospital requirements; at the schedule completion stage, an optimization model allocates the unfilled shifts to the nurses who have not yet met their minimum required hours [21]. Sundaramoorthi *et al.* develop two numerical policies to make nurse-to-patient assignments when new patients are admitted during a shift: a heuristic policy and a partially-optimized policy that minimize the workload unbalancing among the nurses for the entire shift [40]. A recent review on nurse scheduling models is also reported in the chapter of Bard [4]. Brunner *et al.* focus their analysis on the extra overtime to be paid. They develop a mixed-integer program model for a flexible shift scheduling of physicians in a German hospital. The objective is to find an assignment that minimizes the total number of hours that have to be paid out as overtime [13]. They also present a method to solve the scheduling of physicians given flexible start times, variable shift lengths and overtime to cover the demand [14].

Finally, the problem of scheduling staff is largely addressed for years for different services (see, for example, [7,24]).

These analyses show that the problem has been addressed with numerical approaches, such as mathematical programming and column generation, while no attempts of formalizing structural policies can be found. Knowledge about the structure of optimal policies could be helpful for three major reasons: HC providers could easily apply simplified policies without referring to software applications; analytical policies could solve the problem with a limited computational effort, with the possibility to easily include the high variability of the demands; and the structure of an optimal policy could help the research for the optimum in heuristic-based algorithms.

With regard to the estimation of future patients' demands, the literature presents a certain number of studies about the development of stochastic models for representing patient conditions in health care systems [19,27,31–36,41]. However, none of them address HC systems.

8.2 Material and methods

8.2.1 Patient stochastic model

The approach described in the following allows to obtain estimates on the time for visits requested within a time frame and other variables of interest for the planning of a HC provider. The input variables of the patient stochastic model are the patient conditions, from admission into the HC service to their current condition, and information about care already delivered (e.g., patient classification and the amount and typology of visits provided). The model integrates a care pathway model and a cost model: the care pathway model describes the stochastic evolution of patient's conditions over time, and the cost model describes the time requested for the visits in a fixed period as a function of the specific care pathway.

The general technique to develop this model is described as a multi-step approach. It is a general methodology that could be adopted by many different HC providers. In Section 8.3.1, the application of the general approach to the analyzed HC provider is described.

- *Identification of state variables.* Patient conditions are described with the values assumed by a set of representative state variables (e.g., pathology, age and presence of a caregiver). Among the variables that are observable and measurable at low cost throughout the patient care pathway, statistical analyses on the historical data identify the significant variables affecting the care duration (*CD*) and the time spent for the provided visits. These significant variables $x_1, x_2, \dots, x_n$ are the state variables of the model and are included as the components of the model state vector **x**. Consequently, the care pathway is described as the sequence of values assumed by the state vector. Values of **x** are related to the patients under the charge, to the patients permanently discharged as a consequence of death or definitive recovery (state *End*) and to the patients temporarily discharged as a consequence of events such as a hospitalization period (state *Pause*).

- *Identification of patient classes.* Patients admitted to the HC service have different initial characteristics and, consequently, different care pathway evolutions. Hence, patients are classified based on their initial conditions. In practice, classification is usually simplified by the service refunding. Indeed, most national and regional policies require that HC providers group the patients into classes depending on the costs incurred in delivering the service. Thus, the already adopted classification can be adopted as is, or it can be considered as the starting point to classify patients for the model.
- *Development of the patient care pathway model.* The care pathway model consists of a stochastic process $X(k)$ that describes the sequence of values assumed by the state vector **x** during the care pathway. Starting from the initial value $\mathbf{x}(1)$, the state vector **x** is assumed to evolve in discrete time from day k to day $k+1$. The process is modelled as a Markov chain, in which the states are the possible values of **x**. These states are the same for all of the patients as well as the cost that is associated with each state, whereas the transition probabilities are differentiated based on the patient classification, with a specific transition probability matrix $P[p_{ij}]$ for each class. The transition probability matrix of each class is obtained from the historical data of patients according to a frequentist approach:

$$p_{ij} = \frac{n_{ij}}{d_i} \qquad i \neq j \qquad i \neq 0 \tag{8.1}$$

where p_{ij} is the transition probability from state $\mathbf{x}_i$ to state $\mathbf{x}_j$, n_{ij} is the total number of observed transitions from state $\mathbf{x}_i$ to state $\mathbf{x}_j$ and d_i is the total number of days spent by all of the patients of the class in the state $\mathbf{x}_i$. The case $i = j$ is derived considering $\Sigma_j p_{ij} = 1$. Different from the other states, the state *End* (named $\mathbf{x}_0$ with $i = 0$) is defined as an absorbent state.
The proposed Markov chain is homogeneous, i.e., the transition probabilities are assumed to be invariant with time; this assumption has already been reported in the literature [34]. A further assumption of Markovian modelling is the geometric distribution of sojourn times in the states. The accuracy of these assumptions depends on the specific application and must be evaluated during the validation process.
- *Validation of the pathway model.* The pathway model is cross-validated by analyzing the *CD* and the number of patients who are cared for over time.
- *Development of the cost model.* A cost in terms of the time requested for visits N_i in a fixed reference period is ascribed to each patient state $\mathbf{x}_i$. The empirical distribution of each N_i is defined from the historical data by adopting a frequentist approach: for each sojourn in state $\mathbf{x}_i$, N_i is obtained as the ratio between the time spent for visits during the sojourn and the days spent in state $\mathbf{x}_i$, scaled to the reference period. Conversely, states *End* and *Pause* are characterized by zero

visits. Moreover, it could be necessary to differentiate N_i based on the day the care was given (counted starting from the beginning of the care pathway). In this case, a specific distribution of N_i is considered for each group of days that is significant according to a statistical analysis. Hence, the probabilities $P[a \leq N_i < b|\alpha_i;\beta_i]$ are defined, indicating that the specific N_i distribution refers to a day of care $k \in [\alpha_i;\beta_i)$.
This procedure can be used to determine the time for visits received from a specific category of operator (e.g., nurse, physician) or the overall time of the visits received.

- *Validation of the entire model.* The entire model (patient pathway and cost) is cross-validated by analyzing the time for visits that is requested by a patient along his/her care pathway.

The variables of interest for human resource planning can be obtained from the model.

For each patient class, the state probability vector $\boldsymbol{\pi}(k) = [\pi_i(k)]$, which contains the probabilities of being in each state $\mathbf{x}_i$ on day k, allows for estimation of CD and the number n of patients in charge. In detail, the probability that $CD \leq k$, including temporary interruptions of care, is equal to $\pi_0(k+1)$; the expected number of patients $n(k)$ of the examined class still in charge after k days, not including new arrivals of patients, is equal to $n_0[1-\pi_0(k)]$, where n_0 is the initial number of patients in the class.

The state probability vector $\boldsymbol{\pi}(k)$ and the N_i distributions together allow for estimating the time for visits requested by a patient during his/her care pathway. The distribution of the time for visits $V(k)$ on day k (scaled to the reference period) is given by the weighted average of N_i distributions, where the weights are the probabilities $\pi_i(k)$.

The number of patients and the time for visits can be used for dimensioning the provider. With regard to the nurse-to-patient assignment, the model allows for predicting the individual nurse's workload once his/her set of assisted patients is defined. Hence, these estimates are the basis for developing algorithms that optimally manage human resources in HC organizations (such as the policies presented in the chapter).

8.2.2 Assignment policies

The policies address the assignment of a newly admitted patient to his/her *reference nurse* under stochastic patients' demands and nurses' workloads while respecting the continuity of care constraint. Among the possible nurses who are compatible in terms of skill and territory, the reference nurse of a patient is chosen in such a way that the variable costs of the HC provider are reduced. These costs depend on the visits that each nurse supplies in surplus to his/her capacity (in accordance with his/her working contract) and the increase in the surplus of visits. Hence, the policies assign a new patient to the reference nurse by considering the minimum increase in the variable costs that are sustained by the HC provider.

The following assumptions are introduced to derive the policies; they are consistent with the real situations of several HC providers [16].

The new patient must be assigned to only one reference nurse in the set $\boldsymbol{\Omega}$ of the compatible nurses. Each nurse $i \in \boldsymbol{\Omega}$ has a contract capacity υ_i that has been partially charged by the already allocated patients. This initial workload X_i, expressed as the time spent for visits, is modelled as a continuous positive stochastic variable with the probability density function $\Phi_i(x)$. This variable is assumed to be distributed as a triangular function characterized by a minimum value a_i, a modal value b_i, a maximum value c_i and asymmetry r_{bi}:

$$r_{bi} = \frac{b_i - a_i}{c_i - a_i}. \tag{8.2}$$

υ_i is assumed in the second part of the triangular distribution ($b_i < \upsilon_i < c_i$) for each nurse i because the other possibilities are not of interest for a practical application of an assignment policy.

The initial workload X_i of each nurse i and the demand Y of the newly admitted patient are assumed to be stationary in the planning period. This assumption leads us to consider planning horizons that are shorter than the evolution of patients' demands. For the majority of patients, this horizon is equal to one or two months.

The variable cost C_i related to the workload X_i of nurse i before the new assignment depends on the time for visits that he/she provides in surplus to the capacity υ_i:

$$C_i = \begin{cases} 0 & x_i \leq \upsilon_i \\ (x_i - \upsilon_i)^m & x_i > \upsilon_i \end{cases}. \tag{8.3}$$

C_i increases with the time for visits that exceeds the capacity ($m > 1$, with m assumed to be the same for all of the nurses of the provider). Therefore, minimizing the cost increase also corresponds to balancing the workloads allocated to the nurses, which is a goal that is pursued in practice. Hence, the policies assign the newly admitted patient to the nurse according to the lowest value of cost increase.

These policies are also graphically represented by considering nurses with the same r_{bi}. This situation is frequent in real HC providers, where the nurses of a district show very similar asymmetries in their workload densities. In this case, nurses are only characterized by a_i and c_i, and these parameters are expressed in terms of the time for visits that can be loaded (*assignable workload* $|\tilde{a}_i|$) or that exceed the capacity (*excess workload* $\tilde{c}_i$). In detail, $\tilde{a}_i$ is defined as $a_i - \upsilon_i$, and $\tilde{c}_i$ is defined as $c_i - \upsilon_i$.

Hence, in the plane $\{\tilde{c}_t; |\tilde{a}_t|\}$, each point of the admissible region that respects the relationships among the parameters corresponds to a nurse, while the policies are represented as curves dividing the admissible region in zones.

The cost increase is a random variable, and different criteria can be applied to minimize it. Therefore, the presented policies differ in the specific cost increase measure that they minimize: the maximum cost increase, the expected cost increase or the entire distribution of the cost increase.

- *Maximum cost policy.* For minimizing the maximum value that the cost increase can assume, the new patient must be assigned to the nurse i with the lowest value of the maximum cost C_i before the assignment. This relationship arises from the independence between the demand Y of the newly admitted patient and the workload X_i that is already assigned to each nurse i. The maximum C_i is assumed when $x_i = c_i$, which is independent of the new patient's demand.
Hence, the maximum cost policy states that, given two nurses i and j, the newly admitted patient must be assigned to nurse i if $c_i - v_i < c_j - v_j$ and vice versa. This policy generates two regions in the plane $\{\tilde{c}_t; |\tilde{a}_t|\}$: points j to the left of point i lead to assigning the new patient to nurse j and vice versa (Fig. 8.1A).
- *Stochastic order policy.* The minimization of the cost increase can be provided in terms of the entire probability density function, by means of stochastic order theory [39]. The lowest distribution of cost increase corresponds to the lowest distribution of cost before the assignment because of the independence between the demand Y of the newly admitted patient and the initial workload X_i of each nurse i. Therefore, in this case, the reference nurse is the nurse with the lowest cost distribution before the assignment, independent of the patient characteristics. We demonstrated the following policy: given two nurses i and j, $C_i \leq_{lr} C_j$ (i.e., C_i is smaller than C_j in the *likelihood stochastic order* [39]), and the newly admitted patient must be assigned to nurse i if the following holds:

$$\begin{cases} c_i - v_i \leq c_j - v_j \\ \frac{c_i - v_i}{r_i (c_i - a_i)^2} \leq \frac{c_j - v_j}{r_j (c_j - a_j)^2} \end{cases} \tag{8.4}$$

where $r_i = 1 - r_{bi} - r_{vi}^2$ and r_{vi} is the ratio $c_i - v_i$ to $c_i - a_i$.
In contrast, $C_j \leq_{lr} C_i$ and the newly admitted patient must be assigned to nurse j in the opposite case. In the remaining cases, no stochastic order is possible between the costs. This policy is represented in the plane $\{\tilde{c}_t; |\tilde{a}_t|\}$ by four regions and, in two of them, it is not possible to stochastically order the costs C_i and C_j (Fig. 8.1B).
- *Expected cost increase policy.* In this case, the assignment also depends on the new patient's demand Y (stochastic variable with probability density function $\Psi(y)$) and not only on the initial costs C_i.
The expected cost increase $\Delta\bar{C}_i$ of a nurse is obtained as the difference between the expected costs after and before the analyzed assignment. The expected cost $\bar{C}_i$ before the assignment is derived from its probability density function, which is obtained by including $\Phi_i(x)$ in equation (8.3). Then, if the new patient is assigned to nurse i, the probability density function of the new workload after the assignment is determined by the convolution between $\Phi_i(x)$ and $\Psi(y)$, the probability density function of the new cost is derived, and the expected new cost is extracted.
Therefore, the expected cost increase policy states that, given two nurses i and j, the newly admitted patient is assigned to nurse i if $\Delta\bar{C}_i < \Delta\bar{C}_j$ or to nurse j if $\Delta\bar{C}_j < \Delta\bar{C}_i$. However, $\Delta\bar{C}_i$ strongly depends on m and the shape of $\Psi(y)$; hence, it is not possible to obtain a general expression that is valid in all of the cases.

For a representative case, the policy is derived and graphically reported in the case $m = 2$ and Y uniformly distributed between a minimum value α and a maximum value β (Fig. 8.1C). In this case, two regions are generated in the plane $\{\tilde{c}_t; |\tilde{a}_t|\}$, and the choice is to assign the new patient to nurse j in the upper left region, while the patient is assigned to nurse i in the lower right region. The separation between the regions also depends on α and β, with a part within each region where the choice is independent of Y (gray regions).

Detailed demonstrations of these policies can be found in Lanzarone *et al.* [28].

The same assignment is provided by all of the policies in most of the cases (see Fig. 8.1). However, even if the stochastic order policy is the most robust approach, it cannot be applied in a part of the plane and, in this part, there is a region where the choice is different between the two other policies. Hence, for a practical application, the choice should be between the maximum cost policy and the expected cost policy. We suggest adopting the maximum cost policy because it is independent from m and the new patient's demands.

The policies assign one patient at a time. Therefore, a simple rule that is coherent with the adopted policy must be coupled along with it to choose the assignment order for the case in which more than one patient must be assigned at the same time. This situation is frequent in the real practice of middle/large HC providers, where a certain number of patients are admitted into the service on each day. In this case, the index k referring to each newly admitted patient is introduced, and new patients are ranked according to their criticality for the HC provider. After having identified the best nurse for each new patient k, the first patient assigned is the one that determines the highest cost increase (according to the adopted policy). Then, this ranking process is repeated for the remaining new patients.

8.2.2.1 Comparison with the current practice of HC providers

HC providers usually neglect the variability of future demands, and new patients are assigned to the nurse with the smallest utilization value scaled to his/her capacity. We model this practice with the approach of the policies. The newly admitted patient is assigned to the nurse i with the highest expected available capacity W_i, given by the difference between the capacity v_i and the expected workload, extracted from the triangular density function $\Phi_i(x)$:

$$W_i = v_i - \frac{a_i + b_i + c_i}{3}. \tag{8.5}$$

Additionally, this case is graphically represented in the plane $\{\tilde{c}_t; |\tilde{a}_t|\}$, with two regions (see Fig. 8.1D). When more than one patient must be assigned, new patients are ranked starting with the patient with the highest expected demand.

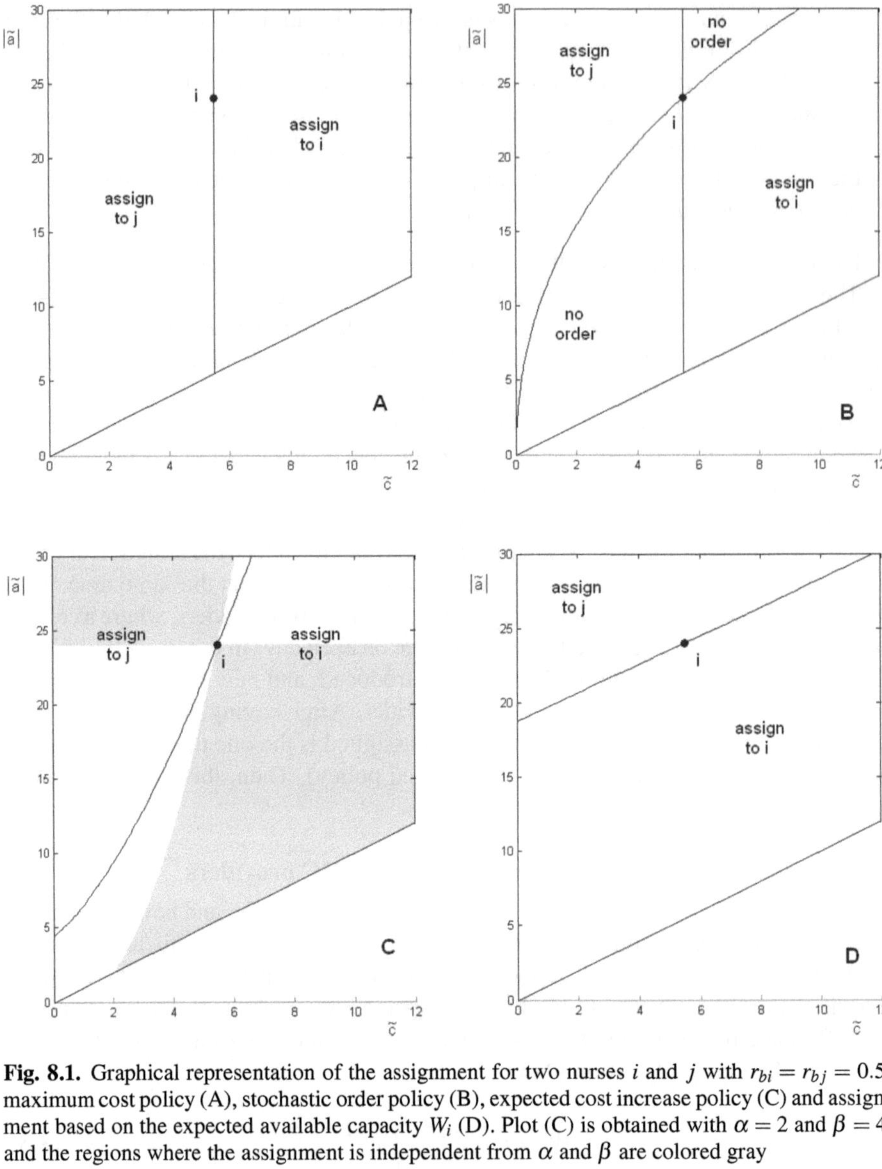

Fig. 8.1. Graphical representation of the assignment for two nurses i and j with $r_{bi} = r_{bj} = 0.5$: maximum cost policy (A), stochastic order policy (B), expected cost increase policy (C) and assignment based on the expected available capacity W_i (D). Plot (C) is obtained with $\alpha = 2$ and $\beta = 4$, and the regions where the assignment is independent from α and β are colored gray

8.3 Results and discussion

The presented policies and the patient stochastic model are validated and evaluated in the real case of one of the largest Italian public HC providers. This provider operates in the north of Italy and covers a region of approximately 800 km^2, with approximately 1,000 patients assisted at a given time by 50 nurses. The provider pursues continuity of care; therefore, each newly admitted patient is assigned to only one ref-

Table 8.1. The *CD* mean value, standard deviation and skewness averaged on the ten random splits, for the six most important FCPs in terms of the requested workload. FCP = 1 refers to the extemporary care, FCP = 6 to the palliative care and the others to the integrated Home Care (Reproduced with permission from [30])

	FCP = 1	*FCP = 3*	*FCP = 4*	*FCP = 5*	*FCP = 6*	*FCP = 9*
Mean – *Set A*	205.26	169.32	159.81	195.36	57.48	184.04
Mean – *Set B*	206.98	171.99	162.39	193.16	58.49	184.98
Standard deviation – *Set A*	237.03	206.60	192.32	230.11	83.27	254.38
Standard deviation – *Set B*	283.52	252.50	221.75	267.07	106.54	272.15
Skewness – *Set A*	2.31	2.48	2.59	2.31	4.12	2.46
Skewness – *Set B*	1.90	2.83	2.40	2.28	5.62	2.21

erence nurse. The skill of the nurses (patients and nurses are divided into palliative care and non-palliative care) and their territorial distribution are taken into account in the assignment.

8.3.1 Patient stochastic model

The patient stochastic model is applied to the analyzed HC provider, considering the historical data of 7,277 assisted patients. First, the general approach for developing the model is applied to this case, and then, the model that is obtained is cross-validated.

8.3.1.1 Application of the model

The analyzed provider includes 14 CPs that are related to as many cost levels and are grouped into three main categories of service (extemporary, integrated and palliative care). CPs related to the palliative care refer to a homogeneous class of terminal patients who have terminal-state pathology. CPs related to the extemporary and integrated care refer to non-palliative patients, and each CP includes a large range of patients in terms of age, pathology and social context.

Statistical analyses suggested to consider the CP as the only state variable of the Markov chain. Hence, the state vector is reduced to a scalar, which is the CP, and the state space includes 16 values (the 14 CPs, together with states *End* and *Pause*). The set of CPs is also used to build the patient classification according to the provider practice. Specifically, the classification is based only on the initial patient characteristics, and the patients are consequently classified according to their First CP (FCP). Thus, 14 classes are included in the model.

The model is then developed using the described frequentist approach. A detailed report of the transition probability matrices and the cost distributions of the states can be found in Lanzarone *et al.* [30].

8.3.1.2 Validation of the model

The model is validated in two steps with a random sub-sampling cross-validation, performed by randomly splitting the historical data into two sets ten times. For each split, data from the training *Set A* are used to develop the model, while data from the testing *Set B* are used to verify it. The validation analysis is reported for the six most important FCPs in terms of workload. These FCPs include 5,973 patients among the 7,277 analyzed patients and cover approximately 86% of the total workload.

The first validation concerns only the care pathway model. The results show a good superposition between the model outcomes of *Set A* and the real data of *Set B*: the *CD* mean value is reproduced well by the model, as well as the skewness (Table 8.1). The Markov chain also captures the high variability of the data, even if the *CD* standard deviation is always lower in *Set A*.

The second validation concerns the entire model, considering the total time for visits requested for all of the operator categories. The results are analyzed by means of the scatter plots of the expected total time for visits requested by a patient during the time. The ordinate values of the points are computed from *Set A*, while the abscissa values are the corresponding data in *Set B*. The plots for the six most important FCPs are reported in Figure 8.2: a cloud of points is obtained on the diagonal, showing the superposition between the model outcomes and the provider historical data.

8.3.2 Assignment policies

The performances of the policies are evaluated by analyzing the activity of the provider over a period of 26 weeks, following the period over which the data used for the patient stochastic model are obtained. The provider is divided into three separate divisions, and the largest division consists of six independent districts (one for each combination of skill and territory). The analysis is provided in four of these districts, where more than one nurse is allocated: NPA (non-palliative care in territory A – 8 nurses), NPB (non-palliative care in territory B – 4 nurses), NPC (non-palliative care in territory C – 5 nurses) and PA (palliative care in territory A – 3 nurses).

8.3.2.1 Experimental setup

An initial assignment of the reference nurse is performed at the initial week (named week 0) for all of the patients in charge, while the other assignments are performed rolling from weeks 1 to 25: at the beginning of each week, the new patients admitted in the service during the previous week are assigned. Experiments are conducted with three types of assignments: *MC* (according to the maximum cost policy), *EC* (according to the expected cost increase policy with $m = 2$ and Y uniformly distributed) and *EAC* (following the current practice of HC providers).

The weekly arrivals of new patients are taken from the historical data of the provider, in terms of patient numbers and patients' classes for each district, while their demand distributions are estimated by means of the patient stochastic model reported in Section 8.2.1. The current data of each patient are used as input to the

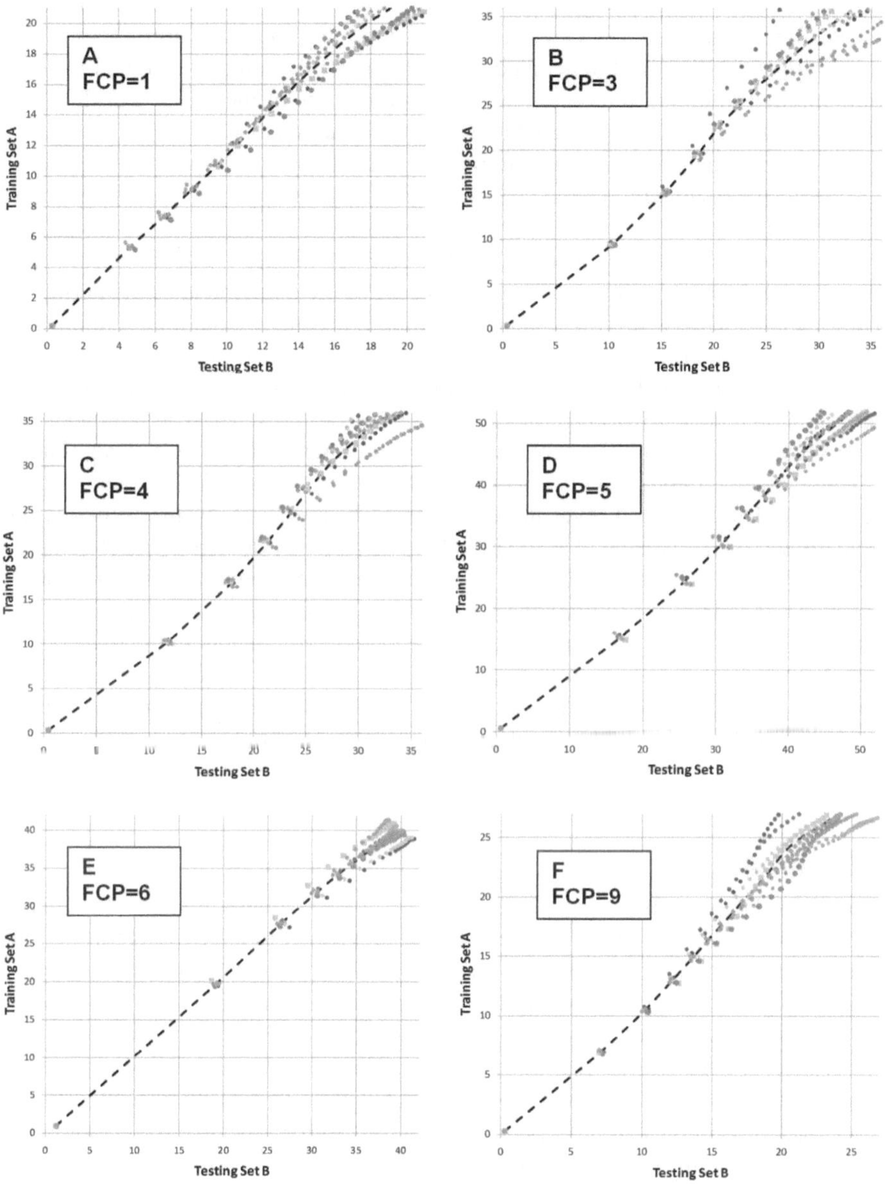

Fig. 8.2. Scatter plots of the cumulative number of visits for the six most important FCPs. The points of each random split are reported, while the line represents the average of the values among the splits. The values are plotted every 30 days for a better visualization, even if each day is considered in the model (Reproduced with permission from [30])

patient model, thus obtaining estimates of patients' demands in terms of empirical density functions. Estimates of each new patient k are used for fitting the uniform density function $\Psi(y)$ of the demand Y. Estimates of the already assigned patients are combined to obtain the empirical density functions of the initial workloads X_i for each nurse i, which are then fitted to derive parameters a_i and c_i (assuming $r_{bi} = 0.467$ for each nurse i based on the data collected from the provider). Specific expedients are assumed to include cases of operators that exit from the assumptions of the policies.

The initialization at week 0 does not follow the hypotheses of the policies. Hence, only at week 0, assignments are provided for all of the experiments considering all of the patients as new arrivals, using the empirical density functions without any fitting and minimizing the expected cost increase with $m = 2$.

In each experiment, the results are obtained in terms of the newly provided assignments and the planned workload of each nurse at each week. These assignments are then executed in a set of 30 sample paths, generated with a Monte Carlo approach.

These executed assignments are evaluated in terms of the workload and cost for the nurses. The workload level indicator for each nurse i along the weeks is the mean utilization $\bar{u}_i$, calculated as the ratio between the workload provided by nurse i and his/her υ_i in each week, averaged from weeks 1 to 25. Hence, a first performance indicator is the range of $\bar{u}_i$ among the operators of a district (named Z). This indicator denotes the workload balancing performance of the assignments in the district: for a stricter value of Z that is obtained, the greater is the workload balancing that is accomplished. A second performance indicator is the total variable cost TC of nurses who belong to a district; it is computed as the sum of the variable costs of each nurse who belongs to the district, from weeks 1 to 25, averaged over the same nurses (with $m = 2$).

8.3.2.2 Results

A total of 1,046 patients are present in the division: 581 patients are under the charge of nurses at week 0, while 465 are assigned from weeks 1 to 25. Results for the four analyzed districts of the division are reported in Table 8.2. *MC* and *EC* show very similar Z and TC for all of the districts (overlapped confidence intervals). Moreover, *MC* and *EC* guarantee a significantly better workload balance and a lower total cost with respect to *EAC* for non-palliative patients. With regard to the palliative patients, *EAC* also guarantees a comparable workload balance. This result is related to the lower variability of the palliative patients' demands with respect to the other patients' demands. Therefore, in the last case, the benefit of considering uncertainty in the nurse assignment problem is not significant.

Table 8.2. Z and TC for the three experiments, executed in 30 sample paths (mean value ± half-width 95% confidence interval). The normality of the data is assessed with the Anderson-Darling test

District	*Variable*	*MC*	*EC*	*EAC*
NPA	Z	0.2790 ± 0.0226	0.2901 ± 0.0244	0.4552 ± 0.0245
	TC	211.45 ± 29.55	198.19 ± 25.65	353.47 ± 42.65
NPB	Z	0.3060 ± 0.0463	0.3245 ± 0.0377	0.5761 ± 0.0430
	TC	762.58 ± 105.25	772.85 ± 109.45	1577.99 ± 188.70
NPC	Z	0.1704 ± 0.0231	0.2151 ± 0.0282	0.3777 ± 0.0283
	TC	510.34 ± 70.45	564.13 ± 90.20	776.79 ± 92.10
PA	Z	0.2904 ± 0.0429	0.3629 ± 0.0414	0.3285 ± 0.0457
	TC	102.25 ± 35.15	115.42 ± 37.80	138.37 ± 43.05

8.4 Conclusions

In this chapter, we propose a general approach for solving the nurse-to-patient assignment problem in HC under continuity of care. This problem is a crucial aspect of HC planning that deeply influences all of the planning levels and affects the dimensioning of the providers.

The proposed methodology of coupling a patient stochastic model to an assignment policy provides useful instruments and yields good results when applied to a representative HC provider.

First, the methodology allows the development of a tool for automatically assigning patients to operators. In contrast, in the majority of HC providers, the assignment problem is still solved by hand. Specifically, in the analyzed HC provider, this tool has been inserted into the management software and is currently adopted by planners to assign patients and to evaluate the workload of the nurses.

Moreover, the inclusion of patient demand variability into the entire process proved to increase the quality of the assignment for non-palliative patients who have a very high variability of the care pathway evolution and demand. In fact, the proposed policy allows us to exploit the benefits derived from considering this variability. In contrast, it is not possible to fully include this variability in numerical approaches such as stochastic programming because of the extremely high number of scenarios to be solved simultaneously [29].

Finally, the analyzed HC provider is representative of a general class of providers [16, 18, 37] in terms of organization and resource planning; therefore, the proposed approach and the implemented tool can be considered general and applicable to other similar structures and can be expected to have similar favourable results.

References

1. Aickelin, U., White, P.: Building better nurse scheduling algorithms. Ann. Oper. Res. **128**, 159–177 (2004)
2. Akjiratikarl, C., Yenradee, P., Drake, P.R.: PSO–based algorithm for home care worker scheduling in the UK. Comput. Ind. Eng. **53**(4), 559–583 (2007)
3. American Geriatrics Society AGS: Geriatric healthcare statistics: Demography of aging. In: Reported resources – Statistics (2006)
4. Bard, J.F.: Nurse Scheduling Models. In: Cochran, J.J. *et al.* (eds.) Wiley Encyclopedia of Operations Research and Management Science, Topic 4.3. Medicine and Health Care **5**, 3617–3627, John Wiley & Sons, New York (2010)
5. Bard, J.F., Purnomo, H.W.: Preference scheduling for nurses using column generation. Eur. J. Oper. Res. **164**(2), 510–534 (2005)
6. Bard, J.F., Purnomo, H.W.: Cyclic preference scheduling of nurses using a Lagrangian-based heuristic. J. Scheduling **10**(1), 5–23 (2007)
7. Beaumont, N.: Scheduling staff using mixed integer programming. Eur. J. Oper. Res. **98**(3), 473–484 (1997)
8. Belien, J., Demeulemeester, E.: A branch-and-price approach for integrating nurse and surgery scheduling. Eur. J. Oper. Res. **189**(3), 652–668 (2008)
9. Ben Bachouch, R., Fakhfakh, M., Guinet, A., Hajri-Gabouj, S.: Planification de la tournée des infirmiers dans une structure de soins à domicile. Proceedings of the IV Conférence Francophone en Gestion et Ingénierie des SystèmEs Hospitaliers GISEH2008 (2008)
10. Bennett, A.R., Erera, A.L.: Dynamic periodic fixed appointment scheduling for home health. IIE Transactions on Healthcare Systems Engineering **1**(1), 6–19 (2011)
11. Bertels, S., Fahle, T.: A hybrid setup for a hybrid scenario: combining heuristics for the home health care problem. Comput. Oper. Res. **33**(10), 2866–2890 (2006)
12. Borsani, V., Matta, A., Beschi, G., Sommaruga, F.: A home care scheduling model for human resources. Proceedings of the International Conference on Service Systems and Service Management ICSSSM06, 449–454 (2006)
13. Brunner, J.O., Bard, J.F., Kolisch, R.: Flexible shift scheduling of physicians. Health Care Manag. Sci. **12**(3), 285–305 (2009)
14. Brunner, J.O., Bard, J.F., Kolisch, R.: Midterm scheduling of physicians with flexible shifts using branch and price. IIE Trans. **43**(2), 84–109 (2011)
15. Burke, E.K., De Causmaecker, P., Berghe, G.V., Van Landeghem, H.: The state of the art of nurse rostering. J. Scheduling **7**(6), 441–499 (2004)
16. Chahed, S., Marcon, E., Sahin, E., Feillet, D., Dallery, Y.: Exploring new operational research opportunities within the home care context: the chemotherapy at home. Health Care Manag. Sci. **12**(2), 179–191 (2009)
17. Cheang, B., Li, H., Lim, A., Rodrigues, B.: Nurse rostering problems – a bibliographic survey. Eur. J. Oper. Res. **151**(1), 447–460 (2003)
18. Chevreul, K., Com-Ruelle, L., Midy, F., Paris, V.: The development of hospital care at home: an investigation of Australian, British and Canadian experiences. Istitute de recherce et documentation en économie de la santé (IRDES) 1610 (2005)
19. Congdon, P.: The development of Gravity models for hospital patient flows under system change: a Bayesian modelling approach. Health Care Manag. Sci. **4**(4), 289–304 (2001)
20. Cordes, C., Dougherty, T.: A review and an integration of research on job burnout. Academy of Management Review **18**(4), 621–656 (1993)
21. De Grano, M.L., Medeiros, D.G., Eitel, D.: Accommodating individual preferences in nurse scheduling via auctions and optimization. Health Care Manag. Sci. **12**(3), 228–242 (2009)
22. Eveborn, P., Flisberg, P., Ronnqvist, M.: LAPS CARE – an operational system for staff planning of home care. Eur. J. Oper. Res. **171**(3), 962–976 (2006)
23. Eveborn, P., Ronnqvist, M., Einarsdóttir, H., Eklund, M., Lidén, K., Almroth, M.: Operations research improves quality and efficiency in home care. Interfaces **39**(1), 18–34 (2009)
24. Gamache, M., Soumis, F., Marquis, G., Desrosier, J.: A column generation approach for large-scale aircrew rostering problems. Oper. Res. **47**(2), 247–263 (1999)

25. Hertz, A., Lahrichi, N.: A patient assignment algorithm for home care services. J. Oper. Res. Soc. **60**(4), 481–495 (2009)
26. Kellogg, D.L., Walczak, S.: Nurse scheduling: from academia to implementation or not? Interfaces **37**(4), 355–369 (2007)
27. Koizumi, N., Kuno, E., Smith, T.E.: Modelling patient flows using a queuing network with blocking. Health Care Manag. Sci. **8**(1), 49–60 (2005)
28. Lanzarone, E., Matta, A.: Stochastic nurse assignment in home care services under continuity of care. Under review (2011)
29. Lanzarone, E., Matta, A., Sahin, E.: Operations Management Applied to Home Care Services: the Problem of assigning Human Resources to Patients (2011). Under review
30. Lanzarone, E., Matta, A., Scaccabarozzi, G.: A patient stochastic model to support human resource panning in home care. Prod. Plan. Control **21**(1), 3–25 (2010)
31. Marshall, A.H., Mc Clean, S.I.: Using coxian phase-type distributions to identify patient characteristics for duration of stay in hospital. Health Care Manag. Sci. **7**(4), 285–289 (2004)
32. Marshall, A.H., Mc Clean, S.I., Shapcott, C.M., Millard, P.H.: Modelling patient duration of stay to facilitate resource management of geriatric hospitals. Health Care Manag. Sci. **5**(4), 313–319 (2002)
33. Marshall, A., Vasilakis, C., El-Darzi, E.: Length of stay-based patient flow models: recent developments and future directions. Health Care Manag. Sci. **8**(3), 213–220 (2005)
34. Mc Clean, S.I., Mc Alea, B., Millard, P.H.: Using a Markov reward model to estimate spend-down costs for a geriatric department. J. Oper. Res. Soc. **49**(10), 1021–1025 (1998)
35. Mc Clean, S.I., Millard, P.H.: A three compartment model of the patient flows in a geriatric department: a decision support approach. Health Care Manag. Sci. **1**(2), 159–163 (1998)
36. Mc Clean, S.I., Millard, P.H.: Where to treat the older patient? Can Markov models help us better understand the relationship between hospital and community care? J. Oper. Res. Soc. **58**(2), 255–261 (2007)
37. Medicare Payment Advisory Commission MEDPAC: Home health services (Chapter 8). In: Report to the Congress: medicare payment policy (2011)
38. Purnomo, H.W., Bard, J.F.: Cyclic preference scheduling for nurses using branch and price. Nav. Res. Log. **54**(2), 200–220 (2007)
39. Shaked, M., Shanthikumar, J.G.: Stochastic orders. Springer Series in Statistics. Springer, New York (2007)
40. Sundaramoorthi, D., Chen, V.C., Rosenberger, J.M., Kim, S.B., Buckley-Behan, D.F.: A data-integrated simulation-based optimization for assigning nurses to patient admissions. Health Care Manag. Sci. **13**(3), 210–221
41. Taylor, G.J., Mc Clean, S.I., Millard, P.H.: Stochastic models of geriatric patient bed occupancy behaviour. J. R. Statist. Soc. A **163**(part 1), 39–48 (2000)
42. Thomsen, K.: Optimization on home care. Thesis in Informatics and Mathematical Modeling, Technical University of Denmark (2006)
43. Punnakitikashem, P., Rosenberger, J., Behan, D.: Stochastic programming for nurse assignment. Comput. Optim. Appl. **40**(3), 321–349 (2008)
44. Topaloglu, S.: A multi-objective programming model for scheduling emergency medicine residents. Comp. Ind. Eng. **51**(3), 375–388 (2006)
45. Woodward, C.A., Abelson, J., Tedford, S., Hutchison, B.: What is important to continuity in home care? Perspectives of key stakeholders. Soc. Sci. Med. **58**(1), 177–192 (2004)

Chapter 9

Prioritizing health care interventions: A multicriteria resource allocation model to inform the choice of community care programmes

Mónica D. Oliveira, Teresa C. Rodrigues, Carlos A. Bana e Costa, and Armando Brito de Sá

Abstract. Many countries, including Portugal, are currently dealing with budget cuts and a shortage of resources in the health sector, while the demand for health care services is increasing. The Group of Health Centres (GHC) of Northern Lisbon faces the challenge of prioritizing community care programmes in order to decide which programmes to fund. We describe the development with the GHC of a *Multi-criteria model to allocate human resources in community care programmes* (MARCCO). Building MARCCO was a socio-technical process using multi-criteria decision analysis (MCDA) in a decision conferencing environment. The GHC used the results obtained by MARCCO to select programmes and to redesign its information system. MARCCO contributes to the literature by showing how a constructive approach using MCDA methods and decision conferencing is an alternative to conventional approaches used in the prioritization of interventions in the health care sector.

Keywords: resource allocation, portfolio decision analysis, multicriteria analysis, primary care

---

M.D. Oliveira
CEG-IST, Centre for Management Studies of Instituto Superior Técnico, Av. Rovisco Pais, 1049-001 Lisbon, Portugal
e-mail: monica.oliveira@ist.utl.pt

T.C. Rodrigues (✉)
CEG-IST, Centre for Management Studies of Instituto Superior Técnico, Av. Rovisco Pais, 1049-001 Lisbon, Portugal
e-mail: teresacrodrigues@ist.utl.pt

C.A. Bana e Costa
CEG-IST, Centre for Management Studies of Instituto Superior Técnico, Av. Rovisco Pais, 1049-001 Lisbon, Portugal
e-mail: carlosbana@ist.utl.pt

A. Brito de Sá
Institute of Preventive Medicine, Faculty of Medicine, University of Lisbon, Av. Prof. Egas Moniz, 1649-028 Lisbon, Portugal
e-mail: abritosa@fm.ul.pt

Tànfani E., Testi A. (Eds.): Advanced Decision Making Methods Applied to Health Care.
International Series in Operations Research & Management Science 173
DOI 10.1007/978-88-470-2321-5_9, © Springer-Verlag Italia 2012

9.1 Introduction and problem addressed

Many countries, and Portugal in particular, are currently dealing with budget cuts and a shortage of resources in the health sector, while the demand for health care services is increasing. This calls for transparent prioritization of health care interventions by carefully balancing their multiple costs and benefits [21]. There is a clear "need for multi-criteria decision analysis" [3] (MCDA) and decision conferencing [23] to support resource allocation in health care organizations. In fact, the use of MCDA and decision conferencing within a "socio-technical process improves communication within the organisation, develops shared understanding of the portfolio and generates a sense of common purpose about those projects that will best realise the organisation's objectives" [24]. Previous studies have already shown the usefulness of MCDA to help prioritize health care interventions [3,22].

Based on a national health service (NHS) structure created in 1979, the Portuguese health care system is defined as universal, nearly free at the point of use and funded by general taxation [2]. The first level of contact in the NHS is primary care, which has been undergoing major reforms since 2005. Groups of health centres (GHC) were organized in 2008 to promote quality and equity of access and reorganize the existing health centres (HC) into operative divisions with complementary responsibilities [25]. This was followed by the creation of a community care division (CCD) in each HC, responsible for providing health care services and health education, offering both social and psychological services to people, families, vulnerable and risk groups and handicapped people with physical and functional dependence [20]. In 2010, each of the four HCs of the Northern Lisbon GHC started the process of creating their own CCD. The first step was developing an action plan consisting of several community care programmes to be appraised by the GHC board. Preliminary analysis of the four action plans showed that it was not realistic to implement all the proposed programmes, because of a shortage of financial and human resources, nurses in particular. Programmes thus had to be chosen and others discarded within each action plan. A common framework to appraise costs and benefits of the programmes was necessary. The authors suggested to the GHC board a socio-technical approach using MCDA [11] to construct a ***M**ulti-criteria model to **a**llocate human **r**esources in **c**ommunity care pro**g**rammes* (MARCCO).

9.2 Materials and methods: Building MARCCO

9.2.1 Activities and methods

MARCCO was the result of a socio-technical process framed within a multicriteria resource allocation model [24] structured and built with the decision-making group (DM) – the members of the Clinical Board and the Executive Director of the Northern Lisbon GHC – in a sequence of decision conferences during which the group was involved in the model building activities depicted in Figure 9.1. Decision conferencing is a process, guided by a neutral facilitator, that helps DM to built a computer-

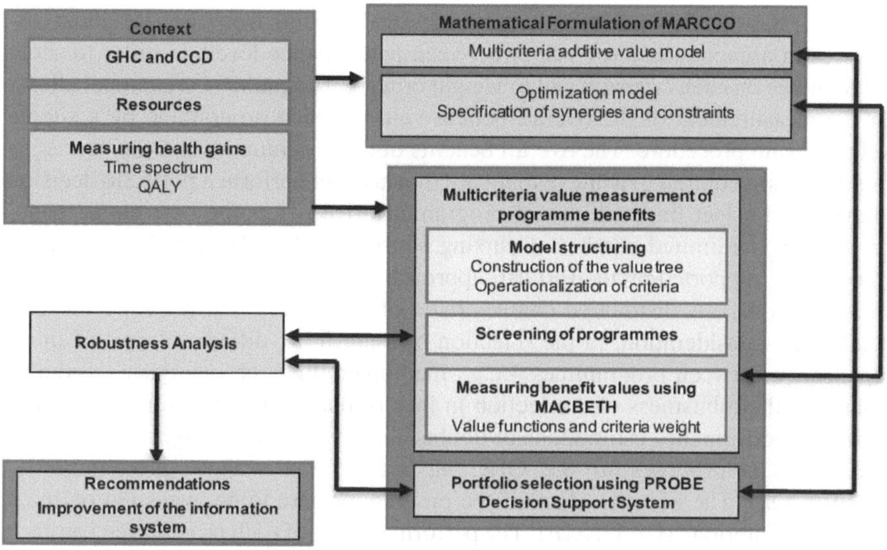

Fig. 9.1. Activities developed to build MARCCO

based model, on-the-spot, that reflects the collective view of the group [23,24]. The role of the facilitator is to guide the group during the construction of the model, providing structure to the group's tasks, but abstaining from contributing to the content of discussions [23]. This socio-technical process allows the DM to develop a shared understanding of the issues, generate a sense of common purpose, and gain commitment in the way forward and confidence in model results [23,45].

The group started by discussing the specificities of the GHC/CCD decision context and concluded that the key resource constraining the approval of all proposed programmes was the shortage of nursing hours available in each HC. Strategic objectives of the Northern Lisbon GHC for which community care programmes should contribute and corresponding criteria for benefit evaluation were specified and structured in a value tree (see Fig. 9.2). The next activity consisted of associating with each criterion a measure of the extent to which the criterion can be satisfied, from a most attractive to a least attractive level of performance. This measure is called a descriptor of performance and can be a quantitative indicator or a qualitative scale (see Table 9.1), depending on which is most adequate to describe programme performance, "because the more objectively performance is appraised, the better understood (less ambiguous) and therefore the more accepted (less controversial) the evaluation model will be" [10]. Two reference levels were identified in each descriptor: "good" (unquestionably attractive benefit) and "neutral" (neither attractive nor unattractive). They are not necessarily the most and least attractive levels of the descriptor, although this may sometimes be the case (as in Table 9.1).

The multicriteria method MACBETH (***M**easuring **a**ttractiveness by a **c**ategorical **b**ased **e**valuation **t**ec**h**nique* [7, 8]) and its software (M-MACBETH [4, 6]) were used to construct the multicriteria evaluation model. A distinctive characteristic of

MACBETH is that it requires only qualitative judgements from the DM about differences in attractiveness (or value) between performance levels in order to score programmes on each criterion and to weight criteria. The multicriteria model allows for the measurement of the overall benefit value of each programme by a simple weighted sum procedure. The overall benefits of the programmes and the "costs" in nursing hours required to achieve them are then used to perform a portfolio decision analysis and select the portfolio of programmes that offers the best global benefit value for the limited number of nursing hours available. The portfolio selection process was supported by the PROBE approach and software (***P**ortfolio **rob**ustness **e**valuation* [19]). A distinctive characteristic of PROBE is that it allows the DM to take into consideration, in the selection of a portfolio, different forms of interdependence between programmes – e.g., incompatibilities or synergies – and also to analyse the robustness of a selection in face of uncertainty phenomena (such as imprecise performance estimations or doubts about values and weights).

Each CCD proposes to the GHC an action plan with m programmes j $(j = 1,\ldots,m)$. The benefit values of the programmes are to be evaluated on the n evaluation criterion i $(i = 1,\ldots,n)$. The performance x_{ij} of each programme j on each benefit criterion i is measured by one level of the respective descriptor X_i. The partial value of j on i is measured by converting x_{ij} into a value score $v_i(x_{ij})$ by a value function constructed with MACBETH, such that $v_i(neutral_i) = 0$ and $v_i(good_i) = 100$. On the other hand, the comparison, with MACBETH, of the differences between $good_i$ and $neutral_i$ $(i = 1,\ldots,n)$ of the several criteria allowed the DM to assign a weight k_i to each criterion i. In this way, the common critical mistake [17] was avoided, i.e., "the attempt to assign weights that reflect the 'importance' of the criteria without reference to any considerations of ranges on the value scales and how much each one of those ranges matters to the decision-maker" [24]. The activities of scoring and weighting are further described in Section 9.2.2.

Consider a proposed programme j with benefits $x_{1j},\ldots,x_{ij},\ldots,x_{nj}$ $(i = 1,\ldots,n)$. The overall benefit value v_j of that programme j is determined by the multicriteria additive value model defined in Equation (9.1):

$$v_j(x_{1j},\ldots,x_{nj}) = \Sigma_{i=1}^{n} k_i v_i(x_{ij}), \quad \text{with } \Sigma_{i=l}^{n} k_i = 1 \text{ and } k_i > 0 \ (i = 1,\ldots,n). \quad (9.1)$$

The use of the additive model (9.1) should acknowledge that the difference independence condition is respected, i.e., the difference in attractiveness between performance levels on each criterion can be measured independently of the performance levels on the rest of the criteria, this being considered a working hypothesis in the model building process [5, 18].

Would the overall value of a proposed programme result negative from model (9.1), the programme would be globally unattractive and therefore should be screened out and sent back to the CCD to be revised and resubmitted. Consequently, the baseline to screen for programmes that need to be revised is a hypothetical programme that is neutral in all criteria [9, 12]. For simplicity of exposition and without loss of generality, we assume that each programme $j(j = 1,\ldots,m)$ has $v_j > 0$ and "costs" c_j

of nursing hours; and this information will enter the MARCCO resource allocation process.

Let B designate the total number of hours available. Assume that B is not fixed and can vary within a certain range. The best portfolio of programmes, that is the one offering the highest global benefit under these conditions, can be found by solving the basic optimization problem (9.2) (such that $l_j = 1$ if programme j is included in the best portfolio and zero otherwise):

$$\begin{aligned} \text{maximize: } & \sum\nolimits_{j=1}^{m} v_j l_j \\ \text{subject to: } & \sum\nolimits_{j=1}^{m} c_j l_j \leq B \\ & l_j \in \{0.1\}, j = 1, \ldots, m. \end{aligned} \tag{9.2}$$

Other (linear) constraints enabling model interdependencies between programmes can be added to model (9.2). For example: programme j must be chosen given past commitments ($l_j = 1$); j cannot be carried out this year ($l_j = 0$); j can only be chosen if programme h is also selected ($l_j - l_h \leq 0$); j and h need to be implemented simultaneously ($l_j - l_h = 0$), or the opposite ($l_j + l_h \leq 1$). It is also possible to take into account restrictions in other type of resources, for instance, other human resources such as nutritionists, physiatrists, etc. Let h_{kj} represent the hours of a human resource k consumed by programme j and H_k the total number of hours of k that are available. This restriction can be considered in the selection by simple adding to the basic model (9.2) the linear constraint $\sum_{j=1}^{m} h_{kj} l_j \leq H_k$.

9.2.2 Building MARCCO at the GHC

The DM agreed that the evaluation and selection of programmes should consider the HC core objective of maximizing health gains and also other benefit dimensions, as specified in the value tree in Figure 9.2. Several of these dimensions are interdependent and were therefore clustered together, giving rise to four evaluation criteria defined as follows: a) *Effective health gains* (the extent to which a programme provides health gains to the population covered by the programme); b) *Equity* (the extent to which a programme contributes to equity improvements); c) *Achievement of GHC goals* (the extent to which a programme contributes to the achievement of goals agreed with the Lisbon and Tagus Valley Regional Health Authority); and d) *Agreement with the portfolio of services and the community* (the extent to which a programme belongs to the services to be delivered to the community and is essential according to the most pressing needs of the community).

A descriptor of performance was associated with each of these criteria. For example, performance on *Effective health gains* is measured by a quantitative product index defined by multiplying the predicted health gain, measured in quality adjusted life years (QALYs), by the effective population and by the (percentage) level of accomplishment of objectives (a similar procedure was used in [1]). *Good* and *neutral* levels of *Effective health gains* were defined as 50 and 0 QALYs, respectively. On

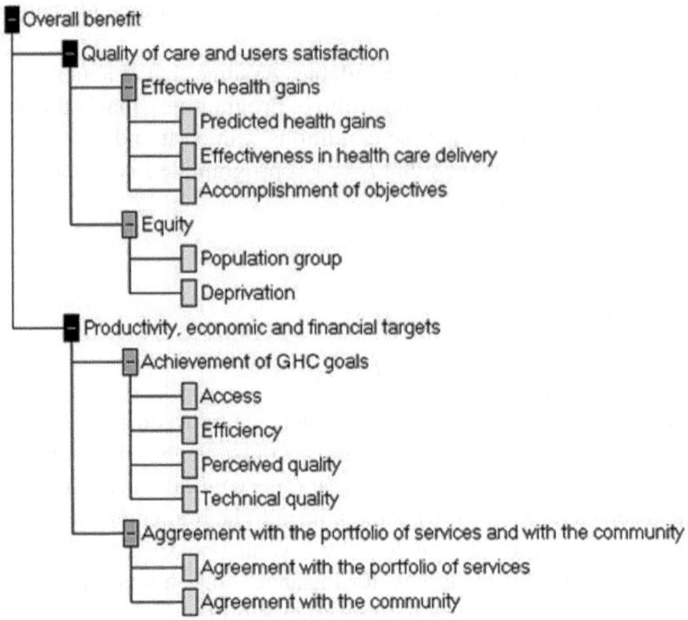

Fig. 9.2. Value tree (evaluation criteria in bold)

Table 9.1. Qualitative descriptor for the *Equity* criterion

Levels	*Descriptor: The programme targets...*
N1 *(Good)*	... the youth or children or pregnant women and that group mostly lives under deprived conditions and/or suffers from family problems and negligence; or functionally dependent individuals or individuals with chronic diseases, and that group mostly lives under deprived conditions.
N2	... the elderly and that group mostly lives under deprived conditions.
N3	... individuals with high risk behaviour (e.g. prostitutes, drug addicts); or individuals living in the HC area, and that group mostly lives under deprived conditions.
N4	... functionally dependent individuals or individuals with chronic diseases or the elderly.
N5	... the youth or children or pregnant women.
N6 (Neutral)	... individuals living in the HC area.

the other hand, an example of a qualitative descriptor is the six-level *Equity* scale shown in Table 9.1.

Subsequently, in order to construct the value function for each of the four criteria, one at a time, the DM was asked to express MACBETH pairwise comparison judgements between performance levels of the respective descriptor. Figure 9.3a shows the consistent matrix of MACBETH judgements for the *Equity* criterion. According

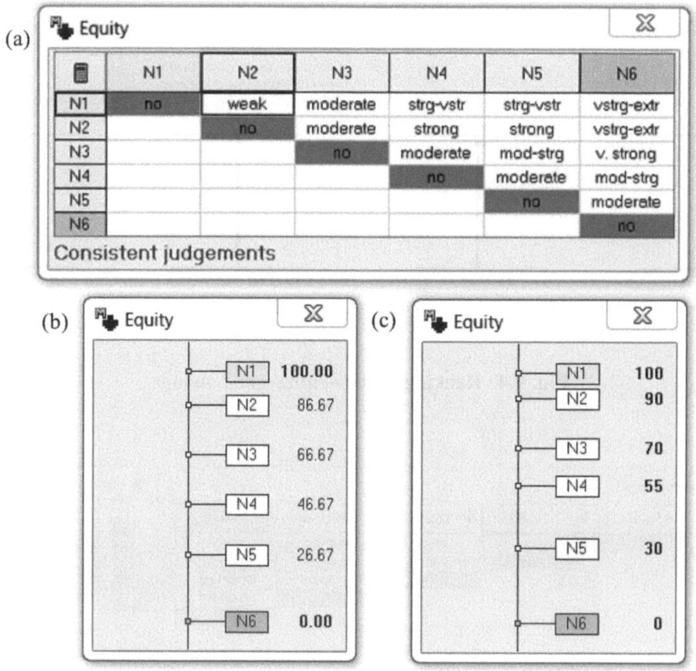

Fig. 9.3. (a) M-MACBETH judgements for the *Equity* criterion. MACBETH allows the DM to hesitate or disagree between judgements, therefore more than one category can be chosen, for example: mod-strg (moderate or strong), strg-vstr (strong or very strong), vstr-extr (very strong or extreme); (b) corresponding basic MACBETH scale; (c) interval scale chosen by the DM

to Bana e Costa *et al.* [8], "deriving a MACBETH scale from a consistent set of judgments is not an end in itself but a path in the learning process of measuring attractiveness in an interval scale". The software M-MACBETH assisted in that path: from the consistent set of judgements (for instance, judgements in Fig. 9.3a), M-MACBETH proposed value scores for the performance levels (the "basic MACBETH scale" in Fig. 9.3b) by solving a linear programming problem [7, 8] (see Appendix). In order to validate the scale, the sizes of the intervals between the proposed scores were compared and, if necessary, scores were adjusted [8]. For the *Equity* criterion, the DM chose the final interval scale shown in Figure 9.3c.

When the value scales for all criteria were built, the next stage was the weighting of the criteria (following the procedure used in [10]). First the DM was asked to rank, in decreasing order of overall attractiveness, the swings from *neutral* to *good* in the four criteria, as shown in Figure 9.4. Then the DM qualitatively judged the overall attractiveness of each swing, filling in the last column of the MACBETH matrix of weighting judgements in Figure 9.5a. Finally, the DM pairwise compared each two swings, thus completing the matrix. Questions were asked so that the DM could validate the weights proposed by MACBETH and sensitivity analysis on differences in participants' views on weights was also carried out, until an agreement was reached on the final weights shown in Figure 9.5b.

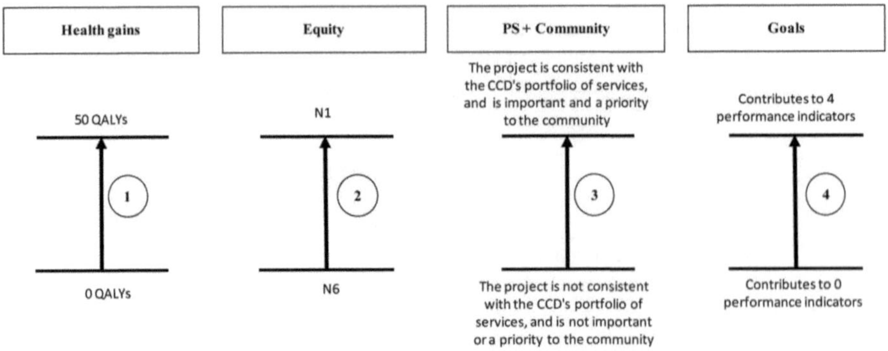

Fig. 9.4. Ranking of the *neutral-good* swings

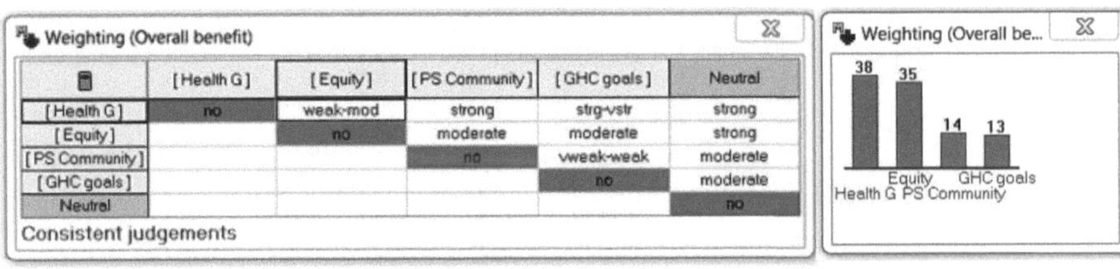

(a) (b)

Fig. 9.5. (a) MACBETH matrix of weighting judgements; (b) histogram of criteria weights (*vweak-weak*, equal to very weak or weak; *weak-mod*, equal to weak or moderate; *str-vstr*, equal to strong or very strong)

9.3 Results and discussion

9.3.1 Results from using MARCCO

MARCCO was applied to the CCDs of the Northern Lisbon GHC, in particular to the Alvalade and Sete Rios CCDs. Regarding the criterion *Effective health gains* the DM decided that the results for two different time horizons should be analysed: for the one-year duration of each action plan (*short time horizon*); and for a time horizon long enough to capture all the future outcomes of the programmes (*long time horizon,* using a discount rate of 5%). MARCCO was applied under different scenarios, which the DM defined by combining those two time horizons with different constraints.

Results from applying MARCCO to the selection of a portfolio of community care programmes for the Alvalade CCD are here presented considering a *long time horizon*. Table 9.2 shows the values of the partial and overall benefits of the proposed programmes, calculated by the multicriteria model, presented by decreasing order of overall benefit. It can be read that only the integrated long-term care programme

Table 9.2. Table of scores for Alvalade programmes, considering a long time horizon

Programmes [j]	*Overall Benefit* $[v_j]$	*Health gains*	*PS+ Community*	*GHC goals*	*Equity*
P10 – Integrated long-term care	143.7	192.0	100.0	167.5	100.0
Good	100.0	100.0	100.0	100.0	100.0
P7 – Support to the child and youth vulnerable groups	68.6	41.3	100.0	30.0	100.0
P12 – Promoting family parenting for vulnerable families	53.3	1.1	35.0	100.0	100.0
P2 – Domiciliary visits: healthy lives	53.3	1.0	35.0	100.0	100.0
P1 – Social integration income	51.7	33.6	35.0	60.0	100.0
P5 – Reproductive health and family planning	51.6	10.1	35.0	60.0	75.0
P6 – Group support for teenagers	45.2	20.2	100.0	100.0	100.0
P4 – Prevention of domestic accidents for the elderly	44.4	0.4	35.0	60.0	29.9
P8 – Preparation for maternity/paternity	23.7	1.3	35.0	60.0	90.0
P9 – Preparation for post-delivery	23.1	9.9	35.0	30.0	29.9
P3 – Physical exercise for the elderly	19.0	0.4	35.0	0	40.0
P11 – Health at home	4.9	0	35.0	0	
Neutral	0	0	0	0	0
Weights		0.38	0.14	0.13	0.35

Table 9.3. Ranking for Alvalade programmes by the benefit/cost ratio

Programmes [j]	*Overall Benefit* $[v_j]$	*Nursing hours required* $[c_j]$	*Benefit/ Cost ratio*	*Cum. Overall Benefit*	*Cum. Overall Cost*
P1 – Social integration income	51.7	0	$+\infty$	51.7	0
P2 – Domiciliary visits: healthy lives	53.3	5.5	9.69	105	5.5
P3 – Physical exercise for the elderly	19.0	4	4.76	124	9.5
P4 – Prevention of domestic accidents for the elderly	44.4	64	0.69	168.4	73.5
P5 – Reproductive health and family planning	51.6	96	0.54	220	169.5
P6 – Group support for teenagers	45.2	182	0.25	265.2	351.5
P7 – Support to the child and youth vulnerable groups	68.6	1002	0.068	333.8	1353.5
P8 – Preparation for maternity/paternity	23.7	464	0.051	357.5	1817.5
P9 – Preparation for post-delivery	23.1	464	0.050	380.6	2281.5
P10 – Integrated long-term care	143.7	2940	0.049	524.3	5221.5
P11 – Health at home	4.9	204	0.024	529.2	5425.5
P12 – Promoting family parenting for vulnerable families	53.3	4164	0.013	582.5	9589.5
TOTAL	**582.5**	**9589.5**	—	—	—

(P10) is globally better than a programme that is good in all criteria; and the health at home programme (P11) has the lowest overall benefit, performing at the least attractive level in three of the criteria.

Table 9.3 shows the overall benefits values and 'costs' in nursing hours (in a total of 9589.5 nursing hours required) of the programmes, which are presented in decreasing order of their benefit/cost ratios (a measure of their efficiency). A first finding for the DM is that the two rankings in Tables 9.2 and 9.3 are quite different. A second finding was that a significant number of programmes have a low level of efficiency and little value (in any case, as the overall budget is 8820 nursing hours, some programmes have to be excluded).

The overall benefits and the required nursing hours of the programmes were the inputs to perform a portfolio decision analysis, with the PROBE software, in several scenarios. Figure 9.6 depicts the PROBE results for the scenario in which one linear constraint was defined to ensure that the programmes 'Preparation for post-delivery' and 'Preparation for maternity/paternity' are only chosen together. Supposing that the available nursing hours varies from 0 to 9589.5 hours, Figure 9.6 presents the main screen of PROBE, in which the dots represent the efficient portfolios (a portfolio is efficient when any other portfolio with higher global benefit requires more nursing hours); they form the efficient frontier. Figure 9.7 helps to make clear that when moving from the left to the right in the efficient frontier, from one portfolio (A) to the next one (B), what matters is the ratio between added benefit and added cost, while maximizing the global benefit.

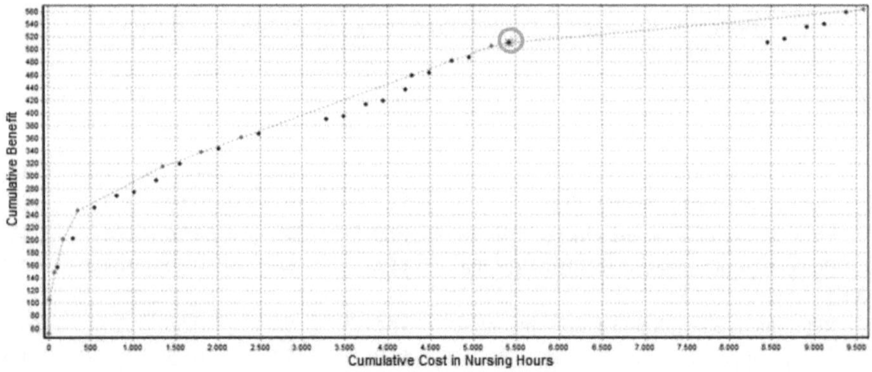

Fig. 9.6. Efficient portfolios for Alvalade's CCD analysed using the PROBE decision support system for a *long time horizon*

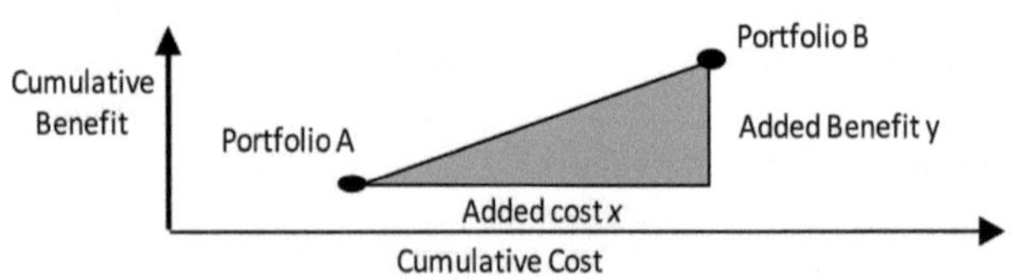

Fig. 9.7. Cost-benefit triangle

Three zones of the graph in Figure 9.6 were observed: a first zone (corresponding to portfolios totalling less than 500 nursing hours), almost vertical, where the added global benefit per added nursing hour is very high; a second zone (between 500 and 5500 hours) with smaller but still high efficiency; and a third zone (demanding more than 5500 hours) in which an additional benefit unit "costs" a lot of hours. This observation made the DM decide that it is not worthwhile spending more than 5500 nursing hours and therefore the portfolio represented by a star dot in Figure 9.6 was selected (this portfolio included all programmes with the exception of P12).

A robustness analysis confirmed that the portfolios chosen by the DM for the Alvalade and Sete Rios CCDs were highly stable to uncertainty in criteria weights, to the use of both the short and the long time horizons and to imprecise performance for some programmes.

Following the results from applying MARCCO, the CCDs were asked to reconfigure current programmes or propose alternative ones, in order to spend the remaining nursing hours available more efficiently (more than 3000 hours for the case of the Alvalade CCD). MARCCO has also helped to improve the GHCs' information system by building guidelines and a template for preparing future action plans, so that CCDs could propose programmes to be compared on a common basis and so that, when defining programmes, CCDs could better understand which programme features are valued by the GHC.

9.3.2 Discussion

The members of the Clinical Board and the Executive Director of the Northern Lisbon GHC agreed with the results obtained by using MARCCO and utilized them in selecting programmes and re-designing the information system.

The structure of the multicriteria model reflects the importance of organizational and incentives structures (based on goals and targets) for prioritizing programmes at the local level. In fact, GHCs are required to respond to many different local and national goals and targets, which are often weakly related to QALY gains, usually used in economic evaluation in health care [27]. When applying MARCCO, two main difficulties had to be overcome. First, as the literature in the area does not provide estimates of QALYs for all the interventions, QALYs for similar preventive interventions had to be used to measure performance for some programmes. Second, the group initially felt uneasy about deciding which definition(s) of equity was meaningful for the delivery of community care programmes (similar difficulties were reported in [1]). The process of identifying criteria and building value functions and weights in the multicriteria value model and of analysing the triangles of value for money provided a clear and transparent framework for the group comparing the programmes; and the use of the M-MACBETH and the PROBE decision support systems was critical to analyse results when there were disagreements between participants and helped participants to change their views.

9.4 Conclusions

MARCCO allowed for transparent prioritization of health care interventions by balancing programmes' costs and benefits for the GHC within a multicriteria resource allocation model structure, and decision conferencing enabled an agreement on the way forward to be achieved. Previous studies stated that MCDA can help DM to make transparent and more robust decisions in health care [27] according to their preferences and values [10, 14]. Despite this, little work has been done so far on the development of comprehensive MCDA approaches [3]. MARCCO contributes to the literature by demonstrating how a constructive approach using MCDA methods and decision conferencing is an alternative to conventional approaches used in the prioritization of interventions in the health care sector, highlighting the usefulness of MCDA in priority setting in the health sector as suggested in previous studies [3, 3, 7, 10, 27, 31]. In the health care sector models applied are usually normative or prescriptive, not always reflecting the concerns and values of the people who best know the system and are directly related to management decision [21]; previous studies have also reported a low use of those models/methods at the local level [16, 39]. MARCCO intends to be a model that helps the DM to allocate resources according to their concerns and values, helping them to have confidence in results and to gain commitment to move forward.

Acknowledgements. The authors gratefully acknowledge that this chapter is based upon work developed at the Group of Health Centres of Northern Lisbon, which they would like to thank for the opportunity given to publish the case. The authors would also like to thank Dr Manuela Peleteiro, Dr Lucília Martinho and all the members of the Clinical Board that participated in the development and application of the model; and to thank José Ferrão, who assisted in the decision conferences.

Appendix: The MACBETH linear programming formulation

The basic MACBETH scale (Fig. 9.3b) suggested by M-MACBETH for a matrix of judgements (Fig. 9.3a) is obtained by linear programming [8]. Let:

- $C_k, k = 0.\ldots,6$, be the seven MACBETH categories of difference in attractiveness: "null" (C_0), "very weak" (C_1), "weak" (C_2), "moderate" (C_3), 'strong' (C_4), "very strong" (C_5) and "extreme" (C_6);
- X be a finite set of performance levels (as in Table 9.1);
- x^+ and x^- be the most and least preferred levels of X, respectively;
- x and y be two elements of X such that x is at least as attractive as y;
- $(x,y) \in C_k(k = 0,\ldots,6)$ be a MACBETH judgment of the difference in attractiveness between x and y expressed by the single category C_k;
- $(x,y) \in C_l\text{U}\ldots\text{U}C_s(l,s = 1,\ldots,6 \text{ with } l < s)$ be a MACBETH judgment of the difference in attractiveness between x and y expressed by a subset of categories from C_l to C_s (in cases of judgmental hesitation or disagreement).

The "basic MACBETH scale" is obtained by solving the following linear program, where$u(x)$ is the score assigned to performance level x:

minimize $u(x^+)$
subject to:

- $u(x^-) = 0$;
- $\forall (x,y) \in C_0 : u(x) - u(y) = 0$;
- $\forall (x,y) \in C_l \text{U} \ldots \text{U} C_s$ with $l,s \in \{1,2,3,4,5,6\}$ and $l \leq s : u(x) - u(y) \geq l$;
- $\forall (x,y) \in C_l \text{U} \ldots \text{U} C_s$ and $\forall (w,z) \in C_{l'} \text{U} \ldots \text{U} C_{s'}$
  with $l,s,l',s' \in \{1,2,3,4,5,6\}, l \leq s, l' \leq s'$ and $l > s'$:
  $\text{u}(x) - u(y) \leq \text{u}(\text{w}) - \text{u}(\text{z}) + 1 - \text{s}'$.

When this linear program is infeasible, the set of judgments is inconsistent. When it is feasible, the optimal solution may not be unique. If multiple solutions exist, there is more than one possible score for at least one performance level $x \in X \backslash \{x^-, x^+\}$, in which case their average is taken to ensure the uniqueness of the basic MACBETH scale (see details in [7]).

References

1. Airoldi, M., Morton, A., Smith, J., Bevan, G.: Healthcare prioritisation at the local level: a socio-technical approach. Priority Setting for Population Health. Working paper no. 7, London School of Economics (2011)
2. Assembleia da República: Constituição da República Portuguesa. Assembeia da República, Lisbon (1992)
3. Baltussen, R., Niessen, L.: Priority setting of health interventions: the need for multi-criteria decision analysis. Cost Effectiveness and Resource Allocation **4**(14) (2006)
4. Bana Consulting: M-MACBETH Version 1.1: User Manual. Lisbon (2005)
5. Bana e Costa, C.A., Carnero, M.C., Oliveira, M.D.: A multi-criteria model for auditing a Predictive Maintenance Programme. European Journal of Operational Research **217**(2), 381–393 (2012)
6. Bana e Costa, C.A., De Corte, J.M., Vansnick, J.C.: MACBETH. Working Paper LSEOR 0356, London School of Economics, London (2003)
7. Bana e Costa, C.A., De Corte, J.-M., Vansnick, J.C.: On the mathematical foundations of MACBETH. In: Figueira, J., Greco, S., Ehrgott, M. (eds.) Multiple Criteria Decision Analysis: The State of the Art Surveys, vol. 76, pp. 409–442. International Series in Operations Research & Management Science. Springer, New York (2005)
8. Bana e Costa, C.A., De Corte, J.M., Vansnick, J.C.: MACBETH (Measuring Attractiveness by a Categorical-Based Evaluation Technique). In: Cochran, J.J. (ed.) Wiley Encyclopedia in Operational Research and Management Science, vol. 4, pp. 2945–2950. Wiley, New York (2011)
9. Bana e Costa, C.A., Fernandes, T.G., Correia, P.V.D.: Prioritisation of public investments in social infrastructures using multicriteria value analysis and decision conferencing: a case study. International Transactions in Operational Research **13**, 279–297 (2006)
10. Bana e Costa, C.A., Lourenço, J.C., Chagas, M.P., Bana e Costa, J.C.: Development of reusable bid evaluation models for the Portuguese Electric Transmission Company. Decision Analysis **5**(1), 22–42 (2008)
11. Belton, V., Stewart, T.J.: Multiple Criteria Decision Analysis: An Integrated Approach. Kluwer Academic Publishers, Boston (2001)
12. Clemen, R.T., Smith, J.E.: On the choice of baselines in multiattribute portfolio analysis: A cautionary note. Decision Analysis **6**(4), 1–7 (2009)

13. Dolan, J.G.: Shared decision-making – transferring research into practice: The Analytic Hierarchy Process (AHP). Patient Education and Counseling **73**, 418–425 (2008)
14. Dolan, J.G.: Multi-criteria clinical decision support: A primer on the use of multiple criteria decision making methods to promote evidencebased, patient-centered healthcare. Patient **3**(4), 229–248 (2010)
15. Goetghebeur, M.M., Wagner, M., Khoury, H., Levitt, R.J., Erickson, L.J., Rindress, D.: Evidence and Value: Impact on DEcisionMaking – the EVIDEM framework and potential applications. BMC Health Services Research **8**(270) (2008)
16. Hoffmann, C., Von der Schulenburg, J.-M.: The influence of economic evaluation studies on health care decision-making. In: Von der Schulenburg, J.-M. (ed.) The Influence of Economic Evaluation Studies on Health Care Decision-Making: A European Survey, pp. 3–16. IOS Press, Amsterdam (2000)
17. Keeney, R.L.: Value-Focused Thinking: A Path to Creative Decision Making. Havard University Press, Cambridge, MA (1992)
18. Kirkwood, C.W.: Strategic Decision Making: Multiobjective Decision Analysis with Spreadsheets. Duxbury, Belmont (1997)
19. Lourenço, J.C., Bana e Costa, C.A., Morton, A.: PROBE – A Multicriteria Decision Support System for Portfolio Robustness Evaluation. Working Paper LSEOR 09.108 (revised version), London School of Economics, London (2011)
20. Missão para os Cuidados de Saúde Primários: Unidade de Cuidados na Comunidade. Available at: http://www.mcsp.min-saude.pt/engine.php?cat=95. Consulted in May 2010 (2008)
21. Mitton, C.: Priority setting for decision makers: using health economics in practice. European Journal of Health Economics **4**, 240–243 (2002)
22. Peacock, S., Mitton, C., Bate, A., McCoy, B., Donaldson, C.: Overcoming barriers to priority setting using interdisciplinary methods. Health Policy **92**, 124–132 (2009)
23. Phillips, L.D.: Decision conferencing. In: Edwards, W., Miles, R., von Winterfeldt, D. (eds.) Advances in Decision Analysis: From Foundations to Applications. Cambridge University Press, New York (2007)
24. Phillips, L.D., Bana e Costa, C.A.: Transparent prioritisation, budgeting and resource allocation with multi-criteria decision analysis and decision conferencing. Annals of Operations Research **154**(1), 51–68 (2007)
25. Pisco, L.: A Reforma dos Cuidados de Saúde Primários. Cadernos de Economia, 60–66 (2007)
26. Williams, I., Bryan, S.: Understanding the limited impact of economic evaluation in health care resource allocation: A conceptual framework. Health Policy **80**(1), 135–143 (2007)
27. Wilson, E., Sussex, J., Macleod, C., Fordham, R.: Prioritizing health technologies in a Primary Care Trust. Journal of Health Services Research **12**(2), 80–85 (2007)

Chapter 10

An analysis of the financial statements of Italian health care providers through correlation-based networks

Marina Resta

Abstract. We examine the balance score of 300 Italian health care providers (HCPs), using the data to build a network. In such network, nodes are HCPs, and each pair of them is connected by an arc whose weight is related to the cross-correlation coefficient between the corresponding HCPs balance scores. By connecting all the vertices through the most correlated link, without forming any loop, we have obtained the Minimum Spanning Tree (MST) on data. We were then able to provide a quite unusual representation of the overall financial situation of Italian HCPs. Our major findings include: (*i*) an original representation of the relations among various HCPs; (*ii*) the emergence of HCPs patterns: HCPs tend to cluster according to shared accounting and financial features; and hence (*iii*) the evidence that a global representation of the financial situation of HFs generates information that can be of help to policy makers, in order to realize a more efficient allocation of financial resources among the existing HCPs.

Keywords: health care providers, financial statements, correlation based-networks

10.1 Introduction and problem addressed

In an ideal world the health system should be effective, and it should be able to achieve the specified outcomes in a way to maximize access, outputs and outcomes within the available resources: the higher the budget allocation to hospital facilitators (clinics, regional or local community hospitals, medical centers) is, the higher should be the overall quality of services they provide, and so their probability to reach their financial goals without any additional external intervention, namely: to reach efficiency.

M. Resta (✉)
Department of Economics and Quantitative Methods (DIEM), University of Genova, Via Vivaldi 5, 16126 Genova, Italy
e-mail: resta@economia.unige.it

Tànfani E., Testi A. (Eds.): Advanced Decision Making Methods Applied to Health Care.
International Series in Operations Research & Management Science 173
DOI 10.1007/978-88-470-2321-5_10,

In the real world, however, this does not happen. Just to make an example, looking at the situation of Italy, it is a matter of fact that health care expenditure plays a crucial impact into the financial resources of the country, however it is not easy to explain why our health care system may be lesser efficient than others. The basic difficulty is to find a common platform to compare the efficiency of health systems, because of their intrinsic complexity, and of certain ambiguity in what does efficiency itself consist and how to measure it.

For what it concerns the complexity of health systems, a quite recent study for the Australian National Health and Hospitals Reform Commission [14] found low relation between relative efficiency and the level of health spending: among the best performers were high spending countries like Australia and Iceland, but also low spending countries like Korea. The same study outlined that grouping countries with respect to the type of health system they have does not seem helping to explain their performance relative to one another. If we look, for instance, at Denmark, Iceland and Norway, they have very similar health systems, but their relative performance differs markedly. Finally, [24] undertook an analysis of efficiency in public health spending in G7 countries relative to other OECD countries, showing that countries which spend a relatively large share of health budgets on labour costs tend to be less efficient.

On the other hand, with respect to the ambiguity of the definition of efficiency and to the way to measure it, the existing literature mainly focuses on three issues. The first one relates to the method used to generate efficiency scores. Most commonly used approaches include Data Envelopment Analysis (DEA) and Stochastic Frontier Analysis (SFA) [10, 13]. Both are similar in that efficiency is measured relative to a best practice (or efficient) frontier. Deviations from this frontier (usually measured as a geometric distance) give measures of (relative) efficiency. A large literature has developed comparing the two techniques, and evaluating their statistical properties. Examining the statistical properties of DEA efficiency estimates, in particular, has encompassed a significant portion of the recent literature [2, 8, 18, 19]. A second major area of research uses one of the approaches outlined below (DFA, SFA) to examine efficiency in a single area of health care production: [2] and [6] focused on hospitals; [15] on pharmaceutical industry, [9] on Health Maintenance Organizations (HMO) industry, [5] on long term care, and [7,21] on cluster of hospitals, just to cite some. Finally, a third area of research uses a combination of different efficiency calculations to measure other aspects of health care practice. As an example, there is an extensive literature using technical efficiency calculations to create the so called Malmquist indices of technological change [13]. Other studies [9, 16] have used technical efficiency scores to create indices of quality change.

Our approach, however, differs from all the aforementioned ones, since we focused on efficiency from the accounting point of view rather than the economic one. In particular, we try to offer new insights to the subject by using the balance sheets of 300 Italian public Health Care Providers (HCPs) to build a network and to perform graph mining. In such network, nodes are HCPs, and each pair of them is connected by an arc whose weight is related to the cross-correlation coefficient between the corresponding HCPs financial statement.

The main contributions of our chapter may be briefly summarised as follows.

- The wellness of firms has been traditionally addressed according to a single unit approach, by examining with quite sophisticated techniques (see for instance, [1], and [11]) the vulnerability of single enterprises. In our case, on the other hand, we try to offer a global view on elements of either weakness or force for a bunch of firms. This, in turn, should be the starting point to investigate how to soften the former and empower the latest.
- To the best of our knowledge, the use of graph mining on balance sheets data to assess the efficiency of HCPs is completely new. In particular, following the work of [23] we used a correlation based filtering procedure on the available data thus obtaining a Minimum Spanning Tree (MST) representation of the italian HCPs.
- We were then able to provide a quite unusual representation of the overall financial situation of Italian HCPs, observing the emergence of very surprising patterns: we will show how those could be of help to policy makers, in order to realize a more efficient allocation of financial resources among the existing HCPs.

10.2 Materials and methods

10.2.1 Dataset background

The Italian health system assumes that health services can be provided both by public and private structures, the former essentially totally funded. Here the term public identifies two kind of structures: Aziende Sanitarie Locali (ASL) and Aziende Ospedalierie (AO). The main difference between the two enterprises stands in the fact that while AO are generally single structures (namely: hospitals), ASL, on the other hand, are more composite, since, by definition of law, they can include more than one local (regional, district, municipal) units that provide health care to citizens.

According to the more recent reform statements of the public health sector, ASL and AO are required to act like autonomous units to control their financial flows. This means that:

- each unit of the system should exhibit capabilities concerning the management of economic and financial flows;
- the efficiency of each unit does not only depend on factors of technical type (such as quality of the provided health service, innovation, satisfaction of the final consumer), but also by more strictly financial factors;
- the capability of the whole system to maintain satisfying levels of solvency and efficiency depends, in turn, on those of every component of the system (ASL and AO).

The efficiency of the system becomes therefore something that includes in a broad sense the bare management of financial variables: for this reason we have analyzed

Table 10.1. Name of Italian Regional Districts, and the ID associated to them throughout the chapter

Name	*ID*	*Name*	*ID*	*Name*	*ID*
Abruzzo	ABR	Aosta Valley	VDA	Apulia	PGL
Basilicata	BAS	Calabria	CAL	Campania	CAM
Emilia-Romagna	EMR	Friuli-Venezia Giulia	FRI	Lazio	LAZ
Liguria	LIG	Lombardy	LOM	Marche	MAR
Molise	MOL	Piedmont	PIEM	Sardinia	SAR
Sicily	SIC	Trentino-Alto Adige	TAA	Tuscany	TOSC
Umbria	UMB	Veneto	VEN		

the balance sheets of 300 public enterprises (ASL and AO), as resulting from the more recent Italian Statistics Institute (ISTAT[1]) database[2].

The goal was to retain information that might help to monitor the actual level of the (accounting) efficiency of the National Health System, and, eventually, to find some suggestions to improve it.

The data under examination were arranged into two different aggregation levels: regional, and by single unit. Since Italy is organized into twenty regional districts (as resulting from Table 10.1), we managed twenty files, and within each of them, a variable number of financial statements of public health care providers operating into the region itself.

Every unit is identified by a string code whose first part is the region ID, and the second part is a number varying from 101 to 999. For instance, PIEM101 identifies the first ASL of Turin in Piedmont, while VEN112 is associated to the ASL of Venice, and so on.

The records in the balance sheet, on the other hand, are organized according to the principles of the International Accounting Standards (IAS) and their modifications, as resulting from the consolidation model introduced by the law act DM Salute, 31 December 2007 [20], so that they capture the financial flows of each single unit. Examples of such flows are given by fundings (either from public institutions or from private organizations), inflows deriving from the provision of health services, or costs and liabilities, for an overall number of 164 variables.

If we examine the data in the traditional accounting way, we should move to set apart from the balance sheet those variables that are generally employed to calculate financial ratios, but we decided to behave differently, for at least two reasons. The first one is that although financial ratios should accomplish to simplification purposes, the number of ratios that can be built from the balance sheet does not sensitively differ from the number of records in the balance sheet. In addition, building financial ratios requires a non trivial knowledge of accounting variables, to combine them in a meaningful way, while the technique we are going to explain basically relies on simply statistical calculations.

[1] www.istat.it.

[2] 2008 data.

A more technical explanation of our choice comes by looking to the peculiarity of data under examination. Both ASL and AO, in fact, are enterprises almost uniquely devoted to provide health care services, so that the greater part of the records we can read in their balance sheet pertains costs and inflows related to such specific activity; on the other hand, the accounting literature does not provide proper financial ratios that can be able to capture such specificity.

As a result, we decided to consider all the available data from the financial statements of ASL and AO, thus obtaining an input matrix of dimensions 300×164, where each row represents either ASL or AO with their 164 normalized determinants.

10.2.2 Methodology

We employed the graphs formalism to analyze the available data. To make clearer the framework we are merging into, on following we will recall some basic definitions and notational conventions.

A graph $G = (V, E)$ consists of a (finite) set denoted by V, and a collection $E \subseteq V \times V$, of unordered pairs $\{u, v\}$ of distinct elements from V.

Each element of V is called a vertex (point, node), and each element of E is called an edge (line, link). Typically, it is assumed that self-loops (i.e. edges of the form (u, u), for some $u \in V$) are not contained in a graph.

A sequence of connected vertices forms a path. The number n of vertices, (i.e. the cardinality of V), is called the order of graph and denoted by $|V| := n$. The number m of edges (the cardinality of E), is called the size of graph and denoted by: $|E| := m$. The degree of a vertex $v \in V$ is the number of its neighbours in the graph.

Moreover, the graph G will be claimed to be:

- directed, if its edge set is composed of ordered vertex (node) pairs; undirected if the edge set is composed of unordered vertex pairs;
- simple, if it has no loops or multiple edges;
- acyclic if there is not any possibility to loop back again from every vertex; cyclic if the contrary holds.
- connected, if there is a path in G between any given pair of vertices, otherwise it is disconnected;
- regular, if all the vertices of G have the same degree;
- complete, if every two distinct vertices are joined by exactly one edge. The complete graph with n vertices will be denoted by K_n;
- a path, if consisting of a single path. The path graph with n vertices will be denoted by P_n;
- bipartite, if the vertex–set can be split into two sets in such a way that each edge of the graph joins a vertex in first set to a vertex in second. A complete bipartite graph is a bipartite graph in which each vertex in the first set is joined to each vertex in the second set by exactly one edge;
- a tree, if it is connected and it has no cycles. If G is a connected graph, the spanning tree in G will be a subgraph of G which includes every vertex of G and is also a tree. The minimum length spanning tree is called Minimum Spanning Tree.

$$\begin{pmatrix} 1 & 1 & 0 & 0 & 1 & 0 \\ 1 & 0 & 1 & 0 & 1 & 0 \\ 0 & 1 & 0 & 1 & 0 & 0 \\ 0 & 0 & 1 & 0 & 1 & 1 \\ 1 & 1 & 0 & 1 & 0 & 0 \\ 0 & 0 & 0 & 1 & 0 & 0 \end{pmatrix}$$

(a)

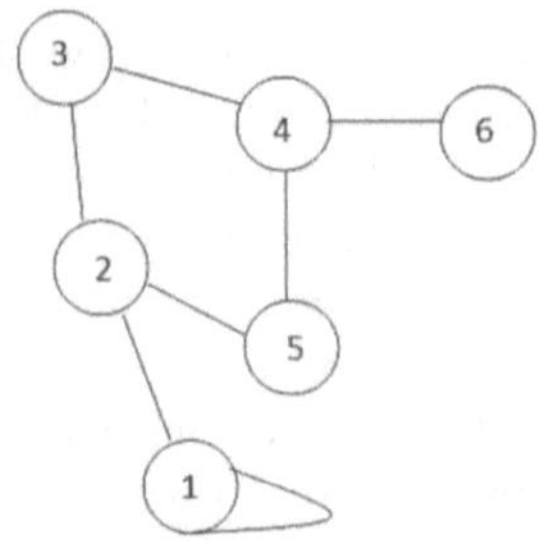

(b)

Fig. 10.1. For left to right: the adjacency matrix for an undirected graph (a), and the corresponding graph (b). In (a) ones indicate the existence of connection among nodes, while zeroes mean no connection. The adjacency matrix provides then complete information bout the graph: without looking at (b) we can claim that the graph has a loop in node 1, and ties between nodes 1 and 2 (2 and 1), 2 and 3, 2 and 5 (3 and 2, 5 and 2), 3 and 4 (4 and 3), 4 and 5, 4 and 6 (5 and 4, 6 and 4)

Commonly, the representation of graphs passes through the building of the adjacency matrix, i.e. a matrix that marks neighbour vertices with one, and labels with a zero those nodes that are not adjacent.

Figure 10.1 explains the idea behind in deeper detail.

In our case, in order to build such adjacency matrix we used as starting point the correlation matrix obtained from the 300×164 input matrix described in the previous subsection.

In practice, for each ASL and AO we used the 164 normalized variables of the corresponding financial statements to fill in arrays (in the overall number of 300). Then, for each couple (i, j), $(i = 1, \ldots, 300)$, and $j = (1, \ldots, 300)$ we proceeded to evaluate the correlation distance of such arrays one to each other, according to the well-known formula:

$$\rho_{ij} = \frac{\sigma_{ij}}{\sigma_i \sigma_j}$$

where σ_{ij} is the covariance between the $i-$th and $j-$th array, while σ_i and σ_j are the corresponding standard deviations. As final step, we have built the adjacency matrix $A^* = \{b_{ij}\}$, being $b_{ij} = 1$, if $\rho_{ij} \neq 0$, and $b_{ij} = 0$ otherwise.

Figure 10.2 shows the network of relations among Italian ASL and AO, as it appears after the creation of the matrix $A^* = \{b_{ij}\}$.

One can immediately notes the huge number of connections per node: at this point, however, only a low level of information can be retained, since almost all nodes seem to be reciprocally connected.

This *excess of information* is similar to that we can find managing financial stocks data: very often data need to be refined, in order to get the best from them. Many different tools can be suitable to such purpose: a common practice, for instance, is to set a threshold level ϑ on the correlation, to flatten at zero all the correlation values under such ϑ. However, we decided to act a filtering procedure which runs jointly on the correlation and on the adjacency matrix.

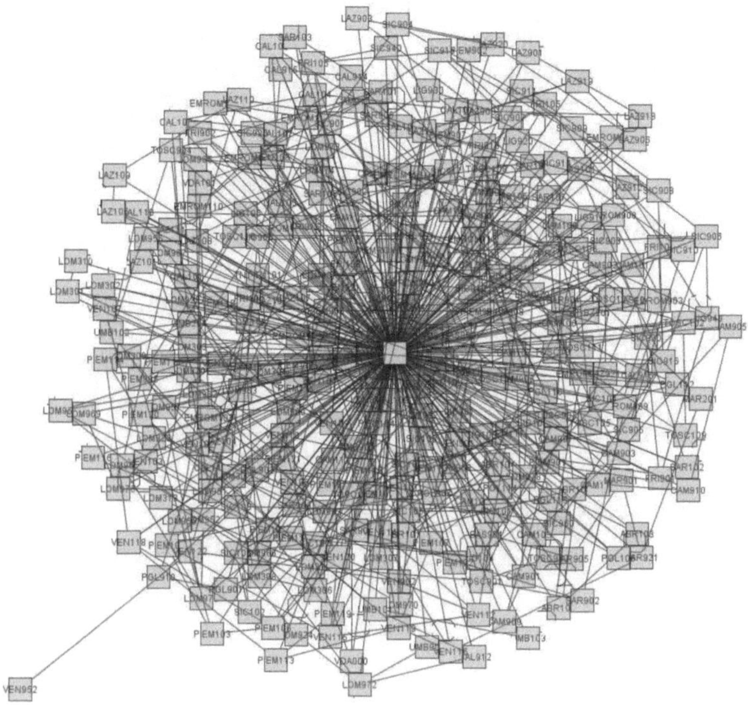

Fig. 10.2. The network of Italian ASL and AO as resulting by the correlation matrix obtained from their financial statements

More in detail, we selected as relevant only those interactions associated to the strongest correlations in the input matrix, such that to assure the graph to be maintained acyclic. In this way, we have formed the adjacency matrix corresponding to the Minimum Spanning Tree (MST) on the correlated data.

Pseudo code for the whole procedure is provided on following; we assume to denote by C the original 300×300 correlation matrix $C = \{\rho_{ij}\}$, $(i = 1, \dots, 300;$ $j = 1, \dots, 300)$. Clearly C is symmetric, allowing us to focus only on its lower (upper) triangular part L (U). Then:

1. sort the elements of L (U) in decreasing order, thus moving from L to the list L_{ord} (from U to U_{ord});
2. the coordinates in C of the first element of L_{ord} (U_{ord}) are those of the first two nodes of the MST;
3. for each element in L_{ord} (U_{ord}) add the corresponding couple from C to MST; in particular, if the graph still maintains acyclic (i.e. no loops are added to MST), then hold the inserted link, otherwise discard it;
4. repeat step 3 until all the elements in L_{ord} (U_{ord}) have been examined, and then stop the procedure.

Clearly, in this way the available information is filtered, and basically this is our idea: to use a filtering procedure and hence to let the more significant patterns to emerge. To achieve this latter goal, we visualized the MST and performed network analysis: to such aim we used mainly two software suites both open source: Gephy [4] and Yed[3].

10.3 Results and discussion

Our analysis has been performed at different levels, economic and technical, this latter related to the graph representation of data.

We start from Figure 10.3 that shows the network resulting after our filtering procedure.

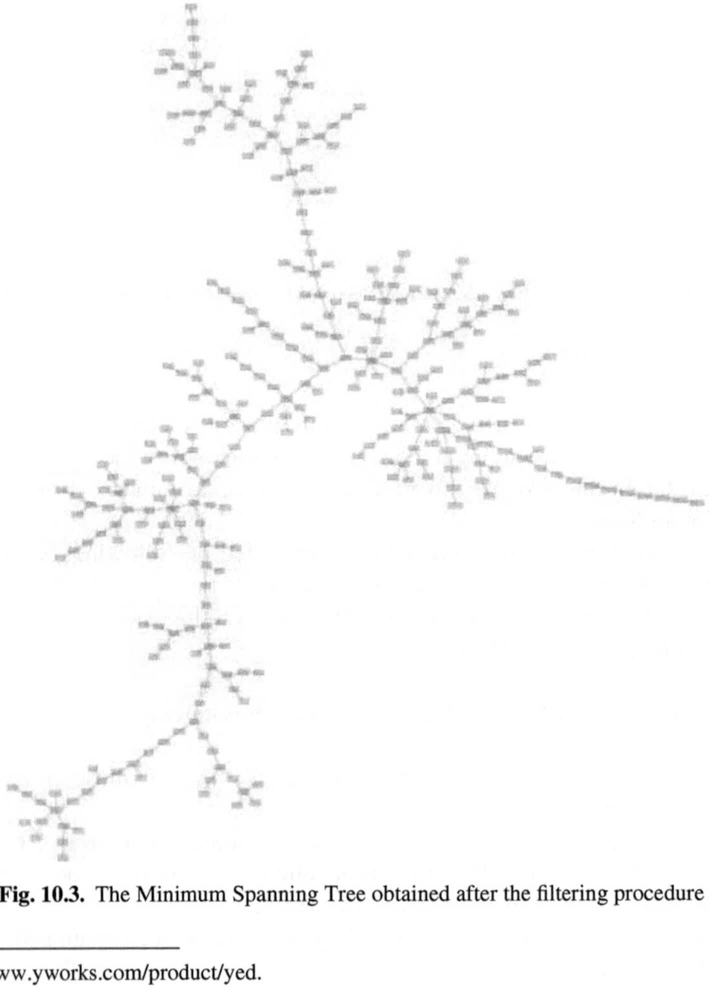

Fig. 10.3. The Minimum Spanning Tree obtained after the filtering procedure

[3] http://www.yworks.com/product/yed.

Table 10.2. Measures of network organization. A comparison between the original correlation network (Net1), and the MST (Net2) obtained after the filtering procedure

Metrics	*Net1*	*Net2*
Average Degree Centrality	10.236	1.993
Network Diameter	27	27
Graph Density	0.83	0.07
Modularity	0.75	0.674
Average Clustering Coefficient	0.82	0.79

A first look impression suggests that, with respect to the graph of Figure 10.2, information has been refined, and only relevant connections have been left.

Obviously, the difference between the two networks is not only a matter of graphical appearance, but it can monitored through a number of specific indicators that are generally employed to measure the level of complexity and organization of a network. The values for the networks under examination are provided in Table 10.2.

In order to discuss those values, we start from the Average Degree Centrality (ADC). ADC expresses the average number of ties of the networks nodes; its interpretation is in terms of the immediate risk of nodes for catching whatever is flowing through the network: the higher this value is, the greater is the exposure of the net to equilibria variation. In the case under examination, for instance, higher scores should mean wider exposure to abrupt changes in the financial asset of HCPs, and they could be used to act a sort of Early Warning System (EWS) to monitor the economic/financial wellness of healt care providers. Moving from Net1 to Net2, ADC decreases from 10.236 to 1.993. The explanation is quite trivial: focusing only on very relevant ties made us possible to cut a number of connections, and hence to reduce the risk of false alarms of such EWS.

Network Diameter shows the longest graph distance between any two nodes in the network: this value has been maintained unchanged from Net1 to Net2. This fact is reasonable, since the filtering procedure cuts only redundant and negligible information from each node.

The Graph Density (GD) measures how close the network is to be complete: since a complete graph has all possible edges, its GD will be 1: the lower this value, the farther the graph is to be complete. The values for Net1 and Net2 are markedly different: Net1 is closer to be complete, but this does not apply to Net2. Once again the reason is in the acted filtering procedure that cleaned the original net from lesser significant ties.

The Modularity, on the other hand, is a concept close to that of clustering, since it examines the attitude to community formation in the net, and it is then strictly related to the possibility to disclose clusters in a net. In order to be significant, values need to be higher than 0.4. This threshold has been largely exceeded in both the examined nets. Related to such values are those of the Average Clustering Coefficient which measures how network nodes are embedded into a neighbourhood.

Looking at the examined results, our filtering procedure has therefore disclosed from the original network (Net1) another one (Net2) with small average degrees, small average distances and high clustering, i.e. a net exhibiting a *small world* effect [25].

We can now focus on Net2, examining it in deeper detail.

We have already said that from Net2 it emerges that HCPs tend to group into clusters: in particular we searched the net for natural clusters, in the sense discussed in [12].

A grouping into natural clusters should fulfill the following properties:

- each node is member of exactly one group;
- each node should have many edges to other members of its group;
- each node should have few or even no edges to nodes of other groups.

Doing so natural clusters emerged, as given in Figure 10.4. Clusters' composition is provided in full detail in Tables 10.3 and 10.4, where data have been split only for readability purposes.

Although not expressely searched, a sort of regional effect dominates on ten of the fifteen clusters, where the totality (or at least a greater part) of nodes belongs to a single region. This, in particular, is the case of clusters labelled by: CL01, CL03, CL04, CL05, CL06, CL07, CL9, CL10, CL12 and CL13.

The emerging groups have been also examined in their economic and financial features. In accordance to the guidelines provided in [20] for each cluster five different determinants have been studied:

- regional fundings (A), including contributions directly assigned to HCPs by the regions;
- outflows deriving from internal costs (B);
- additional revenues (C), including inflows derived from the management of HCPs financial portfolio;
- outflows for third parts products (D), derived from the assessment of immaterial items;
- contribution to the economic result from atypic budgeting administration (E).

The discussion of clusters' features with respect to such determinants was performed with the aid of a box plot [22] for each of them. This is a convenient nonparametric way of graphically depicting groups of numerical data through their five-number summaries: the smallest observation (sample minimum), the lower (first) quartile, the median, the upper (third) quartile, and the largest observation (sample maximum). A rectangle (the box) spans from the lower to the upper quartile, thus defining the so called interquantile range. Spacings between the different parts of the box help indicate the degree of dispersion (spread) and skewness in the data.

In Figure 10.5 we can observe clusters' main features with respect to the aforementioned determinants. Note that due to the choice to work with standardized data, upper and lower tails of the boxes are uniformely set at zero and one levels respectively.

In the case of flows related to regional fundings (A) boxes are positively skewed, with the exception of those referring to clusters CL03 and CL12.

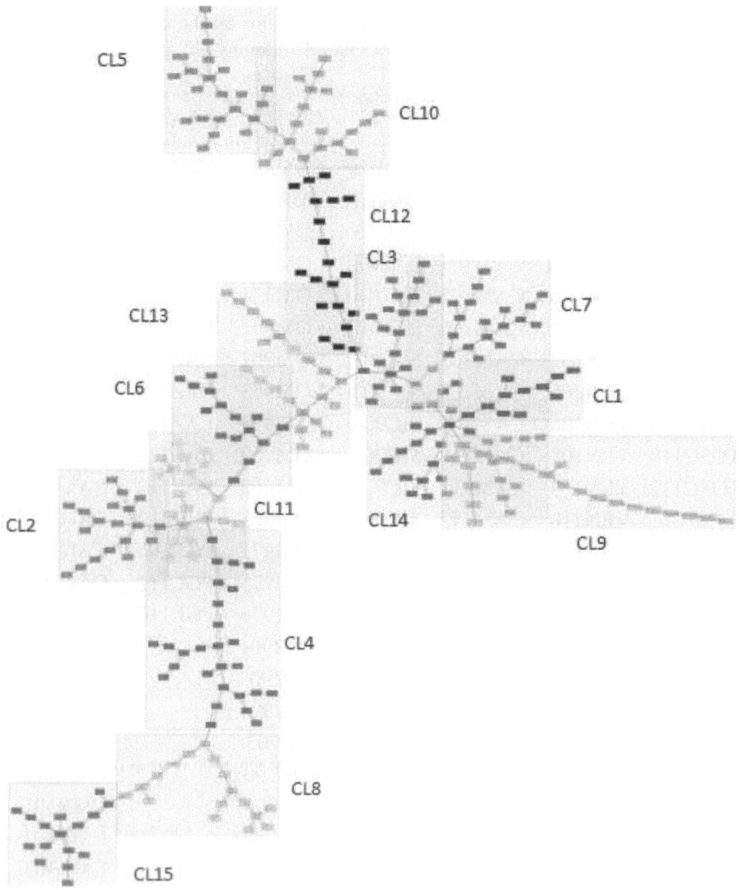

Fig. 10.4. Natural clusters emerged from Net2

From the point of view of a policy maker this fact should be of quite clear interpretation, being a signal of strongest regional investments to support ASL and AO performance. In other words, the majority of the examined HCPs seem to be strongly dependent on regional intervention. Higher results towards such direction are (not very surprisingly) those of cluster CL09 which is prevalently made by HCPs belonging to the region Emilia Romagna (EMR). On the other hand, clusters CL03, CL04 and CL07 are those corresponding to more compressed boxes in the graph, i.e. HCPs belonging to them seem to do not rely very much on such flows. Once again this is not surprising at all, if we look at the regional composition of such clusters.

Outflows deriving from internal costs (B) confirm to a certain extent the distinguishing peculiarity of clusters CL09, CL03 and CL07. In the former case the box shape seems to span over a wider range, meaning that such costs can be very different depending on the HCPs included into the cluster. In the latter two cases, costs appear *compressed* into very smaller ranges, to indicate that such records are lesser

Table 10.3. Cluster components after the filtering procedure on the correlation matrix. Clusters from 1 to 8. COD is the acronym for Clusters Overall Dimension, and provides the number of elements belonging to each cluster

	CL01	*CL02*	*CL03*	*CL04*	*CL05*	*CL06*	*CL07*	*CL08*
	TOSC101	PIEM109	CAM101	FRI102	BAS902	LAZ101	CAL101	FRI901
	TOSC102	PIEM111	CAM102	FRI103	EMR902	LAZ102	CAL102	FRI902
	TOSC103	PIEM118	CAM103	FRI105	LOM920	LAZ103	CAL103	FRI913
	TOSC104	PIEM121	CAM104	LAZ921	LOM922	LAZ104	CAL104	LAZ901
	TOSC105	PIEM122	CAM105	LIG101	LOM924	LAZ106	CAL105	LAZ902
	TOSC106	VEN101	CAM106	LIG940	LOM951	LAZ107	CAL106	LAZ903
	TOSC107	VEN102	CAM107	SIC901	LOM952	LAZ108	CAL107	LAZ906
	TOSC108	VEN105	CAM108	SIC902	LOM953	LAZ109	CAL108	LAZ908
	TOSC109	VEN106	CAM109	SIC903	LOM955	LAZ110	CAL109	LAZ912
	TOSC110	VEN108	CAM110	SIC904	LOM959	LAZ111	CAL110	LAZ918
	TOSC112	VEN109	CAM111	SIC905	LOM960	LAZ112	CAL111	LAZ919
		VEN110	CAM112	SIC906	LOM963	PIEM108	CAL912	LAZ920
		VEN112	CAM901	SIC907	LOM971	PGL106	CAL914	LIG950
		VEN113	CAM902	SIC908	LOM975	PGL112	CAL915	PIEM901
		VEN114	CAM903	SIC909	LOM976	PGL114	CAL916	PIEM902
		VEN115	CAM906	SIC910	MAR901		CAM113	PIEM903
		VEN117	CAM908	SIC911	MAR905		CAM904	PIEM904
		VEN118	CAM909	SIC912	MAR921		CAM905	
		VEN121	CAM910	SIC913	SAR903		CAM907	
			LOM304	SIC914	TOSC901		CAM912	
				SIC915	TOSC902		UMB101	
				SIC916	TOSC903		UMB102	
				SIC917	VDA000		UMB103	
				SIC920			UMB204	
				SIC930				
				SIC940				
				SIC960				
COD	11	19	20	27	23	15	24	17

relevant than in other clusters to determine the final economic result. For the remaining clusters, on the other hand, costs seem to stay within intermediate ranges.

For what it concerns additional revenues (C), the boxes of the plot are quite longer in almost all clusters, to indicate that clusters values span over wild intervals. In this case the information that can be retrieved is therefore similar for all the examined clusters, and it suggests that this kind of variable cannot be effectively used by the policy maker as budgeting tool.

Similar remarks apply also in the case of records referred to atypic budgeting administration (E).

Table 10.4. Cluster components after the filtering procedure on the correlation matrix. Clusters from 9 to 15. Like in Table 10.3, COD is the acronym for Clusters Overall Dimension, and provides the number of elements belonging to each cluster

	CL09	*CL10*	*CL11*	*CL12*	*CL13*	*CL14*	*CL15*
	TAA201	CAL913	LIG102	LOM301	FRI101	ABR101	FRI912
	TAA101	LOM923	LIG104	LOM302	FRI104	ABR102	FRI916
	EMR101	LOM925	LIG105	LOM303	FRI106	ABR103	LIG910
	EMR102	LOM954	PIEM110	LOM305	LAZ105	ABR104	LIG920
	EMR103	LOM957	PIEM112	LOM306	LIG103	ABR105	LIG930
	EMR104	LOM958	PIEM116	LOM307	PIEM101	ABR106	PIEM905
	EMR105	LOM962	PIEM117	LOM308	PIEM102	BAS101	PIEM906
	EMR106	LOM965	PIEM119	LOM309	PIEM103	BAS102	PIEM907
	EMR109	LOM966	PGL113	LOM310	PIEM104	BAS103	PIEM908
	EMR110	LOM968	PGL116	LOM311	PIEM105	BAS104	PGL901
	EMR111	LOM969	SIC101	LOM312	PIEM106	BAS105	PGL902
	EMR112	LOM970	SIC102	LOM313	PIEM107	BAS901	PGL907
	EMR113	LOM972	SIC103	LOM314	PIEM113	MAR201	PGL910
	EMR903	LOM973	SIC104	LOM315	PIEM114	SAR102	VEN901
	EMR904	LOM974	SIC105	LOM956	PIEM115	SAR103	VEN902
	EMR908	LOM977	SIC106	LOM964	PIEM120	SAR104	VEN952
	EMR909	LOM978	SIC107	LOM967	PGL115	SAR105	
	EMR960	LOM979	SIC108		VEN116	SAR106	
	SAR101	LOM980	SIC109		VEN119	SAR107	
	SAR902	UMB901	VEN103		VEN120	SAR108	
	SAR904	UMB902	VEN104		VEN122	SAR901	
			VEN107			SAR905	
						SAR906	
						TOSC111	
						TOSC904	
						VDA101	
COD	21	21	22	17	21	26	16

Finally, in the case of flows for third part costs (D), the results suggest that such kind of cost is generally maintained at lower levels. Margins to intervenue are possible only in four clusters (CL01, CL02, CL09, and CL13), although due to the mainly technical nature of these items, their management seems matter for HCPs managers rather than for policy makers.

Due to the complex articulation of flows related to the B determinant, we have also provided some further investigation on its components. To such purpose, we have decomposed B into twelve relevant elements:

- $b1$: generic health care costs, such as those for purchasing of medical drugs, vaccines, oxygen, and so on;
- $b2$: costs related to basic health care provisions;

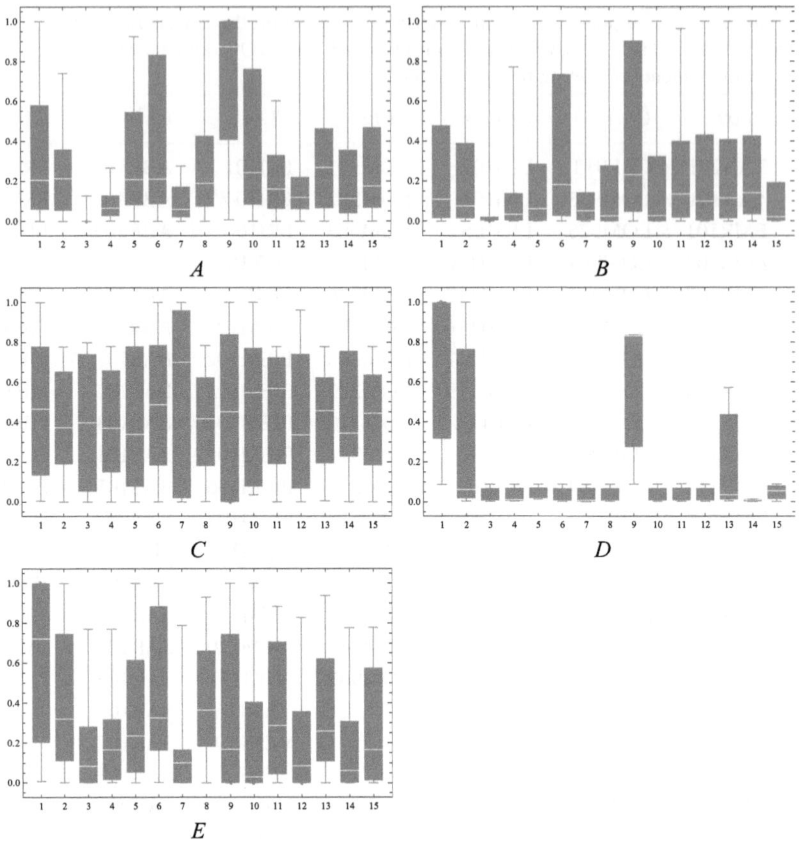

Fig. 10.5. Box Plots for the five determinants of HCPs clusters balance sheets. In each plot, clusters ID are on x–axis, and standardized variables value on y–axis

- $b3$: pharmaceutical costs, related to the distribution of pharmaceuticals over the land of pertinence;
- $b4$: specialised health care services;
- $b5$: rehabilitation;
- $b6$: assistance;
- $b7$: intramoenia, pertaining the exercise of medical activity to external patients inside the HCPs buildings;
- $b8$: consultancy;
- $b9$: HCPs Personnel Training;
- $b10$: building maintenance;
- $b11$: loans;
- $b12$: personnel retributions.

The results are provided in Figure 10.6.

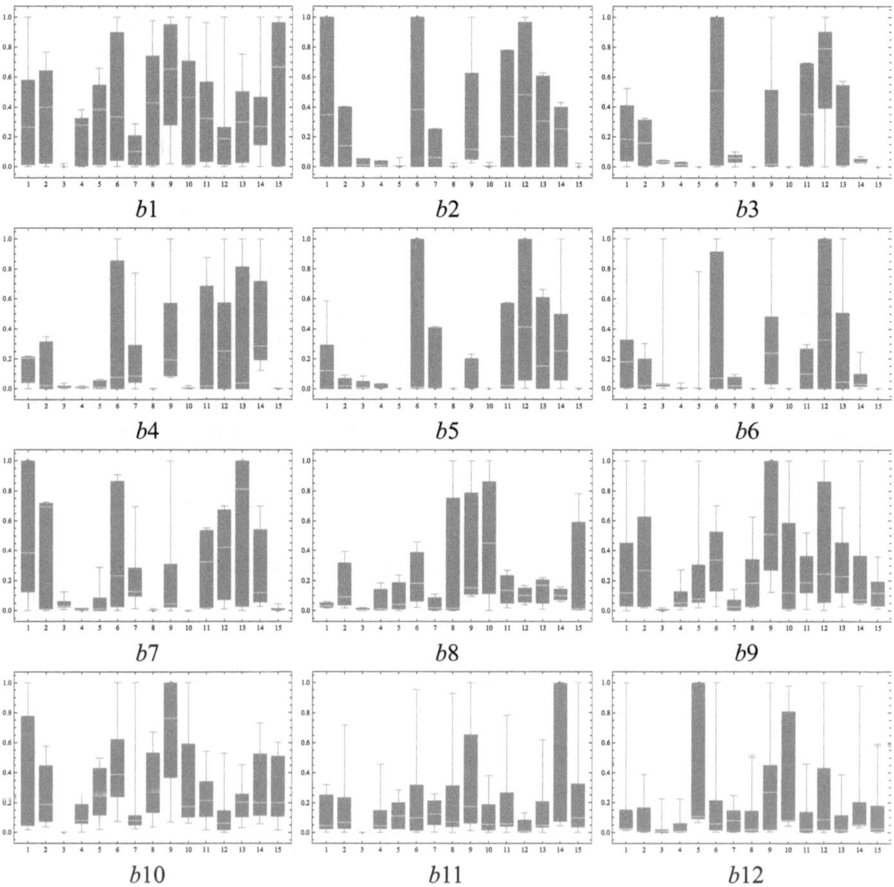

Fig. 10.6. Box Plots, details related to costs organization in various clusters. In each plot, clusters ID are on x-axis, and standardized variables value on y-axis

The analysis of Figure 10.6 confirms the existence of both compression and sparsity effects in the HCPs flows. In addition, looking at the box shapes, it is suggested (Fig. 10.6, *b*1) a possible field of intervention for what concerning the provision of generic health care services. Stronger monitoring activity should be probably due in the case of HCPs belonging to clusters CL06 and CL12, that exhibit heavy variations for all the examined components.

10.4 Conclusions

In this work we have introduced a technique to analyse financial statements based on graph mining. The rationale was inspired by the need for a common platform to compare the efficiency of health systems, and to drive the action of policy makers. While traditional approaches try to reach this goal with methods estimating the economic efficiency of Health Care Providers (HCPs), we have moved towards an alternative direction, since we focused on the concept of efficiency from the accounting point of view.

To such purpose, we have considered the balance sheets of 300 public enterprises (ASL and AO), as resulting from the more recent Italian Statistics Institute (ISTAT) database. We then filtered twice the available information, once building from the HCPs financial statements the correlation matrix C, and in a second time we derived from C the djacency matrix A^* through a filtering procedure taylored to maintain only correlation values maintaining acyclic the graph. As result we have obtained a representation of HCPs and their relevant ties that offered various arguments for debate.

Our first finding was of technical type: taking only relevant information from the network of relations among HCPs balance sheets let us possible to evidence in the resulting net a small world effect. This is important: if we look to such net as model of spreading contagion, we are sure that the probability to generate false alarms is quite smaller.

As second remark, we offered a global view into the system of HCPs, but we also evidenced the presence of natural clusters, i.e. we show that HCPs tend to group according to their financial similarities. This tendence for grouping does not necessarily correspond to a regional criterion: while a notable number of clusters groups firms belonging to the same region, this is not a general rule.

More importantly, the analysis of the features corresponding to the various HCPs clusters put into light their weaknesses as well as their points of force. The study via box plots also suggested perspective directions for interventions.

We can then conclude that in perspective, the availability of data like those examined for a wider time extension could made graph mining a very effective tool to address the action of policy makers.

Acknowledgements. This work has been funded by MIUR within the FIRB project N. RBFR081 KSB.

References

1. Altman, E.I., Marco, G., Varetto, F.: Corporate Distress Diagnosis: Comparisons Using Linear Discriminant Analysis and Neural Networks. Journal of Banking and Finance **18**(3), 505–529 (1994)
2. Banker, R.: Maximum Likelihood, Consistency and Data Envelopment Analysis: A Statistical Foundation. Management Science **39**(10), 1265–1273 (1993)
3. Bastian, M., Heymann, S., Jacomy, M.: Gephi: an open source software for exploring and manipulating networks. International AAAI Conference on Weblogs and Social Media (2009)
4. Bjorkgren, M., Hakkinen, U., Linna, M.: Measuring Efficiency of Long Term Care Units in Finland. Health Care Management Science **4**(3), 193–201 (2001)
5. Braithwaite, J., Westbrook, M., Hindle, D., Ledema, R., Black, D.: Does Restructuring Hospitals Result in Greater Efficiency? – an Empirical Test Using Diachronic Data. Health Services Management Research **19**(1), 1–13 (2006)

6. Brennan, A., Sampson, F., Deverill, M.: Can we Use Routine Data to Evaluate Organizational Change? Lessons from the Evaluation of Business Process Reengineering in a UK Teaching Hospital. Health Services Management Research **18** (4), 265–277 (2005)
7. Brockett, P., Chang, R., Rousseau, J., Semple, J., Yang, C.: A Comparison of HMO Efficiencies as a Function of Provider Autonomy. Journal of Risk and Insurance **71**(1), 1–19 (2004)
8. Burgess, J. Jr., Wilson, P.: Variation in Inefficiency among US Hospitals, INFOR **36**(3), 84–102 (1998)
9. Fare, R., Grosskopf, S., Roos, P.: Productivity and Quality Changes in Swedish Pharmacies. International Journal of Production Economics **39**, 137–147 (1995)
10. Cooper, W.W., Seiford, L.M., Tone, K.: Data Envelopment Analysis: a Comprehensive Text with Models, Applications, References and DEA-solver software. Kluwer Academic Publishers, Boston (2000)
11. Fantazzini, D., Figini, S.: Random Survival Forest Models for SME Credit Risk Measurement. Methodology and Computing in Applied Probability **11**(1), 29–45 (2009)
12. Girvan, M., Newman, M.E.J.: Community structure in social and biological networks. Proc. Natl. Acad. Sci. USA **99**, 7821–7826 (2002)
13. Hollingsworth, B.: Non-Parametric and Parametric Applications Measuring Efficiency in Health Care. Health Care Management Science **6**(4), 203–218 (2003)
14. Hurley, E., McRae, I., Bigg, I., Stackhouse, L., Boxall, A.M., Broadhead, P.: The Australian health care system: the potential for efficiency gains. Working paper, Australian Government National Health and Hospitals Reform Commission (2009)
15. Key, B., Reed, R., Sclar, D.: First-order Economizing: Organizational Adaptation and the Elimination of Waste in the U.S. Pharmaceutical Industry. Journal of Managerial Issues **17**(4), 511–528 (2005)
16. Maniadakis, N., Thanassoulis, E.: Assessing Productivity Changes in UK Hospitals Reflecting Technology and Input Prices. Applied Economics **32**, 1575–1589 (2000)
17. Mirmirani, S., Li, H.C., Ilacqua, J.A.: Health Care Efficiency In Transition Economies: An Application Of Data Envelopment Analysis. International Business & Economics Research Journal **7**(2) (2008)
18. Murillo Zamorano, L.: Economic Efficiency and Frontier Techniques. Journal of Economic Surveys **18**(1), 33–77 (2004)
19. Ozcan, Y.A.: Health Care Benchmarking and Performance Evaluation. An Assessment using Data Envelopment Analysis (DEA). Springer, Newton, MA (2008)
20. Salute, D.M., 31 dicembre 2007: Nuovi modelli di rilevazione del conto economico e dello stato patrimoniale delle aziende sanitarie locali, aziende ospedaliere, istituti di ricovero e cura a carattere scientifico pubblici, anche se trasformati in fondazioni e aziende ospedaliere universitarie integrate con il Servizio sanitario nazionale (già policlinici universitari a gestione diretta di diritto pubblico), integrati con le codifiche informatiche, G.U. Serie Generale n. 14 del 17/01/2008
21. Sikka, V., Luke, R.D., Ozcan, Y.A.: The Efficiency of Hospital-Based Clusters. Health Care Management Review **34**(3), 251–261 (2009)
22. Tukey, J.W.: Exploratory Data Analysis. Addison-Wesley, Reading, MA (1977)
23. Tumminello, M., Aste, T., Di Matteo, T., Mantegna, R.N.: A tool for filtering information in complex systems. PNAS **102**(30), 10421–10426 (2005)
24. Verhoeven, M., Gunnarsson, V., Carcillo, S.: Education and Health in G7 countries: Achieving better outcomes with less spending. International Monetary Fund (IMF) working paper, WP/07/263 (2007)
25. Watts, D., Strogatz, S.: Collective dynamics of small-world networks. Nature **393**(6684), 440–442 (1998)

Chapter 11

Using data envelopment analysis for formative evaluation of radiotherapy services: An exploratory study

Sérgio P. Santos and Carla A.F. Amado

Abstract. Radiotherapy is an important element in cancer treatment, both for cure and for palliation. Whilst performance measurement and performance improvement are major concerns of most radiotherapy departments, measuring and managing the performance of these departments is particularly challenging. This article critically explores the use of Data Envelopment Analysis (DEA) for formative evaluation of radiotherapy services. Following a review of the literature, a conceptual framework for performance assessment of radiotherapy departments is developed and its use illustrated. Our empirical analysis uses mostly data from 2007 and compares the fairness of access to services, technical efficiency, and clinical effectiveness across the English strategic health authorities. The analysis shows that whilst the application of DEA in this context meets some difficulties, it also has great potential by providing valuable information to improve services, especially if used in a formative mode.

Keywords: data envelopment analysis, performance measurement, radiotherapy services

11.1 Introduction and problem addressed

Cancer has become one of the most significant health care problems in the western world and it is a leading cause of premature death. Every year hundreds of thousands of patients are diagnosed with cancer and it is estimated that more than one in three

S.P. Santos (✉)
Faculty of Economics, University of Algarve, Campus de Gambelas, 8005-139 Faro, Portugal
CEFAGE-UE, University of Evora, Largo Marquês de Marialva 8, 7000-809 Evora, Portugal
e-mail: ssantos@ualg.pt

C.A.F. Amado
Faculty of Economics, University of Algarve, Campus de Gambelas, 8005-139 Faro, Portugal
CEFAGE-UE, University of Evora, Largo Marquês de Marialva 8, 7000-809 Evora, Portugal
e-mail: camado@ualg.pt

Tànfani E., Testi A. (Eds.): Advanced Decision Making Methods Applied to Health Care.
International Series in Operations Research & Management Science 173
DOI 10.1007/978-88-470-2321-5_11,

people will develop cancer at some stage in their lives and one in four will die from it [7]. As a consequence, the direct and indirect effects to the economy resulting from cancer are enormous. To minimise the impact of these effects it is fundamental to ensure an efficient use of resources.

As emphasised by Appleby and Thomas [1], an inefficient use of resources in the health care context means not only that money is wasted, but more importantly that the opportunity is lost to save lives, avert pain, and provide care to those in need. While this applies to all health care areas, it is particularly meaningful in the case of cancer care, including radiotherapy.

Radiotherapy along with surgery is a major modality in the management of cancer and it is used as a primary treatment for many types of cancer. It uses beams of high-energy waves or particles to kill or damage cancer cells, and it may be used individually or in combination with surgery and/or chemotherapy, depending on the location, pathology and stage of the cancer.

Most commonly, radiotherapy is delivered from an external source, usually a linear accelerator, with the beam being concentrated on the tumour. It may be part of a programme of treatments intended to cure the patient's tumor (radical radiotherapy), or it may be used to relieve symptoms of advanced disease (palliative radiotherapy). It is estimated that, about half of all cancer patients should receive radiotherapy at some point in their illness, either as part of their primary treatment or in connection with recurrences or palliation.

Whatever the intent, the use of radiation for the treatment of cancer is a complex, multi-step process, involving trained personnel who carry out a variety of interrelated activities. An appropriate measurement and management of the performance of radiotherapy departments can therefore play an important role in ensuring an efficient and effective use of their resources in the different stages of this process and, ultimately, in saving lives.

One method to measure performance is to benchmark a radiotherapy facility against others performing similar activities. A benchmarking exercise allows the radiotherapy facility to evaluate how well it is doing when compared to best-observed practice according to a particular criterion. Also, a good benchmarking exercise should allow the facility to learn about how other facilities are able to do better. However, the challenge is in identifying 'best practice', as what constitutes 'best practice' is in itself dependent upon the perspective taken. Furthermore, what constitutes 'best practice' is dependent upon the priorities of the radiotherapy facility under evaluation. Therefore, what constitutes 'best practice' to one organization might not constitute 'best practice' to another.

Data envelopment analysis (DEA) is a non-parametric linear programming technique which has proved very effective in determining best practices. This article explores the potential of using DEA for formative rather than summative evaluation in radiotherapy. In particular, it discusses the need to use DEA as a learning tool for radiotherapy services. To this purpose, the chapter is organized in three further sections. Section 11.2 gives an overview of the DEA methodology and comments on the extent to which its use in the health care area is reflected in the literature. Informed by the literature review, an illustrative example and by previous research undertaken in this and other contexts, Section 11.3 discusses how DEA can be used in a formative way to assess and improve the performance of radiotherapy departments. Section 11.4 concludes with some closing remarks and an outline of the ongoing research agenda.

11.2 Materials and methods

DEA is a non-parametric technique used to measure the efficiency of Decision Making Units (DMUs) and was first proposed by Charnes, Cooper and Rhodes in 1978 [3]. This technique uses a production metaphor. It considers that each DMU is engaged in a transformation process, where by using some inputs (resources) it is trying to produce some outputs (goods or services). With the provision of these services, the DMU intends to achieve certain outcomes, which measure the impact of the services on the patients. One of the interesting features of DEA is that it allows each unit to identify a benchmarking group; that is, a group of units that are following the same objectives and priorities, but performing better. In this respect DEA aims to respect the priorities of each DMU by allowing each one of them to choose the weight structure for inputs and outputs that most benefits its evaluation. As a result, it aims to classify each unit in the best possible light in comparison to the other units. In one of its simplest forms, the formulation of the problem for unit Q is as follows:

$$\text{Max} \qquad H_Q = \frac{\sum_{i=1}^{I} w_i y_{iQ}}{\sum_{j=1}^{J} v_j x_{jQ}}$$

$$\text{subject to} \quad \frac{\sum_{i=1}^{I} w_i y_{is}}{\sum_{j=1}^{J} v_j x_{js}} \leq 1 \qquad \forall s, with\ s = 1,\ldots Q \ldots S,$$

$$w_i, v_j \geq \varepsilon \qquad \forall i, with\ i = 1,\ldots,I; \forall j, \quad with\ j = 1,\ldots,J,$$

where S is the number of DMUs; I is the number of outputs; y_{is} is the amount of outputs i generated by unit s; J is the number of inputs; x_{js} is the amount of input j used by unit s; w_i is the weight associated with output i; v_j is the weight associated with input j; ε is a small positive number. H_Q is the radial efficiency measure for DMU Q. $H_Q \in [0, 1]$, and will be equal to 1 if the DMU is efficient, and smaller than 1 if the DMU is inefficient when compared with the other DMUs. A comprehensive review of the DEA technique can be found in Cooper *et al.* [5,6].

The use of DEA in the health care context is not new. Indeed, since the mid-1980s, DEA has been used increasingly to measure the performance of health care services. Hollingsworth *et al.* [10], Chilingerian and Sherman [4] and more recently Hollingsworth [9] review applications of DEA to health care.

However, the applications of DEA in oncology services are very rare. Some exceptions include the works of Dervaux *et al.* [8], Johnston and Gerard [11] and Langabeer II and Ozcan [14]. The former two studies discuss the use of DEA to investigate the relative efficiency of cancer screening units. The latter discusses the use of DEA to better understand the degree to which greater specialization and scale of cancer centres contribute to higher efficiencies. To the best of our knowledge no study has been carried out to explore the potential of DEA to assess performance in radiotherapy departments. This is the main objective of this chapter. By developing a comprehensive framework to assess the performance of radiotherapy services and by illustrating its use with an example at the Strategic Health Authority (SHA) level, we aim to contribute to the literature in this under-researched area.

While the use of DEA in the radiotherapy context faces several difficulties, some of which will be discussed later, there are also several distinct reasons that make it suitable and convenient for comparing the performance of radiotherapy departments:

Firstly, DEA can handle the existence of several non-commensurate inputs and outputs, without requiring unit prices for each of them. This is a clear advantage in health care studies, including radiotherapy, when we consider that we are usually confronted with processes characterized by the use of several resources, involved in the delivery of several distinct services, in order to achieve several distinct outcomes. Whilst unit costs for the resources may be obtainable, it is considerably more challenging to obtain information regarding the unit value of outputs and outcomes.

Secondly, DEA uses all the data available to construct a best practice empirical frontier, to which each non-optimal production point is compared. This is a distinct advantage when compared to regression-based techniques that focus on average units and construct an average production function.

Thirdly, in contrast with parametric techniques, such as Stochastic Frontier Analysis, DEA does not require the specification of the functional form that links the inputs to the outputs. Moreover, if information is available, it allows the incorporation of several distinct assumptions regarding the relationships operating at the frontier, regarding the returns to scale, the disposability of the inputs and outputs, and the convexity of the production function.

Fourthly, the performance of DMUs can be assessed using several alternative orientations to the best practice frontier, depending on the context of the study. The DEA projections to the best practice frontier can reflect an output maximization, an input minimization, or a combination of both.

Finally, given that most DEA models can be conceptualized as a linear program, a vast range of useful information becomes available for research, decision-making and policy making. This information is very valuable for performance improvement.

In our view, performance improvement is the ultimate goal, the most important reason for measuring performance. We consider that performance measurement is an integral element of continuous improvement and that even the best performance information is of limited value if it is not used to ultimately improve results. From a formative perspective, there must be a clear focus on using performance information to drive action, in particular improvement and learning, otherwise measurement efforts will be worthless. Measuring performance and learning from results are essential criteria for achieving continuous improvement in an organization [13].

However, to learn from the results and to achieve continuous performance improvement, it is fundamental to use performance evaluation in a formative rather than summative way. As distinguished by Scriven [18], summative evaluation involves the collection and analysis of data with the aim of determining whether an organization is performing better or worse than another. Its aim is solely descriptive and classificatory. In contrast, formative evaluation involves the collection and analysis of data with the aim of developing and improving the organizations. Formative evaluation studies are characterized by an effort to involve the stakeholders and to provide useful feedback to the decision-makers and policy makers in terms of organizational improvement and knowledge development. The ultimate aim of a formative evaluation study is the promotion of learning.

While some progress has been made in this regard, most evaluation studies have used DEA in a summative way, involving rankings, classifications and targets. This article argues that for DEA to reach its full potential in performance improvement in radiotherapy care it needs to be deployed in the formative mode. It is, therefore, critical to define DEA models that are acceptable to their users and that can be used to identify the causes of poor performance, to identify key learning networks, and to develop strategies for performance improvement.

To this purpose, it is fundamental to identify what an ideal radiotherapy facility would look like from the point of view of the main stakeholders and what the main objectives of such a system would be.

A system of ideal radiotherapy cancer care would, among other things, ensure that: (1) all clinically eligible cancer patients within a facility's catchment area have timely access to radiotherapy services; (2) the care provided is clinically effective, in line with agreed standards, and is delivered with the minimum disruption to the patients' lives; (3) equipment is utilized at maximum efficiency and staff workload levels allow the delivery of a safe and high quality service; and (4) there are enough resources available to ensure the provision of an effective, efficient and accessible radiotherapy service (Fig. 11.1). These four main themes – Fair Access to Services, Clinical Effectiveness and Outcomes, Efficiency, and Capacity and Capability – strongly reflect those found in other frameworks to assess performance in health care, including the Performance Assessment Framework [15].

Based on the key features of an ideal radiotherapy facility, it is our belief that any performance measurement system developed to assess radiotherapy departments should include the key dimensions of fair access to services, efficiency, and clinical effectiveness and outcomes. The capacity and capability dimension can, in its turn, play a fundamental role in better understanding the results achieved in the other three dimensions. It is well known that the provision of an effective, efficient and accessible radiotherapy service greatly depends of the availability of resources. Therefore, if patients are to receive adequate and timely radiotherapy treatment, giving them an opportunity to achieve the best outcomes, appropriate equipment and staffing is fundamental.

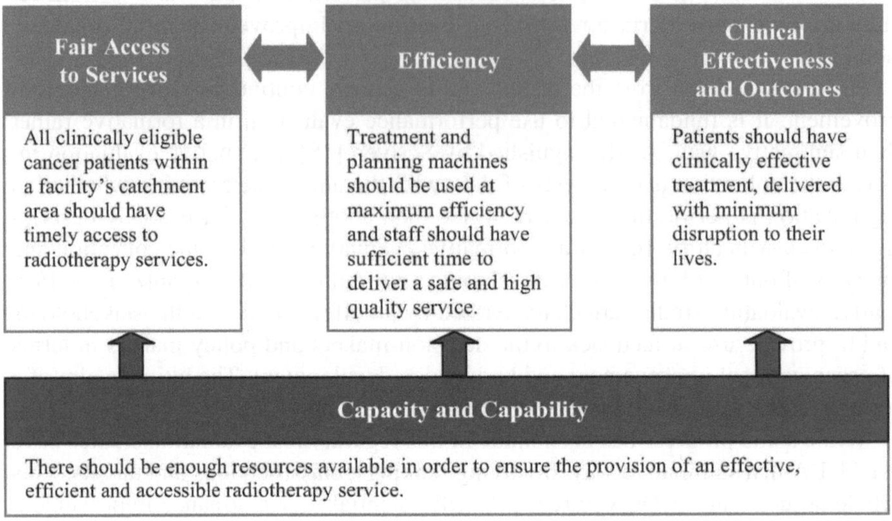

Fig. 11.1. Features of an optimum radiotherapy facility

In what follows we suggest three DEA models for assessing the performance of radiotherapy departments (each one of them capturing one of the dimensions mentioned above), illustrate their use with data from radiotherapy services aggregated at the SHA level, and discuss the importance of this assessment and the learning that can derive from it.

11.3 Results and discussion

Presently there are ten Strategic Health Authorities across England, each with regional responsibility to implement directives and policies laid down by the Department of Health. Each SHA is responsible for various NHS Trusts which run or commission local NHS services, including radiotherapy services. Within this remit, SHAs are under increasing pressure to deliver high quality healthcare services whilst reducing costs and achieving greater economies.

Whilst the DEA analysis can be carried out at a different level (e.g. cancer networks or cancer centres), the availability of data at the SHA level, together with the exploratory nature of this study, were influential regarding the level of analysis adopted. The data used in the models refers mostly to 2007 and was collected from several data sources, including The Information Centre for Health and Social Care, the UK Office for National Statistics, the Royal College of Radiologists website and the study by Williams and Drinkwater [23]. The DEA models have assumed an output orientation and a variable returns to scale (VRS) technology because this type of specification was considered the most appropriate in this context. From one side, SHAs attempt to maximize their outputs with the resources available, and from another side, it cannot be assumed that full proportionality exists between the inputs and outputs.

11.3.1 Fair access to services

One of the main characteristics of an ideal cancer care system is that all patients, wherever they live, should have equality of access to high quality cancer care services. In the context of radiotherapy treatment, this means that all clinically eligible cancer patients within a facility's catchment area should have timely access to high quality radiotherapy services. This is extremely important because there is clinical evidence that the use of radiotherapy improves the outcomes of cancer care.

It is well known that radiotherapy can cure many different types of cancer either alone or in combination with surgery and/or chemotherapy. When the cancer cannot be cured by radiotherapy, either because it is 'locally advanced' or because it has spread to other parts of the body, radiotherapy can still be used with palliative intent to ease symptoms, increase patients' survival time, and improve the patients' quality of life.

It is therefore fundamental to ensure that all clinically eligible cancer patients within a facility's catchment area have timely access to radiotherapy. To measure the extent to which radiotherapy departments achieve this goal we can use as an indicator the percentage of patients diagnosed with cancer who receive radiotherapy (i.e. that receive at least a course of treatment). It is important to emphasize, however, that the local access rate to radiotherapy services must not be used in isolation to evaluate the fairness of access to radiotherapy treatment. The access to radiotherapy has several facets and, even if the percentage of patients diagnosed with cancer and receiving radiotherapy treatment is high, there will be little improvement in the outcomes unless definitive treatment is rapidly available. The interval between the time of diagnosis and initial treatment is crucial to high quality care, and should therefore be minimized wherever possible. The Joint Council of Clinical Oncology [12] defines guidelines for the waiting time targets. Due to the impact that waiting times might have on treatment outcomes and on patients' satisfaction, it is also important to include this measure in any model developed to evaluate fairness of access to radiotherapy services. Furthermore, to achieve optimal outcomes, most cancer care delivery should be planned and coordinated by a multidisciplinary team of oncologic health professionals. Therefore, it is also important to take into account the number of patients who are managed in accordance with evidence based protocols by specialist teams. Considering that information regarding some of these variables is not publicly available, we propose a simpler, but still comprehensive model to assess fairness of access to services. This model uses a single input (the cancer incidence rate per million population) and two outputs (the number of new courses of radiotherapy per million population and the number of courses delivered within the recommended period per million population). Whilst not inclusive of all the information discussed above, this model still provides a more complete assessment of the fairness of access to radiotherapy services than the use of a single access rate, as is commonly suggested in the literature.

Table 11.1. Summary statistics for the variables used in the Fair Access Model

	Cancer incidence rate	*New courses of radiotherapy*	*Courses of radiotherapy delivered within the recommended target*
Average	4873	1892	1662
St Dev	532	433	250
Max	5688	2389	1981
Min	3618	1241	1289

Unit: Per million population of the catchment area
Note: The values for the variable courses of radiotherapy delivered within the recommended target are estimated based on the audit results reported on Williams and Drinkwater (2009).

Table 11.2. Summary of the fair access results across SHAs

Fair access results *DEA results of a VRS model output-oriented*	
Average	91.9%
St Dev	11.3%
Max	100%
Min	66.3%
Number of SHA which score 100%	5

Table 11.1 presents a descriptive summary of the data used in the DEA model adopted to assess the fairness of access to services and Table 11.2 presents a summary of the results obtained for the 10 SHAs compared.

The analysis of the results in terms of fair access to radiotherapy services suggests that whilst the average of the DEA scores is high (above 90%), there is still a significant variation across SHAs. In particular the minimum score of 66.3% achieved in one of the SHAs suggests that, considering the cancer incidence rate in that SHA, the radiotherapy centres belonging to it should be able to increase the levels of new courses and the number of courses of treatment delivered within the recommended periods by around 50%.

Valuable insights can be drawn from these results. Considering the clinical evidence suggesting that the timely use of radiotherapy improves the outcomes of cancer care, whenever the level of performance in this dimension is 'poor', local clinical traditions or working practices, machine and staffing levels, productivity levels and equipment downtime should be investigated to establish the main causes of the poor performance. These factors, to a certain extent, are under the control of the radiotherapy facilities and consequently acting upon them can lead to considerable performance improvements.

Care must be taken, however, when analyzing the access rates to radiotherapy given that local clinical referral protocols and some comorbidity conditions may affect the choice of treatment for cancer. In this respect, a relatively low utilization rate of radiotherapy services in a particular region may simply reflect that the population is too ill to receive radiotherapy, and not necessarily reflect poor access to services. In addition to the comorbidity issue, another factor that may affect utilization rates is patients' choice. A radical course of radiotherapy may last for about six or seven weeks of daily visits to the cancer centre. Some patients may decide that, notwithstanding the clinical recommendation, they prefer not to undergo radiotherapy. This decision may be influenced by factors such as the prospective wait for treatment, the availability of treatment alternatives, and the distance to the cancer centre where the radiotherapy treatment is delivered.

In addition to these factors, there are others that also need to be taken into consideration. It is important to bear in mind that the different SHAs differ significantly in population, geographical size, population density and deprivation characteristics. These are important contextual features that must be taken into account when analyzing the results of the DEA models. As pointed out by Williams and Drinkwater [23], deprivation is a major unrecognized influence on radiotherapy access rates. According to these authors, in regions with higher levels of deprivation, it is likely that fewer patients with cancer receive radiotherapy and the proportion treated radically is lower. This might reflect late presentation with advanced disease, poor performance status and co-morbid illness.

To explore the extent to which deprivation might explain the DEA results discussed above, we depict the deprivation scores in 2007 by Local Authority (LA) grouped by SHAs against the DEA fair access scores (Fig. 11.2).

The English indices of multiple deprivation [16] combine a number of indicators on seven domains. These domains have been chosen to cover a range of economic, social and housing issues into a single deprivation score for each super output area, of which there are 32482 in England, each containing an average of 1500 people.

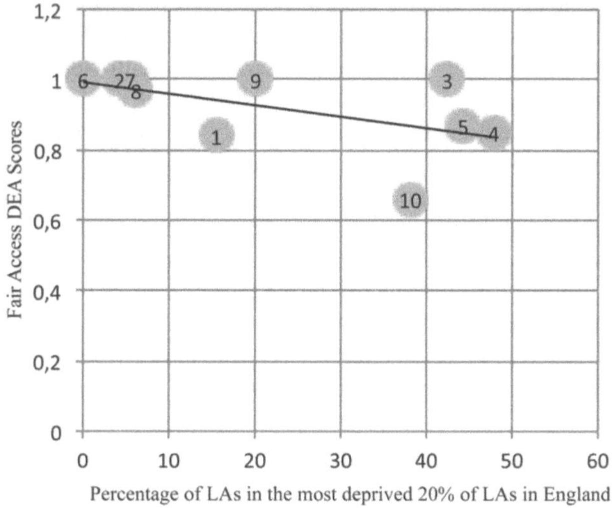

Fig. 11.2. Relationship between the fair access DEA scores and the deprivation scores

The negative inclination of the trend line depicted in Figure 11.2 seems to corroborate the findings of Williams and Drinkwater [23]. As can be seen from Figure 11.2, three of the five SHAs with the highest DEA scores on fair access to radiotherapy services are simultaneously the least deprived SHAs in England. SHAs 6, 7 and 2 have a 100% DEA score and have the lowest percentage of LAs in the most deprived 20% of LAs in England. Contrarily, SHAs 10, 4 and 5 are amongst the most deprived SHAs in the country, which appears to have an impact on the poorer performance of these SHAs regarding the fairness of access to radiotherapy services.

11.3.2 Efficiency

Efficiency is a major concern in the area of cancer care and it has been the subject of considerable attention and discussion by health care authorities. As previously emphasized, inefficiency means that money is wasted, but more importantly it means that the opportunity to provide appropriate care to those in need is lost.

Several performance indicators can be used to assess how efficiently a radiotherapy facility is using its resources, including both staff and equipment workload levels. On the staff side the following inputs can be used: the number of clinical oncologists, radiographers and physicists. Although other staff groups are involved, these are the three main categories of staff needed to plan and deliver a course of radiotherapy. The model would be, however, incomplete if it neglected the inputs related to the availability of equipment. The prime performance indicator to consider in this regard is the number of linear accelerators (LinAcs) available. Although there is a variety of other equipment that forms an essential part of any radiotherapy service (e.g. simulators, image-based planning and treatment planning systems as well as mould room, branchytherapy and unsealed source facilities), LinAcs are the most important piece of equipment in a modern radiotherapy department and, as such, the number of LinAcs per million head of population is usually used as the prime performance indicator to assess a radiotherapy department's capacity. It is, however, important to bear in mind that radiotherapy is a complex multi-step process involving other equipment which might, to a greater or lesser extent, explain the performance results achieved by a radiotherapy facility. Finally, it is important to consider that some cancer centres conduct fundamental research in this area. It is therefore important to assess their research efficiency. To this purpose, the inclusion of the budget allocated to research could also be considered as an input measure.

Regarding the outputs, there are several measures that can be used. The dose delivered at each visit for radiotherapy is referred to as a fraction, therefore, the number of fractions delivered is a good indicator to measure the efficiency in the use of resources. The average number of fractions per LinAc per working hour is usually considered a suitable indicator of equipment workload. Another measure that can give us some evidence of an inefficient use of radiotherapy resources, and which may negatively affect the outcomes of treatment, is the number of unscheduled gaps in treatment. An appropriate prevention or management of unplanned gaps has the potential to increase the local tumor control rates in certain tumor types, reducing long-term health care costs involved in dealing with local recurrences. It is therefore critical to minimize the percentage of patients with unplanned gaps in overall treatment and the average duration of these gaps.

Furthermore, while it is highly desirable to achieve an efficient use of resources, staff workload should not be so large that it becomes impossible to provide a good quality clinical service and to carry out essential non-clinical duties (such as academic/scientific requirements). The enrolment of staff in academic work and scientific research is critical for the development and diffusion of knowledge on cancer care. Apart from this, it is important to emphasize that staff overload greatly contributes to increasing levels of stress and lower job satisfaction, which is highly undesirable because of the risk of error and the effect that this may have on the quality and safety of treatment. In this respect, and whenever data is available, it is important to also include in the model output indicators capturing these aspects (e.g. the number of scientific publications in major cancer research journals by the staff and the staff satisfaction with the work environment).

Bearing in mind the data that is publicly available, we have used a DEA model with two inputs (number of machines in clinical use – i.e LinAcs or equivalent machines – and WTE clinical oncologists) and one output (number of fractions delivered). Table 11.3 presents a descriptive summary of the data used in this model and Table 11.4 presents a summary of the results obtained for the 10 SHAs compared.

The results on Table 11.4 show a fairly efficient sector with an average efficiency score of 95%. In spite of this, some SHAs present considerable scope for improvement as is the case of SHA 4, which presents the minimum efficiency score at 77%. The same is to say that the radiotherapy centres belonging to this SHA should, with the current capacity level, be able to deliver more 30% of fractions, and conse-

Table 11.3. Summary statistics for the variables used in the Efficiency Model

	Number of machines in clinical use	*WTE consultant clinical oncologists*	*Fractions delivered*
Average	4.4	8.8	29341.5
St Dev	0.6	1.2	6615.9
Max	5.2	11.2	36426.0
Min	3.3	7.6	17678.0

Unit: Per million population of the catchment area
Note: The values for the variable WTE consultant clinical oncologists refers to 2008.

Table 11.4. Summary of the efficiency results across SHAs

Efficiency Results *DEA results of a VRS model output-oriented*	
Average	95.0%
St Dev	7.8%
Max	100%
Min	77.0%
Number of SHA which score 100%	5

quently, deliver treatment to more patients. Once again, valuable insights can be drawn from these results. More important than discovering which SHAs (or radiotherapy departments) are efficient and which are not, is to discover the main reasons for their inefficiency. Variation in efficiency may be associated with several factors which are department-related, including unplanned downtime caused by old equipment; higher complexity of LinAcs, which decreases the number of patients that can be treated per hour and then the number of fractions delivered. There are, however, some causes that are patient-related, and which cannot be neglected (e.g., transport difficulties; intercurrent illness; radiotherapy reactions; personal circumstances, and so on).

11.3.3 Clinical effectiveness and outcomes

In addition to the timely access to treatment, and the efficiency in the use of resources, it is fundamental to evaluate the quality of the services provided. It is of paramount importance to ensure that the treatment patients receive in a radiotherapy unit is clinically effective.

Certainly, there are several different indicators that can be used to assess clinical effectiveness and outcomes. These include, for example, local cancer control rates, patients' satisfaction, cancer survival rates, morbidity and mortality statistics, as well as quality of life indicators. In spite of the interest in monitoring outcomes, in practice, the data available for clinical outcomes is very limited or inaccurate. For instance, whilst considerable progress has been done in recent years in measuring patients' quality of life, the assessment of this indicator is often inaccurate [21], which prevents its use on a systematic basis in DEA analyses. These facts impose serious restrictions on the DEA models that can be developed to assess this dimension of performance. In spite of this, we believe that it is possible to develop simple DEA models that still can provide valuable insights regarding the clinical effectiveness of the treatments delivered by the different cancer centres. The model we have used to illustrate the usefulness of DEA has two inputs (number of radical courses delivered and number of palliative courses delivered) and two outputs (1 year survival rate following diagnosis of prostate cancer and 5 years survival rate following diagnosis of prostate cancer). The survival rates are age standardized relative survival rates for patients diagnosed between 2001 and 2003 and followed up to 31st December 2008. Age standardization allows control for differences in the age structure of the population between SHAs, and allows unbiased comparisons between rates. Although there are a variety of malignant conditions for which radiotherapy is currently the recommended treatment, radiotherapy is the most common radical treatment used in prostate cancer, and therefore, we decided to use the survival rates from this cancer as a reasonable proxy for cancer survival following radiotherapy.

Two weight restrictions linking each input with the respective output were also used to ensure meaningful results. For example, the weight attributed to the first input must be similar to the weight attributed to the second output, as these two measures refer to the treatment of radical patients. The summary statistics for the

Table 11.5. Summary statistics for the variables used in the Clinical Effectiveness and Outcomes Model

	Radical courses per million population	*Palliative courses per million population*	*1 Year prostate cancer survival rate*	*5 Years prostate cancer survival rate*
Average	1246	1041	92%	78%
St Dev	293	242	1%	3%
Max	1592	1339	94%	82%
Min	727	621	89%	71%

Table 11.6. Summary of the clinical effectiveness and outcomes results across SHAs

Clinical Effectiveness and Outcomes Results *DEA results of a VRS model output-oriented*	
Average	78.0%
St Dev	13.0%
Max	100%
Min	67.0%
Number of SHA which score 100%	2

variables used on this model are displayed in Table 11.5 and its results are shown on Table 11.6.

In consistency with the results obtained for the previous performance dimensions, the results presented in Table 11.6 suggest that there is considerable scope for improvement with regard to the effectiveness of treatments across SHAs. In this particular case, according to the DEA scores, only two SHAs are considered clinically effective.

The DEA model we have used to assess clinical effectiveness and outcomes presents, however, some limitations that cannot be neglected. In addition to the difficulty in measuring some of the outcomes, as discussed above, and having considered the survival rates of only one type of cancer, it is also important to take into consideration that the performance measures related with survival rates are 'delayed' outcomes, which means that lower rates are a symptom of poor performance in the past, and not necessarily an indicator of the actual performance of radiotherapy departments. Whilst the inputs considered in the model refer to 2007, the survival rates refer to patients diagnosed between 2001 and 2003 and followed up to 31st December 2008. It is not known from the data available, when the radiotherapy treatments were delivered. Therefore, some care must be taken in analyzing the results obtained. Furthermore, it is important to bear in mind that many factors other than health care can affect and explain variations in outcomes. For example, a finding of a lower-than-expected 5-year survival rate in one cancer centre relative to another could simply reflect differences in patients' comorbidity status, as opposed to poor quality of care received. In this respect, it is desirable to include in the model some variables related with patient case-mix, in order to capture the environmental factors that may affect the performance of the departments.

Furthermore, it is well known that securing improvements in cancer survival rates requires continuing efforts on many fronts, not just in treatments. As pointed out by the Department of Health [7], better awareness and prevention, earlier diagnosis, and better and faster treatment, all play an important role in reducing both the incidence of cancer and the deaths it causes.

11.4 Conclusions

Data envelopment analysis is probably one of the most widespread OR/MS techniques used to compare the performance of organizational units and its use in the health care sector has been prolific. Surprisingly, however, its use on the context of cancer care has been very rare.

In this article we have illustrated and discussed the potential of using DEA for formative evaluation of radiotherapy services. The theoretical framework we propose is inclusive of structure, process and outcomes, and portrays the views of different stakeholders, including patients, clinicians, and managers. Whilst the models we have used to assess fairness of access, efficiency and clinical effectiveness of radiotherapy services present some limitations due to data unavailability, they still provide valuable information for decision makers. The fact that the analysis was carried out at the level of the English SHAs, meant that we only had 10 DMUs, which further imposed some limitation on the models used, as in these cases it is important to keep the number of inputs and outputs to a minimum in order to obtain some discrimination in the results. It is important to mention, however, that the use of DEA on small population sizes is not rare (e.g. [14]) and researchers have shown that DEA is a reliable technique as long as the total number of DMUs is greater than the total number of input and output variables [2, 22].

Despite the difficulties encountered in obtaining data for some models and their illustrative nature, there are some important empirical findings from our study. Firstly, we found wide variation in terms of the fairness of access to radiotherapy services across SHAs. This variation ought to be investigated in order to ensure equitable access to the services across the country. A significant variation was also found in terms of efficiency and effectiveness of the services delivered, suggesting that a better use of the resources could lead to more services being delivered to the patients in need and that there is potential to improve the clinical effectiveness and outcomes of these services. Secondly, considering that performance is multidimensional, our empirical analysis seems to suggest that trade-offs exist between some of the performance dimensions assessed. With the exception of SHA 3, which presents above average scores in all three dimensions (Fig. 11.3), and therefore is a SHA that could serve as a learning benchmark to other SHAs, all the other SHAs seem to achieve above average performance results in some of the dimensions at the expense of poorer performance results in the others.

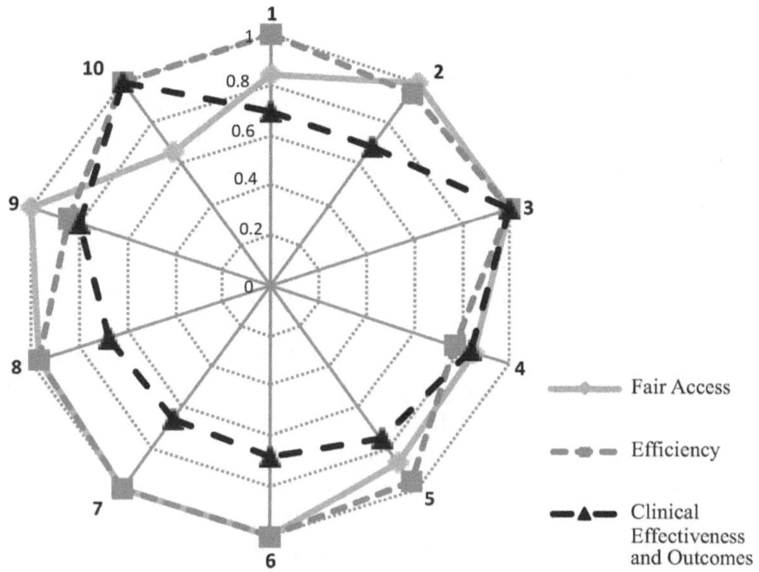

Fig. 11.3. Trade-offs between performance dimensions

The fact that the DEA analysis allows the identification of suitable learning peers to each SHA, as well as targets for performance improvement is a major advantage of this technique. Furthermore, by considering simultaneously multiple inputs and/or multiple outputs, the DEA technique offers a more comprehensive assessment of performance and more robust findings than the traditional single ratios approach, where standard ratios such as fractions per LinAc or the percentage of cancer patients receiving radiotherapy treatment are analyzed over time and used for comparison between cancer centres. Indeed, it has long been recognized that single factor productivity analyses are not adequate to perform comprehensive performance assessments and gain a sense of the overall performance of health care organizations.

The full potential of DEA can only be reached, however, if it is used in a formative mode. That is, the main goal in performing the DEA assessment should not be to rank radiotherapy services but rather to catalyze further analysis about the underlying reasons for performance variation, identify potential areas for improvement and calibrate future targets on the basis of comparative benchmarks.

Despite the potential of DEA to assess the performance of radiotherapy departments, there are some limitations that have to be understood and dealt with carefully in order to get meaningful results from the use of this technique. Some of these limitations are related with the DEA technique, others are related with the particular context of our analysis. These limitations include the following:

- DEA assumes that it is possible to fully characterize the production of health care by identifying a set of inputs, outputs and outcomes of production. However, some of the outputs and outcomes of radiotherapy treatment are not measurable.

Furthermore, there are an extensive number of factors operating at different levels which impact on this transformation and which may lead to the violation of the linear input-output relationship.

- DEA assumes one-way causality between inputs to outputs. In this respect, it is assumed that higher levels of inputs should lead to higher levels of outputs. However as pointed out by Smith [20], in a context where the level of output achievement is published, poor levels of outputs can generate pressure for increased resources. In this respect, a negative correlation may exist between inputs and outputs. Smith [20] refers to this problem as 'negative political feedback'. Orme and Smith [17] examined the effects of this problem for DEA studies and concluded that, in the presence of 'negative political feedback', DEA estimates of efficiency may be subject to bias against DMUs using fewer resources. These DMUs may be asked to make greater improvements in efficiency than DMUs using higher levels of resources. In this respect, the use of DEA for target setting in a context where the output data is subject to great political scrutiny, as is the case of radiotherapy services, requires further caution.
- Measuring outputs represents a utilitarian approach that values the consequences of actions above anything else. In this respect, the use of DEA to assess performance in radiotherapy services can lead to a biased representation of their success. The delivery of these services is also governed by non-consequentalist principles and it is essential to provide alternative representations of success.
- Given the arbitrariness involved in the selection of variables used in a DEA model (particularly output and outcome variables), a DEA analysis can lead to biased and potentially misleading results. This is one of the reasons why it is important to use DEA for formative evaluation rather than for judgmental assessment. In the case of radiotherapy, when defining the inputs, outputs and outcomes to compare the performance of departments it is very important to bear in mind that a radiotherapy department may provide treatment to different kinds of patients including urgent, radical, palliative and post-operative patients, each of these groups having different needs and different treatment complexities. For example, the use of simple outputs like the number of patients treated, or the number of courses or fractions of treatment delivered, do not account for factors such as treatment complexity or the performance status of the patients, suffering clear limitations. Therefore, when output/outcome measures are selected, case mix, risk or severity adjustment is strongly recommended to account for determinants of outcome that are outside of the control of the health care provider.
- Standard DEA models do not take into account stochastic variability in the data and are therefore very sensitive to data errors. Considering that stochastic variability exists in some of the variables discussed above (e.g. survival rates) it is important to bear in mind some of the developments in DEA modeling that take into account the stochastic variability in the data [19].
- DEA assumes proper envelopment of all the DMUs. That is, a meaningful measure of efficiency can only be calculated if the DMU under evaluation has a comparison set. Otherwise, the DMU will be classified as efficient, simply because no comparison can be established. This is a limitation that results from the fact that

DEA allows full flexibility in the weights applied to each input and output. In this respect, if a DMU is characterized by a peculiar mix of inputs or outputs, it can find a set of very extreme weights under which it is efficient. This is a problem likely to occur in the context of radiotherapy treatment as some of the cancer centres are very specialized, and therefore present very specific characteristics. This problem can be solved by separating the radiotherapy centres into homogeneous clusters and performing separate analyses for each cluster.

Awareness of these factors and of their potential impact on the results is necessary if useful information is to be obtained. Furthermore, considering that performance measurement may result in responses from individuals quite different from those intended by the organization, great attention needs to be given to the design, implementation and use of performance assessment models. It is fundamental to have a good understanding about the way individuals perceive, process and respond to performance information. In this respect, it is our conviction that performance assessment in radiotherapy departments can be most useful if the perceived purpose is one of learning and improvement, and as long as the results are interpreted very cautiously, in a formative rather than judgmental way.

Despite all the challenges, we believe that DEA has great potential in this context, given its ability to take into account multiple inputs, outputs and outcomes, without requiring a specification of the functional form for the transformation process. Moreover, if used in a formative mode, engaging the decision-makers, it can provide valuable information that can lead to the establishment of learning networks and the development of improvement action plans.

The longer term aims of this research are three fold. Firstly, to implement and refine the framework proposed in this chapter using a sample of radiotherapy departments. Secondly, to apply the DEA technique in a formative way, in order to assess its potential to contribute to performance improvement in practice. In particular we aim to identify key learning networks, and to design strategies for performance improvement of radiotherapy services. Thirdly, to undertake in-depth analyses of the performance results, with the aim of drawing conclusions for radiotherapy delivery, management and policy making.

Acknowledgements. We would like to thank Graeme Doherty for useful comments during the preparation of this manuscript. Funding support for this research was provided by Fundação para a Ciência e a Tecnologia (FEDER/POCI 2010).

References

1. Appleby, J., Thomas, A.: Measuring performance in the NHS: what really matters? British Medical Journal **320**, 1464–1467 (2000)
2. Camanho, A.S., Dyson, R.G.: Data envelopment analysis and Malmquist indices for measuring group performance. Journal of Productivity Analysis **26**, 35–50 (2006)
3. Charnes, A., Cooper, W.W., Rhodes, E.: Measuring the efficiency of decision making units. European Journal of Operational Research **2**(6), 429–444 (1978)

4. Chilingerian, J.A., Sherman, H.D.: Health care applications: From hospitals to physicians, from productive efficiency to quality frontiers. In: Cooper, W.W., Seiford, L.M., Zhu, J. (eds.) Handbook on Data Envelopment Analysis. Kluwer Academic Publishers, New York, Chapter 17 (2004)
5. Cooper, W., Seiford, L., Tone, K.: Data Envelopment Analysis: A Comprehensive Text with Models, Applications, References and DEA-Solver Software. Kluwer Academic Publishers, Massachusetts (2000)
6. Cooper, W., Seiford, L., Zhu, J.: Handbook on data envelopment analysis. Kluwer Academic Publishers, Massachusetts (2004)
7. Department of Health: The NHS Cancer Plan – A plan for investment, a plan for reform. Department of Health, London (2000)
8. Dervaux, B., Eeckhoudt, L., Lebrun, T., Sailly, J.C.: A cost-effectiveness analysis using data envelopment analysis – an application to colorectal-cancer screening. Medical Decision Making **11**(1), 68–68 (1991)
9. Hollingsworth, B.: The measurement of efficiency and productivity of health care delivery. Health Economics **17**, 1107–1128 (2008)
10. Hollingsworth, B., Dawson, P.J., Maniadakis, N.: Efficiency measurement of health care: a review of non-parametric methods and applications. Health Care Management Science **2**, 162–172 (1999)
11. Johnston, K., Gerard, K.: Assessing efficiency in the UK breast screening programme: does size of screening unit make a difference? Health Policy **56**(1), 21–32 (2001)
12. Joint Council for Clinical Oncology. Reducing delays in cancer treatment: some targets. London: Royal College of Physicians and Royal College of Radiologists (1993)
13. Kaye, M., Anderson, R.: Continuous improvement: the ten essential criteria. International Journal of Quality & Reliability Management **16**(5), 485–506 (1999)
14. Langabeer, J.R., Ozcan, Y.A.: The economies of cancer care: longitudinal changes in provider efficiency. Health Care Management Science **12**, 192–200 (2009)
15. NHS Executive: The NHS Performance Assessment Framework. NHS Executive, London (1999)
16. Office of the Deputy Prime Minister: The English indices of deprivation 2004 (revised). HMSO, London (2004)
17. Orme, C., Smith, P.C.: The Potential for Endogeneity Bias in Data Envelopment Analysis. Journal of the Operational Research Society **47**, 73–83 (1996)
18. Scriven, M.: The methodology of evaluation. In: Tyler, R.W., Gagne, R.M., Scriven, M. (eds.) Perspectives on Curriculum Evaluation, pp. 39–83. Rand McNally, Chicago (1967)
19. Sengupta, J.K.: Transformations in stochastic DEA models. Journal of Econometrics **46**(1–2), 109–123 (1990)
20. Smith, P.C.: Negative Political Feedback: An examination of the Problem of Modelling Political responses in Public Sector Effectiveness Auditing. Accounting Auditing & Accountability Journal **5**(1), 5–20 (1992)
21. Tassinari, D.: Surrogate end points of quality of life assessment: have we really found what we are looking for? Health and Quality of Life Outcomes **1**, 71 (2003)
22. Thanassoulis, E., Boussofiane, A., Dyson, R.G.: A comparison of data envelopment analysis and ratios as tools for performance assessment. Omega International Journal of Management Science **24**(1), 229–244 (1996)
23. Williams, M.V., Drinkwater, K.J.: Geographical Variation in Radiotherapy Services Across the UK in 2007 and the Effect of Deprivation. Clinical Oncology **21**, 431–440 (2009)

Chapter 12

A simulation-based decision support tool to analyze clinical pathways in hospital

Elena Tànfani and Angela Testi

Abstract. In this chapter we analyze the patient flow inside a hospital surgical department, adopting a patient-centered perspective focused on clinical pathways (CPs). The specific aim is to develop a decision support tool to make the clinical point of view, implicit in the CP approach, compatible with the economic and managerial requirements of the hospital. The simulation-based modeling framework herein proposed analyzes the three main operative areas, or sub-processes, of the flow of surgical patients within the hospital, i.e. waiting list management, operating theatre planning and bed ward organization. The framework has been applied to a university public hospital in Genova (Italy). Firstly, the simulation model has been used to compare alternative scenarios, changing waiting list and bed management strategic decisions, through a complete set of indexes able to capture the performance of the three sub-processes, with parity of resources. Secondly, the model has been adapted to evaluate the impact on the overall department performance of iteratively introducing the solutions given by a 0-1 optimization model developed to solve the tactical operating room planning problem. The reported results show that the integrated decision tool can be helpful in supporting decisions that are particularly hard in healthcare delivery because they usually imply a tradeoff between different performance indexes.

Keywords: patient flow, clinical pathways, hospital surgical department, simulation, optimization, performance analysis

---

E. Tànfani
Department of Economics and Quantitative Methods (DIEM), University of Genova, Via Vivaldi 5, 16126 Genova, Italy
e-mail: etanfani@economia.unige.it

A. Testi (✉)
Department of Economics and Quantitative Methods (DIEM), University of Genova, Via Vivaldi 5, 16126 Genova, Italy
e-mail: testi@economia.unige.it

Tànfani E., Testi A. (Eds.): Advanced Decision Making Methods Applied to Health Care.
International Series in Operations Research & Management Science 173
DOI 10.1007/978-88-470-2321-5_12,

12.1 Introduction and problem addressed

In all industrialized countries, where health system sustainability is challenged by fast medical progress, population aging and increasing demand for quality care by more informed patients, the so-called clinical pathways (CPs) are receiving growing attention [37]. A CP is "the path" followed by an ill person through the healthcare system, describing spatial and temporal sequences of activities to be performed, based on scientific and technical knowledge and organizational, professional and technological available resources [7]. In this sense, CPs can be considered as an operational tool in the clinical treatment of diseases, from a patient-focused point of view [20].

The medical literature is very rich and a plethora of papers have been put forward to develop CPs for specific diseases and pathologies. Many studies show that, appropriately implemented, CPs have the potential to reduce patient length of stay and limit variability in care, thereby yielding cost savings [22].

On the contrary, the operations research and management science (OR&MS) literature that focused on giving modeling insights to make CPs operative in the current health service delivery system and improve their impact on the organization is particularly poor. It seems that no consolidated agreement exists to fine tune clinical CP requirements with the optimal management of resources. This is, however, a crucial issue because different patients compete for the same resources, at a system level as well as at a facility level. In order to fill this gap some authors have proposed discrete-event simulation models aimed at investigating the global flow of patients belonging to different paths, focusing on hospital or ambulatory facilities [4,26]. Maliapen and Dangerfield [17] have used a system dynamics-based simulation approach to examine the development of clinical pathways in a hospital in Australia, while Cote and Stein [6] have developed a semi-Markovian queuing model for modeling the flow of a single patient during a treatment given in an ambulatory structure.

In this chapter we focus our attention on the flow of surgical patients through a hospital department, following different CPs and requiring hospital resources such as operating rooms (ORs), ward beds, surgeon and nurse time, and so on.

How to decide how to allocate hospital resources to the different homogeneous CPs grouped in specialties remains a challenge. In other words, it is necessary, for instance, to decide how many OR blocks should be assigned to orthopedic, cardiologist or endocrine surgeons, such that the clinical pathways for hip replacement can be compatible with angioplasty and thyroidectomy interventions.

In this chapter we suggest a holistic decision tool, based on a simulation framework, to solve this problem As mentioned, our proposed framework is patient-centered to match clinical decisions following a CP approach with resource utilization. This means, therefore, identifying the relevant patient characteristics for supporting organizational and management decisions taking into consideration the doctor's and hospital's point of view as well as the patient's

From the patient's point of view, the most important characteristic is his/her need, measured, as we will explain in Section 12.2, using the Urgency Related Group (URG) assigned by the surgeon and the waiting time. From the doctor's point of view, patients are classified into specialties following the pathology problem they face in accordance with the CP as prescribed by evidence-based guidelines and specific protocols. Finally, the characteristics pertaining to the hospital's point of view are related to how many resources he/she requires. In our framework we utilize the operating time and the length of stay as proxies for resource utilization. The first is proportional to operating room costs and the second to the stay area ones.

Note also that the proposed decision tool faces all three usual levels of business organization: strategic, tactical and operational. In particular, the strategic level is the decision process at which a hospital determines objectives and uses resources to achieve these objectives. The main activities, at this level, establish how to best meet demand while controlling costs. In this chapter, this aspect regards waiting list management as well as organization of bed wards (see Sections 12.2.1.1 and 12.2.1.3). Tactics uses resources to accomplish the objectives stated at the strategic level. In our framework we face tactical decisions by means of the optimization model aimed at determining the optimal use of the operating theatre facility (see Section 12.2.1.2). This means determining how many OR sessions from the total available should be assigned to each specialty and on which day of the week they should be scheduled. Finally, the operational level is devoted to linking tactical decisions to achieve the strategic objective in the current daily activity. In our framework the operational level consists in deciding which patients are selected to be admitted each day and their sequencing order.

The chapter is organized as follows. In Section 12.2, the modeling framework is given, with particular attention given to the system representation and its subdivision into operative areas and decisions to be taken. Application to a real case study is provided in Section 12.3, together with a discussion of the results herein reported. Finally, some conclusions and directions on future research are given in Section 12.4.

12.2 Materials and methods

This chapter analyzes how patient flow, following different CPs in a surgical department, can be made mutually compatible with respect to the available resources. We suggest a holistic decision tool based on a simulation modeling framework

From the analysis of the literature it appears that simulation has been extensively used to support decisions arising in hospitals, where direct experimentation is too costly and almost impossible to pursue [12, 13].

In particular, some authors use simulation for improving waiting list management and scheduling patient admission in hospitals [24, 34]. Tuft and Gallivan [31] use simulation to compare different strategies for determining admission dates for patients awaiting cataract extraction, while Ratcliffe et al. [21] evaluate alternative allocation policies for the management of a waiting list for liver transplantation.

Other works deal with the use of simulation for operating room planning and scheduling. Among them, a practical and efficient simulation model to support OR scheduling decisions concerning patients waiting for elective surgery is proposed in [8], while in [2] simulation is used to assess proposals for improving the utilization of orthopedic trauma theatre sessions. In [29] a discrete event simulation model has been developed in order to compare different priority rules for the OR scheduling problem.

Simulation has also been used for planning bed capacity [11] and for balancing bed unit utilizations [5], while Akkerman and Knip [1] use simulation to reallocate hospital beds, taking into account the relationships between patient length of stay, bed availability and hospital waiting lists.

From a more "holistic" point of view, Harper [10] develops an integrated simulation model for the planning and management of operating theatre, beds and workforce needs, while VanBerkel and Blake [33] propose a discrete event simulation model to support capacity planning and wait time reduction in a general surgery department.

We argue that, to be most effective, the decisions at different levels should be based on an integrated approach and, consequently, we propose a simulation-based framework integrated under two points of view. Firstly, because it includes the three main operative areas, or sub-processes, into which the flow of surgical patients can be broken down into, i.e., waiting list management, operating theatre planning and bed ward organization. Secondly, because it embodies a 0-1 model in order to iteratively solve the OR planning problem and determine how many OR blocks must be assigned to each specialty in a given planning horizon, as well as a cyclic timetable that assigns a specialty to each OR during each day.

12.2.1 Modeling framework and system representation

We focus our attention on the flow of homogeneous groups of patients, grouped by their CPs, within a surgical hospital department. Within each group, the pathway is characterized not only by clinical characteristics proxied by the specialty, but also by a set of attributes that describe the resource requirement. In particular, in our framework we consider the following attributes: i) the Urgency Related Group (URG); ii) the Expected Operating Time (EOT) and iii) the Length of Stay (LOS). Such attributes manage the pathway of the patient through the system, where a given amount of resources is given. In particular we can take as proxies of hospital resources the number of "beds" and "OR blocks", assuming that they include all other inputs, such as staff, materials, drugs, etc. We can, therefore, refer to a surgical department made up of n different specialties, each of them responsible for one specialty managing a single waiting list and sharing a given number m of ORs and b of stay beds

In Figure 12.1 a synthetic flow chart representation of the system under study is given. This is the first step for the development of the discrete event simulation model since it identifies the elements of the system and the functional relationships between them.

As usual, the system representation requires abstraction of only the most important features of the system that generate the underlying process. In our framework, we take into consideration only the elective surgery pathways followed by patients that present to the department because they need a surgical intervention.

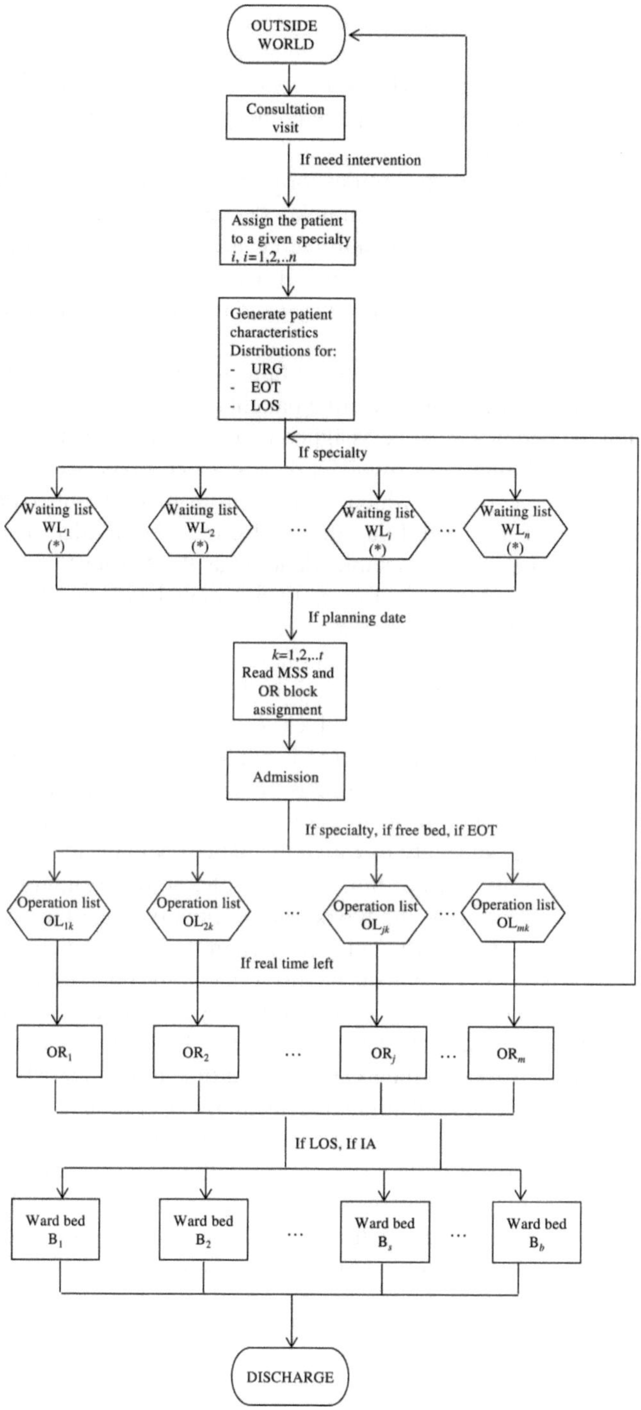

Fig. 12.1. System representation overview

Moreover, we have ignored the causes of removal from the waiting list without admission, for example in the case of renunciation or death, and we have assumed that after admission all patients will be operated on. Note that, in the case study reported in Section 12.3, the flow of patients here depicted represents 90% of all cases entering the department.

Elective patients, which are the entities, or parts, of the model, start the care process with a consultation visit when a clinician decides if they need an intervention or not. In the latter case additional examinations are prescribed and they should be checked later, i.e., they re-enter the system. However, if they need an intervention, the surgeon assigns the patients to a specialty i and registers them in the corresponding waiting list (WL_i).

The first decision, as we will see later, pertains to the queue discipline (*) of the waiting list, i.e., the order in which elective patients are admitted to be operated on. After admission the patients must be assigned to an OR on a given day.

Planning and scheduling ORs involves different decisions. At a tactical level, the available OR time capacity, which is split into a given number of OR block times (usually one half to one full day in length), must be divided over the surgical teams. Secondly, the cyclic timetable, denoted as the Master Surgical Schedule (MSS), which determines the surgical specialty associated with each OR during each day, must be decided. At the beginning of each planning horizon, the simulation model reads for each day k of the planning horizon (usually a week) the MSS parameters, i.e., the specialty assigned to OR j on day k. Before including a patient in the Operation List (OL_{jk}) of a given OR block jk, the model firstly verifies if there is a free ward bed and afterwards that the EOT is not longer than the time left available in the assigned OR block time. If the time is not adequate to include the patient in the operation list, the patient returns to the waiting list to be scheduled in the next OR block assigned to the specialty to which the patient belongs to. The model goes on trying to fill the operation list as much as possible, until the sum of the EOTs of the patients included is equal to the block length. Finally, once the operation lists for each day k are created, the last decisions pertain to the sequencing order of the interventions on each block, i.e., the queue discipline of the operation lists. The ORs are modeled as machines with service times given by the durations of the interventions, which can be different to the EOTs. Note that if the surgery durations of the first patients operated on exceed the EOTs, the real time left in a block might not be enough to start the intervention of some patients in the operation list. These patients are, therefore, shifted and their operation postponed to another day.

Finally, after the intervention the patient is pushed into a ward bed where he/she remains for a given number of stay days, according to his/her length of stay, before being discharged. The stay area organization sub-process consists of decisions regarding bed organization. Different strategies can be used, such as associating the beds to surgical specialties, and differentiating/reallocating stay areas and beds according to the patient length of stay (if LOS) and/or Intensity of Assistance (if IA).

By the system representation it appears that from the hospital's point of view the main decisions affecting the flow of patients can be broken down into three sub-processes or operative areas, each of which require appropriate decision making: i) waiting list management; ii) operating theatre planning and scheduling; and iii) ward organization.

In the following we will briefly give some details on the operative assumptions and rules that can be stated for each sub-process, thus showing better how our integrated model works.

12.2.1.1 Waiting list management

Waiting list management affects the order in which patients are admitted to be operated on. Some hospitals simply admit patients according to a generic "first in–first out" rule, with some exceptions for more urgent cases. However, today attention is focused on the determination of a prioritized order of admission based on clinical conditions and several urgency criteria.

In our framework we consider two different rules for the queue discipline of waiting lists. The first is the representation of what happens in current practice (real order), which is more or less based on a first in–first out rule, giving some pre-emption to urgent cases but without following any explicit rule. The second recognizes the so-called "time appropriateness" of health care services. This means ensuring that everyone is treated within his individual "right" time, assessed on a "need" principle [28]. The interest in evaluating individual needs has a long history, beginning in the late 1960s and early 1970s when several prioritization formulae were developed (see [19] for a complete literature review on prioritization).

Accordingly, waiting list policies have been implemented all over the world following two main approaches: (i) determining priority scores directly and (ii) categorizing patients into urgency classes according to the maximum time they can wait without deteriorating [30]. In this chapter, we pursue the idea of combining the two approaches, in such a way as to integrate "urgency" and "priority" [32]. In more detail, when a patient is registered in the elective waiting list, the surgeon assigns him/her to an Urgency Related Group (URG), i.e., recognizes he/she must be operated on within a Maximum Time Before Treatment (MTBT). In the department under study, five urgency categories (A1, A2, B, C and D) are stated with MTBTs of 8, 30, 60, 180 and 360 days, respectively.

The queue discipline is, therefore, based on the priority scores of patients, assessed on the basis of both the URG and the amount of time they have already waited. In particular, following the prioritization algorithm used herein, the patients are characterized by an "urgency coefficient", associated to their MTBT, which gives the speed at which the clinical need of the patient increases over time. For instance, if a patient must be treated within 30 days, and another within 60 days, one day spent on the list for the first patient equals two days spent by the second patient, because they both must obtain the treatment at their individual MTBT. The urgency coefficient of the second patient is, therefore, double that of the first one. Patients proceed in the list according to their urgency and gain different relative priorities, given the same time spent in the list. Therefore, for each patient the priority score is computed by multiplying the chronological time already waited by the urgency coefficient of his/her URG.

12.2.1.2 OR planning and scheduling

The OR planning and scheduling sub-process received the closest attention in recent international literature [3], because this is one of the most critical decisions arising in any surgical department due to the high costs of the operating theatre facility. The problem of planning and scheduling ORs implies strategic as well as tactical and operational decisions [35]. At a strategic level the number and type of ORs available for the department and the hours that ORs will be open must be decided. Then, at a tactical level, the ORs' capacity must be shared between the surgical groups, or specialties, and a cyclic timetable, denoted the Master Surgical Schedule (MSS), is constructed on a medium-term stand point to define the assignment between specialties and ORs for each day of the planning horizon considered. Finally the operational level of decisions is related to the so-called "surgery process scheduling" and splits into two sub-problems called "advance scheduling" and "allocation scheduling" [15]. The first sub-problem solves a planning phase by assigning a surgery date and OR to each patient over the planning horizon. The second sub-problem solves a scheduling phase which determines the sequence and resource allocation of procedures in each OR and day.

In this chapter we assume that the strategic decisions pertaining to the ORs' capacity are given. At a tactical level, we propose a 0-1 linear programming model, which is an extension of the one presented in [27], to determine the number of OR block times to be assigned to each specialty and construct the MSS to be used as input data for the simulation model for a given planning period. The MSS can then be updated as a response to changes in the waiting list consistency and to fluctuations in the relative demand of the specialties belonging to the department. Note that in our case study, we propose to revise the MSS every three months [35]. Also, historical data could be used as input and compared to the optimized MSS, as we will show in Section 12.3.

Afterwards, once the MSS parameters are input, the simulation model solves the surgery process scheduling and determines for each day of the planning horizon the subset of patients to be operated on and their order of intervention. By means of what-if scenario analysis, different operative decisions for planning patient admissions and sequencing their intervention, for example Longest Waiting Time (LWT), Longest Processing Time (LPT) and Shortest Processing Time (SPT), could be easily compared and analyzed.

The 0-1 LP model to solve the tactical OR planning problem

Given a set O of υ OR block times available in a given planning horizon and a set I of n surgical specialties belonging to the surgery department, the tactical decisions herein addressed are those of determining how many OR block times should be assigned to each specialty i, as well as the day of the week they should be scheduled. Note that the o-th block time is actually addressed by indexes j, k representing the OR and the day of the planning horizon, respectively. We denote by J and K, respectively, the set of ORs and days, and by m and t their corresponding cardinality.

The objective function is aimed at leveling the Weighed Waiting Lists (WWL) of the surgical specialties belonging to the department. The WWL is a measure of the clinical complexity of the specialty, computed by multiplying the length of the waiting list by the average urgency coefficient of the waiting patients.

The main assumptions of our model are: i) the number of ORs as well as the number and length of OR block times are fixed in the planning horizon; ii) only one specialty should be assigned to a given block time, i.e., a block scheduling approach is considered [15]; iii) OR blocks are completely homogeneous regardless of the day of the week. Note that the last assumption can be easily relaxed to manage different block time length and special OR equipment.

The model for the OR planning problem has been designed to take into consideration the strategic decisions, related to the introduction of the Week Surgery model in the ward stay area. In order to introduce such decisions as model constraints (see (12.8)–(12.9)), let η_i be the number of short-stay patients on the waiting list of specialty i at the beginning of the planning horizon, and $F \subset O$, the subset of OR block times available for surgery in the subset of days $S \subset K$ related to the first days of the week (usually Monday and Tuesday), where $|F| = f$. For each specialty i, we compute the average number of block times β_i that represents the relative demand of block times in the first days of the week of specialty i:

$$\beta_i = f\frac{\eta_i}{\sum_i \eta_i} \qquad \forall i = 1,2,\ldots,n. \tag{12.1}$$

We assume x_{ijk} as binary decision variables of the problem, with the following specification:

$$x_{ijk} = \begin{cases} 1 \text{ if specialty } i \text{ is assigned to OR } j \text{ on day } k \\ 0 \text{ otherwise.} \end{cases}$$

Considering a t-days length planning period, the weighted waiting list w_i of specialty i, as found by the model solution, is computed as follows:

$$w_i = \left\{ \left(h_i + t\lambda_i - r_i \sum_j \sum_k x_{ijk} \right) \cdot \rho_i \right\} \qquad \forall i = 1,2,\ldots,n \tag{12.2}$$

where h_i is the waiting list length of specialty i at the beginning of the planning horizon, r_i is the average block service rate of specialty i, i.e., the average number of patients operated for block time by specialty i, while λ_i and ρ_i are, respectively, the average daily arrival rate and average urgency coefficient of patients belonging to specialty i. The summation $\sum_j \sum_k x_{ijk}$ determines the number of OR block times assigned during the planning horizon to specialty i, $\forall i = 1,2,...n$. Note that, if $\rho_i = 1$, $\forall i =1, 2,\ldots, n$, the objective function is to reduce deviations between the resulting numbers of patients on the specialty waiting lists, thus recognizing that each CP has the same average urgency.

The definition of variables x_{ijk} and macros w_i and β_i, $\forall i = 1,2,\ldots,n$, enables an easy formulation of the underlying model for OR planning:

$$\text{Minimize} \max_{i=1,2,..,n} \{w_i\} \tag{12.3}$$

$$\sum_i \sum_j \sum_k x_{ijk} \leq \upsilon \tag{12.4}$$

$$\sum_i x_{ijk} \leq 1 \qquad \forall j,k \tag{12.5}$$

$$l_i \leq \sum_j \sum_k x_{ijk} \leq u_i \qquad \forall i \tag{12.6}$$

$$\sum_j x_{ijk} \leq e_{ik} \qquad \forall i,k \tag{12.7}$$

$$\lfloor \beta_i \rfloor \leq \sum_j \sum_{k \in S} x_{ijk} \leq \lceil \beta_i \rceil \qquad \forall i \tag{12.8}$$

$$\sum_i \sum_j \sum_{k \in S} x_{ijk} = f \tag{12.9}$$

$$x_{ijk} \in \{0,1\}. \tag{12.10}$$

(12.3) is the objective function that minimizes the maximum of the resulting WWL of the specialties. Constraint (12.4) is the capacity constraint that limits the sum of the OR block times assigned to all specialties to be not greater than the total number υ of block times available during the planning horizon. Constraints (12.5) are the assignment constraints that impose that each OR block time can be assigned to no more than one specialty. Constraints (12.6) bound the total number of block times signed to specialty i to be greater and less than some given lower (l_i) and upper bound (u_i) values, respectively. Constraints (12.7) are the so-called team constraints that limit the number of parallel OR block times, assigned to specialty i on a given day k, to be not greater than the number of teams e_{ik} available to operate simultaneously. Constraints (12.8) are the week surgery stay constraints that allow the nearest integer number of average block times in the first days of the week, β_i, computed by (12.1), to be assigned to specialty i. Finally, (12.9) provides that all blocks $o \in F$ must be assigned.

12.2.1.3 Ward organization

With reference to the decision on how stay areas can be organized, literature analysis revealed that in recent years, progress in medical technology and research in cost-effectiveness have provided new general surgery models focused on reducing length of stay, with beneficial effects on patients and hospital costs [16].

In our framework we evaluate a new organizational model, i.e., the "Week Surgery" model. It consists in separating a particular ward where the so-called short-stay patients stay a maximum of five days. This organization represents an important contribution to surgical therapeutic strategies, allowing an excellent compromise between safety, convenience for the patient and economic savings for health care structures. In fact, this model allows closure of the relevant ward over the weekend, thus saving staff time.

Results suggest that the week surgery model can be considered a valid and achievable alternative organization compared to conventional hospitalization, as a retrospective seven-year study of Veneto Region (Italy) public hospitals shows [23]. Exploiting all possible benefit from this organizational setting requires re-organization of patient flow across the week, reallocating hospital workloads also for OR blocks, to allow operations for short-stay patients in the first days of the week to be able to discharge them before the weekend.

12.2.2 Performance indexes

The discrete event simulation model acts as a decision support tool to compare alternative "what if" scenarios by means of a complete set of performance indexes able to assess the performance of the three sub-processes (Table 12.1).

In particular, for waiting list management the indexes are intended to evaluate the demand addressed by the hospital and the extent to which patient clinical needs are met. In particular, the first index, referred to as "WL length", indicates how many people are waiting at the end of the simulation period. From a different point of view, the "WWL length" index measures the average clinical complexity of the future demand of the specialties. Remember that (see Section 12.2.1.2) for each specialty the WWL length is computed by multiplying the WL length by the average urgency coefficient of the waiting patients. The last index, usually computed for assessing the waiting list performance, is the average waiting time. In our framework, however, we argue that a more informative index could be a comparison of how long people have been waiting with respect to how long they should have been waiting. Note that the latter is the stated MTBT of the URG the patient belongs to (see Section 12.2.1.1). The new index is the so-called "MTBT achievement index", computed as the percentage of patients that have been operated on within their MTBT. The latter is an equity index, or more properly, a horizontal equity index, because for each URG (same need) it measures how many people have been delivered the necessary intervention in the right time.

The performance of the ORs is measured, firstly, by the number (#) of patients operated on during the period which, is the main output of the OR activity. The "OR utilization rate" assesses the efficiency of the OR planning system measuring whether OR blocks, which are the most costly resources of the hospital, are exploited as much as possible. The index is computed as the average ratio between the real oc-

Table 12.1. Integrated performance indexes

Index	*Sub-process*	*Dimension*
WL length	Waiting list management	Demand
WWL length	Waiting list management	Demand
MTBT Achievement Index for each URG	Waiting list management	Equity
# operated patients	OR planning & scheduling	OR activity
% of shifted patients	OR planning & scheduling	Equity
OR utilization rate	OR planning & scheduling	OR efficiency
# dismissed patients	Stay area organization	Bed efficiency
Bed utilization rate (ws)	Stay area organization	Bed efficiency
Bed utilization rate (long)	Stay area organization	Bed efficiency
Bed utilization rate (total)	Stay area organization	Bed efficiency

cupation and the OR block length for all blocks. The last OR index, i.e., the % of shifted patients, could be considered, in some sense, an index of equity of the ORs, measuring the percentage of patients planned to be operated on and then rescheduled to other days.

Finally, the stay area performance is assessed by the number of dismissed patients and by the bed utilization rate. The first is an activity index, whilst the second an efficiency one. Note that the second index is separately computed for the beds devoted to short stay (week surgery) and long stay and, also, as an average for the whole department (total).

12.3 Results and discussion

The simulation framework has been applied to model the patient flows into a General Surgery Department of the San Martino University Hospital in Genova, Italy. The patients can be grouped by their care pathways into homogeneous groups proxied by the specialty to which the patients belong. Into the department under study, $n = 7$ specialties share the hospital resources, i.e., operating theatre and hospital stay area facilities. In particular, the operating theatre includes $m = 6$ ORs open from 8 a.m. to 2 p.m., five days a week, for a total of $\upsilon = 30$ OR blocks available for surgery each week. With reference to the stay area, $b = 102$ beds are available for the post-intervention stay of patients.

12.3.1 Patient data collection

Patient data was collected with the collaboration of the department under study, between 1 January 2009 and 31 December 2009. In this period 3715 patients following different CPs were operated on. For all patients we collected the whole set of characteristics necessary to generate the distribution functions for the attributes used to manage the flow of patients through the system (see Section 12.2.1).

In Table 12.2, the case-mix characteristics related to the length of stay (more or less than a week) and URG of the patients operated on during the study period are given for each homogeneous group of patients (specialty S_i, $i = 1, 2, \ldots, n$).

Table 12.2. Length of stay and URG classification of the patients grouped by CPs

	S_1 (# and %)		S_2 (# and %)		S_3 (# and %)		S_4 (# and %)		S_5 (# and %)		S_6 (# and %)		S_7 (# and %)		*Department* (# and %)	
LOS																
Long stay	607	0.68	207	0.30	169	0.21	248	0.39	128	0.49	110	0.46	117	0.54	1586	0.43
Short stay	280	0.32	475	0.70	618	0.79	393	0.61	133	0.51	131	0.54	99	0.46	2129	0.57
URG																
A1	74	0.08	68	0.10	78	0.10	55	0.09	19	0.07	19	0.08	13	0.06	326	0.09
A2	198	0.22	220	0.32	238	0.30	139	0.22	57	0.22	68	0.28	76	0.35	996	0.27
B	348	0.39	261	0.38	301	0.38	243	0.38	105	0.40	101	0.42	81	0.38	1440	0.39
C	227	0.26	94	0.14	128	0.16	176	0.27	65	0.25	42	0.17	35	0.16	767	0.21
D	40	0.05	39	0.06	42	0.05	28	0.04	v15	0.06	11	0.05	11	0.05	186	0.05
Total	887	0.24	682	0.18	787	0.21	641	0.17	261	0.08	241	0.06	216	0.06	3715	1.00

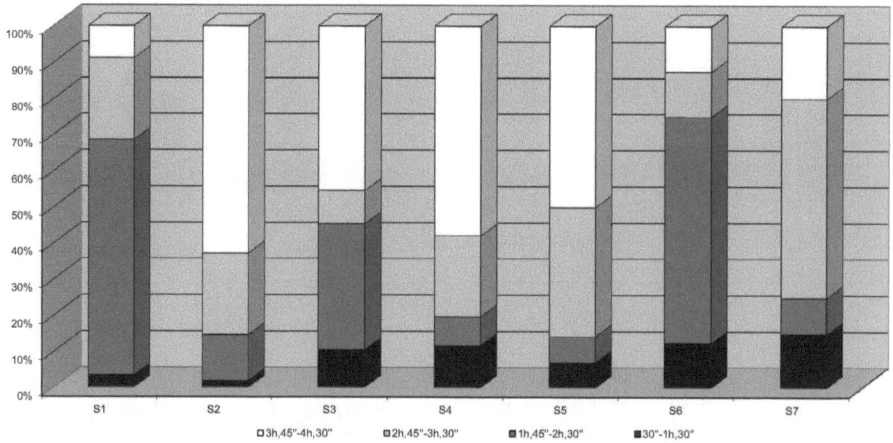

Fig. 12.2. Frequency distribution of the patient EOT classes within each CP group/specialty

The collected data were sorted and various statistics were derived using a statistical modeling package, such as SAS System, for estimating the inter-arrival time distribution function for each specialty and obtaining the empirical distributions of the URG, EOT and LOS attributes.

Patients were observed to arrive following Poisson distributions and, as usual, neg-exp distributions have been used for the inter-arrival time distributions and mean parameters varying between the specialties and equal to 9.9, 12.7, 11.2, 13.4, 30.7, 34.1 and 40.0, for $S_1, S_2, \ldots, S_7$, respectively.

The histogram reported in Figure 12.2 gives the distribution of the EOT collected for the operated patients of each specialty during 2009, showing the different EOT patterns among the different care pathways. Note that the EOT are split into classes used by clinicians during the consultation visit to categorize patient interventions.

Note that to introduce the difference between the EOT and the real service time a triangular distribution with different parameters has been added to the generated EOT of each patient. The real service time in fact includes an allowance for cleaning and preparation between patients and could be greater than the EOT due to possible complications occurring during the intervention.

Finally, in Figure 12.3 the LOS empirical distributions for the patients belonging to the seven CP groups, i.e., specialties, are depicted. The LOS classes are expressed in days and for each specialty the frequency distribution function is derived for all patients.

12.3.2 Scenario analysis

Once the discrete event simulation model for the case study has been implemented in WITNESS [36], it has been validated to ensure its ability to represent the real system under investigation.

In the first phase a face validation [14] was performed with the clinicians and nurses of the department to verify the overall behavior and the rules introduced.

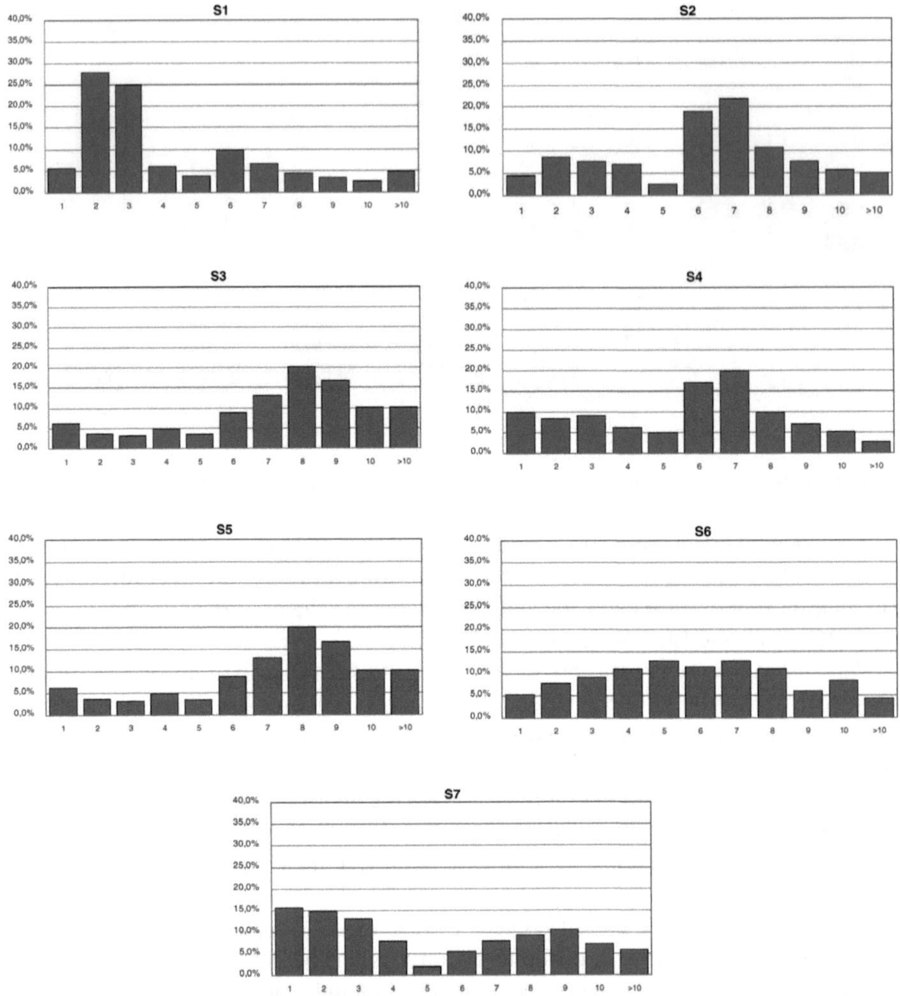

Fig. 12.3. LOS empirical distributions of patients belonging to the different specialties

The personnel involved gave us many insights to help us adapt the model to the current practice and render it a truer representation of the real system. Afterwards, the simulation outputs were compared to the real measures under investigation by adopting appropriate validation tests [14]. We compared the steady-state length of the waiting lists of the seven specialties at the end of a one-year simulation run, obtained with 10 IID replications, with the real measures collected at the end of the data collection period. We used the t-test for testing the null hypothesis H_0 under a probability of rejecting the model fixed to the $\alpha = 0.05$ level, obtaining for all specialties a value inferior to the critical value.

Table 12.3. Scenario operative assumptions for each sub-process

	Waiting list discipline	*Stay area*	*OR planning*	*OR scheduling*
Scenario 1	Current	Current	Real data	LWT
Scenario 2	Current	Current	Real data	LPT
Scenario 3	Current	Current	Real data	SPT
Scenario 4	Prioritization	Current	Real data	LWT
Scenario 5	Prioritization	Current	Real data	LPT
Scenario 6	Prioritization	Current	Real data	SPT
Scenario 7	Current	Week surgery	Real data	LWT
Scenario 8	Current	Week surgery	Real data	LPT
Scenario 9	Current	Week surgery	Real data	SPT
Scenario 10	Prioritization	Week surgery	Real data	LWT
Scenario 11	Prioritization	Week surgery	Real data	LPT
Scenario 12	Prioritization	Week surgery	Real data	SPT
Scenario 13	Prioritization	Week surgery	Optimiz model	LWT
Scenario 14	Prioritization	Week surgery	Optimiz model	LPT
Scenario 15	Prioritization	Week surgery	Optimiz model	SPT

The validated model has been used to perform a quite extensive scenario analysis aimed at comparing different decisions for the sub-processes into which the patient flows have been organized.

In Table 12.3 the set of scenarios herein analyzed is given. Note that the first two columns give the rule adopted for the strategic decisions related, respectively, to waiting list management and stay area organization (see Sections 12.2.1.1 and 12.2.1.3), while the final columns are related to the tactical and operational OR planning and scheduling decisions. A group of scenarios (1–3 and 7–9) assumes that the patient admission is based on the current logic, while the others assume a prioritized order of admission.

The first six scenarios use the current stay area organization while the remaining ones are based on the assumption that the Week Surgery model is implemented. With reference to the decisions pertaining to the tactical OR planning, the first 12 scenarios use the historical MSS coming from the real data collection. In contrast, Scenarios 13–15 include the OR allocation among the specialties resulting from the optimization model (3)–(10) reported in Section 12.2.1.2. Finally, other differences between scenarios depend on the scheduling rule (LWT, LPT, SPT) used to schedule patients in each block time.

Note that the optimization model (3)–(10) has been run four times for each simulated year, i.e., each three months [35], and the formulation for a generic instance of the case study requires 232 variables and 115 constraints. The model instances have been implemented in MPL [18] and solved with CPLEX 12.10. The optimal solutions are obtained on a PC Intel Core i5, with 6GB RAM, and the average CPU time is less than 1 second.

12.3.3 Steady-state computational results

In Table 12.4 the one-year steady-state results, based on 10 IID replications, related to the set of "what-if" scenarios reported in Table 12.1, are given. Note that all scenarios are run starting from the real situation of the surgical department, as resulting after one year of model running and one year of warm up.

Remember that the first three scenarios are developed assuming that all decisions are based on current practice, without any organizational innovation, only changing the intervention scheduling rule.

The performance indexes of the three sub-processes show that the worse situation is in waiting list management. The MTBT Achievement Indexes are, in fact, very low, especially for the more urgent URGs. Prioritization seems, therefore, to be the first strategy to be implemented to let more urgent patients be operated on sooner, as their clinical condition requires.

Scenarios 4–6 explore what should happen if prioritization is applied. As prioritization consists in changing the admission ordering, but does not change either the inter-arrival or service rates, we don't expect shorter waiting lists (first column). The WWL length, however, is strongly reduced: approximately the same number of people are waiting but in some sense they "can" wait because their condition is not so severe. From an economic point of view, we can say that there is less total remaining need, which means that prioritization can, by itself, increase the efficiency of given resources. Even more importantly, prioritization entails a consistent gain from the point of view of the patients that are operated on in the period, since the MTBT Achievement Index increases with respect to the initial situation. This means that most patients (though with different percentages among URGs) can be treated within the time assigned them. From an economic point of view this means attaining equity.

According to analysis of Scenarios 7–9, it appears that when, together with prioritization, stay areas are re-organized, waiting list indexes worsen. In this case, in fact, a tradeoff arises between cost reduction (week surgery model) and equity. This means that saving costs entails loss of some equity of treatment. Note, however, that following the week surgery model improves the activity indexes, not only for the stay area, as expected, but also for OR utilization. In Scenarios 7–9 both the number of dismissed patients and operated patients are larger than in Scenarios 4–6. More importantly, the bed efficiency improves consistently, from values 0.77, 0.77 and 0.74 to 0.80, 0.81 and 0.76, as a direct effect of this re-organization.

Finally we consider what happens when the OR optimization model is integrated in the simulation model (Scenarios 13–15 versus 10–12). Three main effects can be detected. The first is the direct effect on OR utilization. Using the optimized MSS resulting from model (3)–(10) instead of the historical one allows an increase in the OR activity: the numbers of patients operated on increase from 3658, 3717 and 3528 to 3679, 3740 and 3560, respectively. Moreover, the other indexes also improve. In particular, the equity index, that is the percentage of the shifted patients, is lower and the efficiency index, i.e., the OR utilization rate, reaches the highest values of all considered scenarios. The second is the indirect effect on the stay area indexes. The impact is positive: both activity (dismissed patients) and efficiency indexes improve.

Table 12.4. Comparison of the performance indexes

Scenario	*Waiting list* Total WL length	Avg WWL length	MTBT Achievement Indexes A1	A2	B	C	D	*Operating theatre* # operated patients	% shifted patients	OR utilization rate	*Stay area* # dismissed patients	Bed utilization rate (ws)	Bed utilization rate (long)	Bed utilization rate
Scenario 1	659	899	0.00	0.10	0.52	1.00	1.00	3662	0.17	0.86	3654			0.76
Scenario 2	584	791	0.00	0.10	0.71	1.00	1.00	3734	0.18	0.88	3723			0.78
Scenario 3	750	1016	0.00	0.08	0.42	1.00	1.00	3569	0.14	0.84	3562			0.75
Scenario 4	642	387	0.61	0.84	0.94	1.00	1.00	3676	0.18	0.87	3657			0.77
Scenario 5	592	358	0.67	0.86	0.95	1.00	1.00	3725	0.17	0.88	3705			0.77
Scenario 6	774	461	0.54	0.72	0.80	1.00	1.00	3547	0.14	0.84	3543			0.74
Scenario 7	650	888	0.02	0.20	0.47	1.00	1.00	3669	0.16	0.86	3659	0.92	0.77	0.80
Scenario 8	584	786	0.02	0.19	0.54	1.00	1.00	3733	0.17	0.88	3724	0.93	0.78	0.81
Scenario 9	799	1099	0.02	0.16	0.42	1.00	1.00	3523	0.14	0.83	3519	0.94	0.72	0.76
Scenario 10	662	403	0.40	0.66	0.79	1.00	1.00	3653	0.18	0.86	3649	0.93	0.76	0.79
Scenario 11	600	368	0.44	0.69	0.81	1.00	1.00	3717	0.18	0.87	3705	0.93	0.77	0.80
Scenario 12	791	478	0.32	0.56	0.66	1.00	1.00	3528	0.14	0.83	3520	0.93	0.73	0.76
Scenario 13	639	436	0.33	0.49	0.62	1.00	1.00	3679	0.17	0.89	3673	0.93	0.77	0.80
Scenario 14	576	403	0.39	0.50	0.63	1.00	1.00	3740	0.17	0.88	3726	0.94	0.78	0.81
Scenario 15	758	505.29	0.32	0.46	0.59	1.00	1.00	3560	0.13	0.84	3553	0.91	0.73	0.76

Dismissed patients increase as an immediate consequence of the increased throughput of the OR. Bed occupancy improves also as a consequence, both for long and short stay. Therefore, the overall bed utilization rates become 0.80, 0.81 and 0.76, which is very satisfying and maybe even "too high" for short-stay beds. The third indirect effect on the waiting list, however, is not so good. Even though, at first glance, the number of patients waiting reduces, the WWL index shows that patients are more urgent and the equity index, MTBT Achievement Index, decreases. This confirms that a tradeoff usually arises between improving the point of view of the hospital (better OR utilization) and achieving equity of treatment (prioritization). The decision tool presented here allows quantification of the cost and benefit of different re-organization strategies to assist in solving this dilemma. As explained, some differences between scenarios depend on the scheduling rule (LWT, LPT, SPT) even though no general rule seems to be preferable to others

The results reported in Table 12.4 are the summary for the whole department resulting sometimes from different impacts on each care pathway. In Tables 12.5 and 12.6 the waiting list indexes for each specialty are reported, comparing the expected results after one year in two different scenarios. The first relates to the scenario where everything goes on like the current situation, while the second assumes that all three sub-processes will be re-organized. In both cases, to facilitate the comparison, only the scheduling rule LWT is reported (Scenario 1 and Scenario 13).

Comparison allows assessment of how the re-organization can impact on the performance indexes referred to in the clinical pathway groups. We do not expect, of course, that the proposed integrated approach can reduce waiting lists, because resources are exactly the same and the number of patients joining the different pathways are different (see Table 12.2), thus resulting in different WL lengths among the specialties. Moreover, what we expect is that the WWL, that is, the weighted number of patients in the waiting lists of the specialties, should be almost similar. In effect, we observe that from the current situation (Table 12.5) to the re-organized one (Table 12.6) they are more leveled, even if not perfectly the same, as the SD row shows. Also the MTBT Achievement Indexes, though generally improved (from the

Table 12.5. Impact on equity of treatment for specialty pathways (Scenario 1)

Specialty	*WL length*	*WWL length*	*Avg urgency coefficient*	*MTBT Achievement Indexes* A1	A2	B	C	D
S1	152	1640	10.79	0.00	0.00	0.60	1.00	1.00
S2	120	977	8.14	0.00	0.00	0.51	1.00	1.00
S3	109	1100	10.09	0.00	0.00	1.00	1.00	1.00
S4	151	1460	9.67	0.00	0.00	0.14	1.00	1.00
S5	72	506	7.03	0.00	0.00	0.00	1.00	1.00
S6	44	489	11.11	0.00	0.00	0.36	1.00	1.00
S7	11	125	11.36	0.00	0.72	1.00	1.00	1.00
Total	659	6297	68.27					
Avg	94.14	899.57	9.74	0.00	0.10	0.52	1.00	1.00
SD	49.84	511.57	1.50	0.00	0.25	0.36	0.00	0.00

Table 12.6. Impact on equity of treatment for specialty pathways (Scenario 13)

Specialty	*WL length*	*WWL length*	*Avg urgency coefficient*	*MTBT Achievement Indexes* *A*1	*A*2	*B*	*C*	*D*
S1	103	388	3.77	0.59	0.84	0.94	1.00	1.00
S2	72	348	4.83	0.49	0.64	0.83	1.00	1.00
S3	93	535	5.75	0.62	0.78	0.92	1.00	1.00
S4	107	568	5.31	0.37	0.63	0.79	1.00	1.00
S5	61	223	3.66	0.13	0.24	0.42	1.00	1.00
S6	80	408	5.10	0.00	0.03	0.04	1.00	1.00
S7	60	354	5.90	0.50	0.37	0.45	1.00	1.00
Total	576	2824	34.36					
Avg	82.29	403.43	4.90	0.39	0.50	0.63	1.00	1.00
SD	17.79	108.71	0.83	0.22	0.28	0.31	0.00	0.00

initial average values of 0.00, 0.10, 0.52, 1.00 and 1.00 to 0.39, 0.50, 0.63, 1.00 and 1.00), are quite different among the specialties, meaning that equity should be still improved. This can be done by improving the way resources are distributed.

12.4 Conclusions

In this chapter we have developed an integrated framework for the evaluation of clinical pathways inside a hospital surgery department, taking advantage of both simulation and optimization ability to support decisions. The framework has been applied to a real case study, showing that the integration of the two methodological approaches can provide a useful tool to compare and analyze different operative scenarios, following a re-organization process. The purpose of this process was to meet the double objective of increasing the equity of treatment of patients and increasing the efficiency of the resource utilization, in particular beds and operating rooms.

The main conclusion is that, in principle, a decision tool cannot individuate the best solution. However, it can help in assessing the direct and indirect impact of each choice on the different sub-processes into which patient flows can be broken down, from an organizational point of view within a hospital.

Our computational model, therefore, proves that supporting decisions does not mean replacing decisions. Choices are, as usual, in economic decisions subject to a tradeoff and improving a performance index often means worsening another. This is an additional reason why the impact should be carefully measured and evaluated through an integrated approach that concerns the complete patient flow, i.e., from the moment the patient enters the system as outpatient, flows through it as inpatient and then is discharged to return home.

Of course the model is quite general and other patient characteristics, implying different organizational models, could be included, for instance the new models differentiating stay areas by means of the level of assistance requiring different typology of stay beds, from the more intensive beds to the less intensive ones.

Future research will be devoted to utilizing the integrated approach herein presented to study the potentialities of a simulation optimization approach [27]. Starting from the computational results herein reported, it can be noted that introducing a prioritization system for waiting lists is not sufficient to achieve good values of MTBT Achievement Indexes, which in many cases are still far from the optimal values. After ensuring that the existing resources are allocated in the best possible way, the only effective strategy would be increasing the hospital resources (especially OR blocks) and distributing them among the different care pathways. The exact amount of additional resources able to make the waiting list equity indexes equal to 1, for all urgency classes, could be computed by means of the optimization packages provided by the main simulation software. This new integration could be extended also to other resources, for instance, to find the optimum number of short- and long-stay beds, as well as their proportion, to guarantee adequate levels of bed utilization rates.

Acknowledgements. The authors acknowledge support from the Italian Ministry of Education, University and Research (MIUR), under the grant FIRB n. RBFR081KSB. The authors wish to thank the Director of the General Surgery Department of the San Martino Hospital for providing data and helping in model implementation and validation.

References

1. Akkerman, R., Knip, M.: Reallocation of beds to reduce waiting time for cardiac surgery. Health Care Management Science **7**(2), 119–126 (2004)
2. Bowers, J., Mould, G.: Managing uncertainty in orthopaedic trauma theatres. European Journal of Operational Research **154**, 599–608 (2004)
3. Cardoen, B., Demeulemeester, E., Beliën, J.: Operating room planning and scheduling: A literature review. European Journal of Operational Research **201**(3), 921–932 (2010)
4. Cardoen, B., Demeulemeester, E.: Capacity of Clinical Pathways - A Strategic Multi-level Evaluation Tool. Journal of Medical Systems **32**(6), 443–452 (2008)
5. Cochran, J.K., Bharti, A.: Stochastic bed balancing of an obstetrics hospital. Health Care Management Science **9**(1), 31–45 (2006)
6. Cote, M.J., Stein, W.E.: A stochastic model for visit to the doctor's office. Mathematical and Computer Modeling **45**, 309–323 (2007)
7. De Blaser, L., Depreitere, R., De Waele, K., Vanhaecht, K., Vlayen, J., Sermeus, W.: Defining pathways. Journal of Nursing Management **14**, 553–563 (2006)
8. Everett, J.E.: A decision Support Simulation model for the management of an elective surgery waiting system. Health Care Management Science **5**, 89–95 (2002)
9. Fu M.C.: Optimization for simulation: Theory vs. practice. INFORMS Journal on Computing **14**(3), 192–215 (2002)
10. Harper, P.R.: A framework for operational modeling of hospital resources. Health Care Management Science **5**(3), 165–173 (2002)
11. Harper, P.R., Shanani, A.K.: Modelling for the planning and management of bed capacities in hospitals. The Journal of the Operational Research Society **53**(1), 11–18 (2002)
12. Jacobson, S.H., Hall, S.N., Swisher, J.R.: Discrete Event Simulation of Health Care Systems. In: Hall, R.W. (eds.) Patient Flow: Reducing Delay in Healthcare Delivery. International Series in Operations Research and Management Science, vol. 91, pp. 211–252. Springer, New York (2006)
13. Lagergren, M.: What is the contribution of models to management and research in health services? A view from Europe. European Journal of Operations Research **105**(2), 257–266 (1998)

14. Law, M.A.: Simulation Modeling & Analysis, 4th ed. McGraw-Hill, New York (2007)
15. Magerlein, J.M., Martin, J.B.: Surgical demand scheduling: A review. Health Services Research **13**, 418–433 (1978)
16. Major, S.: New approach to surgical care aims to improve recovery and reduce length of hospital stay. British Medical Journal **334**(7598), 816–817 (2007)
17. Maliapen, M., Dangerfield, B.C.: A system dynamics-based simulation study for managing clinical governance and pathways in a hospital. Journal of the Operational Research Society **61**, 255–264 (2010)
18. Maximal Software, Inc.: MPL Modeling System, USA (2010)
19. Mullen, P.M.: Prioritising Waiting Lists: How and Why? European Journal of Operational Research **150**, 32–45 (2003)
20. Panella, M., Marchisio, S., Di Stanislao, F.: Reducing clinical variations with clinical pathways: Do pathways work? International Journal for Quality in Health Care **15**, 509–521 (2003)
21. Ratcliffe, J., Young, T., Buxton, M., Eldabi, T., Paul, R., Burroughs, A., Papatheodoridis, G., Rolles, K.: A simulation Modelling Approach to evaluating alternative policies for the management of the waiting lists for liver transplantation. Health Care Management Science **4**, 117–124 (2001)
22. Ronellenfitsch, U., Rössner, E., Jakob, J., Post, S., Hohenberger, P., Schwarzbach, M.: Clinical Pathways in surgery-should we introduce them into clinical routine? A review article. Langenbeck's Archives of Surgery **393**(4), 449–457 (2008)
23. Saia, M., Barra, S., Mantoan, D., Pietrobon, F.: Feasibility of week surgery model in general surgery. Ann. Ig. **20**(5), 477–483 (2008)
24. Sciomachen, A., Tànfani, E., Testi, A.: Simulation models for optimal schedules of operating theatres. International Journal of Simulation **6**, 26–34 (2005)
25. Strum, D.P., May, J.H., Vargas, L.G.: Modeling the uncertainty of surgical procedure times: comparison of the log-normal and normal models. Anesthesiology **92**, 1160–1167 (2000)
26. Swisher, J., Jacobson, S., Jun, J., Balci, O.: Modeling and analyzing a physician clinic environment using discrete event-event (visual) simulation. Computers & Operations Research **28**, 105–125 (2001)
27. Tànfani, E., Testi, A.: Improving surgery department performance via Simulation and Optimization. Proceedings of the IEEE Workshop on Health Care Management, Venezia, Italy. (2010)
28. Testi, A.: Rationalizing Waiting Lists in Health Care Delivery: An International Comparison. Economia Internazionale (In press) (2012)
29. Testi, A., Tànfani, E., Torre, G.: A three-phase approach for operating theatre schedules. Health Care Management Science **10**, 163–172 (2007)
30. Testi, A., Tànfani, E., Valente, R., Ansaldo, G., Torre, G.C.: Prioritising surgical waiting list. Journal of Evaluation in Clinical Practice **14**(1), 59–64 (2008)
31. Tuft, S., Gallivan, S.: Computer modelling of a cataract waiting list. British Journal of Ophthamology **85**, 582–585 (2001)
32. Valente, R., Testi, A., Tànfani, E., Fato, M., Porro, I., Santori, G., Santo, M., Ansaldo, G., Torre, G.C.: A model to prioritize access to elective surgery on the base of clinical urgency and waiting time. BMC, Health Services Research **9**(1) (2009). doi: 10.1186/1472-6963-9-1
33. VanBerkel, P.T., Blake, J.T.: A comprensive simulation for wait time reduction and capacity planning applied in general surgery. Health Care Management Science **10**(4), 373–385 (2007)
34. Vissers, J.M., Adan, I.J., Dellaert, N.P.: Developing a platform for comparison of hospital admission systems: An illustration. European Journal of Operations Research **180**(3), 1290–1301 (2007)
35. Wachtel, R.E., Dexter, F.: Tactical increases in operating room block time for capacity planning should not be based on utilization. Anesthesia & Analgesia **106**, 215–226 (2008)
36. Witness: User guide. Lanner Group, London, UK (2010)
37. Zander, K.: Integrated care pathways: Eleven international trends. Journal of Integrated Care Pathways **6**, 101–107 (2002)

Chapter 13

Patient mix optimisation for inpatient planning with multiple resources

Jan Vissers, Ivo Adan, Nico Dellaert, Jully Jeunet, and Jos Bekkers

Abstract. This contribution addresses the planning of admissions of surgical patients, requiring different resources such as beds and nursing capacity at wards, operating rooms and operating theatre personnel at an operating theatre, intensive care beds and intensive care nursing capacity at an intensive care ward. We developed a modelling approach for this planning problem, starting from a very simplified base model with deterministic resource requirements only for elective patients to a model with also stochastic resource requirements and finally a model extended to emergency patients. We developed the consecutive models over a period of 6 years together with a cardiothoracic surgeon who acted as problem owner and user of the model in healthcare practice. Each of the steps taken in the development of the models provided new insights and added to the knowledge of the planning problem and

J. Vissers (✉)
Institute of Health Policy and Management, Erasmus University Rotterdam, Burgemeester Oudlaan 50, 3062 PA Rotterdam, The Netherlands
e-mail: vissers@bmg.eur.nl

I. Adan
Department of Mathematics and Computer Science, Eindhoven University of Technology, P.O. Box 513, 5600 MB Eindhoven, The Netherlands
e-mail: iadan@tue.nl

N. Dellaert
Industrial Engineering School, Eindhoven University of Technology, P.O. Box 513, 5600 MB Eindhoven, The Netherlands
e-mail: n.p.dellaert@tue.nl

J. Jeunet
CNRS, Lamsade, Université Paris Dauphine, Place de Lattre de Tassigny, 75775 Paris Cedex 16, France
e-mail: jully.jeunet@dauphine.fr

J. Bekkers
Thorax Centre Rotterdam, Erasmus University Medical Centre, P.O. Box 2040 3000, CA Rotterdam, The Netherlands
e-mail: j.a.bekkers@erasmusmc.nl

Tànfani E., Testi A. (Eds.): Advanced Decision Making Methods Applied to Health Care.
International Series in Operations Research & Management Science 173
DOI 10.1007/978-88-470-2321-5_13, © Springer-Verlag Italia 2012

approach. We present the steps taken and the models developed, show the results obtained and the lessons learned.

Keywords: admission planning, operating theatre planning, patient mix, resource allocation, integer linear programming, simulation

13.1 Introduction and problem addressed

Planning and scheduling of patients in hospitals has been a topic of research for many years [4]. This popularity can be explained by the many challenges a hospital poses to researchers in terms of complexity of the system, the contribution of modelling to improved performance of the system and the implementation of research findings.

Much of the research efforts focus on the planning or scheduling of patients for a single department, such as an outpatient department, a radiology department, an inpatient ward or an operating theatre department.

Less work has been done on planning and scheduling of patients for a process involving a number of departments [5,7]. A patient referred to a hospital not only visits the outpatient department but also diagnostic departments such as radiology or pathology; it may also involve a surgical procedure in a day surgery centre. The planning and scheduling of the outpatient process of a patient involves multiple resources and asks for a coordination of the process for the patient. A similar problem exists for the inpatient process, when a patient requires an inpatient admission to be investigated and treated. An inpatient admission requires different resources, ranging from a bed and nursing staff at a ward, to equipment, room and personnel at diagnostic departments, surgical staff and facilities at an operating theatre department, a bed and specialized nursing staff at an intensive care unit, et cetera.

Several authors have studied this topic from a multiple resource perspective. Beliën and Demeulemeester [3] for instance, see development of effective operating room schedules as a three stage process: allocation of OR time to surgical specialties at strategic level, development of a master surgery schedule at tactical level, scheduling individual patients at operational level. Van Oostrum et al. [8] also look at cyclic master scheduling for operating rooms and the impact on departments downstream. They use data on actual surgical procedures and their stochasticity and focus on the optimisation of the use of operating theatre resources. More studies on the same topic can be found in the review papers mentioned before [4,5,7].

We focus in this chapter on improving the performance of hospitals in inpatient planning for a flow of patients in a surgical specialty, leaving out the interactions between specialty flows in shared resources. This simplifies the planning problem as we have only to concentrate on the flow of patients of one specialty, but it helps us to investigate the possibilities of a specialty to manage their own flow of patients. We performed this study in a cardio-thoracic surgery centre with dedicated resources for the specialty. This helped us to concentrate on the objective of the study to investigate the possibilities of the specialty to improve their planning performance by deciding on the mix of patients in a master schedule that would fulfil the volumes of patients agreed upon in the contracts, optimise the use of resources and take into account the restrictions on resources such as the number of operating rooms available. The case study setting of thoracic surgery was therefore an excellent starting point for our study.

13.2 Materials and methods

We performed a series of studies that aimed at modelling the system and offering modelling support for the thoracic surgeon that is in charge of the planning of surgical procedures. We first provide more information on the case study setting (Section 13.2.1). Then we perform a problem analysis in which we discuss and define the variables that play a role in the planning problem (Section 13.2.2).

13.2.1 Case study setting

The Thorax Centre Rotterdam is a department of the Erasmus Medical Centre, providing care to patients suffering from malfunctions of the heart, lung and the intrathoracic vessels. The Department of Cardiothoracic Surgery performs surgery of coronary heart disease (coronary artery bypass grafting-CABG), surgery of valvular and congenital abnormalities in children and adults, lung operations as well as heart transplants. The department has a surgical staff of eight Cardio-Thoracic surgeons, trained to perform all adult cardiac and pulmonary operations, including heart transplants. Two surgeons are specialized in congenital heart operations.

The patient flow of the Thorax Centre can be distinguished in scheduled patients (elective patients from the waiting list) and non-scheduled patients (emergency patients requiring immediate surgery). The flow of elective patients in the Thorax Centre is shown in Figure 13.1. Most patients are waiting at home for an operation and are admitted to the Medium Care unit (MC) one day before the operation. Also patients waiting in another hospital are admitted to the MC unit one day before the operation. In case the patient stays before the operation in another department of the University Hospital, the patient is taken directly to one of the operating theatres.

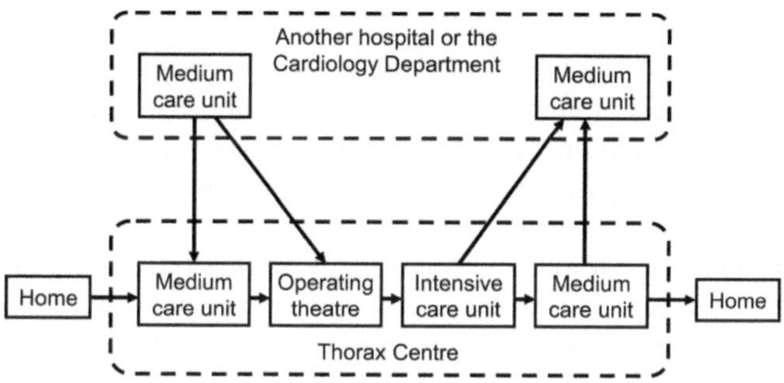

Fig. 13.1. The flow of elective patients in the Thorax Centre

Table 13.1. Patient groups, use of OT, IC and MC, and 4 week volumes

Patient group	*Example*	*OT*	*IC*	*MC*		*number of*
				pre-op	*post-op*	*patients*
		hours	*days*	*days*	*days*	*per 4 weeks*
1 Child simple	Closure venticular septal defect	4	1.1	0	1.5	7.36
2 Child complex	Arterial switch	8	1.1	0	1	9.36
3 Adult, short OT, short IC	Coronary bypass (CABG)	4	1.3	1	5.9	66.00
4 Adult, long OT, short IC	Mitral valve plasty	8	1.5	1	7.4	12.73
5 Adult, short OT, middle IC	CABG with medium IC stay	4	1.6	1	8.7	2.64
6 Adult, long OT, middle IC	Heart transplant	8	4	1	15.3	1.55
7 Adult, long OT, long IC	Thoraco-abdominal aneurysm	8	7	1	9	0.36
8 Adult, short OT, no IC	Cervical mediastinoscopy	2	0.2	1	2.3	6.91
Total						106.91

Children are admitted to the Children's Department before the operation. After the operation the patient stays for some days in an Intensive Care unit (IC) within the Thorax Centre, and after recovery he may use the Medium Care unit (MC) for a few days until he returns home or to the referring hospital or department. Children will return to the Children's Department after their IC stay. In the sequel we consider the treatment process only within the boundaries of the Thorax Centre.

The most important resources for cardiothoracic surgery are the operating theatres with its capacities, the intensive care ward with IC-beds and specialized nursing staff, and the medium care ward with a number of beds. We limit our study to these four most important resources.

Table 13.1 provides information on the patient groups distinguished based on the use of OT and IC resources. For each patient group information is given on the number of hours scheduled for the OT, the average number of days in the IC, and the average length of stay in the MC. Also the average number of patients that need to be scheduled for each period of 4 weeks is defined. The 4 weeks is the length of the planning period that allows for every patient group to be scheduled at least once.

As we are in this study not interested in the overrunning of theatre sessions we can use the planned durations of operations instead of data of realized durations.

For IC nursing we assume that patients in categories 1–4 use 12 hours of capacity per day at the IC and that patient categories 5–6 use 24 hours of capacity on the day of operation; patient group 7 requires also 24 hours of capacity at the day after the operation.

There are four operating theatres available for 9 hours per day, 10 IC-beds, 36 MC beds and 133 hours of nursing capacity per day at the IC. Table 13.2 provides information on the availability of resources for each day of the week. As about 20% is reserved for emergency patients, the targets that are used for scheduling elective patients are also defined.

For the planning of cardiothoracic surgery two types of restrictions can be distinguished. The first type of restriction is that some categories need to be operated at a specific day within the week. This can be due to the availability of specialized surgeons required for this type of operations. Another reason can be that scheduling patients with a specific length of stay on a fixed day in the week is beneficial to

Table 13.2. Available resources per day of the week

Day	*OT-hours*		*IC-beds*		*MC-beds*		*IC-Nursing*	
	Capacity	*Target*	*Capacity*	*Target*	*Capacity*	*Target*	*Capacity*	*Target*
Monday	36	29	10	7	36	27	133	91
Tuesday	36	29	10	7	36	27	133	91
Wednesday	36	29	10	7	36	27	133	91
Thursday	36	29	10	7	36	27	133	91
Friday	36	25	10	7	36	27	133	91
Saturday	0	0	4	2	36	27	133	91
Sunday	0	0	4	2	36	27	133	91

the utilization of beds in the weekend. The second type of restriction is to limit the number of patients from certain categories to a maximum per day. This allows for controlling the workload for OT or nursing, generated by categories of patients.

In the current practice the following restrictions were used:

- fix category 5 and 6 operations on Thursday and Friday to improve the use of IC-beds in the weekend;
- a maximum of 3 long operations from Monday to Thursday, and 1 on Friday (because of OT workload);
- a maximum of 8 operations per day from Monday to Thursday and 6 on Friday (because of the available number of theatre personnel staff on Friday afternoon);
- a maximum of 2 operations of category 1 and 2 from Monday to Thursday and 1 on Friday (because of available nurses with children specialization within the IC).

13.2.2 Problem analysis

Though the admission process is dictated by the operating theatre capacity, the surgeon planner in the Thorax Centre sees the IC capacity as the bottleneck resource that needs to be used to its optimum. Within the IC this regards in the first place the IC-beds, as the number of beds in use is already linked to the nursing staffing levels required. The IC nursing staff is a more flexible resource that can adapt better to peaks and troughs in workload. The operating theatres are, of course, also an important resource to be used efficiently. MC-beds are less scarce. In case an extra bed is required, it is possible to borrow a bed from another department. Thus IC-beds, operating theatre time, IC nursing staff and MC-beds is the priority order in the eyes of the surgeon planner.

Now we can formulate the planning problem as follows. How should thoracic surgery patients be scheduled for operating theatres to optimally use the scarce resources, given:

- a master operating theatre schedule as an approach for the operational schedule;
- a planning cycle length of four weeks;
- an aggregated time slot for operating theatre capacity of one day;

- a number of patient categories based on resource requirements, with average resource requirement profiles;
- four resources: operating theatre time, IC-beds and IC nursing staff and MC-beds;
- a priority order for optimization: IC-beds, operating theatre time, IC nursing staff and MC-beds;
- target resource utilization levels that take into account the reserve capacity required for emergency admissions;
- restrictions to the planning of patients, if availability of a specific surgeon or other reasons require that patients be operated upon on a specific day within the week.

The current planning has a strong focus on the operating theatre capacity. It may be improved by also taking into account all other resources involved. This probably leads to a more efficient use of the available resources and to an increase on the number of treated patients.

13.2.3 Modelling the planning problem

We developed methodology for the planning problem in three modelling steps, performed in a series of studies between 2004 and 2010.

- The first model considered only the elective patients, assuming a reservation of 20% for emergency patients [9]. The resource requirements are modelled in a deterministic way, based on averages for operation duration and length of stay in intensive care and medium care.
- In the second model we investigated the influence of stochastic resource requirements on the quality of the master schedules and the optimisation performance [2]. We used empirical distributions to model the stochastic resource requirements.
- The third model covered the elective part as well as the non-elective part, and made it possible to look at the overall performance of the system [1]. We used simulation to test the robustness of the master schedule for deviations in the operational plans derived from the master schedule and to calculate the effects for hospital efficiency and patient service.

We present the first model more detailed and then describe the changes in the subsequent modelling efforts. For more details we refer to the published full papers [1,2,9].

13.2.3.1 Model 1: elective patients, deterministic resource requirements

In the first modeling effort we concentrated on the planning of elective patients, assuming a fixed percentage as a buffer for emergency patients. More-over, we used deterministic resource requirements based on average length of stay.

Clearly, in this case the important decision concerns the master operation schedule, and the planning problem can be briefly formulated as: find a cyclic operation schedule such that the desired target utilization of the resources is realized as close as possible, while satisfying the target throughput and restrictions. Below we describe how the planning problem can be translated into a mathematical model.

Let T denote the cycle length (in days) of the operation schedule. The patients are categorized according to their workloads for the resources; let N denote the number of patient categories. It is convenient to number the resources operating theatre time, IC-beds, MC-beds and IC nursing staff from 1 to 4. For resource r, $r = 1,\ldots,4$, we then introduce the following quantities:

- C_{rd} available capacity of resource r on day d of the operation schedule;
- U_{rd} target utilization of resource r on day d of the operation schedule.

The important decision variables in the planning problem are the number and mix of patients operated on each day of the operation schedule. Let X_{cd} denote the number of patients from category c operated on day d of the operation schedule. Clearly, X_{cd} is a nonnegative integer. Thus

$$X_{cd} \in \{0,|,2,\ldots\}, \qquad c = 1,\ldots,N, \qquad d = 1,\ldots,T, \tag{13.1}$$

and they should satisfy the target patient throughput TPT_c of patient category c, i.e.,

$$\sum_{d=1}^{T} X_{cd} = TPT_c, \qquad c = 1,\ldots,N. \tag{13.2}$$

We now want to determine the values of the X_{cd} variables for which the deviation of the realized and target utilization of the resources is minimized. Below we show how this problem can be modeled by a mixed integer linear programming problem. Introduce the auxiliary variables V_{rdk} satisfying

$$V_{nlk} \geq 0, \quad r = 1,\ldots,4, \qquad d = 1,\ldots,T, \qquad k = 1,2. \tag{13.3}$$

It is possible to formulate linear constraints forcing these variables to be equal to the deviation of the realized and target utilization, i.e., for $k = 1$ the variable V_{rdk} will be equal to the over utilization of resource r on day d, and for $k = 1$, it will be equal to the under utilization. This will be demonstrated for resource $r = 1$, i.e., the operating theatre time. Let o_c be the operation duration (in hours) of a category c patient, $c = 1,\ldots,N$. Then the utilization of the operating theatre on day d is equal to

$$\sum_{c=1}^{N} o_c X_{cd}\,. \tag{13.4}$$

If we require that

$$\sum_{c=1}^{N} o_c X_{cd} - U_{1d} \leq V_{1d1}, \qquad d = 1,\ldots,T, \tag{13.5}$$

$$U_{1d} - \sum_{c=1}^{N} o_c X_{cd} \leq V_{1d2}, \qquad d = 1,\ldots,T, \tag{13.6}$$

and minimize the sum

$$\sum_{d=1}^{T} (V_{1d1} + V_{1d2})\,,$$

then it is easily verified that the minimum is realized for

$$V_{1d1} = \max\left(\sum_{c=1}^{N} o_c X_{cd} - U_{1d}, 0\right), \qquad V_{1d2} = \max\left(U_{1d} - \sum_{c=1}^{N} 0_c X_{cd}, 0\right).$$

So, indeed, V_{1d1} and V_{1d2} are equal to the over, respectively under utilization, and the sum $V_{1d1} + V_{1d2}$ is equal to the (absolute) deviation of the realized and target utilization of the operating theatre on day d of the operation schedule. Note that the utilization of the operating theatre on day d may not exceed the available capacity on day d. Thus

$$U_{1d} + V_{1d1} \leq C_{1d}, \qquad d = 1, \ldots, T. \tag{13.7}$$

Constraints similar to (13.5)–(13.7) can be formulated for the other resources. Before operation a patient is first admitted to the MC unit; after operation, he stays one or more days at the IC unit and then moves again to the MC unit for a few days until he is discharged. Let po_c be the number of pre-operative days at the MC unit, ic_c the number of days at the IC unit and mc_c the number of post-operative days at the MC unit for a patient from category c. Further nw_{cd} denotes the IC nursing workload (in hours) for a patient of category c on day d of his stay in the hospital. The category c patients at the IC unit on day d are the ones that are operated on day $d, d-1, \ldots, d - ic_c + 1$. Thus the total number of patients at the IC unit on day d is equal to

$$\sum_{c=1}^{N} \sum_{t=1}^{ic_c} X_{cd-t+1},$$

and the following constraint expresses that this number should be close to its target,

$$U_{2d} - V_{2d2} \leq \sum_{c=1}^{N} \sum_{t=1}^{ic_c} X_{cd-t+1} \leq U_{2d} + V_{2d1}, \qquad d = 1, \ldots, T. \tag{13.8}$$

Similarly we obtain for the other two resources

$$U_{3d} - V_{3d2} \leq \sum_{c=1}^{N} \sum_{t=1}^{po_c} X_{cd+t} + \sum_{c=1}^{N} \sum_{t=1}^{mc_c} X_{cd-ic_c-t+1} \leq U_{3d} + V_{3d1}, \tag{13.9}$$

$$d = 1, \ldots, T,$$

$$U_{4d} - V_{4d2} \leq \sum_{c=1}^{N} \sum_{t=1}^{ic_c} nw_{ct} X_{cd-t+1} \leq U_{4d} + V_{4d1}, \qquad d = 1, \ldots, T, \tag{13.10}$$

and

$$U_{rd} + V_{rd1} \leq C_{re}, \qquad r = 2, 3, 4, \qquad d = 1, \ldots, T. \tag{13.11}$$

In the above constraints we used the convention that the subscript d in X_{cd} (indicating the day of the operation schedule) should be read modulo T: day 0 is the same as day T, day -1 is day $T-1$, day -2 is day $T-2$ and so on. Then, minimizing the deviation of the realized and target utilization of all resources amounts to minimizing the sum

$$\sum_{r=1}^{4} w_r \sum_{d=1}^{T} (V_{rd1} + V_{rd2}). \tag{13.12}$$

In this sum, the deviation of the utilization of resource r is weighted with coefficient w_r, defined as

$$w_r = K \cdot \frac{a_r}{\sum_{d=1}^{T} U_{rd}}, \qquad r = 1, \ldots, 4, \tag{13.13}$$

where a_r is some nonnegative number, and the normalization constant K is chosen such that

$$\sum_{r=1}^{4} w_r = 1.$$

The coefficients w_r are introduced *i*) to control the relative importance of the resources (by means of a_r) and *ii*) to make the sum (13.12) dimensionless (i.e., it is scaled with respect to the target utilization). The latter is needed, since it is undesirable that the optimal solution will depend on the units used for the resource capacities. Finally, we have to take into account restrictions on operation schedules, such as *i*) the specialty may want to fix the number of patients from a specific category operated on a specific day in the operation schedule, or *ii*) the number of patients from a certain combination of categories that can be operated on a single day is limited. The first restriction means that we fix certain variables X_{cd} to prescribed values. To formulate the second restriction we introduce B_d denoting the maximum number of patients from categories that $c \in S$ can be operated on day d of the operation schedule, where S is a subset of the categories $\{1, \ldots, N\}$. Then the second restriction translates to

$$\sum_{c \in S} X_{cd} \le B_d, \qquad d = 1, \ldots, T. \tag{13.14}$$

The above restriction is formulated for exactly one combination S of categories. Of course, similar constraints may be added for other combinations as well. In Table 13.3 we summarize the input parameters and the variables introduced.

Our planning problem can be formulated as the following mixed integer linear programming problem:

$$\text{Minimize} \sum_{r=1}^{4} w_r \sum_{d=1}^{T} (v_{rd} + V_{rd2})$$

subject to

$$\sum_{d=1}^{T} X_{cd} = TPT_c, \qquad c = 1, \ldots, N,$$

$$U_{1d} - V_{1d2} \le \sum_{c=1}^{N} o_c X_{cd} \le U_{1d} + V_{1d1}, \qquad d = 1, \ldots, T,$$

$$U_{2d} - V_{2d2} \le \sum_{c=1}^{N} \sum_{t=1}^{ic_c} X_{cd-t+1} \le U_{2d} + V_{2d1}, \qquad d = 1, \ldots, T,$$

Table 13.3. Input parameters and variables

Input parameters	*Description*	*Variables*	*Description*
T	cycle length (days)	X_{cd}	number of patients of category c operated on day d
TPT_c	target patient throughput of patients of category c	V_{rd1}	over utilization of resource r on day d
C_{rd}	available capacity of resource r on day d	V_{rd2}	under utilization of resource r on day d
U_{rd}	target utilization of resource r on day d		
o_c	operation duration (hours) of a patient of category c		
po_c	number of pre-operative days at the MC unit of a patient of category c		
ic_c	number of days at the IC unit of a patient of category c		
mc_c	number of pre-operative days at the MC unit of a patient of category c		
nw_{cd}	IC nursing workload (hours) for a patient of category c on day d		
w_r	Relative weight of resource r		
B_d	maximum number of patients from categories $c \in S$ that can be operated on day d		

$$U_{3d} - V_{3d2} \leq \sum_{c=1}^{N} \sum_{t=1}^{po_c} X_{cd+1} + \sum_{c=1}^{N} \sum_{t=1}^{mc_c} X_{cd-ic_c-t+1} \leq U_{3d} + V_{3d1}, \qquad d = 1, \ldots, T,$$

$$U_{4d} - V_{4d2} \leq \sum_{c=1}^{N} \sum_{t=1}^{ic_c} nw_{ct} X_{cd-t+1} \leq U_{4d} + V_{4d1}, \qquad d = 1, \ldots, T,$$

$$U_{rd} + V_{rd1} \leq C_{rd}, \qquad r = 1, \ldots, 4, \quad d = 1, \ldots, T,$$

$$\sum_{c \in S} X_{cd} \leq B_d, \qquad d = 1, \ldots, T,$$

$$V_{rdk} \geq 0, \qquad r = 1, \ldots, 4, \quad d = 1, \ldots, T, \quad K = 1, 2,$$

$$X_{cd} \in \{0, 1, 2, \ldots\}, \qquad c = 1, \ldots, N, \quad d = 1, \ldots, T.$$

13.2.3.2 Model 2: elective patients, stochastic resource requirements

In the second modelling effort we again concentrated on the elective patients but in this case we modelled stochastic resource requirements by using empirical distributions for the length of stay on IC and MC, and then aimed at finding a cyclic operation schedule minimizing the deviations of the expected resource utilizations from their targets.

To describe the constraints for the utilization of the resources we introduce the parameters $C_{r,t}$ and $U_{r,t}$ indicating the available capacity and target utilization, respectively, of resource r on day t, where

$$r \in R = \{ot, ic, mc, nh\}.$$

Let the auxiliary variables $UU_{r,,t}$ and $OU_{r,,t}$ denote the under- and over-utilization (with respect to the target). To formulate the constraints for the expected utilization of the IC unit we introduce the probabilities $p_{ic,c,t}$ denoting the probability that a patient from category c is (still) at the IC unit t days after operation, $t = 0, 1, 2, \dots$

Then the expected utilization of the IC unit should satisfy

$$U_{ic,t} - UU_{ic,t} \le \sum_{c=1}^{C} \sum_{s=0}^{\infty} p_{ic,c,s} X_{c,t-s} \le U_{ic,t} + OU_{ic,t}, \qquad t = 1, \dots, T.$$

In the above constraints we used the convention that the subscript $t-s$ in $X_{c,t-s}$ should be treated *modulo* T: day 0 is the same as day T, day -1 is the same as day $T-1$ and so on. If $nw_{c,t}$ denotes the IC nursing load (in hours) of a category c patient t days after operation, then we get for the expected nursing workload

$$U_{nh,t} - UU_{ic,t} \le \sum_{c=1}^{C} \sum_{s=0}^{\infty} mw_{ct} p_{ic,c,s} X_{c,t-s} \le U_{nh,t} + OU_{nh,t}, \qquad t = 1, \dots, T.$$

Similarly, for the expected utilization of the MC unit we get

$$U_{mc,t} - UU_{mc,t} \le \sum_{c=1}^{C} \sum_{s=1}^{po_c} X_{c,t+s} + \sum_{c=1}^{C} \sum_{s=0}^{\infty} p_{mc,c,s} X_{c,t-s} \le U_{mc,t} + OU_{mc,t},$$
$$t = 1, \dots, T,$$

where po_c is the number of pre-operative days at the MC for category c patients and $p_{mc,c,t}$ is the probability that a patient from category c is at the MC unit t days after operation, $t = 0, 1, 2, \dots$

The length of the chapter does not allow us to present the complete model. See for more details the full paper [2]. For this contribution we can refer to the first model and state that the equations (13.8)–(13.10) describing the deterministic resource requirements need to be substituted by the stochastic formulations above.

13.2.3.3 Model 3: emergency and elective patients

In the third modelling effort we want to combine emergency patients with elective scheduled patients. To model the combined effect of emergency patients with a master schedule for elective patients, we need also to consider the operational plans derived from the master schedule and the actually executed plan, i.e. the operational performance (see Fig. 13.2). As we move towards operational performance we should be aware that the operational plan may deviate in some respect from the master plan, and that the actual plan executed again can show deviations from the operational plan.

The master plan is developed in a similar way as before (see Section 13.2.3.2). Part of the capacity is reserved for emergency patients. Every planning period – in our case four weeks – the master plan is translated into an operational plan, which takes into account the current situation. As we consider a stationary arrival process, the average number of performed elective operations per cycle will be the same for all master plans with a sufficient number of slots. However, we may decrease the waiting time considerably by a larger number of planned slots (overplanning) and by re-assigning unused slots to other patient groups (flexibility). At the operational performance level the handling of emergency patients can lead to changes in the number of elective admissions. If for instance more emergency patients arrive than expected, some elective operations need to be cancelled.

We developed three tactical plans with different levels of slack for handling more patients (no slack, medium slack, large slack). For details of the slack options we refer to paper [1]. For each of these tactical plans we allow three flexibility options (no flexibility, medium and large flexibility in replacing patients with patients from other groups). For these nine alternative short term plans of elective patients we

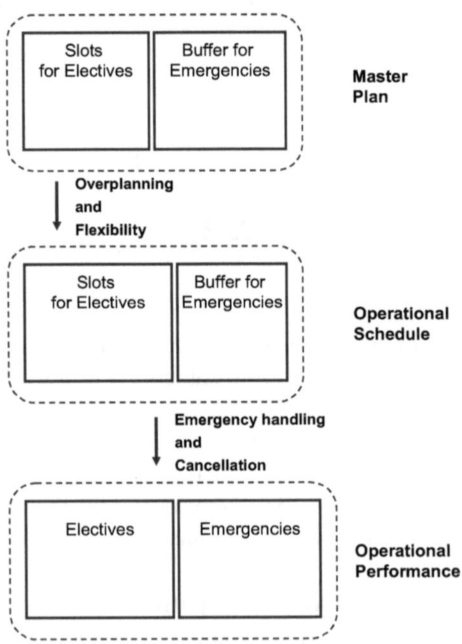

Fig. 13.2. From master plan to operational performance

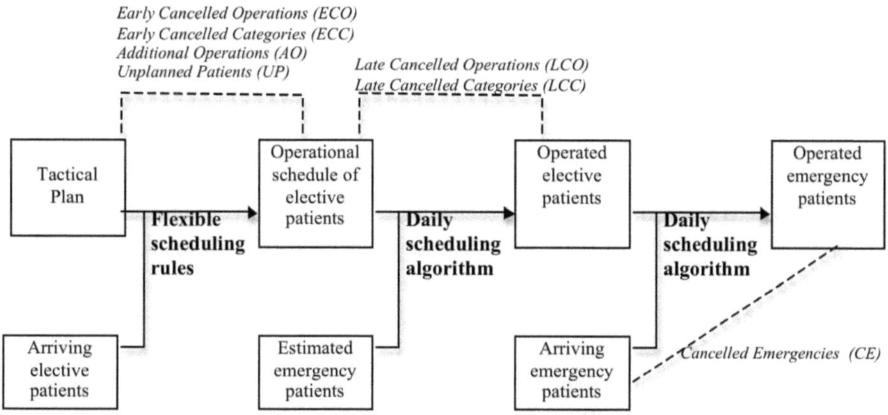

Fig. 13.3. Plan changes from tactical plan to operational plan and actual plan, and indicators of performance

consider next how these plans are actually executed in combination with the arrival of emergency patients.

The performance of the whole scheduling procedure (scheduling rules and daily scheduling algorithm) is assessed by several indicators reflecting the changes between the tactical plan, the operational schedule of elective patients and the stream of actually operated patients.

Figure 13.3 illustrates the plan changes. Using one of the flexible scheduling rules to deal with arriving elective patients leads to an operational schedule that can differ from the initial tactical plan. Some categories of patients may be added or cancelled compared to the tactical plan. There can also be more or less operations. Then the cancellation rule is applied to the operational schedule containing the scheduled elective patients. We refer to late cancellations, as these cancellations are decided on the day of operation.

Arrivals of emergency and elective patients were simulated through a Poisson process with a parameter depending on the day of the week for emergencies and a fixed weekday parameter for electives. For each scheduled patient, we drew an actual IC stay and MC stay according to the empirical distributions that were obtained from the hospital.

13.3 Results and discussion

The results of the three step modelling approach to the planning problem will be illustrated for the case study setting of thoracic surgery. Though the three steps were developed as stepping stones towards a more complete coverage of the practice setting, it also had benefits as well as for the modelling contribution as for the lessons learned for practice development.

13.3.1 Model 1: elective patients, deterministic resource requirements

The first model we developed focused on elective patients and made use of average length of stay data for IC and MC.

13.3.1.1 Illustration of results

Using the input data as described in Section 13.2.1 (patient numbers, demand requirements, available capacities and type two restrictions on the number of operations), then the model developed provided the following output for a 4-week cyclic operation schedule (see Fig. 13.4).

From these graphs it appears that the OT utilization on most days stays above the target level, IC utilization (beds and nursing) stays below the target level, and

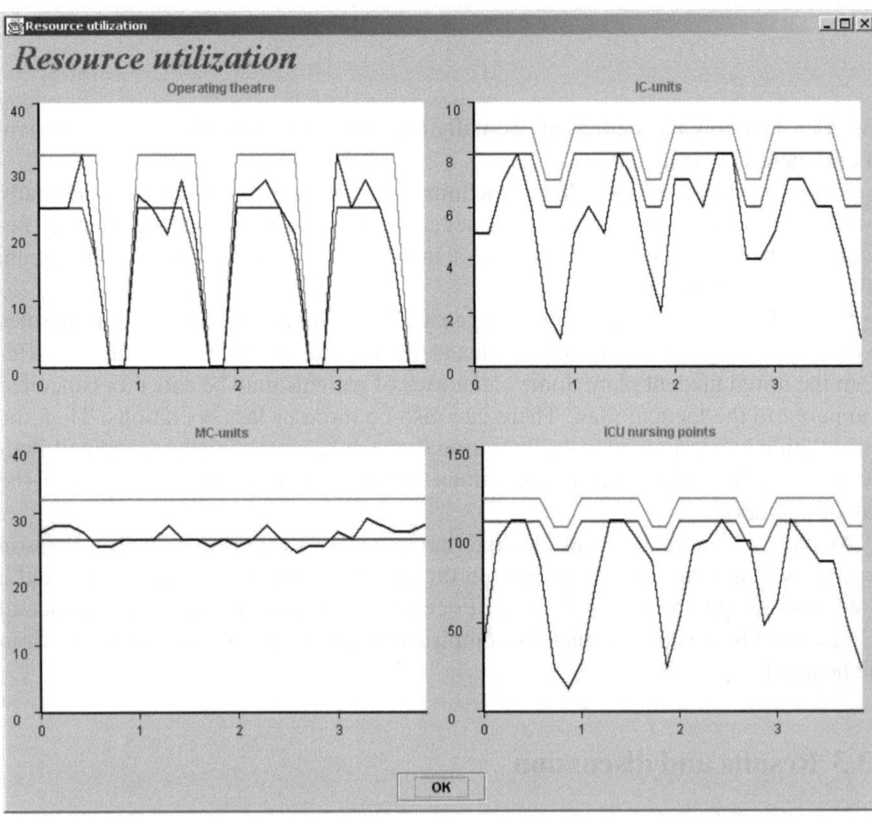

Fig. 13.4. Results of a setting with 9 IC beds. In each graph the red line represents the maximum capacity available, the blue line represents the target capacity utilization and the black line refers to the projected realization of resource use; the week number within the planning cycle is on the horizontal axis, the amount of capacity is on the vertical axis: operating theatres in number of hours, IC units in number of beds, MC units in number of beds, and IC nursing in number of nursing hours

Table 13.4. Summary of results of the different scenarios

	1	*2*	*3*	*4*
Scenario Measure	9 IC beds	8 IC beds and weekend scheduling policy	Ideal plan	350 extra bypass
Number of patients treated	89	89	89	116
Capacity required				
• OT (hours)	32	32	32	38
• ICb (beds)	9	8	8	9
• MC (beds)	30	30	32	40
• ICn (hours)	120	112	112	124
Average occupancy during the working week				
• OT	108%	109%	108%	104%
• ICb	78%	88%	88%	93%
• MC	102%	102%	106%	101%
• Icn	84%	84%	85%	88%
Average occupancy during the weekend				
• OT	42%	65%	63%	56%
• ICb	100%	98%	96%	96%
• MC	38%	63%	60%	58%
• Icn				
Score fit	70.9	46.6	48.0	49.7

the MC utilization stays above the target level. Close to the target line represents in our case the best fit. Exceeding the target line can create difficulties in handling the emergency patients. Staying below can pinpoint the existence of overcapacity.

To demonstrate the use of the model we applied the model to different scenarios relevant to the setting of the Thorax Centre. Each of these scenarios has its own resource allocation and target setting for resource utilization and throughput. The model produces results in terms of the utilization of resources and a score indicating the fit with the targets set for the utilization of resources in that particular scenario. The optimality gap of the solutions produced by the model was at most 5-10%, which, in this case, is regarded as sufficiently accurate to indicate the impact of scenarios. Of course, we could have easily produced more accurate results by increasing the computational effort, i.e., the number of nodes examined.

The results of the different scenarios Table 13.4.

For each scenario we have shown the number of patients treated, the capacity required to treat these patients, the results in terms of utilization of resources during the working week and the weekend, and the score as a measure of the deviation from the target utilization level.

Comparison of the scores for fit shows that the scenarios 2 ('8 IC-beds and weekend scheduling policy'), 3 ('ideal plan') and 4 (350 extra bypasses) produce much better fits with the targets than scenario 1 ('9 IC-beds'). Also the utilization levels of resources show a comparable performance in these scenarios.

Furthermore, Table 13.4 shows that the IC-capacity in terms of beds as well as nursing staff can be used better, especially in the weekend. It seems to be possible to reduce the capacity during the weekend and to use this to increase production during the week.

The different scenarios provide insight into the range of questions that can be investigated with the model. The graphical output (an overview of impacts on all resources) did help very much in creating ideas for better solutions.

We can conclude that the model is able to generate a master operation schedule for longer term planning purposes, with small deviations between the realized and the target resource utilization, while the total available capacity of the different resources is not exceeded, the target patient throughput is met and the given restrictions are not violated. Also the model can provide support for calculating the amount of resources required in case of an increase in contracts with purchasers.

13.3.1.2 Learning points

Though the model was based on (deterministic) average resource requirements, the model makes clear that there are imbalances in the system. The intensive care has overcapacity compared with the operating theatres and medium care. A further contribution to practice was that there was an increased awareness of system impacts when scheduling surgical patients. The mathematical model was implemented in a software tool that could also be used by the thoracic surgeon. The optimisation procedure worked very well. In a few minutes a (often not optimal) solution was found. For a better (possibly optimal) solution the maximum number of nodes to be evaluated in the (Brach-and-Bound) optimization method was set at 300,000 nodes.

13.3.2 Model 2: elective patients, stochastic resource requirements

The second model also focused on elective patients but we used stochastic resource requirements for IC and MC.

13.3.2.1 Illustration of results

Figure 13.5 illustrates the results obtained by using the deterministic lengths of stay at IC and MC and by using the stochastic lengths of stay. For the deterministic lengths of IC and MC stay we used similar data, as shown in Table 13.1. For the stochastic lengths of IC and MC stay we used empirical data from the hospital. Based upon these data, we determined the best 4-week schedule for the deterministic data and the best 4-week schedule for the stochastic data; so both the deterministic model and the stochastic model were solved to (near) optimality (by application of CPLEX). At first sight, the two schedules look quite similar. However, when we measure the performance of the 4-week cyclic schedules by assuming the stochastic

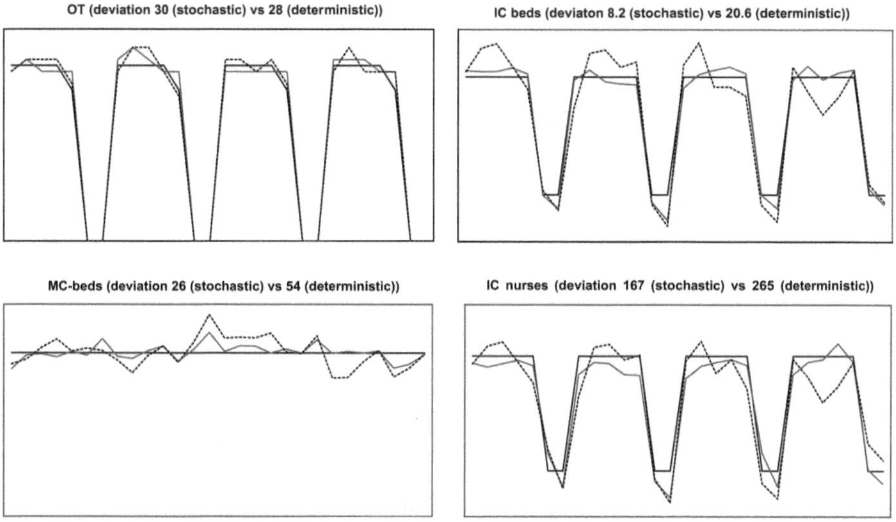

Fig. 13.5. Comparison of performance with stochastic and deterministic lengths of IC and MC stay (target level in dark solid line, stochastic realization in light solid line, deterministic realization in dotted line)

data to be the real ones, we notice quite some differences. The resulting expected utilization levels of resources for both schedules are depicted in Figure 13.3. Above each of the graphs we display the total deviation of the expected utilization from its target over the whole planning period for the stochastic versus deterministic model.

The blue line represents the target capacity utilization. The black dashed line refers to the expected utilization level for deterministic lengths of stay and the pink dotted line refers to the expected utilization level for stochastic lengths of stay. We limit ourselves in Figure 13.5 to show expected utilization levels, but it is also possible to calculate the corresponding standard deviations. This would illustrate the variability of utilization levels. The results in Figure 13.5 demonstrate that the stochastic model performs much better than the deterministic model; for the IC, IC nursing and the MC the pink dotted lines are more close to the target line than the black dashed ones.

Using the weight function, the score for the combined performance of the resources for the deterministic and the stochastic model are given in Table 13.5. The total weighted deviation from the target resource levels turns out to be 17.33 when we use stochastic data and 30.52 when we use deterministic data.

Table 13.5 shows that at the costs of some performance at the OT, big improvements can be obtained for the other resources when we use the stochastic empirical data. This supports the initial feeling of the cardiothoracic surgeon planner, and is also in line with other studies reported by McManus et al. [6] and Wachtel and Dexter [10].

Table 13.5. Difference between realized and target utilizations for the stochastic and the deterministic data model

Resource	*Performance Model*	
	Stochastic	Deterministic
OT-hours	30	28
IC-beds	8.22	20.64
MC-beds	26.38	53.66
IC-nursing	166.56	264.66
Overall score	17.33	30.52

13.3.2.2 Learning points

The second model looked at the added value for using more detailed data on the distribution of the length of stay of patients on the intensive care and medium care. The extension of the model with stochastic resource requirements demonstrates that the quality of the model improved. The model could generate master schedules that had a better fit with the targets for the use of the resources.

13.3.3 Model 3: emergency and elective patients

In the third model we combined elective patients and emergency patients. By doing this we also had to investigate the changes tactical plans undergo when they are translated into short term operational plans and finally in execution. In order to generate data on the operational performance we used a simulation approach.

13.3.3.1 Illustration of results

We considered the indicators described in Section 13.2.3.3 (see Fig. 13.3) and averages were computed for each option of slack planning, flexibility as well as different arrival intensities (ρ) for both elective and emergency patients. Table 13.6 provides these averages. The effects for the patients are aggregated in the indicator 'Dissatisfaction for Patients' and the effects for the hospital are aggregated in 'Hospital Inefficiency'. From the results displayed in Table 13.6, we may draw several comments, analyzing each strategy individually.

- *Slack planning.* Increasing the number of planned patients reduces the average waiting time and increases the number of cancelled emergencies as more resources are allocated to elective patients. However, late and early cancellations for elective also increase: with no slack planning, there is a stronger tendency to stick to the initial plan (see *(ECO)* and *(ECC)*) or to the operational schedule (late cancellations represented by two indicators: *(LCC)* and *(WLCO)*. With more planned patients, there is more freedom to allocate resources differently. Thus, slack planning tends to create more schedule instability (single indicators like *(UP)* and *(ECO)* increase with the number of planned patients). Slack planning creates more possibilities for cancelling or adding operations through the use of flexibility strategies. On a global basis, an increase in the number of planned pa-

Table 13.6. Numerical results: indicators of inefficiency (indicators for schedule changes, patient dissatisfaction and hospital inefficiency are compound indicators)

	(WT) Waiting Time	(CE) Cancelled Emergencies (%)	(WLCO) Weighted Late Cancelled Operations (%)	(AO) Additional Operations of planned categories	(UP) Patients of Unplanned categories	(ECO) Early Cancelled Operations	(ECC)+(LCC) Total cancelled categories	(ECC) Early Cancelled Categories	(DR) Dissatisfaction of elective	(DE) Dissatisfaction of Emergency	(E) Exceeding capacities	(SC) Schedule Change	(DRE) Dissatisfaction of all patients	(HI) Hospital Inefficiency
Overplan														
No (O1)	22.56	6.73	1.40	5.42	2.33	4.99	4.73	4.62	2555	1207	33.02	64.94	3762	6549
Intermediate (O3)	13.59	7.97	2.50	9.12	3.78	8.15	11.10	10.86	1894	1429	38.33	114.00	3323	9533
Large (O2)	11.97	8.95	4.61	8.90	5.32	11.59	12.54	12.09	2183	1604	44.16	134.83	3787	11157
Flexibility														
No (F1)	23.80	6.68	1.23	0.00	0.00	3.28	5.36	5.25	2643	1197	32.71	14.12	3840	3977
Intermediate (F3)	13.25	8.45	2.84	10.82	0.00	9.12	8.48	8.20	1931	1516	40.59	80.44	3447	8081
Large (F2)	11.06	8.52	4.45	12.63	11.43	12.33	14.52	14.12	2058	1527	42.20	219.21	3585	15181
Exc. Capa. El. (p_{elec})														
No (option 1)	15.64	9.11	3.17	7.80	3.74	8.15	9.41	9.09	2242	1633	20.31	103.72	3875	7217
Yes (option 2)	16.64	6.04	2.34	7.84	3.91	8.37	9.53	9.34	2164	1084	65.78	105.89	3247	11873
Exc. Capa. Em. (p_{emer})														
No (option 1)	16.22	15.43	2.51	7.87	3.83	8.18	9.55	9.30	2160	2766	7.75	105.18	4926	6034
Small (option 2)	16.33	8.70	2.85	7.73	3.82	8.19	9.43	9.16	2243	1559	29.87	104.10	3802	8192
Large (option 3)	15.65	3.30	2.99	7.88	3.79	8.32	9.44	9.17	2204	591	62.50	104.79	2795	11490

tients leads to a decrease of the waiting time and to an increase of the number of cancelled emergencies.

The improvement of waiting times compensates for the increased cancellations to a certain extent: for the large slack planning option, the decrease of waiting time is minor compared to the one we get with medium slack planning therefore entailing a satisfaction decrease for electives (see indicator *(DR)*). Thus elective patients reach the best satisfaction with medium slack planning (however, the satisfaction of emergency patients degrades). The dissatisfaction of all patients reaches its minimum value for medium slack planning. Slack planning creates more schedule instability and -when allowed- capacities are more exceeded for larger numbers of planned patients. This results in a decrease of the overall hospital efficiency.

- *Flexibility.* An increased flexibility decreases the overall waiting time as some unused slots will be filled with other patients. This leads to scheduling other patients than initially planned. Additional operations *(AO)* are only zero for the no flexibility option, and scheduled patients from unplanned categories *(UP)* are obviously only positive for the large flexibility option. The medium and large flexibility options induce a large increase of the schedule change indicator *(SC)* compared to the no flexibility option. With flexibility, early and late cancellations of electives are increased and the number of cancelled emergencies also is increased. Although there are more cancellations, there are also more additional operations from other categories. Therefore the average waiting time decreases, and of course, with a shorter queue length, the probability becomes much larger that there is no patient at all from a certain category, so that the session has to be cancelled.

  Due to increased schedule changes, the hospital inefficiency increases as the flexibility level increases. Although there are more patient cancellations, there is also less waiting time which globally entails a lower dissatisfaction for emergency patients; the highest service for elective patients is reached with the medium flexibility option. Indeed large flexibility induces only a slight decrease of waiting time that does not compensate for cancellations. We obtain the best overall service for all patients with the medium flexibility option.

- *Capacity excess for elective patients.* This strategy uses a tight capacity when making the operational schedule, but allows for capacity excess on the operation day. Therefore, we find a small increase in waiting time, but a reduction in the cancelled operations. It also reduces the cancelled emergencies because more capacities are made available for emergency. It has no significant impact on schedule changes. The hospital inefficiency is obviously increased due to the increase of capacity excess. The satisfaction of both types of patients is increased.

- *Capacity excess for emergencies.* Increasing the capacity violations for emergencies mechanically leads to a decreased number of cancelled emergencies and thus to an increased satisfaction for emergency patients. There is no significant impact on the schedule change indicators. Obviously, hospital inefficiency is increased due to capacity violations.

Table 13.7. Pareto efficient strategies

Solution name	*Slack planning*	*Flexibility*	*Exc. Capa. Elective*	*Exc. Capa. Emergency*	*Patients Dissatisfaction (DRE)*	*Hospital Inefficiency (HI)*
(a)	Large	No	Yes	Large	2086	8555
(b)	No	Medium	No	Large	2292	6535
(c)	Large	No	No	Large	2488	4931
(d)	Medium	No	No	Large	2662	4753
(e)	No	Medium	No	Small	3387	3344
(f)	Large	No	No	Small	3483	1980
(g)	Medium	No	No	Small	3507	1616
(h)	No	No	No	Small	4288	1145
(i)	No	No	No	No	6301	1088

Table 13.7 provides the Pareto efficient combinations of strategies in terms of patients' dissatisfaction and hospital inefficiency. Slack planning and flexibility strategies produce Pareto efficient solutions when used in alternation: large slack planning is associated with no flexibility and no slack planning is associated with medium flexibility. The large flexibility option never appears as an efficient solution since it produces only a slight decrease in the waiting time that does not compensate for cancellations. The best alternative for patient satisfaction is large slack planning, no flexibility and large capacity excesses allowed for both types of patients. Conversely, the best hospital efficiency is reached when none of the strategies developed here is applied. Indeed, slack planning and flexibility create schedule instability that is detrimental to the hospital efficiency.

Allowing for capacity excess also decreases the hospital efficiency. There is obviously a trade-off between patient dissatisfaction and hospital inefficiency: an increase of the hospital efficiency can only be made at the expense of a decreasing patient service for all solutions along the efficient frontier, by definition. Figure 13.6 plots Pareto efficient solutions as well as non-efficient solutions, where patient dissatisfaction appears along the x-axis and hospital inefficiency along the y-axis. Figure 13.7 provides a sharper display of the efficient frontier where values along the x-axis were inverted to make the reading of the graph easier. Thus, patients' dissatisfaction increases as we move from the left to the right of the graph. All the line segments joining any pair of points have an increasing slope meaning that an increase of patients' satisfaction (or equivalently a decrease in patients' dissatisfaction) always implies an increase of the hospital inefficiency. As we did not consider a wider range of options and parameter values for the flexibility and the slack planning strategies as well as capacity excesses, we obtain uneven marginal rates of substitution between patients' satisfaction and hospital inefficiency. For instance, moving from solution (i) to (h) allows for a large improvement in patients' satisfaction at the expense of a slight degrade in the hospital efficiency. Conversely, from solution (b) to (a), patients' satisfaction is only slightly augmented whereas hospital efficiency

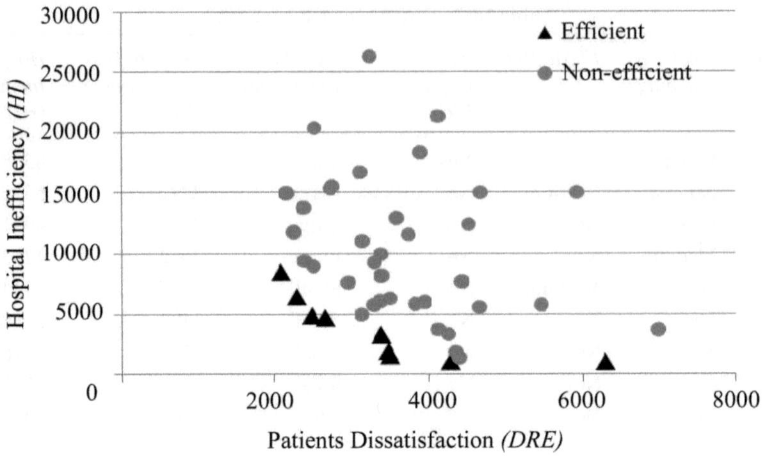

Fig. 13.6. Efficient and non-efficient strategies

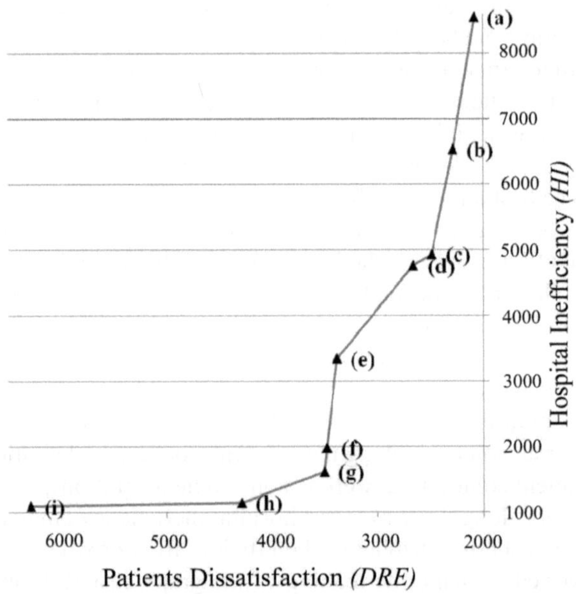

Fig. 13.7. The efficient frontier

strongly decreases. Still, the efficient frontier in Figure 13.7 clearly supports the existence of a trade-off between patients' dissatisfaction and hospital inefficiency. Let us also note that allowing for large capacity excess especially for emergency patients provides the highest patient satisfaction and the worst hospital efficiency. With little or no capacity excess, we obtain the opposite situation.

13.3.3.2 Learning points

The third model had an extension of the non-elective part. To assess the performance of the overall system, we modelled the arrival process of emergency and elective patients and used a simulation model. We also used this model to consider the robustness of the solution for deviations in the operational plan derived from the master schedule, by overplanning, flexibility between patient groups and cancellations.

Of course, an important contribution of model 3 is the combining of elective and emergency patients. However, more importantly was the contribution to test the robustness of master plans for deviations that arise in the translation of master schedules into operational schedules and in the actual operational performance when the operational plans are executed. This forced us to take a much closer look at healthcare practice, but it also made clear hat master plans can add value to that healthcare practice.

13.4 Conclusions

Though the different models were developed in a stand alone setting with dedicated resources, the approach can be used for any surgical specialty in a hospital to improve the planning of the patient flow of the specialty. The approach can help to make a specialty more aware of the possibilities to manage its own patient flows, by manipulating the number of admissions per patient category and the development of a stable master surgical schedule.

Future work could focus on overcoming the limitation of this study to only one patient flow. The lessons learned from this modelling approach of a more simple setting could be that this extension to more patient flows and interactions between patient flows at shared resources should not be tried in one go but be built up in a number of steps. This could add valuable insight in each step rather than trying to encapsulate all complexities in one modelling attempt.

References

1. Adan, I., Bekkers, J., Dellaert, N., Jeunet, J., Vissers, J.: Improving operational effectiveness of tactical master plans for emergency and elective patients under stochastic demand and capacitated resources. European Journal of Operational Research **213**, 290–308 (2011)
2. Adan, I., Bekkers, J., Dellaert, N., Vissers, J., Yu, X.: Patient mix optimisation and stochastic resource requirements: A case study in cardiothoracic surgery planning. Health Care Management Science **12**, 129–141 (2009)
3. Beliën, J., Demeulemeester, E.: Building cyclic master surgery schedules with levelled resulting bed occupancy. European Journal of Operational Research **176**, 1185–1204 (2007)
4. Brailsford, S., Vissers, J.: OR in healthcare: A European perspective. European Journal of Operational Research **212**, 223–234 (2011)
5. Cardoen, B., Demeulemeester, E., Belien, J.: Operating room planning and scheduling: A Literature Review. European Journal of Operational Research **201**, 921–932 (2010)
6. McManus, M.L., Long, M.C., Cooper, A., Litvak, E.: Queuing theory accurately models the need for critical care resources. Anesthesiology **100**, 1271–1276 (2004)

7. Van Berkel, P.T., Boucherie, R.J., Hans, E.W., Hurink, J.L., Litvak, N.: A Survey of Helth Care Models that Encompass Multiple Departments. International Journal of Health Management and Information **1**, 37–69 (2010)
8. van Oostrum, J.M., van Houdenhoven, M., Hurink, J.L., Hans, E.W., Wullink, G., Kazemier, G.: A master surgical scheduling approach for cyclic scheduling in operating room departments. OR Spectrum **30**, 355–374 (2008)
9. Vissers, J.M.H., Adan, I.J.B.F., Bekkers, J.A.: Patient mix optimization in cardiothoracic surgery planning: a case study. IMA Journal of Management Mathematics **16**, 281–304 (2005)
10. Wachtel, R.E., Dexter, F.: Tactical increases in operating room block time for capacity planning should not be based on utilization. Anesthesia & Analgesia **106**, 215–226 (2008)

MIX
Papier aus verantwortungsvollen Quellen
Paper from responsible sources
FSC® C105338

If you have any concerns about our products,
you can contact us on
ProductSafety@springernature.com

In case Publisher is established outside the EU,
the EU authorized representative is:
Springer Nature Customer Service Center GmbH
Europaplatz 3, 69115 Heidelberg, Germany

Printed by Libri Plureos GmbH
in Hamburg, Germany